WHAT ARE JEWS FOR?

What Are Jews For?

HISTORY, PEOPLEHOOD, AND PURPOSE

ADAM SUTCLIFFE

PRINCETON UNIVERSITY PRESS

PRINCETON & OXFORD

Published by Princeton University Press
41 William Street, Princeton, New Jersey 08540
6 Oxford Street, Woodstock, Oxfordshire OX20 1TR

press.princeton.edu

Library of Congress Cataloging-in-Publication Data

Names: Sutcliffe, Adam, author.
Title: What Are Jews For?: History, Peoplehood, and Purpose / Adam Sutcliffe.
Description: Hardcover ed. | Princeton ; Oxford : Princeton University Press, 2020. |
    Includes index.
Identifiers: LCCN 2019032983 (print) | LCCN 2019032984 (ebook) |
    ISBN 9780691188805 (hardcover) | ISBN 9780691201931 (epub)
Subjects: LCSH: Jews—Election, Doctrine of.
Classification: LCC BM613 .S88 2020 (print) | LCC BM613 (ebook) |
    DDC 296.3/117—dc23
LC record available at https://lccn.loc.gov/2019032983
LC ebook record available at https://lccn.loc.gov/2019032984

British Library Cataloging-in-Publication Data is available

Editorial: Ben Tate and Charlie Allen
Production Editorial: Debbie Tegarden
Jacket/Cover Design: Layla Mac Rory
Production: Brigid Ackerman
Publicity: Katie Lewis and Kate Hensley

This book has been composed in Arno

Printed on acid-free paper. ∞

Printed in the United States of America

10 9 8 7 6 5 4 3 2 1

CONTENTS

PREFACE AND ACKNOWLEDGEMENTS

THIS BOOK was a very long time in gestation, but once I had found my way to the right formulation of my question it was relatively swift in execution. My question is about purpose, and asking it has itself been for me strongly imbued with a sense of purpose. This isn't only because Jewish purpose is personally important to me: though it is, and the reach and shape of the book inevitably to some extent reflects my own particular vantage point. As much as possible, though, I have attempted to write from an ethnically, religiously, politically and nationally neutral perspective, and to offer all the varied voices I discuss a fair and sensitive hearing.

I here offer what I hope is a scholarly but nonetheless accessible exploration of over four centuries of debate, among both Jews and non-Jews, on what I call 'the Jewish purpose question'. I am an intellectual historian by training and profession, and my primary aim is to explain the historical unfolding of these ideas and arguments, and to capture both their local contextual nuances and their deep continuities and connections across centuries. The concerns of many other disciplines—philosophy, theology, sociology, literary studies, economics and politics—are also prominent in these pages. My subject, most importantly, is by no means significant only for Jews, or for those who have a special interest in them or their history. Jewish purpose, I centrally argue, is the perennial starting-point in Western thought for reflections on the collective purpose of any and all forms of human group affiliation. This book, in other words, concerns the purpose of all of us.

I have whenever possible used readily accessible editions and reliable published translations of the texts I discuss. In many cases, though, no such translations exist, and quoted translations are my own. Jewish Bible quotations are from the Jewish Publication Society version, and New Testament quotations from the King James version, in both cases occasionally very slightly modified. All web links in the endnotes were functioning shortly before publication.

My debts to those who helped this project take shape are innumerable and immense. Even restricting my thanks to those who have most directly assisted my research and writing, the list is long. My colleagues at King's College London, particularly but not only in the History Department, have been inspirational, supportive and sustaining in very many ways. I am particularly grateful to Simon Gaunt for his mentorship during my term as Head of Department, and to Evelyn Welch for a turning-point conversation in which she advised me to write the book that I most wanted to write. Several audiences in London, and also in Cambridge, Oxford, Southampton, Cape Town, Illinois and Pennsylvania, helped me test out my arguments: many thanks to Jessica Cooperman, Dara Goldman, Brett Kaplan, Hartley Lachter and Adam Mendelsohn for the international invitations that enabled these encounters. I would also like to thank the many people at Princeton University Press who have worked so assiduously on this manuscript, and in particular my ever-enthusiastic editor Ben Tate, my meticulous copyeditor Francis Eaves and my efficient production editor Debbie Tegarden.

Very special thanks are due to those colleagues and friends who generously found time to read and critique substantial portions of my draft text: Jim Bjork, Hannah Dawson, David Feldman, Shirli Gilbert, Peter Howarth, David Kaskel, Andrea Schatz, Esther Schor and Elliot Wolfson. My triumvirate of rabbinic advisors—Janet Burden, Judith Rosen-Berry and Mark Solomon—offered invaluable encouragement and insights. Brian Klug read the entire manuscript, and offered detailed and extremely shrewd feedback. Jonathan Price provided advice from a publisher's perspective. I am extremely grateful for all this assistance, and also to the two anonymous readers on behalf of Princeton University Press.

My most heartfelt thanks, though, are to my family. My brother, William, and my father, John, both read and encouragingly commented on sections of the project. My mother, Susan, read every word, not only picking up my proofreading slips and stylistic clangers, but also helping me disentangle many garbled or over-long sentences. If this book is a clear and pleasurable read for the 'educated general reader', this is in large measure thanks to her. The wonderful scholarship of my wife, Nadia Valman, is cited thirteen times in my endnotes; engaging closely with it has been one of the special pleasures of this project. This is only the publicly visible tip of the privately submerged immensity of our intellectual, amorous and parental life together. I am boundlessly grateful, as ever, for her loving support, probing critique and constant mental stimulation, during the writing of this book and throughout the past sixteen years.

This book took shape in parallel with asking, together with Nadia, how we might organize a bar mitzvah for our son Orlando that would explore and convey as meaningfully as possible the significance of embracing Jewish adulthood and responsibility. I'm not sure to what extent we succeeded, but the attempt to do so richly cross-fertilized with the writing of this book. The challenges and joys of fatherhood over the past fifteen years, the last eleven of them with Lucian also, have been the sustaining centre of my life. If, within the meaner inner recesses of my psyche, there's a part of me that wants to hold my sons, and the delightful distraction they provide, responsible for the errors and infelicities that remain in this book, then I certainly wouldn't have wished it any other way. Perhaps this book will one day help Orlando and Lucian find or clarify their Jewish purpose. They have already, though, helped me find mine.

London
January 2020

What Are Jews For?

HISTORY AND THE PURPOSE QUESTION

We are not obliged to justify our existence by working for the world. Nobody, no other nation, has ever been put under such an obligation, and some of us see it as scandalous that unlike everyone else, we have to justify being Jews by serving some further purpose. No one asks a Frenchman why he is there. Everyone asks a Jew why he is there; no one would be content with the statement, I am just a Jew. Yet the Jew has every right to be just a Jew and to contribute to what he is by being just what he is. We are always asked to be something exceptional, something supreme, something ultimate. Maybe that very expectation will come to fruition one day, and perhaps then even the enigma of being the chosen people, which is not so easily discarded, will be resolved.[1]

—GERSHOM SCHOLEM (1973)

WHAT ARE JEWS FOR? The question is at first sight absurd and impertinent, if not worse. Jews, like anybody else, live for the most part muddled and meandering lives, without any notably clear sense of purpose, either as individuals or as a collective. To single out any group of people as bearers of a designated role or responsibility in the world seems invidious: why them? To single out Jews feels particularly awkward. The perception of Jews as somehow irreducibly different from others has been a feature of various familiar tropes of antisemitism. Is it not high time, then, for this question to be laid unambiguously to rest? Should we not today clearly insist that Jews, of all people, have no need to justify their existence, and should not in any sense be understood as performing some historical function for the rest of humanity?

And yet: this question cannot be easily evaded. The idea that Jews are endowed with a particular historical purpose occupies a central position both in the Jewish tradition itself and in the Christian and post-Christian frameworks that have structured Western thinking about the place of the Jews as a unique minority in the wider world. The question of Jewish purpose follows inescapably from Jewish chosenness, which lies at the heart of Judaism. God chose the Jews: but why, on what terms, and to what end? The biblical 'election of Israel'—the setting apart of the Jews by God, as recipients of divine protection, and bearers of special holiness—gives rise to an array of further questions. What does it mean for a universal God to single out a particular people? Where does this leave those other peoples in the eyes of God, and in relationship to Jews? Can the election of Israel be rescinded, either for all Jews, or for individuals among them? What happens if individual Jews reject their covenant with God (whatever precisely that means)? For what specific role in the world, and in the messianic denouement of human history, did God select the Jews? And why, of all people, them? Cogitating on these questions, the early sages and rabbis developed various theological avenues of reflection, elaborating on the Jews' unique intimacy with God, and their special place in the divine plan for the world. The church fathers, starting from the same biblical texts—particularly the books of Exodus and Isaiah—originated the tradition of Christian theological thinking on the election and historical purpose of the Jews, which both overlaps with Jewish perspectives and has been enduringly central to the tension between the two religions.

In the ancient Near East it was, it seems, unexceptional to believe that one's own God was in some sense the only true God, and was certainly superior to those of other tribes and polities. In this respect the perspective of the Jewish Bible can be taken as broadly representative of the prevailing religious norms of the region around the eighth century BCE. The limited available evidence suggests that neighbouring peoples, such as the Moabites and the Ammonites, understood their intimate relationships with their own deities in terms broadly similar to those of the prophetic books of the Bible.[2] In the Hellenistic and Roman periods, the monotheistic focus of the Jews marked them more clearly apart from the syncretic paganism of the dominant culture. It was only with the emergence of Christianity, though, that Jewish religious and ethnic separateness became firmly welded together, and conceived as the defining hallmark distinguishing Judaism from the universalist message and mission of the self-defined Catholic Church.

The significance of the Jews' separateness, and of their special relationship with God, was a matter of serious reflection among the early and medieval rabbis. However, for as long as Jews lived in a clearly subordinate position within Christian and Muslim states, which not only accepted but enforced their segregation, these issues had no direct practical significance, and were not a focus of contention between the three faiths. Early Islam was much more polemically engaged with Christianity than with Judaism, and evinced no particular concern with these matters.[3] From a medieval Christian perspective, the dispersal and suffering of the Jews reflected their rejection by God for having failed to accept his son as the messiah, and any political implications of their status as nonetheless in some sense still God's chosen people were deferred to a distant future. Only when some Christians came to believe that a transformed future might be not distant but imminent, and, in a related attitudinal shift, that Jews should be treated on a more welcoming and tolerant basis, did Jewish particularity become a prominent topic of confusion and controversy. From the seventeenth century onwards, as European Jews and Christians developed new and shared languages of political thought, the question of the proper place of Jews in the present and future world became a matter of increasingly intense and ramified debate.

The modern history of the Jewish 'purpose question' really begins, then, in the seventeenth century, when Hebraic themes moved to the fore of political discourse in the two most dynamic states of the period—the Dutch Republic and England. Both Protestant polities claimed for themselves the mantle of divine chosenness as a means to justify and sanctify their special place in the world. In both countries there was also a close engagement with Jewish texts, and with Jews themselves. Shared Jewish and Christian excitement over the role of the Jews in the culmination of human history reached a peak in 1665, when Sabbatai Zevi was widely proclaimed as the Jewish messiah. Hebraic themes played a much wider role in the period, however, and this fascination also intensified the non-Jewish reception of the philosophy of Baruch Spinoza—the first Jew emphatically to reject the doctrine of the election of Israel. In the eighteenth century, several leading Enlightenment philosophers defined their ideas in contrast to the particularism represented by Judaism, while Spinoza and Moses Mendelssohn—by far the most influential Jewish philosopher of the eighteenth century—offered starkly contrasting attempts to account for Judaism within an Enlightenment framework. The significance of these debates, for most of the long Enlightenment period, was predominantly intellectual. They intersected, however, with questions of practical policy. Around 1780, the balance between these perspectives abruptly shifted, with the political and cultural transformation of Jews in order to harness their economic utility becoming one of the most intensely debated topics of the revolutionary and Napoleonic eras.

In this period of unprecedented upheaval, many European intellectuals, both Jewish and Christian, believed that the ancient religion served no further purpose, and that with emergence of a new era of rational universalism the 'euthanasia of Judaism', as envisaged by Immanuel Kant, was approaching.[4] Those Jews who rejected this, but otherwise embraced the Enlightenment legacy, felt the need to advance new arguments for the value of perpetuating Judaism in the world. Leading nineteenth-century rabbis, particularly those at the fore of the German Reform movement such as Abraham Geiger, vigorously asserted that the Jews had an indispensable historical mission as teachers of ethics and spirituality to others. They also raised their voices against other very different conceptions of Jewish distinctiveness in this period, which linked the Jews, often but not always in negative terms, to the development of capitalism, or to anticapitalist political radicalism. The Zionist movement emerged in part as an attempt to normalize the place of Jews in the world, and as a challenge to the idea that Jews should justify themselves in the terms of others, which Zionists such as Ahad Ha'am regarded as cravenly assimilationist. However, various notions of Jewish historical mission have played an important role in Zionist thought, including, most famously, the idea that a Jewish state should be 'a light unto the nations'.

In the nineteenth and early twentieth centuries the historical role of the Jews was closely associated with their suffering. This link was drawn, in various ways, by both Jewish and non-Jewish philosophers, such as Hegel, Nietzsche and Hermann Cohen, and writers such as Walter Scott, Grace Aguilar, Heinrich Heine and Stefan Zweig. Antisemitic resentment, when it emerged as a political force in Europe in the late nineteenth century, was readily seen in this light as an unsurprising and perhaps even understandable response to Jewish election and specialness. Since the Holocaust, though, this argument has become almost impossible to entertain. Passive acceptance of Jewish suffering, once witnessed on such a scale, has almost universally been regarded as an untenable position. For many late twentieth-century Jews, particularly in the United States, the idea of Jewish chosenness has been troublesome for a different reason: this highlighting of special status has seemed to brush against the grain of Jewish efforts to 'fit in' within mainstream society. Mordecai Kaplan, the founder of the most

American form of Judaism, Reconstructionism, rejected the concept, and attempted to purge the religion of what he regarded as its unwarranted and outdated claims of exclusivity and superiority. The chosen people idea, however, has retained a tenacious presence in Jewish life in America, Israel and elsewhere.[5] Many Jews today find it awkward to embrace but similarly difficult to abandon.

The leading British rabbi and theologian Louis Jacobs, writing in 1973, encapsulated the diffidence with which Jewish chosenness was approached in the postwar era. Suggesting that medieval Jewish thinkers already found the doctrine 'something of an embarrassment', Jacobs rejected the claim that Jews were superior to others, and was at pains to distance the chosen people idea from Nazi notions of racial supremacy. He nonetheless argued that despite the dangers of the notion, the Jewish people's collective self-understanding as a chosen people valuably affirmed their commitment to the covenant and to a 'sense of destiny'.[6] Within mainstream Judaism, this has remained the consensus view. While the topic is relatively little addressed directly, serious attempts have been made to defend and develop the theology of the election of Israel, paying careful attention to its implications for the relationship between Jews and non-Jews.[7] The question of Jewish purpose is, however, not exclusively a theological matter. The insistence, within the Jewish tradition, on the this-worldly dimension of the final redemption to which the Jews' election in some way points—that this messianic moment will truly transform our world—has itself blurred the boundary between the religious and the secular, or, one might say, the political. Jewish distinctiveness has also been historically associated with a wide range of non-religious qualities and values: rationalism, textuality, intellectuality, idealism, ethical rigour, cultural vitality and collective cohesion.[8] Jews today, if they choose to identify positively with Jewishness, may be integrating these associations into their personal and possibly entirely secular sense of Jewish purpose, without necessarily any sense of affiliation with other Jews or explicit belief in the chosen people idea.

How, then, should we make sense of this vexed and multifaceted topic? I would like to put forward three guiding principles. Firstly, we must approach it historically. Most Jews would probably consider their purpose in the world as Jews—if they acknowledge this as a meaningful question at all—either as a theological or as an existential matter, or perhaps as a mixture of both. However, the doctrine of the election of Israel took shape in the historical context of Jews' diasporic existence among and under Christians and Muslims. In modern history, it has been centrally entangled not only in the evolving religious confrontation between Judaism and Christianity, but also in the attempts, since the seventeenth century, to make sense of difference within a universalistic political and philosophical framework. As these debates developed and diversified, perceptions and significations of Jewish distinctiveness also grew in variety and complexity, and spread into the domains of culture, economics, sociology and nationalism. Our contemporary thinking on Jewish particularity and purpose takes place in the choppy slipstream of these historical debates, further churned and muddled by the central place of Jews in the tragedy and drama of twentieth-century history. We cannot ask, 'What are Jews for?' in innocence of this historical baggage. Rather, we need patiently to tease apart the various strands of thinking on this question, and explore how they have accreted, clashed and mingled, over the past four centuries in particular. Only through such a historical reconstruction is it possible to achieve a lucid understanding of the issues and choices that today rest on this question.

Secondly, and flowing directly from this historicity, we must recognize that the debate on Jewish purpose involves both Jews and non-Jews, in a shared conversation. It is increasingly recognized that in the early centuries CE, Judaism and Christianity took shape in large measure in relation to each other.[9] For Christians, defining themselves as members of a new sort of grouping—a 'religion' in the creed-based sense that we largely understand it today—Judaism was constructed as an antithetical religion in contrast to which Christian truths were clarified. The early rabbis, spurred as much by the destruction of the Second Temple in 70 CE as by the rising challenge of Christianity, at first to some degree responded in kind, but by approximately the sixth century CE they had rejected the Christian conception of religion, and asserted instead a different understanding of Jewishness, defined by the given of ethnic peoplehood rather than by acceptance of a theological orthodoxy.[10] For both Christians and Jews, this dissonance between Jewish ethnic particularity and Christian theological universalism was the central challenge in making sense of the other, and of themselves in relation to the other. The supersessionist theology of early Christianity nonetheless ascribed profound meaning to the Jews as God's chosen people, incurring divine punishment for their failure to recognize Jesus as the messiah, but destined to be restored to favour at the end of days. The early rabbis, rethinking Judaism in the wake of the loss of the Temple and the emergence of Christianity, developed in the Talmud an emphasis on the causal connection between the actions of Israel and the future coming of the messiah. These contrasting and competing notions of the role of the Jewish people in the unfolding of the messianic destiny of human history remain inescapably at the heart of the theological relationship between Judaism and Christianity.

The future-oriented theme of messianism constitutes the theological underlay of the many secular forms into which the question of Jewish purpose has mutated in the modern era. When approaching the question in philosophical, political, economic or sociological terms, both Jews and non-Jews have repeatedly associated the Jewish role in the world with the movement of history toward a transformed future in which the differences and divisions between people would be profoundly altered, and possibly overcome altogether. Jews and Christians (or post-Christian secularists), despite starting from different perspectives on Jewish difference, have nonetheless often put forward very similar accounts of the significance of Jews in the emergence of this future. In conceptual terms, the uniqueness of Jews—as quintessential markers of minority difference, but also as bearers of a special role in the fulfilment of history—was fundamentally the same for both groups. Interpretations of Jewish modernity through the lens of postcolonialism have emphasized the role of Jews as resisters of the dominant cultural discourse.[11] In many contexts, however, and certainly in the educated Western milieux in which, since the seventeenth century, most developed thinking on the idea of Jewish purpose has taken place, Jews have more typically aspired to participate on equal terms within the dominant culture. The matter of their distinctive role in the world, far from necessarily being a focus of division between Jews and others, has often been a particularly rich terrain for Jewish interchange with non-Jews. It has also been a shared source of stimulation and debate on the shape of history and the nature of human purpose in general.

It is temptingly straightforward to assume that group affiliation provides a key for understanding the underlying meaning of any statement a person may make about his or her own or another group. Very similar statements on, for example, the economic prowess of Jews, are on this basis readily ascribed to proud self-assertion when from a Jew (or to self-hatred if this attribute is viewed negatively), but to suspect and possibly antisemitic exceptionalist thinking when from a non-Jew. This crude simplification should, however, be rejected. The layered history of the Western debate on Jewish purpose can only be properly and sensitively understood if a third guiding principle is observed: the avoidance of judgmental categorizations. The study of non-Jewish thinking on Jews has most commonly been filed under the heading 'antisemitism', or the more carefully transhistorical term 'anti-Judaism'. Much of this scholarship is excellent, and provides an essential framework for understanding the exclusionary

hostility and violence that has recurred through Jewish history, and the culmination of this in the Holocaust.[12] Hostility, though, is not the inevitable keynote of all non-Jewish thinking on Jews. The enormity of the Nazi genocide has
very understandably led to an emphasis on this historical current, but as a
result, historians have tended to overlook more positive attitudes to Jews, or
to regard them with suspicion. Both the category 'antisemitism' and its sometimes controversial twin term 'philosemitism' assume the primacy of a binary
determination on the attitudinal valence of a pronouncement on Jews. The two
terms also assume a sharp distinction between what Jews and non-Jews say or
think about Jews: it is not generally considered intelligible to describe a Jew as
either antisemitic or philosemitic. With regard to Jewish purpose, these words
are an impediment to understanding the evaluative openness and nuance of this
idea in many contexts, and the deep interpenetration of Jewish and non-Jewish
thinking on the topic.

Several other terms are also best avoided in our inquiry. Attitudes to Jews
have often been described as 'ambivalent', or as a reflection in the modern era of
a wider ambivalence toward economic and social upheavals, of which the ap-
parently indeterminate status of Jews was widely seen as the archetypal symptom and symbol.[13] As with antisemitism and philosemitism, though, this
middling term carries with it the reductive assumption that reaching an evaluative judgment, as either good or bad, is the underlying aim of all thought on
Jews. Settling on the label of 'ambivalence' to describe a perspective on Jews
foregrounds a sense of uneasy hovering between these two poles, and can often
foreclose careful consideration of the non-evaluative complexity of these ideas.
Within the Jewish domain, reflection on the wider cultural position of Jews or
Judaism is frequently assumed to relate above all to a quest for 'identity': a perspective that implicitly assumes the primacy of introspection and self-definition
over more outward concerns relating to the wider world. Jewish thinkers are
often considered as collectively in dialogue with the non-Jewish world, to
which they offer their 'response'.[14] This last term positions Jews as structurally
external to the cultural mainstream, not participating directly within and to
some degree shaping the dominant culture, but only belatedly reacting to it.
This again assumes a stark divide between the Jewish and the non-Jewish
realms, obscuring the possibility of fine-grained interaction across the boundary between them. In order to approach the history of the Jewish purpose
question with as much openness as possible to its own internal logics and
cross-cultural resonances, we must set aside all these assumptions and the
terms that unreflectively carry them.

Beneath its heavy historical and theological freighting, the issue of Jewish purpose poses an abstract problem that is vexed and pressing for us all: what sort of special role can and should any particular group perform in our shared world? How to live purposively as a Jew clearly has a special lived significance for Jews alone. Discussion of the topic, however, cannot be subject to cultural ownership, above all because it has been so deeply enmeshed over the past two millennia in Western thinking about the general relationships between religion, peoplehood, history and meaning. It is eminently understandable that any group of people might wish to define their own collective purpose without intervention from others. In the Jewish case, the weight of history, including, above all, the role of exceptionalist conceptions of Jews in marking the path to their genocide, has intensified this desire. However, far from leading to a normalization of the place of the Jews in the world, the Holocaust has deepened the overdetermination of Jewish history, peoplehood and purpose. The establishment of the state of Israel, contrary to the hopes and expectations of many, has also not reduced, but rather heightened, the sense of uniqueness, controversy and confusion surrounding the place of Jews in the world. This question is often complicatedly embroiled in heated political controversies over antisemitism and Islamophobia, the Israel/Palestine conflict and the place of utopian radicalism in the world today. However much we might wish it to be otherwise, the meanings of Jewishness, and particularly of Jewish historical purpose, are profoundly intertwined with these central issues of global debate.

We might, though, not wish it to be otherwise. The meanings of minority status—of being different, as a group—have in the Western tradition been most venerably and extensively explored in relation to Jews. These reflections and debates provide a rich starting-point for thinking about the significance of any collective social identity as part of a wider human whole. Zionism was a belated nationalist movement, but the early modern formation of national identities, in the Bible-saturated Protestant world in particular, took place in conscious emulation of the Hebraic example. The actual and potential resonances of the case of Jewish purposiveness extend far beyond the realm of historical nationalism. Many different forms of identity are today jostling for status, meaning and value. What is the worth, though, in asserting a regional, supranational, ethnic, religious or sexual identity, as, say, Scottish, European, Black, Buddhist or bisexual (or any or even all of these at once) in today's mobile and multicultural world, in which our collective affiliations are more fluid and complex than ever? How are these identities defined, and in what way can or should they claim respect not simply as inescapable givens or as self-interested and competing interest groups, but for whatever distinctive element they contribute to our shared planetary existence? These are difficult questions that concern us all. A promising place to begin, I would suggest, is with the modern history of the attempts to answer them with respect to Jews. If the Jewish case indeed proves to be a stimulating and illuminating guide in clarifying our thinking on collective purpose in general, then that itself offers a first answer to the question of Jewish purpose in this world.

The idea that Jews have a special mission to others has a long history. Its most recent forceful rearticulation is by the prominent French Jewish intellectual Bernard-Henri Lévy, who places the chosenness of the Jewish people at the core of his unabashedly self-congratulatory book *The Genius of Judaism* (2017). The Jews, Lévy argues, are a 'treasured people' not because of who they are, but due to their mission in the world. His privileged biblical text is the book of Jonah, in which God sends his prophet to the sinful foreign city of Nineveh, in order to bring its citizens to repentance so that God does not have to punish them. The prophetic corpus, and Jonah in particular, underscores for Lévy 'the obligation of the Jew toward the non-Jew'. The Jewish people have, according to his exegesis, an orientation and a responsibility toward the other nations of the world, in the name of truth and in opposition to evil.[15] Lévy casts this ethical argument in very concrete political terms. The ruins of Assyrian Nineveh stand on the outskirts of the Iraqi city of Mosul, occupied by Daesh ('Islamic State') from 2014 to 2017. The lesson of Jonah, Lévy argues in tenuous connection to this, is that Jews must lead the way in 'looking the devil in the face', by opposing political evil not only in Iraq, but in all its forms. He also relates this moral exceptionalism to what he describes as the extraordinary achievements of the state of Israel and of Jews in France, in both cases in the face of persistent and resurgent antisemitism.[16] Lévy's book is representative of the continuance into the present of attempts to deploy the notion of the Jews' historical purpose in support of particular social and political arguments. Alongside the live question of whether this notion retains any meaningfulness at all, the issue of to what ends and in whose name it should today be mobilized remains a matter of heated contestation and major political significance.

Covenant, Chosenness and Divine Purpose: The Biblical Prooftexts

As soon as Abraham enters the biblical narrative, God declares a special bond with him, promising that 'I will make of you a great nation, and I will bless you' (Genesis 12:2). Twice in the following verses this bond is reaffirmed as a covenant, first with specific lands promised to Abraham's offspring (15:18–21), and the second time with a condition imposed: that Abraham and all his male offspring be circumcised, as a compulsory sign and component of their 'everlasting pact' with God (17:9–14). God's initial declaration, while emphasizing divine protection, already hints that Abraham's descendants are charged with some sort of higher purpose for the whole world: 'all the families of the earth shall bless themselves by you' (12:3). This is soon expanded upon, although somewhat enigmatically. Preparing to punish the city of Sodom for the great sins of its inhabitants, God considers whether to hide from Abraham his intentions, repeating this same phrase and enlarging on it: 'for I have singled him out, that he may instruct his children and his posterity to keep the way of the Lord by doing what is just and right' (18:19). When God does reveal to him the planned destruction of Sodom, Abraham objects to the potential injustice of this collective punishment. He persuades God not to destroy the city if fifty innocent people are found there, and then persistently bargains down this number—first to forty-five, then forty, thirty and twenty, and finally to ten (18:23–32). Abraham here holds God to account, insisting that the judge of the world should indeed act justly.

In the subsequent book of Exodus a divine covenant is forged once again. This time the setting is Sinai, God's interlocutor is Moses, and the covenant is made not only with Abraham's descendants but also with the 'mixed multitude' that fled from Egypt with them (Exodus 13:38). The reciprocity of this covenant is much clearer, being substantiated in a detailed body of law and religious observances that the children of Israel agree to follow. Before revealing any of this, though, God calls Moses from Mount Sinai, commanding him to tell his people these core principles underlying their covenant:

> Now then, if you will obey Me faithfully and keep My covenant, you shall be My treasured possession among all the peoples [*li segulah mikol ha-amim*]. Indeed, all the earth is Mine, but you shall be to Me a kingdom of priests and a holy nation. (Exodus 19:5–6)

These verses are the prime source for the concept of the Jews as a 'chosen people', or, in more formal terms, the doctrine of 'the election of Israel'.[17] The bond established here is grounded on obedience and intimacy. It is not, though, a purely private relationship between God and his treasured people: God is sovereign over all peoples, but has designated the children of Israel as special, both in their value in God's eyes and in their role in the world. Their priestly holiness suggests that they are superior or exemplary to others in some way. But the nature of this is left unclear—as, indeed, are other key aspects of the Sinaitic covenant. The Exodus narrative explicitly states that the people pledge their assent to this agreement. They do so twice, unanimously voicing their obedience, in the same terms, both before and after God has revealed the divine commandments and laws (19:8; 24:3). The first agreement, though, hardly constitutes informed assent; still more problematically, the covenant is also taken as binding for all subsequent generations. An inviolable familial dimension, which is fundamental in the Abrahamic covenant, remains here, but now it is blurred with the conditional and voluntary legal aspect of this second covenant.[18] This has given rise to a core ambiguity within the Judaic tradition: between the potentially inclusive nature of the legal covenant (as anybody can pledge allegiance to a system of laws) and the exclusive familial nature of the first covenant, reiterated at Sinai in its 'chosen people' form.

The ethical aspect of God's design for the Jews, already suggested by Abraham's argument with God over the collective punishment of Sodom, moves to the fore in the prophetic books of the Bible. It is particularly resonantly expressed in the book of Isaiah, in which the Jews are described as a 'light unto the nations'. This is the first and most extensive of the three appearances of this image in the book:[19]

> I the Lord, in My grace, have summoned you, and I have grasped you by the hand. I created you, and appointed you a covenant people, a light unto the nations [or la-goyim], to open eyes deprived of light, rescue prisoners from confinement, and from the dungeon those who sit in darkness. (Isaiah 42:6–7)

Understood in historical context, it seems likely that Isaiah—or 'Deutero-Isaiah', as this section of the book was almost certainly written during the period of Judean exile in Babylon in the sixth century BCE, approximately two centuries later than the likely original authorship of the book's first section—was here seeking to rally the spirits of his people, looking forward to a time in which the exile will be over and Jerusalem will be restored, thanks to the defeat of Babylon by King Cyrus of Persia, who is lauded in this section of the book. However, the ethical resonance of these passages is powerful, and, as we shall see, the 'light unto the nations' idea has featured prominently in some currents of Jewish thought, and particularly as an inspiration and a justification for Zionism.

The high profile of this idea in the modern era is, though, largely due to the special place of the book of Isaiah in Christianity and in polemics between Jews and Christians over the correct interpretation of the Hebrew Bible. Sometimes known as 'the fifth gospel', Isaiah contains many of the passages taken by

Christians as the messianic prophecies most clearly fulfilled by Jesus. In particular, Isaiah's 'songs of the suffering servant' verses are taken in the Jewish tradition to refer to the people of Israel, while Christians have traditionally read them as prophesying the redemptive sacrifice of Jesus Christ. The first of these passages occurs almost immediately before the 'light unto the nations' passage quoted above (42:1–4). The most famous, in Isaiah 53, immediately follows a lengthy prophecy of the redemption of Jerusalem, includes phrases that echo the covenantal language of ethical responsibility to others, and links this responsibility to suffering: 'My righteous servant makes the many righteous; it is their punishment that he bears' (53:11).[20] The association of chosenness with suffering, suggested in this phrase, has risen to prominence over the past two millennia through the diffusion of its Christian interpretation. The elevation of all these verses to the status of central and oft-repeated Christian prooftexts has placed the question of Jewish purpose close to the core of the theological tussle between the two religions, influencing the biblical reading and self-understanding of Jews as well as Christians.

The writings of Paul are by far the most important texts in this debate. Paul's central question was, as Daniel Boyarin has put it, 'How do the rest of the people in God's world fit into the plan of salvation revealed to the Jews through their Torah?'[21] This universalistic concern arose naturally in Paul's Hellenistic philosophical environment, and other Jews of the first century CE were also exploring the same issue. This question was in no sense inherently un-Jewish or anti-Jewish—though this assumption has bedevilled Christian exegesis of Paul, which until recent decades typically read him as an ardent critic of Judaism.[22] It is more accurate to interpret him, following Boyarin, as a 'radical Jew', offering an internal critique of Judaism in the light of the philosophical temperament of the time, and seeking to make sense of the biblical dual covenant. It is the initial covenant, with Abraham, that is for Paul most significant and lofty, because it was made purely on the basis of Abraham's faith in God. Addressing the Galatians, Paul argues that God's promise to Abraham that all the peoples of the world 'shall bless themselves by you' anticipates the extension of God's love to the Gentiles, through faith in Jesus Christ (Galatians 3:8–14). He then poses the question of the purpose of the law revealed at Sinai. He answers that it was 'added because of transgressions' (3:19), and served to guide the children of Israel prior to Jesus Christ's 'promise by faith', and to prepare them for it:

> The law was our schoolmaster to bring us unto Christ, that we might be justified by faith. But after that faith is come, we are no longer under a

schoolmaster. For ye are all the children of God by faith in Christ Jesus. . . . There is neither Jew nor Greek, there is neither slave nor free, there is neither male nor female: for ye are all one in Christ Jesus. (Galatians 3:24–6, 28)

This famous passage, in which Paul asserts the supersession of the Jewish law by faith in Christ, has been widely taken as anti-Judaic or even antisemitic. However, Paul was unequivocal about his own kinship with other Jews, and his personal sense of connection and concern that stemmed from this. In his letter to the Romans, he states explicitly that God has not 'cast away his people', and that their 'stumble' in not embracing Jesus's message does not presage their final fall: quoting from the prophecies of Isaiah, he declares that ultimately 'all Israel shall be saved' (Romans 11:1, 11, 26). Paul's theology of Jews and Judaism was clearly intimate, complex and far from straightforwardly hostile.[23] He regarded the Jews as bearers of a crucial historical purpose, through their double covenant with God, in pointing the way to Jesus Christ. Their historical significance did not, though, end at that point, as their ultimate redemption, through faith in Christ, would mark the final fulfilment of Christ's message.

Paul casts Jewish allegiance to the law as quintessentially particularist, in contrast both to the religious universality of Christian faith and to the philosophical universalism of the dominant Hellenistic culture (Jew versus Greek). This was not an obvious opposition. The Jewish world in the late Second Temple period was very considerably Hellenized. Although the Jews of Palestine were notably distinctive in their insistence on monotheistic worship and on the centrality of the Jerusalem Temple, the Jews as a whole were not in any clear-cut sense a 'particularly particular' people, set apart by differences categorically different from those between other peoples in the Hellenistic world.[24] The contrast that Paul draws between the Jewish and the universal is also highly complex and unstable. He locates in Abraham the originary example of the pure faith on which Christ's message is based. He also does not seem to envisage the extinction of Jewish difference, except at the messianic moment, or in the messianic sense, in which all human oppositions, including gender and social class, will also disappear.[25] Paul's intricate thinking on this issue positioned the Jews as enduringly and inescapably central in debates in the Christian tradition on the significance of the particular within a universalist theological or political framework.

Paul overlays this opposition with a number of powerful and highly influential allegorical binary contrasts, the most important of which is between the flesh and the spirit. The Jewish covenant is inscribed in the flesh through circumcision, while faith in Christ is purely in the spirit: 'circumcision is that of the heart, in the spirit, and not in the letter' (Romans 2:29). The image of the circumcision of the heart occurs in the Torah (e.g., Deuteronomy 30:6), but Paul contrasts this to the mandating of physical circumcision in the Jewish law. While for Jews he sees circumcision as meaningful sign of their covenant with God (Romans 3:1–2), he argues strenuously that with regard to Christ it is an irrelevance, and that Gentile Christians do not need to be circumcised (Galatians 6:12–18). The 'letter' of the law is aligned with the flesh, and against the figural readings offered by Paul, as part of his wider conception of the supersession of the Jewish law by Christ's teachings.[26] In this framework, the law is cast as an infantile phase—'our schoolmaster to bring us to Christ'—in contrast to the maturity of faith. This developmental language is very significant for the future of the idea of Jewish purpose. Paul presents the Jews as blind and child-like: they have signalled the way toward the future that has now become present with the advent of Christ, but they also foreshadow this event and are destined to play a crucial role in its still future final fulfilment. This tangled theological temporality has underpinned the privileged signification of Jews in Western thought on the shape of historical change, particularly in relation to utopian or messianic hopes.

Mainstream Judaism in this period also registered the challenge of explaining the relationship of the Torah to the other peoples of the world. The rise of Christianity made this issue more pressing, as did the destruction of the Temple in 70 CE, which prompted a turn in Judaism from the centrality of priestly rituals to an emphasis on the compilation and study of texts. In the *Sifre* commentary to the book of Deuteronomy, largely compiled in the tannaitic period (first and second centuries CE), an account is given of God offering the Torah to all of the nations of the world, each of whom, after asking for further details, declined it. First God approached the Edomites, who could not agree to the prohibition on murder; next the Torah was offered to the Ammonites and the Moabites, who baulked at the interdict on adultery, as they were descended from the incestuous coupling of Lot with his daughters; the Ishmaelites then refused to assent to the commandment 'thou shalt not steal'. Only after this pattern had been repeated with 'every other nation' did God bestow the Torah on Israel.[27] This account explicitly incorporates the entire world into the narrative of the election of Israel. It superficially appears to imbue that narrative with considerable modesty: for unexplained reasons, Israel was God's last choice. However, the stronger implication is precisely the opposite. Only the children of Israel were ethically worthy of the Torah, and it was for this reason, established according to this account through a thorough process of elimination, that they were chosen by God.

The talmudic tractate *Avodah Zarah*, composed in Babylon between the third and the fifth centuries CE, opens with an elaborate depiction of the Last Judgment, which puts forward a more audacious version of essentially the same argument. God commands each nation to approach separately and to claim their reward for upholding the Torah. The Romans enter first, and claim that all their commercial activity and creation of wealth has been 'for the sake of Israel, that they could occupy themselves with the Torah'. The Persians then make the same claim for their construction and warfare, and the other nations of the world make similar arguments—but God rejects them all, declaring that they have acted only in their own interests. The nations then ask for another chance to accept and follow the Torah. God commands them to perform the 'easy mitzvah' of constructing and living in a *sukkah*. As soon as the sun blazes down on them through the unenclosed roof of this temporary structure, they abandon their test—and God laughs at them.[28] In this account, not only God, but also the higher nobility of the Torah, is in some sense recognized by all, including the Roman and Persian superpowers of the era. The fairness, and thus also the universality, of God is underscored by the granting of a second chance to the nations of the world. The swift abandonment by all the other nations of the burdens of the Torah highlights once again, though, that only Israel is worthy of election.

This passage, like much of the *Avodah Zarah* tractate, was also engaging in polemic against Christianity. God's concluding laughter is an allusion to Psalms 2:4—'He who is enthroned in heaven laughs'—which was widely used as a prooftext for the Christian account of the Last Judgment, and of which the rabbinic sages here offered their own interpretation.[29] The partition of Judaism and Christianity was a protracted process over the course of late antiquity, from which emerged a new notion of 'religion', defined not in terms of allegiance or practice but by a set of doctrines established as theological orthodoxy, and through the rejection as 'heresy' of beliefs deemed incompatible with those doctrines.[30] A matter of particular contestation was the theological meaning of Israel, the mantle of which, for Christians, had through allegorization and spiritualization passed to them. In pointed contrast to this belief, the talmudic sages placed increased emphasis on a familial or genealogical understanding of Israel. Once Christianity became the establishment religion of the Roman world, its challenge to Judaism was also political, and this spurred the sages to conceive of Israel politically, as a nation. Israel was represented in the Talmud as an idealized entity, simultaneously both family and nation. As in the narrative of the Last Judgment given in *Avodah Zarah*, the merit of Israel justified its election and its divinely promised ultimate reward.[31]

Rabbinic Judaism thus consolidated around the notion of the election of Israel, and its messianic redemption in the future. Messianic eschatology is absent from the tannaitic Mishnah, but is frequently present in the later Talmud. The messianic orientation of the Talmud was in part a reaction to the messianism of Christianity, and has been aptly summarized as repeatedly following the formula 'if you do x, the messiah will come; if not, the messiah will tarry'.[32] In this formative period and into the medieval era, the focus of Jewish life was inward, and there was little theological emphasis on outward-oriented understandings of Jewish election and purpose. This was also in part a reaction to Christianity: a caution that stood in contrast to the elaborate theology of Jewish purpose developed by the church fathers, according to which the dispersal and suffering of the Jews was central to their historical purpose for Christians. This 'Jewish witness' doctrine was most influentially articulated by Augustine of Hippo (354–430):

> But the Jews who killed him and refused to believe in him, to believe that he had to die and rise again . . . were utterly uprooted from their kingdom [and] dispersed all over the world. . . . [T]hus by the evidence of their own scripture they bear witness for us that we have not fabricated the prophecies about Christ . . . We recognize that it is in order to give this testimony, which, in spite of themselves, they supply for our benefit by their possession and preservation of those books, that they themselves are dispersed among all nations, in whatever direction the Christian Church spreads.[33]

Like Paul, Augustine believed that the Jews remained God's chosen people, and would ultimately be restored to divine favour. However, he transposed the doctrine of Jewish election and universal mission into a form that justified Christian domination over Jews throughout the medieval period and beyond.[34] In the face of this instrumentalist Christian understanding of their purpose, Jews could only look forward with quietly expectant hope to their own messianic redemption.

At the end of antiquity, Jews and Christians each conceptualized their collective nature largely in relation to the other, and their understanding of history in terms of their very different theologies of the election and mission of Israel. These lines of antagonism established the framework for relations between the two religions for the next millennium and beyond. It is important to note, however, that other religious traditions were also of great importance in the shaping of Christianity and Judaism in this period. For Augustine and other early Christian leaders, the traditional polytheistic practices of the Roman world were of much greater concern than the numerically and politically weaker challenge posed by Judaism. This notably applies to Augustine's contemporary John Chrysostom (349–407), whose polemical *Adversus Judaeos* sermons against the Jews and Judaizing Christians of his home city of Antioch rank among the most intensely anti-Jewish texts of late antiquity. Chrysostom vehemently asserted the sharp separation of Christianity from Judaism in order to present the new religion as the more attractive proposition of the two for the majority pagan population of Antioch.[35] Many Jews, meanwhile, including the Babylonian talmudic sages, lived far to the east of the centres of Christianity, and were soon to find themselves under Islamic rule. Nonetheless, both Jews and Christians came to define themselves most fundamentally in relation to the other, and based their self-understanding on contrasting interpretations of the intertwined notions of peoplehood and purpose put forward in their common scripture. Multiple layers of interpretation—Jewish, Christian and secular—have accreted upon these prooftexts, which have remained a key point of reference in Western debates on universalism, peoplehood and political hope.

In recent years—to offer just one prominent example of the continuing afterlife of these biblical and early post-biblical arguments—the interpretation of Paul has returned to the fore in political philosophy. For the French philosopher Alain Badiou, Paul's message, and his rejection of the particularistic aspects of the Jewish law, stand at the helm of the Western tradition of optimistic, life-affirming and universalistic political activism. Badiou's declared aim is to revivify this tradition, blending Paul and Marx into a new rallying call for mass political agency in the name of all.[36] His Pauline universalism has been criticized for drawing on arguments that echo the Christian *adversus Judaeos* tradition, and has been widely labelled as antisemitic.[37] This controversy highlights the enduring incendiary power of the Jewish purpose question. Whereas for Badiou Paul's stance on this question provides the indispensable basis for a radical universalistic politics, for many of his critics he seeks to wrest the Jewish scriptural message from Jews themselves, and to deny the meaningfulness and value of Jewish difference. In order to understand the significance of these heated current arguments, we need to relate them not only to their antecedents almost two millennia earlier, but also to the intricate and layered intellectual history of the Jewish purpose question over the intervening period.

Jewish Purpose in History: An Outline

In the medieval period Jews and non-Jews developed contrasting and separate concepts of Jewish purpose in the world. In the Jewish world, Judah Halevi took the view that Jews were inherently superior to non-Jews, whereas Maimonides thought that the special feature of the Jews was their philosophical inclination, and that their election was therefore implicitly conditional on the perpetuation of their special role as thinkers. For medieval Christians, meanwhile, building on the 'witness people' theology of Augustine, the purpose of Jews was to provide evidence—through their dispersal and suffering, and their dogged preservation of the scriptural texts that they nonetheless so woefully misinterpreted—of the truth of Christianity. All three of these approaches have remained important through to the present. However, it was not until the aftermath of the Reformation that Jewish and non-Jewish thinking on the subject began to clash and cross-fertilize. In this new environment of theological competition within Western Christendom, the interpretation of Jewish matters became a key ground on which Protestant and Catholics sparred for political and intellectual legitimacy. The seventeenth century was the heyday of 'political theology': the discussion of politics through the language of scripture. This subject, in that period, will therefore be the central focus of the first chapter of this book. In the two most dynamic Protestant states of the early modern period—the Dutch Republic and England—identification with Jews provided the theological underpinning for these nations' own self-image as divinely chosen, and the theological grammar for their internal political arguments. The 'Mosaic Republic' was a key reference point in both polities in the seventeenth century, and political fascination with the Jews was an important force in shaping more welcoming policies toward them (most notably the readmission of Jews to England in 1656). In the Interregnum period in England, arguments from Jewish texts, by thinkers such as John Selden and James Harrington, were fundamental for establishing the case for republicanism and for the primacy of common law. It is erroneous to claim that Jewish texts were therefore the source of these early proto-liberal arguments heralding the advance of democracy and the rule of law: Selden and others knew what they were looking for in their Hebrew texts, and their work should not be seen as a transmission of Jewish arguments into the Christian domain, but as emerging from the interplay and overlap between these traditions. This also applies to the thought of Baruch Spinoza, who in his *Tractatus theologico-politicus* (1670) parochialized the

Jewish Bible as simply the fanciful historical record of one particular people, and thereby profoundly shook the foundations of European political theology.

Spinoza was the hero of radical thinkers in the next two generations and beyond. In the ardent discipleship that characterized the phenomenon of 'Spinozism', we encounter a paradox: Spinoza was feted for his universalistic overcoming of the particular, but this achievement was rooted in his own particularity as a Jew who had rejected Judaism. The special significance of the figure of the ex-Jew as the purest possible universalist extends back to Paul and forward to Badiou (and beyond), but it is in the eighteenth century that it comes most clearly into focus. The second chapter of the book, therefore, will centre on the eighteenth century as the period in which the primary purpose of Jews was to sharpen the elaboration of key philosophical concepts, sometimes by standing as the antithesis of universal reason, but also at times flipping into standing as its embodiment. A particularly rich terrain for exploring this is the work of the Rotterdam Huguenot philosopher Pierre Bayle, whose *Historical and Critical Dictionary* (1700) baffled eighteenth-century readers, and continues to baffle many today, among other things over its elusive positioning of Judaism as the marker of the limits of rational philosophy. The vexed preoccupation of Voltaire with Jews stems from his structurally similar but stylistically and temperamentally extremely different positioning of them as fundamentally antithetical to Enlightenment reason. It is common for these exceptionalist treatments of Jews to be treated with unease, and indeed to be viewed as antisemitic. However, it is important to recognize that the same paradigm of exceptionalism framed the work and reception of Jewish thinkers in the period, including, most significantly, Moses Mendelssohn. The penetrating mind and noble character of Mendelssohn was the model for the dramatic hero of his friend Gotthold Ephraim Lessing's masterpiece *Nathan the Wise* (1779), in which Jewish purpose was cast as the exemplification of rational universalism. For Mendelssohn himself, this flattery was awkward but also indispensable. In his own work, he cautiously embraced Lessing's understanding of Jewish purpose, while simultaneously trying, in his *Jerusalem* (1783), to establish a basis for Jewish normalcy.

In the nineteenth century—the subject of the third chapter of the book—philosophical abstraction was displaced as the crux of thinking on Jewish purpose by efforts to make sense of the dramatic social, political and economic changes of the era. Jews, once they were brought into the political mainstream in the wake of the French Revolution, became the key test case of the reach, not of philosophical ideals, but of political reforms. In many different ways, over the long nineteenth century, both Jewish and non-Jewish thinkers cast Jews as the bearers of a special role in pushing or leading Western society to its developmental destiny in any number of key respects. Jews proudly presented themselves as cosmopolitans (Ludwig Börne, Heinrich Heine), as morally lofty teachers (Heinrich Graetz, Hermann Cohen), or as ethnically superior builders of the future (Benjamin Disraeli). These idealizations overlapped with each other, and drew on earlier traditions. Claims that Jews had a vital mission to perform in the world found wide readerships among non-Jews, and resonated with the admiration for the fortitude of the Hebraic tradition in the writings of non-Jewish thinkers such as Matthew Arnold and Friedrich Nietzsche. The identification of the Jews' mission with the advancement of capitalism had a more complex impact, as this was variably seen in negative, positive or elusively ambivalent terms. A case in point is Werner Sombart's *The Jews and Modern Capitalism* (1911), which has been widely excoriated as an antisemitic blaming of Jews for the ills of modern economic inequality, but at the time of its publication was celebrated by many Jews as a confirmation of the unique resourcefulness of their people. In the work of Sombart's fellow sociologist Georg Simmel, multiple currents of thinking on Jewish purpose are drawn together. In his famous essay on 'The Stranger' (1908), Simmel casts Jews as simultaneously cosmopolitan, capitalist and intellectual. All three features, for Simmel, are hallmarks of the figure of the stranger, of whom the Jew is the quintessential example, and who is also the key driving figure of the connected commercial, cultural and psychological transformations of modernity.

Sombart's most enthusiastic Jewish admirers were Zionists, who saw his research as securing the case for the likely success of a Jewish state. The Zionist movement has throughout its history had a complex relationship to the idea of Jewish purpose. In seeking to establish a state for the Jews in a world increasingly organized around the ethnic nation state, Zionism sought to normalize the place of Jews in the world. The energy and inspirational power of the Zionist idea, however, for non-Jews and for Jews, has however always derived to a large extent from the exceptional hopes and theological significance bound up with the notion of Jewish purpose. The fourth chapter of the book focuses on the purpose of the Jews in relation to the potential and meaning of nationhood, in both Zionist and non-Zionist contexts. This is primarily a twentieth-century story, but it has earlier roots: Moses Hess, writing in Germany in the 1860s, linked a profoundly negative view of the Jews' diasporic role as arch-capitalists to his irenic view of the role of the Jews in his Zionist vision of the future. Zionist grappling with the idea of Jewish exemplarity runs through the twentieth-century history of the movement, and is fascinatingly visible in the cultural Zionism of Ahad Ha'am, and in the political rhetoric of David Ben-Gurion, who repeatedly invoked Isaiah's 'light unto the nations' as his vision for the Jewish state. The relationship of Jewish exemplarity and purpose to the broader political life of the nation state has also been a rich and complicated seam of debate within twentieth-century thought. For Franz Rosenzweig, Jewish exemplarity and purpose resided precisely in standing outside politics. For Jacques Derrida, in contrast, the Jewish case is what one might call, in Weberian terms, the 'ideal type' of collective nation formation, and of the claims to exceptionality that accompany this.

In contemporary debate, we hear frequent calls for Jews, and particularly Israel, to be regarded and judged on the same basis as all others, with any deviation from normal treatment often condemned as antisemitic. However, this call sits somewhat awkwardly alongside the ubiquity, historically and into the present, of the theme of Jewish exceptionality and special purpose. The fifth chapter of the book will focus on the question of normalcy and its relationship to twentieth-century notions of Jewish distinctiveness and purpose. The idea of a special Jewish mission initially thrived within the American Reform movement, but as the urge to integrate within American society gathered strength among Jews, this notion waned in prominence. Jewish exemplarity was most influentially presented in relation to specifics of the American context, through the competing 'melting pot' and 'orchestra' metaphors of Israel Zangwill and Horace Kallen. In Central Europe in the first half of the twentieth century, the hope of Jewish normalization was perceived by sharp observers, such as Karl Kraus, Theodor Lessing and Sigmund Freud, as illusory: all three men put forward their own distinctive analysis of the value of Jews as outsider figures. The horror of the Holocaust cast a profound chill over the idea of Jewish instrumental purpose—but it has also brought about a renewal of the idea, in relation to the ethical and historical lessons imparted by the Nazi genocide itself. The universalistic Jewish Left, meanwhile, has, despite waning in numerical terms, retained its intellectual significance as a prominent current of political argument. From the revolutions in Bavaria and Budapest at the end of the First World War through to recent and contemporary debates on cosmopolitanism and human rights, Jewish arguments for universalism have struck a resonant and paradoxically distinctive note.

———

What, then, *are* Jews for? Across much of the Jewish world in the late twentieth century, anxiety over the long-term viability of Judaism threatened to overwhelm this question. European Jewish life in the aftermath of the Holocaust was shadowed by a sense of mournfully dutiful traditionalism and anxiety over the continued presence of antisemitism. The temptation and increasing ease of assimilation was perceived as a further threat to Jewish continuity, not only in Europe but also in the United States and elsewhere in the New World. Faced with the prospect of a 'vanishing diaspora', it was clear to some Jewish leaders that the postwar focus on communal survival lacked the inspirational power to renew Jewish life.[38] A return to the idea of Jewish purpose, despite its awkwardness, has been an indispensable element in multiple currents of Jewish religious and cultural revival since the 1970s, which in the new millennium have collectively become so robust that earlier anxieties over Jewish disappearance or dilution have been largely allayed.

In recent decades, vigilance toward antisemitism—widely understood as a key lesson of the Holocaust—and identification with the state of Israel have become central to the sense of Jewish meaningfulness of many Jews. As the conflict between Israel and the Palestinians has become increasingly bitter, entrenched and entangled with controversies over antisemitism, two opposing conceptions of Jewish purpose have clashed in public debate. Hard-line Zionist arguments, emphasizing Jewish security and collective interests, are opposed by liberal or leftist perspectives stressing universal ethical and political principles in relation to the conflict. This has exposed a stark cleft within the Jewish world over the essence of the idea of Jewish purpose, and its place in global politics and visions of the future. The broader resonance of the Jewish purpose question has meanwhile in no sense diminished. Intense interest in the question has been important factor in sustaining and framing the prominence in public consciousness across much of the contemporary world of both Holocaust remembrance and the Israel/Palestine conflict. With the rise of nationalist assertiveness and strongman leadership in many countries, including in America under President Trump, this conflict has come to emblematize, with unique symbolic intensity, the profound division in contemporary global politics over the fundamental nature of national collective purpose. The rhetoric of Benjamin Netanyahu and his allies aligns with the unabashedly self-interested outlook of many nationalist governments and political parties across the world; the universalist arguments mobilized on the opposing political wing are widely invoked in support of a range of internationalist and solidaristic visions of collective political responsibility and purpose.

Universalism, at least in the domain of human relations, is a troublesome idea and in an important sense an illusory ideal. We are all, as numerous philosophers and others have argued, bounded in our perspectives on the world by the intellectual and cultural traditions that have shaped us and with which we affiliate. We view the world from our own particular vantage points, and without access to any panoptic position of omniscience or neutrality.[39] The idea of universalism as the ultimate religious or philosophical destination and goal of humanity has, however, been a central feature of the closely connected Jewish, Christian and Western traditions with which this book is concerned. (The significance of universalism in Islamic and other traditions, and the nature and extent of the intertwinement of those lineages with those discussed here, would require careful and separate attention.) The utopian vision of a harmonious future in which the divisions of our world will be overcome has been fundamental to the temporal thinking and to the political energies of Judaism, Christianity and the various avowedly secular outlooks that emerged during and after the European Enlightenment. The idea of universalism is thus an inescapably fundamental cultural and political reference point in Western history.[40] The question of how we can collectively contribute to human progress toward this ideal has been most concretely invested, in Christian and post-Christian thought, in the destiny and purpose of the Jewish people. The Jewish purpose question has therefore been foundational to thinking on collective purpose in these globally dominant traditions. In the early twenty-first century, amid assertive and in some ways unprecedented challenges to universalistic ideals, hopes and commitments, this intellectual heritage is perhaps of crucial importance for the future of the idea of collective purpose itself.

1

Religion, Sovereignty, Messianism

JEWS AND POLITICAL PURPOSE

To the early Jews religion was transmitted in the form of written law because at
that time they were just like children; but later on Moses and Jeremiah told them
of a time to come when God would inscribe his law in their hearts. So while it
was proper only of the Jews of long ago . . . to strive in defence of a law written on
tablets, this does not apply to those who have the law inscribed in their minds.[1]

—BARUCH SPINOZA (1670)

THE PLACE OF JEWS in the early medieval world was, broadly speaking, subordinate but stable. In both the Christian and the Islamic worlds, political authority was underwritten by a theological system of unquestioned supremacy,
which regulated the terms on which Jewish communities were tolerated. Jews
and their texts played an important role in underpinning Christian identity and
intellectual authority. They did not carry this special significance for Muslims,
and in the Islamic world Jewish purpose was therefore a more marginal question, in the main only of interest to Jews themselves. In neither religion, though,
was the material position of Jews a topic of significant controversy. Only in the
twelfth century, in western Europe, did this change, as a new crusading fervour
emerged and religious orders began to engage with rabbinic literature and to
seek actively to convert Jews to Christianity. The purpose of the Jews was not
significantly rethought, though, until the Reformation, when the unity of Western Christendom was dramatically shattered. The theological significance of
Jews emerged in the wake of the Reformation as an important terrain of intellectual competition between Protestants and Catholics. As European political
conflicts became framed through this religious division, so disagreements over

the proper understanding of the purpose of the Jews also became increasingly political.

It was in the seventeenth century, in the wake of the Reformation, that modern 'political theology' was born. Religion and power in medieval Europe were profoundly intertwined, and in the Jewish case the covenants on which Judaism is founded are unmistakably political. When the German jurist Carl Schmitt (1888–1985) coined the term in 1922, however, he focused on the early modern period. Schmitt's discussion of political theology begins with the French thinker Jean Bodin, whose response to the devastation of the civil wars between Protestants and Catholics that raged in France in the late sixteenth century, according to Schmitt, was to theorize the supreme authority and indivisibility of sovereignty. Bodin was the first European thinker, Schmitt argued, to realize that the key feature of sovereignty lay in the power, in exceptional circumstances, to suspend the law, and to rule with absolute authority.[2] Political theology, for Schmitt, is based not on a unity between the religious and political realms (which had, at least in theory, been the case while the pope presided over an undivided Western Christendom), but on the application of theology to politics through analogy, with the omnipotence of God transferred to the omnipotent sovereign. Schmitt's paradigmatic example of political theology is Thomas Hobbes's *Leviathan* (1651). Writing in response to another exceptional crisis of state authority—the English Civil War—Hobbes put forward a starkly rational argument for the necessity of human submission to sovereign authority.[3]

In seventeenth-century European political writings, the Bible was everywhere: in the writings of radicals and of traditionalists, and of those who challenged its authority as well as those who defended it. Precisely because of the controversy surrounding the nature and political place of religion, the Bible, and thus the Jews, were central to political debates in this century, particularly in the Protestant world. Jewish purpose assumed new political significance, in this context, in two distinct but related ways. Firstly, the biblical covenants, as divinely underwritten political arrangements described in the Jewish Bible, were more than ever a foundational political reference point of for Christians. Early Jewish history, and its textual exploration, including rabbinical commentaries on the Bible, thus became a key resource in political debate, used to justify both monarchic and republican government, and a range of positions on the basis, nature and status of popular consent and of the rule of law. Secondly, political arguments for radical change were almost invariably refracted through a future-oriented idea of Jewish purpose. Utopian visions of the future were usually imagined in the seventeenth century in terms of a Christian messianic framework, within which the Jews, as God's errant but nonetheless still chosen people, were ascribed a crucial role. In seemingly secular political arguments from the second half of the century, which looked forward to a transformed future in which theocratic authority would be curbed or even displaced, the idea of Jewish purpose was less explicitly but no less significantly present.

Christian political interest in Jews made a difference to Christian political policies toward them. For Christian scholars of Hebrew texts, Jews were often greatly valued both as teachers and as anthropological specimens. The positive interest in Jews among Protestants led to unprecedentedly close local engagement with the Sephardic (and later Ashkenazic) communities established in the Dutch Republic from the early seventeenth century, and also played an important role in the readmission of Jews to Cromwellian England in 1655/6. By far the most important product of this interaction between Jews and Christians was the philosophy of Baruch (or, as he was known after his expulsion from the Sephardic community of Amsterdam in 1656, Benedict) Spinoza, which was hugely celebrated among radical thinkers in the late seventeenth century and beyond. Spinoza sought, through the application of Cartesian geometric rationalism to ethics and politics, to establish a rigorous logic of social organization according to which, among many other consequences, there would be no further place for Jewish exceptionalism. Nonetheless, biblical exegesis was prominent in his writings. Spinoza ascribed to Jews, for example in the quotation at the head of this chapter, a developmentally immature position in human history, pointing toward a more advanced future in which they could not, as Jews, share. His description of Jews as 'children' echoes Paul, who, as we have seen, cast the Jewish law as 'our schoolmaster', needed at an early stage to signal the way toward Christ and faith, but redundant 'after that faith is come' (Galatians 3:24). For Spinoza's disciples, however, his unflinchingly logical challenge to the authority of all religion took on the status of a revolution, with Spinoza as the Christ-like herald of a new post-religious faith in reason alone. The purpose of Jews as signposts to the future thus assumed a new and enduring secular register.

Special and Subordinate: Jewish Significance in the Early Islamic and Medieval Christian Worlds

Toward the close of the late antique period the heartland of Jewish life moved east. The Babylonian Talmud, redacted by about 500 CE, was constructed upon the base of the Mishnah, the first major work of rabbinic Judaism, which was written in the Hellenistic environment of second-century Palestine; it also responded to the challenge posed by the rise of Christianity. It was shaped, though, in a very different environment, surrounded and influenced by Zoroastrian Iranian culture.[4] Less than two centuries later, Babylonia was under Muslim rule, which soon extended to Morocco and the Iberian peninsula, establishing across this territory a remarkably stable and long-lasting framework for Jewish existence as a minority community. Although the extent of Jewish influence on early Islam remains a highly controversial and uncertain topic, as a politically dominant religion Islam developed no special preoccupation with Judaism. The new faith claimed to have superseded both Christianity and Judaism, and according to the doctrine of *tahrif*, first articulated in the eleventh century, maintained that both Jews and Christians had falsified their sacred texts. However, in contrast to Christianity, Islam did not develop an elaborate supersessionist theology with particular regard to Judaism.

Minority religious communities under Islamic rule were accorded *dhimmi* ('protected') status, subject to special taxation and to various restrictions underscoring their subordinate status, but also allowed considerable internal autonomy. Jewish communities in the medieval Islamic world were treated broadly on the same basis as other minorities. Indeed, when a particular community was singled out in Islamic law, it was much more often the Christians, who were both more numerous and more politically problematic from the point of view of their Muslim overlords, due to their ties with rival Christian powers across the Mediterranean.[5] Not until the nineteenth century, when European colonial powers exported their political orientation points (along with much else) across the Middle East, did Jewish particularity assume any degree of special significance in the Muslim world.

Although the question of Jewish purpose was of little interest to Muslims in the medieval period, it was most certainly of interest to Jews living under their rule. *Dhimmi* status was disadvantageous: whereas in pre-Islamic Babylonia there were no particular inducements to leave the Jewish fold, under Islam this was no longer the case. During the 'golden age' of Jewish culture in al-Andalus (Islamic Iberia) from the tenth to the mid-twelfth century, there were close ties between the two community elites. Many Jews immersed themselves in Islamic philosophy and literature, and a few even rose to prominent political roles in the Cordoba Caliphate. At the same time, however, leading Jewish thinkers powerfully asserted the significance and distinctiveness of Judaism.[6] The most notable example of this is the *Kuzari* of Judah Halevi (c. 1075–1141), a text which purported to recount an earlier instance of proud Jewish self-assertion: the encounter between the king of Khazaria, on the Black Sea, and a rabbinic sage, who gradually persuades him to recognize and adopt the revealed truth of Judaism. (Halevi's account is clearly fanciful, but was taken by many later readers as broadly accurate. It may or may not be the case that, around the eighth century, the Khazar elite had converted to Judaism.[7]) In his eclectic text Halevi unabashedly argues that Jews are different in kind from non-Jews, and that this is the basis for their special role in the world.

Jews, Halevi claims, are ontologically different from non-Jews. They are endowed with godly qualities that are unique to them. He describes them as 'an angelic caste', with purer and godlier souls than those of non-Jews, and the sole possessors of the inherited capability of prophecy (which converts to Judaism cannot acquire).[8] The first argument that Halevi's rabbinic spokesman presents to the Khazar king is the inescapable hierarchy of nature: animate over inanimate; animals over plants; men above beasts. The divine order is the highest of all, and Jews, with their extraordinary potential for prophecy, are uniquely connected to the divine realm.[9] This biological, quasi-genetic argument for Jewish superiority has provoked considerable unease among later Jewish readers—though it has also, as we shall see, been extremely resilient. However, although Halevi's primary focus was on the special qualities of Jews and Judaism, he was also interested in the role of the Jews in the wider world. 'Israel amidst the nations is like the heart amidst the organs of the body', he writes, explaining that Israel is therefore particularly sensitive, being exposed to all the diseases arising in the other organs (representing the non-Jewish nations), but possessing the strength to expel these illnesses before they take root within it, which would be fatal for the entire body.[10] He also compares the Jews to a 'seed', which transforms the earth in which it is planted, and eventually produces a fruit-bearing tree. That tree is the future messiah, who will be recognized by all: 'The nations . . . will all become His fruit.'[11] Intertwined with his pronounced ethnocentrism, then, Halevi ascribes to the Jews a vital role both in sustaining all humanity and in ultimately bringing it most profoundly close to God.

The interpretation of Jewish distinctiveness offered by Moses Maimonides (1135–1204) is very different. Whereas Halevi's work was explicitly anti-philosophical, in the sense that he rejected the notion that all knowledge, including religious knowledge, could be harmonized with philosophical reason, Maimonides was firmly committed to the dominant Aristotelian philosophical tradition of medieval al-Andalus. Although Maimonides clearly shared Halevi's belief in the superiority of Jews over other peoples, he rarely mentioned the notion of the Jews as a chosen people, preferring instead to emphasize their exceptional philosophical knowledge of God.[12] Abraham, he argued in the first volume of his vast *Mishneh Torah*, was before all else a philosopher. As soon as he was weaned he began 'to explore with his mind—to ponder day and night'.[13] This led him to realize the error of the idol-worshippers of Ur, and brought him to God. Abraham's philosophical awakening occurred long before he was first addressed by God, which did not take place until he was seventy-five. The special relationship of the Jews with God, Maimonides argues, was thus based upon Abraham's great philosophical acumen. This 'planted a root' in the hearts of his descendants, which strengthened in subsequent generations.[14] The Jews thus became a nation with a unique knowledge of God, grounded in philosophical understanding and, after the revelation at Sinai, sustained through the observance of the Torah. This revelation, Maimonides argues in his *Guide of the Perplexed* (written in Judaeo-Arabic around 1190), is also rooted in rational understanding: the first two fundamental commandments (the existence and unity of God) were apprehended philosophically at Sinai by all the people of Israel. The specialness of the Jewish people is, according to Maimonides, defined not by any inherent characteristic, but by their philosophically established dual mission: to know and to worship God.[15]

Since the nineteenth century, Halevi and Maimonides, and especially the *Kuzari* and the *Guide of the Perplexed*, have been interpreted in contrast to each other, as romantic particularism pitted against rational universalism. For premodern Jewish readers, however, this was not the case: the two thinkers were widely seen as complementary.[16] Both thinkers, indeed, believed that the Jewish people possessed special qualities; and they both believed that this bestowed on them a vitally important role in the world. Nineteenth- and twentieth-century readers, generally approaching Halevi with the assumption that religion and philosophy are clearly separate and distinct, readily aligned his biological understanding of Jewish uniqueness with an inward-looking, romantic notion of Judaism, at odds with the outward-looking universalism associated with Maimonides. That juxtaposition, though, was a product of modernity. The tension between difference and universalism was posed with particular acuity for Jews during the era of emancipation, in the choice of whether to embrace or resist the transformations that this change of political status made possible. In medieval al-Andalus, despite the high level of cultural integration of men such as Halevi and Maimonides, no such offer existed. Both thinkers proudly assert the superiority of Judaism, and do so in part to boost the self-confidence of the followers of their politically subordinated faith. However, they both also look outward, seeking to articulate a case for being Jewish that they intend to be at least potentially compelling to Jews and non-Jews alike. They both see the Jews as playing a central role in bringing all of humanity closer to God. Halevi emphasizes the sensitivity of the Jews, and their role in leading the way to the future messianic era; Maimonides emphasizes the Jews' philosophical excellence, which he also sees as crucial in preparing the world for its messianic future, in which the distinction between Jew and Gentile would no longer prevail.[17] All these ideas, in many different mixes and guises, are threaded through the later history of thinking on Jewish purpose in the world.

In the Christian world, the Augustinian doctrine of the Jews as a 'witness people' underpinned the medieval understanding of the purpose played by Jews in God's plan for the world. Although this was rooted in the pedagogical value, to Christians, of the dispersion and suffering of Jews as a consequence of their failure to recognize that the New Testament was the fulfilment of the prophecies in the Old, medieval Christian doctrine also insisted on the importance of the future restoration of the Jews to divine favour. Citing, among other things, the biblical prooftext 'slay them not' (Psalms 59:11), popes from Gregory the Great (590–604) to Alexander II (1061–73) spoke out against anti-Jewish violence, on the grounds that this undermined the special purpose of the Jews. According to this theology, the preservation of the Jews was essential in order to enable their ultimate divine salvation.[18] This belief was put to the test at the end of the eleventh century, when the assembly of Christian armies for the First Crusade intensified popular sentiments of religious self-righteousness, expressed though a wave of murderous anti-Jewish violence in the Rhineland in 1096. The protests of local bishops were ineffective in restraining the attacks on the large Jewish communities of Mainz, Speyer, Worms and elsewhere, where, according to Jewish sources, a number of Jews committed suicide in order to escape the choice between forced conversion and slaughter. In the aftermath of these massacres, both Christians and Jews moved away from overlapping notions of Jewish purpose associated with expectations of a universal and ecumenically harmonious messianic future, and toward more hostile views of each other.

The massacres of 1096—in which over a thousand Jews were killed in Mainz alone—were a major jolt to Jewish self-confidence. In their aftermath, the rabbinical leadership asserted with renewed intensity the strength and steadfastness of God's love for the Jews, in order to fortify the cohesion and faith of their communities in the face of Christian claims—even more forcefully asserted following the crusaders' capture of Jerusalem in 1099—that the Jews no longer enjoyed divine favour. This concern is evident in the Torah commentaries of

Rashi (Solomon ben Isaac, 1040–1105), the pre-eminent Ashkenazic rabbi of the period. In his biblical exegesis Rashi repeatedly emphasized that God's love for his chosen people was absolute and unwavering. Commenting on the opening verse of Genesis, he argued that its inner meaning was that the purpose of God's creation was to bestow the Torah, and the land of Israel, on the Jewish people.[19] God's unique intimacy with the Jewish people was, for Rashi, absolutely central, to the extent that this relationship in itself provided the sustaining purpose not only for Jews, but also for God's own actions. In response to the shock of crusader massacres, and to the more combative inter-religious environment of which they were a symptom, Ashkenazic Jews turned inward. Moving away from the idea that they served a purpose for all humanity, they emphasized instead God's ultimate provision for his chosen people, and punishment of their enemies.

The rabbis in Rashi's circle put forward a revised understanding of the messianic future, in which this final reversal of the relationship between Jews and Christians was central. In the Babylonian tradition the messianic process had generally been envisaged in peaceful terms. The messianic era would bring about harmony between the nations of the world, either through the conversion of all 'righteous Gentiles' to Judaism or through the transcendence of all distinctions between peoples. This irenic perspective was maintained among medieval Sephardic Jews living under Islam, such as Halevi and Maimonides. In twelfth-century Ashkenaz, however, the emphasis shifted to a violent vision of messianic redemption, in which God would avenge the blood of Jewish martyrs in a final destruction of the non-Jewish nations.[20] As theological antagonism between the two religions became more entrenched over the course of the twelfth century, visions of the messianic future moved away from intersecting Jewish and Christian understandings of the role of the Jewish people in bringing human history to its ultimate fulfilment. They became instead imagined extensions of the conflicts of the present, in which both sides looked forward to their ultimate triumph.

On the Christian side, the rise of hostility toward Jews in the twelfth century was in part due, paradoxically perhaps, to the increased attention given by Christians in the crusading era to Islam. This to some extent displaced Judaism from its privileged position as the defining 'other' of Christianity: Islam now appeared as a much more significant rival, not just in military but also in theological terms. The positive purpose ascribed to Jews by the Augustinian 'witness people' doctrine was therefore put under some pressure by the more dramatic validation of Christianity provided by the crusading cause itself.[21] Twelfth-century

Christians increasingly conflated Jews with Muslims as enemies of Christendom, and hostility toward these two groups increased in tandem. In addition, Jews in northern Europe were becoming more economically important as moneylenders, which intensified a further dimension of popular resentment toward them. In this charged environment, Christian theologians sought to renew the Augustinian understanding of the purpose of the Jews, by situating it in relation to these intensified currents of cultural and economic enmity.

The most prominent figure among these theologians was Bernard of Clairvaux (1090–1153), the leading figure of the Cistercian monastic order and the principal preacher in support of the Second Crusade (1147–49). For Bernard, the Jews above all embodied carnality, in contrast to Christian spirituality. They were 'the living letters of the law', preserving the cold literalism of their holy texts, of which only Christians were able to grasp the true spiritual meaning. The literalism of Jews was linked to their immaturity: they were like 'green figs', having failed to ripen into Christians. Bernard also linked their lack of feeling and understanding to the immoral materialism of their economic niche. Usury, he argued, was quintessentially Jewish, and therefore any Christian usurer was guilty of 'judaizing'. However, alongside this sweeping condemnation of Jews, Bernard also emphasized their divine purpose: it is vital that they be preserved, so that they can fulfil their function both as 'witness people' in the present and to play their part in the ultimate redemption of 'all Israel'. Bernard actively sought to pre-empt and prevent the anti-Jewish violence that also accompanied the Second Crusade. His concern for the preservation of the Jews was intensified by the fact that he believed that this military mobilization was the prelude to the imminent dawn the messianic age. In Bernard's theology of Jewish purpose, built on clear Pauline and Augustinian foundations, a cluster of themes is yoked together, intensifying connections that foreshadow many later developments of this idea. Jewish immaturity, literalism and materialism had all already been juxtaposed to Christian plenitude, understanding and spirituality. In Bernard's writings, however, this opposition is particularly tightly linked to a highly double-edged notion of the purpose of the Jews, in which their shortcomings are indispensably linked to the eagerly anticipated messianic release of the entire world from the shackles of inflexible law, imperfect understanding and coldly economic human relations.[22]

In the following century, relations between Christians and Jews were given a new twist by the advent of Christian engagement with rabbinic Judaism. Augustine and his early successors had been rigorously uninterested in the development of Judaism after the crucifixion of Jesus, which for them marked the

moment of its supersession by Christianity. However, medieval Christian scholars, stimulated by the twelfth-century intellectual renaissance, the conversionist zeal of the crusading era and also by the advance of Christianity into areas
of Spain where coexistence between Jews and Muslims had previously flourished, began in the thirteenth century to encounter the Talmud and other rabbinic texts, and recalibrated their perceptions of Judaism accordingly. The
error of the Jews, argued the Dominican friars and others who led the Christian condemnation of the Talmud, lay not simply in their failure to understand
the prophecies contained in their own Bible, but also in the entrenchment of
their misreading through their devotion to a vast edifice of rabbinical nonsense.
Thirteenth-century Christians came to regard rabbinic Judaism as profoundly
different from Old Testament Judaism, and guilty not only of a failure to recognize the spiritual truths contained within scripture, but also of deviation from
the literal truth of those very texts which, according to Augustinian doctrine,
they were supposed to preserve. This posed a further challenge to the traditional
Christian view of Jewish purpose, and led to Jews increasingly being regarded,
in less exceptional terms, as straightforward heretics.[23] However, the Christian
discovery of the Talmud also focused attention on, and added complexity to,
the question of what constituted proper reading. A sequence of late medieval
disputations locked Jews and Christians in a protracted argument over the
proper interpretation of the Bible.[24] The Augustinian witness doctrine thus implicitly shifted into a new, semi-secularized register: Jews, and their hermeneu-
tic tradition, now occupied a crucial role in the central scholarly debate on how
one should read and interpret texts.

The theological combat of late medieval Europe was fought not only over
texts, but also, even more intensely, over symbols. For Christians, no object was
more profoundly imbued with meaning than the host; and it was in this
period—starting with a case in Paris in 1290—that Jews were accused of host
desecration, which for Christians constituted a repetition of their abuse of
Christ. These accusations were a form of expression for a wide range of religious,
social, political and economic tensions in late medieval towns, where Jews and
Christians were living in unprecedented proximity and awareness of each other.
They also, perhaps most significantly, enabled Christians to define and feel their
own identity more acutely. Narratives and images of Jewish anti-Christian violence served an important purpose for Christians, producing in them a physically engaged sense of victimhood and pain that was an important experiential
element of religious devotion in *imitatio Christi*.[25] Jews also reinforced their
identity through a sense of being persecuted by Christians, just as they at times

actually did attack or mock the eucharist: there is evidence that Jewish hostility toward Christianity was sometimes the generator of Christian hostility in response.[26] However, the minority religion was constitutive of Christian identity in ways that were not reciprocally the case. In late medieval Europe, the purposes of Jews were multifarious and intense. Layered upon the theological significance that had been ascribed to them a millennium earlier, Jews performed a number of other crucial roles for Christians, enabling them to assert their intellectual superiority as readers of texts, to feel their religious identity experientially as spiritual imitators of Christ and to envision the transformations that would herald the messianic end of days.

Protestant Identity and Hebraic Political Theology

In the early sixteenth century, the tensions between these multiple significances began to come to a head. The friars who had spearheaded the late medieval attack on rabbinic Judaism had been primarily motivated by a determination to use all available resources to cajole Jews to convert to Christianity. However, they were also intellectually drawn to the challenge of mastering the textual sources of their religion. With the emergence of Christian Humanism in the late fifteenth century, this aspect of fascination with Jewish sources intensified. In Germany, Christian Hebraism was pioneered by Johannes Reuchlin (1455–1522), who argued that Jewish sources, and particularly the mystical Kabbalah, provided the original source of all philosophical knowledge. In the early 1510s, Reuchlin was embroiled in a bitter controversy with a Dominican convert from Judaism, Johannes Pfefferkorn, who argued that the copies of the Talmud should be confiscated from Jews and destroyed.[27] This argument, which deeply divided the Church, highlighted two crucial elements that were to reshape the discussion on the place and purpose of Jews in early modern Europe. Firstly, from the early sixteenth century this became a political issue, linked to major tussles of intellectual, spiritual and temporal power. Secondly, these debates now involved both Jews and Christians, in dialogue with each other. Since the thirteenth century, Jewish converts to Christianity had played a prominent role in the Dominican efforts to undermine rabbinic Judaism. Pfefferkorn, however, was the first Jewish convert to be a driving force in shaping Christian debates. He was also the harbinger of many other Jews—traditional, dissident and converted—who were to engage with Christians on these issues over the next two centuries.

One of the many people who weighed into this controversy on Jewish books was Martin Luther (1483–1546), who in 1514 wrote a letter in support of

Reuchlin.[28] In the early years of the Reformation, Luther believed that messianic transformation was imminent, and that this would be heralded by the conversion of the Jews. In his essay *That Jesus Christ Was Born a Jew* (1523), Luther blamed the harsh treatment of Jews by the Catholic Church for keeping them away from Christ; with the emancipation of Christianity from papal bondage, he asserted, the Jews would soon come to see the religion differently, and embrace its truth. In later writings, however, Luther's tone shifted dramatically. His *On the Jews and Their Lies* (1543) is virulently anti-Jewish, calling for the destruction of synagogues and of Jewish books, schools and homes. Moving away from the cornerstone of medieval Christian beliefs on Jewish purpose—that the Jews must be preserved in order to play their crucial role in the advent of the messianic era—Luther in his late writings instead envisaged the displacement of the Jews from their privileged position. Luther's own followers, as the true Christians, had now, he believed, become God's chosen people.[29] The instability of Luther's views on Jews, and the intensity of both his early and late formulations of them, testifies to the heightened importance of Jewish purpose in this period of dramatic religious change. The Jews pointed the way to the future. When, in Luther's eyes, the future seemed to be arriving without the Jews fulfilling their appointed role, a new and drastic revision of their status was required.

Even as a young man, Luther appeared to be in general somewhat hostile to living Jews, who had in any case already been expelled from Wittenberg in the early fourteenth century. He nonetheless felt that his theology required support from the study of Jewish texts. Christian Hebraism was pursued in Wittenberg without contact with Jews, and focused quite narrowly on typology—the interpretation of the Old Testament as a foreshadowing of the New—in support of the claim that Protestants had inherited from Jews the mantle of divine chosenness.[30] Other early Protestant reformers, however, engaged more closely and respectfully with Hebrew texts. This was particularly the case in the Calvinist Reformed tradition. The University of Basel soon emerged as the leading centre of Reformed Hebraist scholarship, where, in contrast to Wittenberg, there was an openness to contact with Jews, who assisted the Hebraist enterprise as teachers or native informants.[31] Most Hebraist tomes written in Basel and other Reformed centres nonetheless took a harshly critical tone toward Judaism, and were justified by their authors as useful tools in persuading Jews to convert to Christianity. This did not, though, fully allay suspicions that Hebraists were inappropriately close to their Jewish collaborators. The theological purpose of their work was also uncertain. It played an important role in inter-confessional polemics against Catholics, in which similarities between rabbinical and papist deviations from the pure meaning of scripture were highlighted. There was, however, an awkward irony to Calvinists' attempts to demonstrate their distance from rabbinic Judaism through their superior mastery of its textual challenges.[32]

As scholarly life developed in Protestant Europe, the prominence and status of Hebraic study increased, driven at least as much by intellectual curiosity and the allure of the ancient and divine associations of Hebrew as by specific theological imperatives. When Isaac Casaubon (1559–1614), the leading French Protestant intellectual of his generation, challenged the historical account of the early Church by the Italian cardinal Cesare Baronio (1538–1607), he deployed his superior mastery of Hebrew to fault Baronio's interpretation of the Jewish milieu from which Christianity emerged.[33] Although this scholarly argument formed part of the intellectual battle between Protestants and Catholics, Casaubon was motivated in large measure by straightforward voracious curiosity, garnished by a passion for philology and for Hebrew in particular: as he wrote in 1610 to the leading Hebraist at the time, the Basel professor Johannes Buxtorf the Elder, 'I have always loved the holy tongue'.[34]

Fascination with Hebrew as a privileged gateway to philosophical wisdom had been central to the awakening of interest in Jewish texts in Renaissance Florence. For Giovanni Pico della Mirandola (1463–94), the Jewish mystical tradition contained precious vestiges of ancient religious truths—the *prisca theologia*—which could be accessed through the hermeneutical techniques of the Kabbalah, particularly those involving numerical and other esoteric forms of analysis of the Hebrew alphabet. Much of Reuchlin's work also focused on the use of the Kabbalah to demonstrate the truth of Christianity. Christian fascination with the Kabbalah continued until the late seventeenth century, culminating with the publication of the *Kabbalah denudata* [Kabbalah Unveiled] (1677–84), a compendium of kabbalistic texts, translated into Latin and annotated by the German Hebraist Christian Knorr von Rosenroth (1636–89). Rosenroth's project was profoundly utopian and irenic: kabbalistic study, he believed, could reveal the inner truths of universal religion, and thus lead to the healing of all confessional divisions.[35] Alongside Christian Hebraist scholarship, translations of a wide range of Jewish literature into Latin brought Jewish intellectual traditions more deeply into Christian scholarly life. The admiration of the Jews as a 'philosophical people' extends back to antiquity, and is also central to the arguments of Maimonides, whose work was translated and studied with particular intensity in the early modern period.[36] While Hebraic scholarship was of great importance as a contested resource in the inter-confessional rivalries of the early modern period, interest in it was also driven by a notion of Jewish purpose that transcended the division between Catholics and Protestants. Despite great ambivalence toward their texts and even toward their physical presence, Jews were widely recognized in sixteenth- and seventeenth-century Europe as playing a unique role as possessors of a unique repository of universal knowledge and wisdom.

Protestant Hebraism, however, was spurred by a particular sense of identi-fication with the ancient Hebrews, whose struggles with their Egyptian and Babylonian neighbours were readily cast as prefiguring the embattled position of godly Protestant polities threatened by the might of the great Catholic pow-ers. In the Dutch Republic, analogies between the Dutch Revolt and the libera-tion of the Jews from their enslavement in Egypt were drawn repeatedly in the literary and visual culture of the seventeenth-century Golden Age. The Dutch saw their young nation as a 'New Israel', blessed with divine protection and a special historical destiny, which had been demonstrated by their successful struggle for freedom from the much mightier Catholic Spain.[37] In England, a similar collective identification as in some sense a divinely chosen nation reso-nated strongly. In both countries, however, the significance of this idea was a key terrain of contestation between competing Protestant camps, in the early seventeenth century in particular. The Puritans in England, and the broadly simi-lar Counter-Remonstrants in the Dutch Republic, restricted their understand-ing of divine election to the community of true believers. For their Arminian adversaries in both countries, the entire nation, and its established rituals and institutions, had inherited the 'New Israel' mantle. Hebraism, in this context, was the standard currency of political argument.[38]

The Christian study of the Old Testament as a political manual also emerged in the late Renaissance. The leading Florentine humanist Niccolò Machiavelli (1469–1527) identified Moses as the most venerable and one of the most outstanding lawgivers in history. The notion that the ancient Hebrew state pro-vided the perfect political blueprint was already a common assumption in medieval Jewish, Christian and Muslim political thought. In his *The Prince* (1513), however, Machiavelli went notably further, claiming Moses as the exem-plar of his concept of political *virtù*, and comparing the subjugated and leader-less Italians of his day to the enslaved Israelites in Egypt, ripe for liberation by a Mosaic lawgiver.[39] Over the next two centuries, the study of the 'republic of the Hebrews' developed into a prominent genre of humanist scholarship. In the Dutch Republic, appeal to the Mosaic example was the most resonant way of advancing political arguments. The most powerful early statement of orthodox Dutch republicanism was Petrus Cunaeus's *De republica Hebraeorum* [The Hebrew Republic] (1617), which was primarily intended as a demonstration of how to preserve civil unity and avoid the perils of factionalism. Published at the height of the power struggle between the Arminian and Counter-Remonstrant camps, Cunaeus highlighted the downfall of the Hebrew polity, which split into two following the death of Solomon. The need to learn from the Hebraic example was urgent, because the Dutch Republic faced a very similar and pressing danger: many citizens, Cunaeus warned, were echoing the conspiratorial machinations of Jeroboam by forming factions and squabbling over obscure issues of religious doctrine.[40]

Cunaeus imagined the ancient Hebraic polity as blissfully agrarian, uncontaminated by the disruptive forces of commerce. The idealization of agrarian simplicity, and its association with the preservation of a just and virtuous *respublica* had been a common refrain in sixteenth-century humanist thought, exemplified most notably in Thomas More's *Utopia* (1516); Cunaeus drew on the Old Testament to add further support to this important current in early modern republicanism.[41] He also found scriptural support for his oligarchic vision of republican government. Almost all decisions in the Hebrew republic, he claimed, were taken by a wise elite of judges or elders, who transmitted their authority through the laying of hands on new appointees. On rare occasions they called together assemblies to consult 'the people', but this occurred only for major decisions such as whether to wage war, or when selecting kings (whose political role, which potentially threw into question whether this polity was truly a republic, he quietly overlooked).[42] For Cunaeus, as for other early modern theoreticians of the Hebrew republic, the political arrangements and events described in the Old Testament were a malleable resource, readily pressed into service as model or as warning to suit the circumstances of the moment.

The most politically contested field of Hebraism, and the most useful area for supporters of republicanism, was Jewish law. Cunaeus was the first to introduce into European legal thought the rabbinic concept, developed in particular detail in Maimonides's *Mishneh Torah*, of the seven universal Noachide laws: the core ethical commandments established by God as legally binding for all the 'children of Noah', the observance of which was required of all peoples with whom the Jews were to sustain peaceful relations.[43] This notion was further developed in the jurisprudence of Hugo Grotius (1583–1645) and John Selden (1564–1654), for whom it assumed fundamental importance in marking the distinction between universal laws, binding on all nations, and 'particular' local laws and regulations. A key figure in the development of early modern natural law theory, Grotius is particularly noted for his foundational work in international law. In his *De jure belli ac pacis* [On the Law of War and Peace] (1625), the Noachide laws serve as the blueprint for the key principles of international law, binding on all, in contrast to which the bulk of Jewish law stood as analogous to the internal legislation of each individual state.[44] This rabbinic distinction enabled Grotius to establish divine endorsement for his view of a legal foundation for universal human morality, clearly distinct from the local laws that vary between polities but must be based upon this common moral groundwork.

Grotius's interpretation of Jewish law also reinforced his wider commitment, as part of the Arminian camp in the Dutch Republic, to 'Erastianism': the supremacy of the state over the church. In the ancient Hebrew polity, he argued, the law was supreme, with diversity of worship among non-Hebrew 'strangers' legally permitted as long as the seven Noachide laws were not contravened.[45] The Jewish law thus underwrote both universalism and a latitude of toleration, bounded by those universal principles. He presented this as a potent rebuttal to those radical Protestants who rejected religious diversity and insisted that the state should enforce their own interpretation of godliness. Fundamental to Grotius's political outlook, and underpinned by his invocation of Jewish sources, was the need to establish a clear basis for the authority and supremacy of the civil law of the state.

For the English legal scholar and parliamentarian John Selden, who shared Grotius's broad perspective but was a much more linguistically competent and agile reader of Jewish texts, establishing this principle was the core purpose of Hebraic scholarship. A vigorous parliamentarian and a trenchant critic of King Charles I's royal authoritarianism, Selden regarded the institutions and traditions of the law, and their continual development within human history, as the core of the English state. The ancient Jewish polity represented, in his view, a detailed example of the supremacy and of the law, and of its sophisticated operation through the structures of the state. This provided a divinely sanctioned model for the status that the law should occupy in England.[46]

In his key work *De jure naturali et gentium juxta disciplinarum Ebraeorum* [On the Law of Nature and of Nations according to the Doctrines of the Hebrews] (1640), Selden explicitly built his theory of natural law on the seven Noachide laws, which despite their universal reach were divinely revealed, he insisted, via Moses at a precise point in Jewish history.[47] The question of the relationship between universalism and revelation was a central point of difficulty in

seventeenth-century natural law theory, as any argument that seemed to separate the two drifted dangerously close to irreligion, whereas the subordination
of the former to the latter left it difficult to explain how natural law could
apply beyond the historical reach of the Mosaic covenant. Nonetheless,
Selden was in this camp: the historical origin of law in God's revelation to
Moses was for him the indispensable root of the English common law tradition. His interest in the minute detail of Jewish civil law stemmed from his
desire to elucidate, by analogy, the relationship between revealed principles
and historical adaptation in societies properly regulated by law. In his *History
of Tithes* (1618), for example, he challenged the claim that tithing was guaranteed by divine right, by showing its basis in law and its variation in historical
practice, just as the tithe payments of the ancient Hebrews had changed over
time, reflecting changing conditions and shifts in the consensus of reasoned
legal opinion.[48] In his extensive and admiring study of Jewish marriage law,
Uxor Ebraica [The Hebrew Wife] (1646), Selden implicitly contrasted the
legal clarity and sophistication of Jewish jurisprudence with the more arbitrary and untidy accretions of canon law on marriage and divorce.[49] The fundamental dividend from the study of rabbinic legal argumentation, Selden
believed, was that this provided the sharpest and most authoritative model
for the analogous development of the English common law from divine and
universal first principles.

Selden was described by a contemporary, only partially in jest, as England's
'chief rabbi', and his Hebraic scholarship has been interpreted by more recent
scholars as a labour of love, imbued with a philosemitic recognition of the humanity of rabbinic exegesis.[50] Selden was certainly passionately devoted to
Hebraica, but he showed no particular warmth toward living Jews: he even at
one point endorsed the medieval 'blood libel' accusation that Jews would kid-
nap and kill a Christian boy each Easter.[51] As with most early modern Christian Hebraists, Selden's fascination with Hebrew texts and arguments was clearly
to some degree animated by the long-standing view of Jews as privileged sources
of distilled wisdom. He was also, through, drawn to his material for instrumental
reasons. The political usefulness of the Hebraic model became increasingly compelling as tensions between parliament and crown intensified over the course
of his career. In the 1640s, when Selden was a member both of the House of
Commons and the Westminster Assembly, he argued explicitly that the 'Jewish church' should be the example on which to base the revised structure of the
Church of England and its relations with the state.[52] In line with most Hebraist
scholarship in the early modern period, Selden deployed his textual sources to

lend authority to his political arguments, arguing against adversaries who were similarly seeking to underwrite their own views with divine sanction.

Hebraic political theology was not, however, simply a tug-of-war. In the thinking of both Grotius and Selden we can clearly perceive the intellectual problem that lay at the heart of their grappling with Jewish sources: the question of what it meant for a particular Christian nation to inherit from the Jews the mantle of divine chosenness. Up to the Reformation, Christians had approached the puzzle of Jewish purpose from a distance: the Jews' status as God's chosen people was given meaning in the context of their relationship to Christian universalism, with which they would ultimately be reconciled when their world historical mission came to be fulfilled. This theology was not discarded by Protestantism, but it was supplemented by a different and more confused one, within which Protestants themselves identified as particular and divinely chosen, while also contrasting their Christian universalism to Jewish particularism. The question of what it might mean to be distinctive or special within a wider framework of universalist meaning is, as we have seen, the nub of the Jewish purpose question. In the writings of these early seventeenth-century natural law theorists we see this question—though not understood in those terms—at work reflexively, as an exploration of how the Dutch or the English could simultaneously be paragons of Christian universalism and God's uniquely chosen people.

Grotius's most enduring work focused on the internationalism of natural law, implicitly casting Dutch or any other body of national law—*jus gentium*—as equivalently particular and parochial. He nonetheless elsewhere argued for the divine status of the Dutch Republic specifically, though he kept this unpublished during his lifetime, leaving the elaboration of this theme to his close friend Cunaeus.[53] The underlying logic of Selden's jurisprudence also suggested an equivalence between all particular legal traditions constructed upon respect for the seven Noachide precepts. However, in the detail of his legal exegesis he criticized legal systems of which he disapproved—such as the convolution of canon law on matters such as divorce and marriage—and vaunted above all the English common law, which he in places clearly elevated above all others. In his posthumously compiled *Table-Talk*, he is recorded comparing the English law directly to the universal laws given by God to all mankind, with the particular laws for the Jews alone compared to the particular laws and privileges of corporations.[54] This uncertainty, which hovered in the background of Selden's work, was a product of the impossibility of any perfect reconciliation between the strains of natural law universalism and national exceptionalism in his jurisprudence.

In Thomas Hobbes's *Leviathan* (1651), the relationship between the biblical Hebraic polity and contemporary English politics is deployed to very different effect. Although the work as a whole is often interpreted as a resolutely irreligious text, the third and longest of its four parts is dense with scriptural citations, and focuses particularly on the political organization of ancient Hebrews. While clearly procedurally influenced by Selden and the extensive 'republic of the Hebrews' tradition, Hobbes presented this regime, in stark contrast with those earlier interpreters, as an exemplar of absolute sovereign authority. As God's 'peculiar people', he argued, the 'nation of the Jews' had forged an everlasting covenant with God, committing itself to be ruled by direct divine sovereignty. This absolute power was exercised first by Moses, as 'God's lieutenant', with authority over all matters passing on his death to the High Priest.[55] The Mosaic polity thus stands as the perfect example of the unified and unlimited sovereign rule for which Hobbes established the logical necessity in the first two books of *Leviathan*. The biblical covenants similarly exemplify the core argument of the book, figuring as a special example of Hobbes's key political idea: the social contract.

The relationship between the theological dimension of the *Leviathan* and its better-known arguments derived from reason and human nature, and the broader question of Hobbes's innermost religious views, continue to stir considerable scholarly controversy and may never reach final determination.[56] It is clear, though, that despite his widespread reputation as an atheist, Hobbes considered it important to establish the case for sovereign authority not just in philosophical but also in biblical terms. The ancient Hebrews, he insisted, were an exceptional case: they alone had been able to communicate with God through the unique mediation of Moses, placing them directly under divine rule, with God as their civil sovereign. Unlike Selden, Hobbes had no interest in rabbinic Judaism, or indeed in Jewish history after the destruction of the First Temple and the Babylonian exile, which extinguished the Jewish commonwealth: after this time, he states, their religion became too corrupted and confused to be of any political salience.[57] Hobbes also stood apart from the prevalent belief that the English nation had in some sense inherited the status of divine chosenness. He holds the Jews at a certain distance with respect to the modern era, while also presenting their ancient state as the most perfect example imaginable of the unitary and absolute political authority that he advocated.

The Jews are not a focus of identification for him, or a model for emulation in the present. They nonetheless serve a vital purpose within his intellectual system, in providing a political ideal type of the highest purity.

Scriptural politics was at an extremely high pitch in Britain at the start of the 1650s. By explicating the very special circumstances of the ancient Hebrews' covenant with God, Hobbes was able sharply to dismiss the claims to covenantal authority of some radicals at the time: he clearly has in mind the Presbyterian Covenanters, who had by then been largely in control in Scotland for a full decade, in condemning as a blatant lie any 'new covenant' supposedly forged directly with God without the essential mediation of 'God's lieutenant'.[58] In England, intense identification with Jews was widespread among radicals during the Interregnum period, with the Fifth Monarchist sect even calling for the national adoption of Jewish law.[59] While Hobbes sought to dampen down this enthusiasm, other scholars were influenced by it. In a sequence of volumes in the later 1650s, James Harrington reasserted the celebration of the Mosaic polity as an exemplary republic. Building on Selden's legal scholarship, Harrington emphasized the longevity, human historicity and most importantly the incipient democracy of the 'Israelite commonwealth', the transmission of authority within it being originally based, he argued, on popular acclaim.[60] For Harrington, the ancient Hebrew polity was an eminently usable model for the British Commonwealth, at a time when the bounds of political possibility seemed dizzyingly open. Hebraic politics mobilized great inspirational power in seventeenth-century Europe, and never more so than in Britain in this tumultuous decade.

It is not the case, however, that Jewish texts were a significant source of new political ideas in this period. Judaism was not—contrary to some recent scholarly claims—the origin of foundational ideas in liberalism, such as toleration, the redistribution of wealth or committed republicanism.[61] Early modern Christian Hebraists approached Jewish texts with a clear idea of what sort of material they were looking for. They quarried these sources for arguments in support of their pre-existing political perspectives, and certainly did not 'discover' startlingly new ideas in the Old Testament or the Talmud. They approached them instrumentally, even if they may often sincerely have believed that they were engaged in disinterested scholarship. However, the fascination with Hebrew texts in early and mid-seventeenth-century political thought extended beyond their usefulness as a potent and polymorphous polemical resource. More profoundly, Hebraism was the terrain on which, in this time of intense political and theological contestation and flux, Dutch and English

Protestants explored how they might reanimate the idea of national specialness and purpose, by breathing new contemporary relevance into its theological encoding in the divine chosenness of the Jews.

Two Jewish Messiahs: Sabbatai Zevi and Baruch Spinoza

The most passionate and politically disruptive identification with Jews in the
mid-seventeenth century took the form of messianism. On the one hand, the
various radical groups of Interregnum England—Levellers, Diggers, Baptists
and Quakers as well as Fifth Monarchists—identified with Jews as an emblem
of their own specialness and separation. Taking further the long-standing Puritan emphasis on the exclusivity of divine election, these groups made heavy
rhetorical use of the morally charged polarities of the Old Testament: Abel and
Cain, Jacob and Esau and, most resonantly of all, Israel versus Amalek.[62] They
also, however, looked forward in various different ways to the millenarian dawn
of a new era in which all such oppositions would dissolve, and a new order of
unity and justice would be established on earth. The dissolution of particularism into universalism was most vividly imagined with reference to God's chosen people: the Jews. For the prophetic preacher TheaurauJohn Tany (born
Thomas Totney, 1608–59), the future of the Jews was the crucial issue of the
moment: In 1650, Tany circumcised himself and declared himself a Jew, and he
largely devoted his remaining years to fulfilling what he believed was his divine
mission to restore the Jews to Zion.[63] In the writings of the leading Fifth Monarchist John Rogers—who, like Selden, was teasingly described as a rabbi—
the tension between the desires to emulate and to transcend Jewish particularism is starkly evident. While festooning his texts with Hebrew words and
phrases, Rogers insisted that he had reached his joyous form of Christianity by
rejecting the sterility of his past religious observance, which he identified with
Judaism. Central to his millenarian vision of the future, however, was the oblit-
eration of all religious differences, including the division between Christians
and Jews. In his considerably Hebraic millenarian tome *Ohel, or Beth-Shemesh:
A Tabernacle for the Sun* (1653), Rogers confidently predicted that the Jews would
imminently become 'most precious' members of Christ's true and universal
church.[64]

   If the Jews occupied a privileged position in the establishment of the messianic future, though, did this not in some way disturb the universalism of that
imagined future? This problem, in various forms, was the crux of much confusion over the place of Jews in messianic and utopian thought. They pointed

the way, as a particular people, toward a universalist future. That future, though, was variously conceived as also Judaic (how could Zion be imagined otherwise?); as its inverse (the fulfilment of Christian universalism as the inversion of Jewish particularism); or perhaps as neither (though this neutrality risked losing all flavour, and was therefore lacking in imaginative power). In this messianic context, Jewish political purpose was both most potent and most confused. Seventeenth-century English millenarians articulated their own sense of purpose through a biblical Jewish idiom. The urgency of their messianic energy, however, pulled into the political present some difficult questions that had hitherto been deferred, as aspects of an only vaguely imaginable divinely shaped future.

This drama took concrete form in the debate in the early 1650s over the 'readmission' of the Jews to England (known as such because they had previously been expelled, by Edward I in 1290). For millenarians, the case was clear: as Baptist Thomas Collier forcefully argued, many of the God-fearing English were eagerly 'waiting for the redemption of Israel', and by welcoming Jews to their shores they could both demonstrate their piety and work to hasten that outcome.[65] These arguments were opposed by more mainstream Puritans such as William Prynne, who was alarmed by the religious diversity and extremism of 'this giddy Apostatizing age', and feared that rather than converting to Christianity, Jews would more probably seduce the English to their religion.[66] Economic arguments also played a role. Established merchants feared Jewish competition, while Collier and others argued in response that the resulting lower prices would benefit the poor majority.[67] The most ingenious compromise suggestion—reflecting the widespread ambivalence over the issue at the time (Cromwell himself was unable to reach a decision in 1655, with an entirely separate chain of events leading to a *de facto* readmission the following year)— came from James Harrington. Rather than admitting Jews to England, where they would remain separate and 'suck the nourishment' from others, Harrington proposed settling them in Ireland, where they would greatly boost the local economy.[68]

This landmark moment in Anglo-Jewish history has generally been interpreted by historians as a significant instance of philosemitism at work.[69] It is clearly true that highly positive associations with Jews were widespread in early and mid-seventeenth-century England, and that these attitudes prevailed, albeit in a hesitant and roundabout fashion, in 1655/6. However, the term 'philosemitism' does not fully capture the complexity of Hebraist and millenarian approaches to Jews and Judaism. The same problems also obviously apply to

'antisemitism': for as long as we use either term, we therefore need the balancing presence of the other within our analytical lexicon.[70] The word 'ambivalence' is also of limited explanatory use in this context. The attitudes expressed
in the Jewish readmission debate certainly seem mixed and even muddled: but
why was this so? The issue of Jewish purpose enables us to offer an answer to
this, and to move beyond the reductive assessment of attitudes to Jews according to their place on a scale of favourability or unfavourability.

Through their intense identification with Jews, Protestant millenarians in the
mid-seventeenth century expressed their own sense of political purpose as a
chosen group performing a crucial historical mission in the world. However,
the denouement of that mission, in the near future, was to be the advent of a
new era in which all particularities—Jewish and Protestant—would be extinguished. Their identificatory theology looked forward to a future that erased
its own particularity, and this cast a puzzling ambiguity over the idea of political particularity itself. This introduced a new complexity into the history of messianism. Medieval notions of the messianic future, both Jewish and Christian,
were usually hazily conceived and remote from the politics of the present. At
times of more pressing messianic expectancy—as for example in the twelfth-
century crusading era—this future was envisaged more as a victory than as a
transformation: Christians such as Bernard of Clairvaux anticipated the final
acceptance by Jews of the universal truths of Christianity, while the rabbinic
followers of Rashi looked forward to the divine triumph of Jews over Christians.
The English millenarians of the 1650s, however, did not understand themselves
in such adversarial or triumphalist terms, but rather as highly particular and special people in the world. Their identity was rooted in particularity, and yet they
were taking active steps to bring all particularity to an end. Their understanding of the distinctiveness and importance of their purpose depended on holding these two elements—their sense of chosenness and the universalism of
their mission—tightly together. This is the structurally fundamental dilemma,
in the modern era, of the question of collective purpose—quintessentially formulated, as in this case, through a Jewish prism. The complexities of these
radicals' attitudes toward Jews are grounded most fundamentally in the internal tensions held within this question. They saw Jews in the same paradoxical
terms as they saw themselves: as simultaneously unique and universal, national
and transnational, and active in the present while also prefiguring the future.

A further complexity that reached new heights in the 1650s was the degree
to which Jews and Christians interacted intellectually, participating in a shared
conversation about the significance of Jews in European society. Messianic

expectancy was at this time in the air among some Jews also. The most notable example is the Amsterdam rabbi Menasseh ben Israel (1604–57), who in 1650 cautiously endorsed the recent claim by a Portuguese crypto-Jew, fêted by Protestant millenarians as of great significance, that he had made contact in the Andes with a remnant of the ten lost tribes of Israel, supposedly still able to recite the Hebrew *Shema* prayer.[71] Menasseh maintained close friendships with a number of radical Christians in Amsterdam at this time. One of his close Christian associates, the millenarian Petrus Serrarius, clearly believed that both Christians and Jews were awaiting the same transformatory event, and was at the centre of a network of like-minded millenarians in both England and Holland.[72] In 1655, Menasseh travelled to London in order to further the campaign for Jewish readmission. He petitioned Oliver Cromwell on the matter, and was warmly welcomed by English millenarian advocates for this cause. Menasseh presented the case for readmission in both millenarian and economic terms, knowing that Cromwell was likely to be receptive to the case that a Jewish merchant presence in London would be beneficial to both parties. His innermost thinking cannot be conclusively determined—but even if, as seems likely, his arguments were in large measure strategic, he was clearly comfortable using a shared messianic language with Christians. Jewish purpose, for Menasseh also, was of broad significance, and required human action for it to be activated as a political force in the present.[73]

The receptivity of European Jewry to messianism was dramatically revealed a decade later, when the charismatic Izmir-born rabbinic scholar Sabbatai Zevi (1626–76) was in 1665 proclaimed as the messiah by his self-declared prophet Nathan of Gaza. Messianic enthusiasm rapidly spread from Nathan's hometown in Palestine to Jewish communities across the Ottoman Empire, in Europe, and beyond. In many communities Jews took steps to prepare for the end of days, selling property, winding down or neglecting their business activities, or making preparations to travel to the Holy Land. In February 1666, Sabbatai was arrested as he approached Istanbul. He was imprisoned in the fortress of Gallipoli, which became a pilgrimage destination for crowds of his devotees from around the Jewish world. In September, with the messianic fervour around him showing no signs of abating, Sabbatai met with the Ottoman sultan, Mehmed IV, after which he announced his conversion to Islam. For the remaining decade of his life, his religious practices straddled Judaism, Islam and, it seems, licentious antinomianism. He sustained his claim to be the messiah even after his exile to Albania in 1673, and cells of his supporters endured after his death in numerous Jewish communities, covertly in some places but openly in others.[74]

Many Christians were extremely interested in this wave of messianic fervour in the Jewish world. Christian millenarians saw these events as extremely portentous, while a number of their critics, in England particularly, saw close parallels between the two movements, and ridiculed the actions of Sabbatai's followers, and the bathetic end of his messianic career, as a means to attack Christian messianic enthusiasm.[75]

Gershom Scholem, whose monumental study of Sabbatianism remains extremely influential, insisted that this movement should be interpreted almost exclusively as a product of internal dynamics within Judaism, and particularly within the history of Jewish mysticism. He ascribed great importance to the use by Sabbatai and Nathan of the Lurianic Kabbalah: a mystical understanding of divine exile and redemption emphasizing the aspiration of *tikkun olam* ('repair of the world'), developed by the rabbi Isaac Luria about a century earlier. Sabbatianism was a crucial stage, he argued, in the history of Jewish 'activist messianism', which he traced forward to modern Zionism, and regarded as the primary inspiration for the various outbursts of similar thinking in the history of the Christian world.[76] There is, however, considerable evidence that the mood of messianic expectancy at this time among Christians, Jews and to a lesser extent also Muslims was to a significant extent a common phenomenon, strengthened by interactions across religious boundaries and a shared interest in the possibility of their dissolution. Menasseh ben Israel's close relationships with Christian millenarians in England and the Dutch Republic is a vivid but not an isolated example of this.[77] Sabbatai's most notable interpreter other than Nathan of Gaza, Avraham Miguel Cardozo (1626–1706), was born into a *converso* family in Spain: for his first two decades he lived outwardly, at least, as a Christian, studying medicine and theology at the University of Salamanca before leaving for Venice in 1648, where he embraced Judaism. Cardozo's Sabbatianism was heavily influenced by his Christian education. Sabbatai's transgression of religious norms and boundaries reflected, Cardozo believed, his messianic transcendence of the limited theological understanding of all three monotheistic religions, while his rejection and imprisonment fulfilled the prophetic association, from Isaiah 53, of messianic redemption with suffering.[78]

Many Sephardic Jews in communities around the Mediterranean, as well as in Amsterdam, London and Hamburg, were similarly shaped by their *converso* background. It is not surprising that some Christian traces, such as the emphasis on suffering in Cardozo's interpretation of Isaiah 53 (a key Christian prooftext), should figure in Sabbatian theology. The prominence of other religions in Sabbatian thought, however, extends beyond such straightforwardly explained instances of syncretic influence. Sabbatians were notably interested in Islam, and even more so in Christianity, engaging closely with the theological debates and internal divisions of both religions. It might even be argued, as one scholar has recently suggested, that their investigations amounted to a form of 'Jewish Christianism': a mirror activity to the 'Christian Hebraism' of Cunaeus, Selden and so many others.[79] These Christians were curious about Judaism, and were interested, in various ways, in exploring and testing the boundaries between the two religions. Sabbatians were similarly curious about Christianity, and additionally about Islam, and they also challenged the traditionally understood lines of separation between these faiths.

The aftermath of Sabbatai's conversion to Islam extended this syncretic blurring into new terrain. A number of his followers—about two hundred families—soon also converted, but obeyed their messiah in continuing to live as a highly segregated community. In 1683, there was a similarly-sized conversion in Salonika, the descendants of which became known as the Dönme: a Sabbatian group within Islam that maintained its distinct identity at least until the early twentieth century.[80] The Dönme, like Sabbatai himself, both did and did not reject the separateness of Judaism. Already before his conversion, a key feature of Sabbatai's messianic performance had been his transgression of Jewish norms: he ate prohibited foods, authorized the reading of the Torah by women, and announced radical changes in forms of worship. For the most radical of the Dönme, the rejection of religious particularism, and the embrace of beliefs and practices from diverse faiths, was part of a conscious embrace of religious universalism.[81] In essence, Sabbatians rejected the rigid authority of the Jewish law, and of the political structures, both within and outside the Jewish world, that maintained the rigid boundary between Jews and their Christian and Muslim neighbours. However, they did not abandon a sense of themselves as a people apart. Indeed, their recognition of a greater unity beyond the divisions between religions paradoxically imbued them with a heightened sense of their specialness. Among the Dönme, who maintained strong traditions of endogamy and cultural distinctiveness while being outwardly assimilated and strongly associated with modernizing trends in Salonika and beyond, this paradoxical duality was maintained for many generations.[82]

The Sabbatians thus faced the same puzzle as the English millenarians of the 1650s. Both groups believed themselves to be at the messianic vanguard, alone in perceiving the unity that transcended the differences between religions. Both groups also expressed their identity through related but distinct articulations of the purpose of Jews in the world. For Christian millenarians, identification with Jews was the primary theological means to express both divinely chosen particularity and the imminent passage to the universalist future that they believed would be the messianic fulfilment of the Jews' unique role in God's plan. Sabbatians were inspired by essentially the same belief in the universal aspect of Jewish messianic purpose. Jewish identification, however, was not available for them as an anchor of particularity, as this was the normative tradition from which they set themselves apart. Instead, they preserved their particularism through a more complex mix of strategies, encompassing endogamy, secrecy and various rituals of moral transgression, particularly with respect to sexuality and gender relations.[83] Both Christian millenarianism and Sabbatianism, though, were seventeenth-century forms of holding together an identity that was simultaneously universalist and highly select, and was understood by its adherents as the true fulfilment of Jewish world historical purpose.

The flourishing Sephardic community of Amsterdam was intensely swept up in the initial wave of Sabbatian enthusiasm. Surviving reports describe wild rejoicing in the Amsterdam streets with the Torah scrolls of the synagogue, leading merchants preparing to sell up their businesses so that they could travel to Palestine and the unrestrained proclamation to non-Jews of the arrival of the messiah.[84] Observing this from a short distance was a former member of that community, who in the long run was to inspire even more intense adulation than Sabbatai Zevi: Baruch Spinoza (1632–77).

At this time Spinoza was no longer living in Amsterdam: he seems to have left the city in 1661, five years after having been expelled from his birth community for his 'abominable heresies', and at this time was living in Voorburg, a village near The Hague. However, he was kept informed of events by his Christian associates, many of whom were themselves inclined toward millenarianism and were therefore fascinated by the drama unfolding in the Jewish world. Relatively little is known about Spinoza's life in Amsterdam in the years immediately following his expulsion from the Sephardic community in July 1656, but he had close contacts at that time with many radical Christians, including the leading millenarian Petrus Serrarius, who died in 1669 while travelling to Turkey in order to meet Sabbatai himself. It is very likely that Spinoza was also in touch with Quakers, who had come to Amsterdam from England precisely in order to make contact with Jews there and to endeavour to convert them to Christianity; he may even be the person who in the late 1650s translated into Hebrew two Quaker conversionist pamphlets.[85] Whether or not this is the case, it is clear that Spinoza's philosophical outlook took shape in an environment heavily charged with millenarian expectancy, in which transformations in Jewish beliefs or practices were regarded as exceptionally significant.

In the 1660s, Spinoza was at the centre of a coterie of radical thinkers, comprised mostly of Protestants from a range of backgrounds but also including the freethinking former Jesuit Franciscus van den Enden. As well as arguing for a more democratic politics and a sharp separation of church and state, members of this group were interested above all in interpreting the Bible in accordance with reason. This was the explicit argument of the book published in 1666 by Spinoza's close friend and personal doctor Lodowijk Meyer, and also, from a more linguistic perspective, of two books of 1668 by another member of the circle, Adriaan Koerbagh. Both these men accorded special significance to the Jews in their complementary visions of the imminent dawn of a new era of true understanding. Meyer's work concluded with a resonantly millenarian call to arms, looking forward to the emergence of a truly universal and rational church, which would then finally embrace 'stranger nations' (the Jews). Koerbagh, meanwhile, was fascinated by the purified, philosophical meaning of the Hebrew Bible, while expressing intense frustration with the 'stiff-necked and servile' Jews for failing to recognize these truths.[86] Koerbagh's arguments were regarded as highly subversive even in the relatively open environment of Amsterdam. The city authorities interrupted printing of his second book as soon as they caught wind of it, and arrested and incarcerated its author, interrogating him about his contacts with Spinoza and others. Koerbagh died while still in custody in late 1669. It was against this background, taking forward a beleaguered intellectual campaign, that Spinoza himself finally went into print, in 1670 anonymously publishing his first major work, his *Tractatus theologico-politicus* [Theological-Political Treatise].[87]

Spinoza shared with Meyer and Koerbagh a close interest in the interpretation of the Bible, and many of the arguments of his *Tractatus* are foreshadowed in their earlier texts. However, Spinoza took a subtly different approach to the central importance of the Jewish people in the biblical narrative. Rather than taking this for granted, he addressed this question directly almost at the outset of the *Tractatus*: in his third chapter, entitled 'On the Vocation of the Hebrews', he offered the first systematic argument for the normalization of the place of the Jews in human history. In the preceding two chapters, he offered his rational and historical explanation for the ubiquity of prophecy in the Hebrew Bible. God adapted his message, Spinoza argued, according to the extreme ignorance of the ancient Hebrews, particularly with regard to the natural world. The supernatural language of the prophets was therefore purely decorative, designed to suit the limited understanding of their audience: only the 'purpose and substance' of their revelations should be taken seriously.[88] His critique of the idea of Jewish chosenness is similarly based on the primacy of reason, and the irrelevance of any pronouncements in the Bible that do not accord with reason. 'True happiness and blessedness', he states at the outset of his argument, 'consists solely in the enjoyment of the good, not in priding oneself that you alone are enjoying that good to the exclusion of others.' The belief that one is more blessed than others because one enjoys wellbeing or fortune that others do not share cannot be 'true blessedness', as such an attitude can only stem either from 'mere childishness' or from 'spite and malice'. God's various declarations that he has chosen the Hebrews 'above all other nations' (e.g., Deuteronomy 10:15) therefore cannot be literal expressions of God's true meaning. This rhetoric of exclusivity, as with the supernaturalism of the prophets, merely reflects the limited understanding of the ancient Hebrews.[89]

Spinoza's biblical exegesis was heavily dependent on the principle of divine 'accommodation', or condescension: the idea that the language of scripture was tailored to the mental capacities of its human audience. This was an established notion in medieval Jewish thought, and particularly in the work of Abraham Ibn Ezra (1089–1167) and Moses Maimonides, with which Spinoza was familiar. It also had a long history in Christian exegesis, playing an important role in the explanations offered by the church fathers for the more 'primitive' legal commandments of the Old Testament, in contrast with the spiritual maturity of Jesus's message.[90] In describing the ancient Hebrews repeatedly as 'children', Spinoza echoed this argument. His view of Judaism as an outlook frozen in an early developmental stage resonates with Christian thinking on Jews as far back as Paul, as we noted at the beginning of this chapter. However, in connecting this to the idea of Jewish chosenness, Spinoza took a new step, arguing that the very idea of having an exclusive relationship with God was inherently and obviously infantile.

If, though, God could not possibly favour the Jews, what *was* the true meaning of the biblical language that seemed to express such divine partisanship? Spinoza offered a detailed answer to this question. There are, he states, three 'worthy objects of desire' in human life: knowledge, virtue and 'to live in security and good health'. The attainment of knowledge and of virtue is dependent on our individual powers, which in all societies similarly vary from person to person. The enjoyment of 'security and good health', however, is equally accessible to 'the fool and the wise', because it is dependent on social and political arrangements, which vary not between individuals, but between organized collectivities. It was only in relation to these arrangements that the Hebrews were in any sense 'chosen': God provided them with bespoke legislation, in order to enhance 'the material success and prosperity of their state'. Spinoza points to biblical evidence that God also guided other nations in developing their own states and 'special laws'. He admits that this evidence is scanty, but ascribes this to the limited scope of the Bible: 'the Hebrews were concerned to record their own history, not that of other nations'. The election of the Jews is thus reinterpreted as their acceptance of divine guidance, which had been similarly available to all peoples, in establishing the political arrangements that were best for them.[91]

This argument implied a radical normalization of the Jews and their place in history. The Jews, according to Spinoza, received no special favour from God, and the very idea of such favour was an infantile absurdity. In his later, posthumously published *Ethics*, Spinoza made it absolutely clear that such favour was incompatible with his conception of God. As he encapsulated it in his famous formulation '*Deus sive natura*' ('God, or nature'), God cannot seek to intervene in human history, deflecting the laws of nature, because God *is* nature.[92] The biblical narrative, on his reading, was simply an example of the early political history of one particular people. However, the particularity of this people was not without interest to him, not only because it was documented in such extraordinary detail, but also because this people happened to be the one into which he was born. In persistently describing the Jews as infantile—not only in the past, but also in their present persistence in observing outdated laws and believing themselves to be divinely chosen—Spinoza appears to harbour a sharply negative view of Jewish particularity. His explanation for why Moses sought special guidance from God reiterates a further stock trope of Christian anti-Jewish rhetoric: it was only the 'obstinate spirit' of the Hebrews, a 'stiff-necked people', that made Moses's appeal necessary.[93] The normalization of the Jews could not readily be reconciled with the textual exceptionality of the Bible, which treated Jewish history in privileged isolation. Spinoza's exegesis of this text therefore inescapably led him back to interpreting the Jews in exceptional terms.

Spinoza's continued interest in the particularity of the Jews was not only expressed in negative terms. Just before the end of his chapter on the 'vocation of the Hebrews', he turns briefly to the recent history of the Jews and to their collective future, in comments that have inspired much fascination among later Jewish generations:

As to their [the Jews'] continued existence for many years when scattered and stateless, this is in no way surprising, since they have separated themselves from other nations to such a degree as to incur the hatred of all, and this not only through external rites alien to the rites of other nations, but also through the mark of circumcision, which they most religiously observe. That they are preserved largely through the hatred of other nations is demonstrated by historical fact. . . .

The mark of circumcision, too, I consider to be such an important factor in this matter than I am convinced that this by itself will preserve their nation forever. Indeed, were it not that the fundamental principles of their religion discourage manliness, I would not hesitate to believe that they will one day, given the opportunity—such is the mutability of human affairs—establish once more their independent state, and that God will again choose them.[94]

These observations combine strains of derision (Judaism discouraging manliness) with original proto-sociological analysis of the reasons for the survival of the Jews as a distinct people, and a hint that these special factors might lead to a dramatic revival of their collective fortune in the future. The idea of an 'ingathering' of the Jews in Zion was, as we have seen, a compelling notion among millenarians at this time, including many of Spinoza's Christian associates, as well as among Sabbatians, some of whom only a few years earlier had taken first steps to make this an immediate reality. Spinoza, we can safely assume, was to some degree influenced by the widely diffused presence of this idea in the intellectual worlds he inhabited. His comments also reflect, though, the significance for him of the present and future life of the people into which he was born. In the context of his universalist philosophy, the Jews have no special importance. However, he allows himself these brief digressive comments on Jewish particularity, which he nonetheless regards as noteworthy, and most probably also of personal interest.

Did Spinoza retain, despite his expulsion from the Sephardic community of Amsterdam, a sense of connection with and perhaps even pride in his Jewish roots? In the early twentieth century, many secular Zionists insisted that he did, using these comments as the basis for the construction of a 'Zionist Spinoza', which, as we will see, played an important role in their attempt to bind together Jewish nationalism and progressive universalism. More broadly compelling, though, has been the idealization of Spinoza as the personification of philosophical detachment. The image of him as a modest lens-grinder, free of all personal attachments or concerns and devoted only to the disinterested development of his rational philosophy, was outlined by his first biographer, his associate Jean Maximilien Lucas, and has remained lodged in popular consciousness ever since.[95] No life, however, can be lived entirely aloof from the specificities of time, space and interpersonal affective relationships. Spinoza's social position of radical disaffiliation made him unique in his period: he stood outside all confessional groupings, an outsider in an even more profound sense than the various dissenting 'Christians without a church', some of whom were his most devoted admirers.[96] He did not, though, seek to erase all traces of his Jewish origins. In a famous letter to a Christian correspondent in December 1675, he discussed his personal knowledge of the religious commitment of some Jewish victims of the Spanish Inquisition.[97] We cannot know Spinoza's innermost identity— but there is no basis, either in what we know of his biography or in the principles of his philosophy, for us to infer that he disavowed any collective identification whatsoever (a position that is any case in practice unsustainable). Despite his desire to dislodge the theological exceptionalism that framed almost all discussion of Jews in the seventeenth century, it was natural for Spinoza, as a Jew by origin, to remain interested in the history and future of this particular people.

For his non-Jewish readers, however, this straightforward reason for a continued interest in the content of the Old Testament did not apply. Over the next few decades, the Bible was attacked across much of Europe in increasingly forthright terms, with frequent emphasis on the alleged absurdity, immorality and barbarism of God's supposedly chosen people.[98] Spinoza's rationalist philosophy and style of biblical exegesis was a key inspiration for these attacks. For many of those in this period who identified with the alluringly transgressive label of 'Spinozist', their hero had laid the groundwork for the discrediting of the Bible *in toto*, and particularly of the nonsensical narratives of the Old Testament, which they typically regarded as worthy only of ridicule.[99]

Spinoza's critique of the Bible was closely linked with his personal idealization. This was neatly emblematized in 1719, when one of the most radical texts that had been circulating in manuscript over the preceding decades—the *Treatise of the Three Impostors* [*Traité sur les trois imposteurs*], which alleged that Moses, Mohammed and Jesus had all invented their divine revelations in order to gain mastery over the gullible masses—was published for the first time, bound together with Lucas's biography of Spinoza, under a new title: *The Spirit of Spinoza* [*L'esprit de Spinosa*]. The unmasking of religion was seen as Spinoza's message, but his authority as messenger was itself imbued with a religious

aura. Lucas identified as Spinoza's most admirable feature his absolute transcendence of his Jewish origins: 'although he was born and bred in the midst of a
gross people who are the source of superstition . . . he was entirely cured of those
silly and ridiculous opinions with the Jews have of God'.[100] Lucas also explicitly conflated Spinoza's philosophy with the core teachings of Jesus Christ.[101]
His account of Spinoza's life resonantly echoed that of Jesus: he too was a former Jew who rejected the tribalism of his origins, and through that rejection
brought into the world a new and universal message. This image of Spinoza, as
in essence the messiah of the Enlightenment, imbued the celebratory reception
of his philosophy, which strengthened over the course of the eighteenth century
and has endured to the present.[102] In this role, Spinoza has continued to fit the
classic template of Jewish purpose: to signal the pathway from the particularism of the past to the universalism of the future.

Both Sabbatai Zevi and Spinoza have been widely cast as messiahs of modernity. For Gershom Scholem, the religious nihilism of Sabbatai played a crucial role in blasting open the ossified rigidity of traditional Judaism and in
enabling the 'dialectic of Jewish history' to move forward. The Dönme and, as
we shall see in the next chapter, another Sabbatian offshoot, the Frankist movement, have fascinatingly combined messianic exclusivity with notably 'modern' commercial, political and sexual attitudes. Spinoza has long been revered
by liberals, and particularly by Jewish liberals; his status as a, or even *the*, founding father of the democratic and emancipatory values of the Enlightenment
has recently been reasserted with renewed vigour.[103] Both Sabbatianism and
Spinoza were strongly influenced by the same strand of cultural hybridity in
seventeenth-century Judaism: the mixed heritage of 'Marrano' Jews, such as
Abraham Cardozo and Spinoza's parents, who had been raised in the Iberian
peninsula living outwardly as Catholics. This background, particularly in the
setting of yet another religious culture (Protestantism or Islam), brought with
it a particularly elevated consciousness of human diversity. It has been argued,
both specifically for Spinoza and for the Marranos in general, that this give
rise to a form of 'split identity' that was in turn the wellspring of modern
subjectivity.[104] This claim constitutes a recent variant of the idea of Jewish
purpose, in the idiom of secular historiography. While the argument is readily over-extended, it is certainly the case that the great impact of both Sabbatai
Zevi and Spinoza was due in large part to their straddling of Jewish and non-
Jewish worlds and intellectual traditions.

There is, then, a striking parallelism between these superficially highly contrasting individuals. Whereas at the start of the seventeenth century serious

intellectual interaction between Jews and Christians had barely begun, in the years around 1670 these two men, in very different ways, inspired many people to regard them as uniquely inspired individuals heralding the dawn of a new historical era. Both men unleashed ripples of messianic energy that continued to register centuries later, and which played, as we shall see, an enduring role in the theological and political unfolding of the Jewish purpose question.

———

The ensnarement of Judaism in the binary oppositions of Christian political theology—literal versus figural; material versus spiritual; childish versus mature—has been viewed by many scholars with extreme suspicion and anxiety. Should we not perhaps reject this pattern of thinking altogether, as irredeemably contaminated with negative caricatures of Jews and Jewishness that fuelled the anti-Judaic prehistory of modern antisemitism?[105] Tempting though such an escape from the weight of history may be, these juxtapositions are too deeply baked into the relationship between Judaism and Christianity for them to be straightforwardly set aside. The implicitly (and sometimes explicitly) hostile aspects of Christian thinking on Judaism are also closely related to other, more positive associations. This duality was particularly evident, as we have seen, in the intensely biblical culture of seventeenth-century Protestant Europe: Jewish particularism inspired identification as well as denigration, and rabbinic literature was seen as a privileged repository of legal and exegetical learning even while simultaneously being derided as sterile and replete with error. Most importantly, the Old Testament was widely seen as offering an admirable political model, of great relevance for those who sought to resolve disputes over power and authority by establishing new forms of covenantal politics.

Judaism was crucial to seventeenth-century politics because it pointed both backward and forward. In the Mosaic 'republic of the Hebrews' Christian political thinkers found a blueprint for the political organization of an elect community living under God's direct rule. The appeal of this idealized vision of circumscribed peoplehood was, though, inextricable from the messianic lure of a future in which all divisions between peoples would dissolve. The Dutch or the English could imagine themselves, in loose terms, as God's new 'chosen people', but they could not throw biblical history into reverse. They could, however, aspire to push it forward, into a messianic future. The forward-looking energies of these two economic powerhouses of the era were theologically framed by hopes of bringing to fulfilment the deepest purpose of the Jews in human history: to lead the world into its culminating era of peace and unity.

In this millenarian endeavour, Christians could feel that they were acting almost as Jews, or at least alongside Jews who shared their millenarian impulses. Both in the Sabbatian movement and in Spinoza's philosophical circle—though in complex and very different ways—we see a degree of messianic communality across the Jewish–Christian divide. This messianic aspect of political theology, which was particularly intense among both Jews and Christians in the third quarter of the seventeenth century, bound these communities closer together, as within both religions it was anticipated that transformations in Jewish life would bear special significance for the world as a whole. In medieval Europe, Christian theology had played a crucial role in holding the Jews in their politically subordinate place. The political theology of the seventeenth century, however, had a very different impact. The divine purpose of the Jews intensified Christian desire for closer contact with them: an attitudinal change that had important consequences, most notably in the readmission of Jews to England. This Judaeocentric messianic outlook also lodged in the political imagination the possibility in the near future of a radically transformed relationship between the two religions.

Over the final two decades of the seventeenth century, the status of the Bible as a pre-eminent political reference point waned rapidly in England, the Dutch Republic and beyond, and by the turn of the century various genres of scriptural satire, unimaginable not long previously, were circulating openly.[106] At one level, this marked a key moment in the rise of secularism, and the 'great separation' of politics from theology.[107] However, this was by no means the end of the theological dimension of politics. Visions of a better future, in which confessional and other human divisions would be overcome, remained central to the political thinking of the following century and beyond. These visions were built upon the messianic hopes of the seventeenth century, and continued to draw energy from these roots. In this fundamental structure of political aspiration, the future was imagined as a transition from particularism to universalism. This was also the essence of the scriptural blueprint for politics, with the purpose of the Jews, as the key agents of this transformation, centrally inscribed within it. After the seventeenth century, Jewish purpose was primarily considered in secular terms, but these various new frameworks were mapped upon this underlying theological template.

For Carl Schmitt, the original theorist of political theology, this term applied, as we have already noted, not to the direct domination of politics by religion, but to the transfer by analogy of theological principles into the political realm. This was why Hobbes was so important for him: his political theory rearticulated the sovereign authority of religion in the emergent language of modernity. Hobbes's sovereign Leviathan, Schmitt admiringly wrote, is 'a combination of god and man, animal and machine, . . . the mortal god who brings to man peace and security'.[108] Spinoza also figured prominently in Schmitt's study of Hobbes—but in the contrasting position of the subverter of Hobbes's thought, and of political theology in general. It was Spinoza, Schmitt argued, who with devastating consequences latched onto the one small restriction to the absolute authority of the sovereign that Hobbes had allowed. This related to the issue of miracles: although Hobbes accorded to the sovereign the power to determine the authenticity of miracles, and forbade public dissent from that official view, he argued that private non-belief in their truth was permissible.[109] Schmitt's words, written in Berlin in 1938, carry an ominous resonance:

> Only a few years after the appearance of the *Leviathan*, a liberal Jew noticed the barely visible crack in the theoretical justification of the sovereign state. In it he immediately recognised the telling inroad of modern liberalism, which would allow Hobbes' postulation of the relation between external and internal, public and private, to be inverted into its converse.[110]

In Spinoza's hands, for Schmitt, Hobbes's attempt to establish a new basis for sovereignty, based upon the acceptance of unified and virtually absolute political and theological authority, was turned inside-out, with the emphasis placed not on social and political unity, but on the liberal tenets of individualism and freedom of thought.

What are we to make of this? Although he was not a supporter of the Nazis before 1933, Schmitt swiftly rallied to their regime, becoming the leading jurist of the Third Reich. The antisemitic inflection of his comments on Spinoza is unmistakable, and is by no means an isolated occurrence in his work.[111] Schmitt's antisemitism was intimately related to his anti-liberalism: Jews, he believed, were the key promoters and beneficiaries of liberalism, which he regarded as a bankrupt political ideology to which the only viable alternative was the acceptance of strong state authority. Schmitt's work remains highly controversial. Many, including thinkers on the Left, regard him as of crucial importance as a theorist of law, ideology and power, while others see him as irredeemably tainted by his Nazism and antisemitism.[112] His reading of Spinoza, at any rate, despite its sneering and conspiratorial overtones, should by no means be bracketed apart from the mainstream of European thought. Schmitt here stands

within a long tradition of ascribing extraordinary acumen and historical significance to this one individual, and associating this with his Jewish origins. Although Schmitt did not like the world that came in the wake of Spinoza's
thought, his belief in its transformatory impact was in accord with the assessment of many of Spinoza's ardent admirers, both in the seventeenth century and
since.

For Schmitt, Spinoza was the inventor of modern secular philosophy—a fatal
achievement that was the direct product of his Jewishness. Individualism, liberalism and other modern ills stemmed from Spinoza's philosophy, and were
thus all in essence also 'Jewish'.[113] Such accusations have figured prominently
in many different guises in the history of modern anti-Judaism and antisemitism. However, this association also has its powerful flipside. Spinoza's Jewishness has often been positively associated with his rational and liberal outlook,
and Jews in general have been frequently fêted (by themselves as well as by non-
Jews) as key originators of modernity.

The idea of Jewish purpose has been central to this positive understanding
of the Jewishness of modernity. Intellectual rationalism, cultural pluralism and
the emancipation of society from theological domination are viewed on this
account as key hallmarks of the modern outlook, in the emergence of which
Jews have played a strikingly prominent or even a crucially determinant role.
The association of the Jewish purpose question with a better future has deep
roots in pre-modern Western thought. This assumed much more concrete shape
and political salience in the seventeenth century, however, as the ideas and ideals that increasingly came to be seen as fundamental to modernity began to
move to the fore of intellectual life, in north-west Europe in particular. Jewish
agency and purpose carried a potent resonance, in this environment, in both
the political application of theology and in the early challenge to the supremacy of this discipline. In the eighteenth century, when theology was decisively
eclipsed by philosophy as the dominant terrain of serious discussion, it was
primarily in relation to the puzzles and potentials of that field of thought that
the Jewish purpose question was most significantly revisited and rethought.

2

Reason, Toleration, Emancipation

JEWS AND PHILOSOPHICAL PURPOSE

O nations, for eighteen centuries you have been trampling on the remnants of Israel! . . . A new era is about to begin; may the palms of humanity adorn its frontispiece, and may posterity applaud in advance the union of your hearts. The Jews are members of that universal family which must establish fraternity between all peoples; revelation is extending its majestic veil over them, as it is over you. Children of the same father, free yourselves of all traces of aversion toward your brothers, who will one day be gathered in the same sheepfold; offer asylum to them, where they can rest their heads and dry their tears in peace. Finally, may the Jew, reciprocating the tenderness of the Christian, embrace me as his fellow-citizen and friend.[1]

—ABBÉ HENRI GRÉGOIRE (1789)

THE DECADES AROUND 1700 were pivotal in the long-term decline in status of theology and the rise of philosophy in Europe. The relationship between these two disciplines had been fractious since the early impact of the work of René Descartes (1596–1650), whose emphasis on deductive reasoning as the source of all reliable knowledge posed a major challenge to defenders of the authority of the Bible. From the 1640s to the 1670s, universities in the Dutch Republic were riven by a factional dispute between those who believed that Cartesianism unacceptably and heretically undermined the supremacy of religion, and those who argued that theology and philosophy (including Cartesian philosophy) were separate pursuits that should be allowed to develop alongside each other.[2] Spinoza's philosophical formation took place against this backdrop, and his work, directly applying a rational approach to scripture itself, was a key contribution to the increasing assertiveness of philosophy. Theologians continued to grapple with the impact of Spinoza, but in the eighteenth century the most significant intellectual debates no longer revolved around the Bible, but instead focused on the nature, scope and impact of philosophical reason. The question of Jewish purpose was also predominantly framed by these ascendant concerns. Theology continued to loom large in eighteenth-century European thinking on Judaism, which therefore figured very prominently in controversies over the relationship between religion and reason. As the reformist aspirations of the Enlightenment era gathered strength, however, Jews assumed importance in a different and more practical context: as the key test case for the remaking of the world on a philosophically rational basis.

What precisely is reason, and what is its relationship to knowledge, belief and certainty? This question was explored with exceptional vigour in this period, which was characterized by extreme epistemological uncertainty and conflict. Exponents of the experimental method of scientific inquiry were rapidly establishing their cultural and intellectual authority, alongside the emergence of a self-consciously transnational scholarly 'republic of letters'.[3] At the same time, both Protestant and Catholic traditionalists sought to shore up the status of religion, while being tested both by internal dissent and by continued rivalry between the two denominations. For many clerics and scholars, the defence of Christianity was dependent above all on establishing a decisive response to Spinoza. This stimulated new attempts to integrate the Bible, and therefore also the place of Jews in history, with reason- and evidence-based forms of argument and knowledge. Alternatively, Judaism was widely deployed as a demonstration of the profound imperviousness of scripture to rational interpretation. This claim could underpin two almost diametrically contrasting arguments, which paradoxically were not always easy to distinguish from each other: the absurdity of both Judaism and Christianity, and the indispensability and inscrutability of non-rational religious faith. In these complex debates, Judaism served a vital purpose, as a keenly contested touchstone in attempts to establish the nature and reach of philosophical reason.

The turn to philosophy was also, though, a turn toward practical, human-centred matters of social and political improvement. A central rallying cause was toleration, over which leading intellectuals associated with the Enlightenment, such as Voltaire, fought a sustained battle against the established hierarchies of church and state. Defining the proper scope and philosophical basis of toleration, however, was not a straightforward matter. Jews and Judaism entered this debate in various ways: as a limit case for the reach of toleration; as a stereotyped negative contrast to the positive values of the Enlightenment; and, most famously in Gotthold Ephraim Lessing's play *Nathan the Wise* (1779), as a counter-stereotypical idealized model of those values. In the final quarter of the eighteenth century a reformist mood rapidly gathered momentum, with the political, cultural and economic transformation of Jews a prominent focus of attention. The extension of political rights to Jews in France was widely seen in the early 1790s as a key fulfilment of the universalist principles of the French Revolution, as was the throwing open of ghettos and the granting of those rights to Jews in other parts of western Europe conquered by Napoleon's armies. This process, which from the 1830s was resonantly known as 'Jewish emancipation', was of vastly greater symbolic than material importance. The transformation of Jewish life in western Europe over this period was driven by profound economic and social changes rather than by the faltering steps toward the civic inclusion of Jews that took place alongside them. The rethinking of the place of Jews in European societies was, however, of immense intellectual significance. For those who embraced the upheavals and reforms of the era as the triumph of Enlightenment reason, this achievement symbolized more powerfully than anything else the epochal significance of that triumph. Opposition to these changes, however, was readily expressed through a refusal to recognize Jews as social and political peers.

Enlightenment thinkers considered themselves as innovators, establishing a new philosophical paradigm for a new historical era. The intellectual models of the past nonetheless undergirded their thought—and this is particularly apparent with respect to the idea of Jewish purpose. In the eighteenth century the Jews continued to denote the essence of tribal particularism, but also to signal the pathway, through their anticipated transformation, to the overcoming of all human divisions in a universalist and quasi-utopian future. This millenarian structure implicitly underlay the future-oriented thought of the Enlightenment era. When the significance of the Jews in human history was addressed explicitly, this current of millenarianism was often explicit. The abbé Henri Grégoire (1750–1831), for example—one of the most ardent advocates for a more amicable policy toward the Jews of France, both in the decade preceding the Revolution and in the years following it—clearly imbued the embrace of Jews by Christians with great significance. This would inexorably lead, as he confidently predicts in the quotation at the head of this chapter, to the reciprocal embrace of Christians (and Christianity) by Jews, ushering the world into a new era of universalism and harmony.

The traditional binary contrasts between Judaism and Christianity, which stretch back to Paul, in no sense lost their significance in the eighteenth century. They were used in various ways as markers of distinction between the old and the new, with Jewish legalism and literalism often juxtaposed to the insights of secular reason rather than to Christian spirit. The emotional valence of these contrasts, however, was more complicated in this era of accelerating and highly contested change. The cultural atavism of the Jews could be regarded in positive rather than negative terms, as a link to an earlier era of noble and simple primitivism prior to the emergence of the theocratic power structures of institutionalized Christianity. The post-particularist future with which their transformation was so closely associated prompted a wide range of responses, which were also readily projected onto Jews themselves. As Theodor Adorno and Max Horkheimer noted in their seminal *Dialectic of Enlightenment* (1944), Jews occupied a confused place in the temporal schema of Enlightenment rationalism: 'they are thought to lag behind advanced civilization and yet to be too far ahead of it; they are both clever and stupid, similar and dissimilar'.[4]

Adorno and Horkheimer developed their analysis of the self-undermining dialectic of enlightened reason in Californian exile from Nazi Germany, and with the twentieth-century legacy of the Enlightenment more in mind than the eighteenth century itself. The association of Jews with both past and future—both childlike immaturity and messianic redemption—also stretches back, as we have seen, to the beginnings of the divergence between Judaism and Christianity. It was in the eighteenth century, however, and in the context of that period's rising historical consciousness, that this Janus-faced view of Jews, as both fossilized remnants from the past and precocious initiators of modernity, established itself most profoundly in Western thought. In the 1940s, these contradictory judgments jointly fuelled murderous antisemitism. Two centuries earlier, however, the significance of these counterposed perspectives was much more fluid and complex. For much of that century the primary purpose of Jews was as a thinking tool, and thus these double-edged evaluations were not straightforwardly applied to the living Jews of the era. However, as the practical application of Enlightenment ideas gathered strength, attitudes and policies toward Jews became a key terrain for the demonstration and contestation of philosophically inspired visions of the future. Advocates of Enlightenment reformism did not share the identificatory philosemitic fervour of the millenarian Protestants of the mid-seventeenth century, but many of them transposed this outlook into a more restrained key, continuing to connect Jewish agency and purpose with the positive forward motion of history. European thinking about Jewish purpose developed in palimpsestic fashion: patterns of meaning established in earlier periods remained in evidence, even as reworkings of these patterns were inscribed over them.

Judaism versus Reason: Pierre Bayle and Voltaire

What is (the) Enlightenment? This question was insistently posed, in various forms, during the eighteenth century, and remains keenly debated among historians today.[5] On one side of this current debate, it is claimed that all the key ideas of modern democratic politics first took shape at the radical cutting edge of the Enlightenment; on the opposing wing the very idea of an eighteenth-century Enlightenment has been called into question, on the grounds that this falsely suggests a rupture with the scholarly practices and perspectives of the seventeenth century.[6] It is clear, though, that an important intellectual transition occurred in western Europe in the period around 1700, even if historians have found it difficult to define its nature. This shift was not only about ideas. It was also shaped by new forms and environments of intellectual communication: this was the period of the rise of the coffee house, the salon, the scholarly academy, the literary journal; which together had a transformative impact on the circulation of thought and argument. This impact was itself reflexive: the promotion of respect and civility within what we now describe as the 'public sphere' became a central concern of that public sphere.[7]

The Enlightenment is perhaps best defined in relation to this self-conscious sense of identity and public purpose among intellectuals at this particular juncture in European intellectual and cultural history. Intellectual excitement over the rise of philosophy was a defining feature of the movement: the self-defined *philosophes* of the French Enlightenment celebrated the triumph of *l'esprit philosophique*.[8] This emphasis on the power of ideas was closely associated, however, with an awareness of the importance of history. The debate between 'ancients' and 'moderns', which raged in both England and France in the period around 1700 was, as has recently been argued, a key event in the emergence of the historical self-understanding of the Enlightenment. Rather than aligning with the 'moderns', proponents of the 'philosophical spirit' of the era were closer to the 'ancients': they recognized the importance of classical sources, valuing them particularly for their freedom from theology. Seeking to learn from the past and to approach it critically, they rejected the moderns' bombastic assertion of the superiority of the present.[9]

This historical turn constituted a major challenge to traditional approaches to the Bible. Whereas for most of the seventeenth century the authority of the biblical text seemed assured, even though Christians argued bitterly over its ownership and interpretation, by around 1700 this was no longer the case. Spinoza's *Tractatus theologico-politicus* had shaken the foundations of biblical interpretation, by reading the Old Testament, in the main, as a non-exceptional and extremely unreliable account of the early history of ancient Hebrews. In response to Spinoza's challenge, numerous attempts were made to integrate the Bible with human history, and to reconcile the sacred text with critical reasoning or with fresh scholarly insights.[10] These debates profoundly destabilized conventional understandings of the historical significance of Jews and Judaism.

Up to the middle decades of the seventeenth century, the traditional Christian theology of Jewish purpose broadly held sway: a remnant from the past, the Jews were nonetheless destined to play a crucial role in the millenarian unfolding of humanity's ultimate destiny. The historicization of the Bible unmoored this temporality, and the political theology with which it was associated. During the early phase of the Enlightenment, the hermeneutical status of the Bible was profoundly uncertain, and this therefore equally applied to the Jews and their history. In this context, the political resonance of Jewish purpose subsided, but a new philosophical resonance moved to the fore. Jews were now the key testing ground for competing interpretations of the relationship of deep history, as narrated in the Hebrew Bible, to philosophical reason.

The first major Christian riposte to Spinoza came from the French Catholic Oratorian priest Richard Simon (1638–1712). In his *Critical History of the Old Testament* (1678) Simon ceded considerable ground to Spinoza's arguments, acknowledging that the Bible was a corrupted and uncertain text. In doing so, he sought to deflect Spinoza's challenge onto Protestantism. Precisely because of the textual difficulties of the Bible, he argued, the Protestant emphasis on the direct interpretation of scripture was foolhardy: it was essential to rely on the authoritative and expert exegetical tradition of the Church.[11] Simon's argument also in a sense turned Protestantism against itself: his biblical criticism built upon the scholarship of French Protestants earlier in the century, particularly that of Louis Cappel (1585–1658), Professor of Hebrew at the Huguenot Academy of Saumur, who had argued that not only the vowel points but also the consonantal text of the Hebrew Bible was unreliable.[12] With Louis XIV's revocation of the Edict of Nantes in 1685, which drove approximately 150,000 Huguenots into exile in neighbouring Protestant countries, the intellectual rivalry between Protestants and Catholics became more heated. In the same year, a trenchant critique of Simon was published by Jean Le Clerc, a leading Swiss Protestant (of Huguenot ancestry) in Amsterdam, accusing him of 'rabbinism' and insisting on the clarity of the Bible on matters of importance.[13] This became a stock accusation in Protestant attacks on Catholic biblical scholarship, in response to which Simon and others cast Protestants as 'Karaites'—a sect of non-rabbinic Jews who had recently been 'discovered' by western European Christians. At times both parties playfully adopted these labels themselves, imagining their contest as an intra-Jewish one.[14] Beneath the surface of this theological drag, however, was a more serious uncertainty among Christian scholars over the intellectual status of Judaism.

The French Catholic establishment, in contrast, emphatically reasserted the traditional view of scripture. After suppressing Simon's book, the leading French bishop Jacques Bénigne Bossuet (1627–1704) published his own *Discourse on Universal History* (1681), in which he put forward a brisk chronological narrative from the creation to Charlemagne. Interleaving sacred and profane history in alternating chapters and sections, Bossuet placed great emphasis on the biblical record of the Jewish past, and its significance both in underwriting the truth of Christianity and in pointing toward an ultimate future of universal reconciliation:

> The Jews, who have been the prey of those ancient nations so celebrated in history, have survived them all, and God, by preserving them, keeps us in expectation of what he will still do for the unhappy remnant of a people once so highly favoured. However, their obstinacy contributes to the salvation of the Gentiles and affords them the advantage of finding in trusted hands the Scriptures, which have foretold Jesus Christ and his mysteries. We see among other things in these Scriptures both the blindness and the misfortunes of the Jews, who so carefully preserve them. Thus we profit by their downfall; their infidelity is one of the foundations of our faith; they teach us to fear God and are a standing example of the judgements he executes upon his ungrateful children, so that we may learn never to glory in the favours shown to our fathers.[15]

Bossuet's theology of Jewish purpose was essentially unaltered from Augustine, inflected with an element of awe in response to the endurance of the Jews, and with a timeless moral lesson on the importance of gratitude. He ascribes to Jews the familiar sins of obstinacy and blindness, which are fundamental to their historical role as bearers of historical truths that they cannot see: the entire history of true religion, he writes, is written on their foreheads.[16] Bossuet's work testifies to the resilience of this traditional view—but his view of history was sustained only by completely ignoring the rapidly mounting challenges to its credibility posed by the scholarship of the period.

Prominent among these challenges was the question of how to integrate into a bibliocentric worldview the histories of non-European civilizations. Bossuet did not directly address this himself, but expressed approval of the recent attempt to do so by his episcopal colleague Pierre-Daniel Huet (1630–1721). In his compendious *Demonstratio Evangelica* [Proof of the Gospel] (1679), Huet echoed Simon in attempting to turn Spinoza's critical method against his heretical conclusions, and in support of Catholic orthodoxy. The tightly logical structure of Huet's text imitated the geometric style of Spinoza's *Ethics*; the thrust of his argument, however, could scarcely have been more contrasting. In this pioneering but extremely fanciful work of comparative religion, Huet purported to demonstrate that the religious narratives of all cultures were corrupted versions of Hebraic history, knowledge of which had in the distant past been diffused to all corners of the world. Osiris, Zoroaster, Bacchus and the leading deities of other civilizations were all disguised representations of Moses, while all principal goddesses were representations of Moses's wife Zipporah.[17] Huet attempted to shore up the intellectual status of Christian orthodoxy by integrating it with global history and adopting the authoritative geometrical format of post-Cartesian philosophy. However, his work met with a lukewarm reception, particularly in the Protestant world. The wilfulness of his argument was glaringly apparent, and could not stand up to the accumulated insights of philological and historical scholarship.

In England in particular, a number of scholars around this time—John Marsham, Ralph Cudworth and most notably John Spencer (1630–93)—were developing a very different approach to the critical historicization of the Hebrew Bible.[18] Most significant was Spencer's monumental *De legibus Hebraeorum ritualibus* [The Ritual Laws of the Hebrews] (1685): an extremely detailed and erudite study of the laws and rituals ordained in the Old Testament, in which Spencer reversed Huet's historical prioritization of Judaism. The Mosaic law, Spencer argued, was itself shaped by Egyptian religious culture. This was by no means a wholly new idea. Various ancient writers, such as Strabo and Tacitus, had described the Jewish religion as having been constructed in pointed opposition to the rituals and rules of Egyptian worship, while Spencer's central argument—that Moses designed his laws in order to wean the Hebrews from the idolatry to which they had been exposed in Egypt—was heavily indebted to Maimonides. Spencer's extensive scholarship underscored, in diametric contrast to Huet, the external derivation of the details of the Mosaic religion, demonstrating, for example, how its sacrificial practices and other rituals of worship were direct inversions of Egyptian customs.[19]

Spencer's readers, both in the seventeenth century and since, have found it difficult to determine the implications of his arguments. He has been widely celebrated as a pioneer of the modern study of the history of religions: according to one recent historian, 'he discovered . . . the laws of religious evolution'.[20] Spencer was, though, deeply embedded in the elite scholarly culture of his own period, and his self-declared aims were far from radical. A conventional mainstream Anglican, he hoped that his careful historicization of the Old Testament would undercut what he regarded as the fanatical Judaizing of the dissenting fringe, and bind sober scholarship to sober religiosity.[21] Despite his intentions, however, Spencer's investigations were theologically extremely destabilizing, particularly with regard to the status and significance of the Jews in human history. Spencer regarded the Jews as a religiously purifying force, purging monotheistic religion of traces of Egyptian idolatry. However, following his Cambridge colleague Ralph Cudworth's *True Intellectual System of the Universe* (1678), Spencer saw the inner significance of the Mosaic religion as also having been derived from Egypt, but in a positive and direct fashion, through Moses's exposure to the esoteric tradition of Egyptian priestly philosophizing.[22] According to the Eyptologist Jan Assmann, Spencer is a key figure in the modern traditions of both 'Egyptophilia' and 'Egyptophobia'.[23] These opposing responses to ancient Egypt invite contrasting assessments of Moses's relationship to the Egypt of his upbringing. Both these views can find support in Spencer's work, which has been interpreted as presenting Moses as an inspired reformer of Egyptian traditions, and also, in negative terms, as a slavish imitator of them. More broadly, Spencer's attempt to insert the Old Testament within Egyptian history undermined the traditional understanding of the exceptionality of the Jews, throwing open many possible alternative ways of rethinking, or rejecting, their chosen status and special purpose.

It did not take long for Spencer's arguments to be used in ways very different from his own intentions. *De legibus* was of great use to the most vociferous deist critic of established religion in the years around 1700, John Toland (1670–1722). In his *Origines Judaicae* [Jewish Origins] (1709), Toland polemicized against Huet's *Demonstratio*, highlighting how the scholarship of Spencer and others undermined his argument for the historical importance of the ancient Hebrews. Drawing on classical sources—particularly Strabo—to develop a counter-history of the origins of Judaism, Toland argued that the Jews were a mongrel race, particularly given to superstition, and burdened with accretions of superfluous laws and rituals.[24] While scorning these Jewish tendencies and religious habits, Toland idealized the pure simplicity of Moses's rational wisdom, which, like Spencer, he regarded as Egyptian in origin, and which he saw as constituting the essence of true, non-mysterious primitive Christianity.[25] In his most provocative claim, which incensed his critics, Toland asserted that Moses had been 'a pantheist, or, in more recent language, a Spinozist'.[26]

Toland's arguments fused Spinoza's rationalist bible criticism with the historical scholarship of Spencer and others. His philosophical theology, while playing an important role in the anticlerical agitation of the period, was nonetheless somewhat confused, particularly with respect to the temporality of Jewish exceptionalism. Not just once, Toland held, but at two points in history the Jews had been the bearers of universal truths—firstly with Moses's transmission of the esoteric mysteries of Egyptian priestly wisdom, and secondly at the time of the emergence of Christianity from, he argued, the Jewish Nazarene sect.[27] In both cases, the special Jewish possession of these truths was complicatedly shared with others in a quasi-universalist framework, which was presented by him as starkly in contrast to normative Judaism. And yet Toland remained fascinated with the history of the Jews, both past and future. In a brief essay also from 1709, he celebrated Moses as the greatest lawmaker in history, and suggested that Christians should 'assist them in regaining their country'. Should the Jews be resettled in Palestine, he wrote, 'they will then, by reason of their excellent constitution, be much more populous, rich and powerful than any nation now in the world'.[28] This excited espousal of proto-Zionism—the first in such explicitly political terms in modern history—sits awkwardly alongside the historicizing impulse that lay behind his scholarly investigations, and his critical insistence on the superfluity and superstition of almost all aspects of Jewish religious life. Despite his aspiration to approach the history of the Jews in a spirit of detached reason, the deep structures of meaning that had long been associated with the Jewish people repeatedly surfaced in his thought. His core commitment to challenging the grip of theology and clerics on thought and culture notwithstanding, Toland regarded both the past and the future as fundamentally shaped by the action of Jews in human history. Eternally particular, and yet also the bearers of universalism, the Jews would, Toland suggested, finally resolve this contradiction and fulfil their ultimate purpose with the re-establishment of their Mosaic polity.[29]

Far from bringing clarity to the interpretation of the Bible, the use of rational argument in the period around 1700 thus gave rise to a multiplicity of different approaches to scripture. Reason was enlisted by all sides, including by
traditionalist clerics seeking to refute the arguments of radicals such as Spinoza
or Toland.[30] In this environment, the basis on which Christians regarded the
Old Testament as meaningful became unprecedentedly uncertain. Whereas for
much of the seventeenth century the political resonance of the Hebrew Bible
had been beyond question, by the end of the century the mutually incompatible attempts by scholars of various camps to renew its intellectual status seemed
only to cause the foundations of its coherence and meaningfulness to subside
still further.[31] While traditional notions of Jewish purpose often rose to the surface even in the minds of otherwise unconventional and anti-establishment
thinkers such as Toland, a general confusion reigned over the place of Jews and
their texts in the wider scheme of human knowledge and history. This confusion reflected, in distilled form, wider uncertainties over the nature and scope
of reason itself. Jews, as we have seen, had since the time of Paul been cast as
bad readers, wedded to the obsolete 'letter' of their law and unable to recognize its deeper spiritual meaning. Spinoza had reworked this binary opposition
in relation to human reason, contrasting infantile Jewish legalism with the maturity of independent thought. In the Enlightenment era, as reason came
under closer scrutiny, this juxtaposition emerged as a new form of Jewish purpose in European intellectual life. By standing as the defining antithesis of
rational existence, Jews played an enabling role in various attempts to articulate more clearly the shape of reason itself.

By far the most profound exploration of reason in this period was that of
Pierre Bayle (1647–1706), a Huguenot refugee from the Pyrenees who settled
in Rotterdam a few years before the revocation of the Edict of Nantes. Founder
and editor of the first of the influential francophone learned journals published
in the Dutch Republic, Bayle was an extremely wide-ranging and incisive scholar
and critic. Above all, though, he was a philosopher, centrally preoccupied with
the relationship between reason and faith. More than any other thinker of the
period, Bayle emphasized the futility of attempts to underpin religious belief
through recourse to reason. He was also vehemently opposed to dogmatism
of any kind, which in his view could emerge from both theological and rational
absolutism. In contrast with Spinoza's confident assertion of the certainties of
philosophy, in bitter argument with many of the leading figures of his own Dutch
Huguenot refugee community, and to the bafflement of many, Bayle persistently
pitted reason and faith against each other. His core belief was that intellectual

inquiry should aim always to defer final resolution, and to remain open to the challenges and contrasting perspectives of others.

In the copious notes of his *Historical and Critical Dictionary* (1697), by far his most famous work, Bayle relentlessly exposed the limits of both reason and Christian faith. This unclassifiable project is the opposite of what it superficially appears to be: it is an anti-dictionary, based on the cataloguing of the errors in other reference works, but more profoundly putting forward the philosophical case for the impossibility of any fully reliable source or repository of intellectual authority. Even scepticism, insofar as its rejection of certainty might itself amount to an inverted dogmatism, is undermined by Bayle's relentless arguments. Truly consistent sceptics, he points out, should apply their arguments reflexively, and therefore 'doubt if it is necessary to doubt'.[32] The most controversial aspect of Bayle's approach, however, was his equal refusal to find any final certainties in religion. He playfully undermined theological orthodoxies in a wide range of ways, but one of his favourite approaches was to highlight the immorality endorsed in the Old Testament. By exposing the moral failings of God's chosen people, and also the absurdity of later attempts, both by rabbis and by Christian theologians, to find explanations and excuses for their behaviour, Bayle tugged apart the claim that reason and faith were straightforwardly reconcilable.

Bayle most potently deployed this argumentative strategy is his lengthy article on King David, which so scandalized his Huguenot peers that he was forced to cut its most provocative passages from the second edition of the work.[33] Bayle here explored with wit and relish the dissonance between David's elevated status and closeness to God and his licentious, merciless and deceitful behaviour. He condemned with particular vigour David's conduct in warfare, which, he wryly noted, made the cruelty of other fearsome warrior nations, such as the Turks or the Tartars, seem mild in comparison.[34] The slaughter of the Amalekites at Siceleg, where David's entourage left no man or woman alive, must be judged, he declared, as 'extremely wicked'.[35] The eternal laws of morality, Bayle insisted, must apply equally in all cases, with no exemption for those acting under divine inspiration. If these standards are not applied to David's actions, then their general applicability is undermined: 'there can be no middle ground: either these actions are unworthy, or actions like these are not wicked'.[36] In his notes to this article Bayle repeatedly returned to David's intimate relationship with God, and to the impossibility of reconciling this with his immoral actions. King David's life thus highlighted the baffling contrast between the moral clarity of rational ethics and the inscrutable manifestations of the authority of God. David's glaring amorality ultimately stood for Bayle as an eloquent reminder of the unfathomability of the Bible, and of the non-rational mystery of faith.

Bayle's scholarly explorations were also highly political and polemical. He was bitterly opposed to the arguments of the leading Huguenot pastor in Rotterdam, Pierre Jurieu, who sought to rally Protestants to overthrow Louis XIV's rule in France. Bayle believed that this approach was both futile and destructive, and devoted great energy to arguing against violence (as in the 'David' article) and in support of toleration.[37] His late writings, however, were primarily directed against Jean Le Clerc and his allies, known as the 'rationaux', who had developed their arguments against Richard Simon into a school of Protestant biblical criticism based on the harmony of reason and faith. Their insistence on this harmony was, Bayle believed, just as dangerously dogmatic as Jurieu's explicitly intolerant zealotry. In a number of essays written in the early years of the eighteenth century, Bayle advanced a 'fideist' position, insisting that many theological puzzles—not only the amorality of the divine voice in the Old Testament, but also the profound problem of the existence of evil—could not be resolved through recourse to reason. These matters, Bayle believed, therefore necessarily remained as mysteries of faith. Le Clerc and his supporters were incensed by these arguments because they believed that Bayle was deliberately undermining religion. For Bayle, though, their condemnation of him demonstrated the intolerance of the 'rationalist' camp, who could not accept any view except their own.[38]

The Jews, for Bayle, occupied a unique position, as they alone had been directly governed by divine legislation. In ancient Judaism, the voice of individual moral conscience, which was the basis on which Bayle believed that David's actions and other instances of barbaric behaviour should be condemned, had no place: God's rule and laws covered all aspects of life, leaving no room for private judgment. Within the framework of Judaism, which Bayle believed was based on the absolute acceptance of divinely revealed scripture, David's actions could not be criticized, because the divine word could not be questioned. (In another comment, Bayle chided Josephus for recounting the past differently from Moses: this stood in contradiction, he suggested, to Josephus's profession of Judaism.[39]) For Christians, natural reason, and the moral absolutes that it suggested, strained against the revealed truths of the Old Testament—but there was no escape from either of these two incommensurable mental spheres, as both were indispensible. For Jews, though, in Bayle's eyes, revelation was all. The Jews alone, then, stood outside the insoluble tension between reason and faith, which was for Bayle the fundamental paradox underlying human existence and the central theme of his philosophical investigations. He represented Judaism as the archetype of a religion of pure faith, which he equated with blind and unthinking obedience to divine commandments, regardless of their utility or morality.

Judaism thus stood as a sharp negative image against which Bayle's own positive understanding of religious and intellectual life—as a never-ending tussle between faith and reason—could be contrasted and more clearly defined. For Bayle, as for orthodox Christians from Augustine to Bossuet, the Jews were also a 'witness people', highlighting for others what they themselves were unable to see. For him, though, Jews bore witness not simply to the truth of the gospels, but to the more fundamental philosophical and existential truth of the incommensurability of reason and faith. This, Bayle sought to demonstrate, was the inescapable consequence of moving beyond the Jewish mode of living purely according to religious laws and commandments, and was the fundamental condition of Christian—or, in alternative terms, modern—thought.[40]

Bayle has perplexed and divided his readers, both in the eighteenth century and since. He has been portrayed both as a devout Calvinist and as an atheist, and as the holder of a wide range of intermediate positions.[41] His view of Jews and Judaism has also been diversely interpreted.[42] His positioning of Judaism as external and impervious to his conception of reason would seem to amount to a semi-secular rearticulation of the patristic view of Jews as lacking the mature insight and spirituality of Christianity. To some degree, this is the case—but Bayle's thought is more subtle. His interest in Jews was not limited to the Bible, and when considering later periods, he showed some awareness that Jews could not live entirely according to scripture. His criticism of Josephus for disagreeing with Moses was teasing in tone, and a starting-point for the highlighting of a classic Baylean paradox: he concludes with the observation that Josephus could not have done otherwise, because embellishment, imagination and invention are part of practice of all historians.[43] Bayle conceived of intellectual inquiry as an unboundedly open activity, not only attuned to puzzles and paradoxes but positively revelling in them. If Judaism, as defined by the Old Testament, served for him the purpose of embodying the antithesis of this outlook, then post-biblical Jews, necessarily leading lives not entirely defined by scripture, implicitly inhabited with particular intensity the intellectual paradoxes that so fascinated him. Bayle was an exceptional case: few if any other thinkers of his period were so philosophically agile and open-minded. He demonstrates, however, how Jews in the Enlightenment period could perform a complicatedly double-edged role as a foil for rational philosophy, simultaneously standing both as reason's antithesis and as its most intriguing and challenging testing ground.

Bayle bewildered many eighteenth-century thinkers because his open, anti-systematic philosophical approach was at odds with the polemical style of argument which defenders of reason increasingly adopted, particularly in France where the battle lines between the *philosophes* and the throne-and-altar estab-lishment were stark. The most pugnacious and prolific advocate for the values of the Enlightenment was Voltaire (1694–1778), who, since his reburial in the Panthéon as the adopted intellectual father of the French Revolution, has been widely regarded as the personification of the embattled and righteous spirit of reason.[44] One prominent feature of Voltaire's writings, however, is difficult to reconcile with this adulatory image: his frequent and often vehement attacks on Jews and Judaism. Repeatedly, throughout his career, Voltaire ridiculed the absurdity of the Old Testament and the primitivism of the Jews, whom he dis-misses in one representative passage as 'this vile people, superstitious, igno-rant, and both scientifically and commercially stunted'.[45] For Voltaire, the Jews were the defining opposite of his own positive values: their ignorance, barba-rism and slavish legalism stood in contrast to his commitment to knowledge, decency and rational inquiry. Jews served a similar structural purpose for Bayle, as we have seen—but whereas for Bayle this was not a wholly negative role, because by standing outside reason Jews valuably highlighted its limits, for Vol-taire this opposition carried no evaluative complexity. Reason, he had no doubt, was the answer to everything. Roland Barthes very aptly characterized Voltaire as 'the last happy writer', confidently condemning with outraged as-tonishment all instances of irrational hatred and cruelty. We have since wit-nessed the Holocaust, Barthes noted, but 'we have not had a single pamphlet against that'.[46]

Voltaire's own sweeping condemnations of Jews, however, seem to be driven by an animus beyond his rational control. The case of the Jews troubled him, and he could not let go of it. He thought of himself as an advocate of universal religious tolerance, and ventriloquistically put forward one of his most power-ful attacks on Christian persecution through the voice of the second-century Rabbi Akiva.[47] However, he expressed his worldview primarily through the negative critique of what he was against, and this adversarial position was filled above all by Judaism. In his *Philosophical Dictionary* (1764)—one of his most accessible and popular works, to some extent imitating the eclecticism of Bay-le's dictionary—almost a third of the entries consist of sustained attacks on the Pentateuch.[48] Developing further the arguments of Toland and others who had used late seventeenth-century biblical criticism against itself, Voltaire sought to show that the textually uncertain and historically derivative nature of the Hebrew Bible discredited it as a text worthy of any special respect. The critical scholars of Spencer's generation had remained fascinated by the intellectual challenge posed by this text, and did not seek to displace its cultural authority; both Toland and Bayle, in different ways, had imbued the Old Testament with their own renewed understanding of the Jews' political or philosophical purpose. Voltaire, in contrast, sought to topple the Jewish Bible entirely, while being heavily dependent on it as the negative polar opposite against which he defined his own positive philosophy. This paradox lay at the heart of his response to Judaism and Jews, and fuelled its angry obsessiveness.

Among other things, Voltaire was a historian, seeking to develop a cosmopolitan account of the past that could plausibly account for the recorded memory and cultural development of all civilizations.[49] In practice, however, given the limited scholarly resources at his disposal, and also his own polemical disposition, this exercise largely amounted to an insistent inversion of the traditional Christian positioning of the Jewish past at the heart of human history. For Voltaire, again extending the arguments of Spencer and Toland, Jews were inveterate imitators, rather than contributors. In his monumental *Essay on Customs* (1765), he sought to demonstrate the richness of the interactions and mutual influences between cultures: the Jews, however, stood as an exception, because they alone merely copied from their neighbours, while teaching them nothing.[50] Voltaire was also an exuberantly patriotic historian of France: his celebration of 'the French genius', which he connected both to the transient influences of government and culture and to the timeless imprint of the local climate and soil, anticipates the nationalist rhetoric of the nineteenth century.[51] The Jews also disturbed this argument. As a dispersed people, with no shared climate or soil, but nonetheless with a much more deeply established collective identity than the French (or any other European people), the Jews represented a very different form of nationhood from Voltaire's model, powerfully sustained by the biblical text that he sought to dismiss. Their enduring existence and strength of identity challenged the foundational assumptions of his historiography. Unable to make sense of the Jews within his historical framework, Voltaire instead repeatedly asserted their exclusion from it, as a uniquely primitive people impervious to the normal human processes of rational progress.[52]

This insistence left Voltaire unable to respond coherently to the Jews of his own era. If Judaism was inherently stranded in the primitive past, what role could Jews play in the Enlightenment present? This question was pointedly brought to the fore in his epistolary exchange with Isaac de Pinto, an Amsterdam Sephardic financier and intellectual, and a great admirer of Voltaire's work. In 1762, Pinto wrote to Voltaire, fulsomely praising the 'immortal writings' of his hero, but objecting to his sweeping attacks on the coarse savagery of Jews, which he insisted did not at all apply to the refined and civilized Sephardim. (Pinto did not express any objection to Voltaire's characterizations with regard to Ashkenazic Jews.) Voltaire's response was slickly ambiguous. Opening with a promise to correct his errors—though in fact he repeatedly made similar statements in many later works—he exhorted Pinto to 'be a philosopher' and also to remain a Jew. However, he also issued him with a challenge that suggested he viewed this dual identity as impossible:

> I shall tell you as frankly that there are many who cannot endure your laws, your books, or your superstitions. They say that your nation has done, in every age, much hurt to itself and to the human race. If you are a philosopher, as you seem to be, you will think as those gentlemen do, but you will not say it.[53]

This double-edged response to Pinto highlights the fracture in Voltaire's thought that was exposed by the Jewish case. Jewish particularism stood for him as the defining negative of his own enlightened universalism. Jews, therefore, could not be coherently incorporated within his philosophical embrace—but neither could they be emphatically excluded, as this would undermine Voltaire's vision of the all-encompassing reach of Enlightenment reason. They were therefore a continual focus of antagonism for him, embodying the failure of his conception of reason to provide a fully convincing alternative account of the origins and nature of peoplehood.[54]

Alongside his heroization as the apostle of Enlightenment, Voltaire has also been ascribed a prominent role in the history of antisemitism. According to this narrative, he was the key 'link' between medieval and modern Jew-hatred, remoulding the long-standing religious animus against Jews as killers of Christ into a new, secular rejection of them as enemies of reason.[55] It is certainly the case that the external position ascribed to Jews in both Christian and Enlightenment thought is structurally the same: in both cases, Jews are marked as the quintessential particular, against which the universalism of Christian love or Enlightenment reason was contrasted and defined. However, Enlightenment thinkers also inherited the Christian anticipation of a transition to a more fully universal future, when Jews would play a crucial role in bringing confessional and all other human divisions to an end. In the period around 1700, there were various attempts to recast in more rational terms this valorizing aspect of the Christian understanding of Jewish purpose, distancing the idea from the millenarian enthusiasm of the mid-seventeenth century that in this more sober era was viewed askance by most. In opposition to the confident reassertion of the Christian view of the primacy of Jewish history by prominent Catholics such as Bossuet and Huet, a range of thinkers, from Hebraist scholars such as John Spencer to deists such as John Toland, tried to integrate Jewish and Gentile history without either overtly privileging the Jewish past or eviscerating it of positive meaning. These two aspirations strained against each other, and could not be fully reconciled.

Both Bayle and Voltaire recognized the impossibility of harmonizing traditional approaches to the Bible with secular history and critical rationality. They responded to this in contrasting ways, which nonetheless led them to structurally similar reformulations of the idea of Jewish purpose. For Bayle, Judaism represented the irreducible kernel of faith that could not be explained or mastered by reason. For Voltaire, Judaism also stood outside and in opposition to reason—but, unlike Bayle, he did not accord any validity or respect to this position. Both these foundational Enlightenment thinkers, however, most sharply defined their conception of reason in contrast to Judaism, which they regarded and portrayed as reason's obverse. Bayle believed both reason and its obverse, in the form of religious faith, to be equally indispensable, while also equally inadequate, as a guide for human life and thought—though his arguments on this point are so intricate that there is still no scholarly consensus that this was his view. Voltaire's belief in the supremacy and sufficiency of reason is, in contrast, unmistakably clear. The temperamental difference in their attitudes to Judaism is also evident: Bayle was fascinated by Judaic topics, whereas Voltaire was aggravated by them. They are in accord, though, in ascribing to Judaism the status of the definitional opposite to Enlightenment rationality. Rejecting the various conceptually fuzzy attempts to integrate the Jewish Bible and Jewish history into the critical scholarship of the period, their sharp separation of Judaism and reason did not overcome the idea of Jewish purpose, but rather added a new twist to it. In their distinct but complimentary contributions to bringing the contours of Enlightenment thought into clear relief, both Bayle and Voltaire cast Judaism as the crucial shadow that enabled those contours to become visible.

Much Enlightenment thought, however, was focused not on philosophical abstraction or historical scholarship, but on practical matters of social and economic improvement.[56] This practical aspect of the Enlightenment was no less concerned with Jews, as from this perspective their inclusion was not merely a theoretical issue, but also a matter of social vision and political policy. As the eighteenth century progressed, Jewish elites became more established in the major cities of western Europe, and Jewish communities as a whole were increasingly regarded as an economic resource of unfulfilled potential. These changes contributed to a rising interest in the reform of the legal and political status of Jews. Discussions of these matters were imbued with the resonance of the idea of Jewish purpose, which in various guises placed the Jews at the centre of hopes for a different future. By the time of Voltaire's death in 1778, the transformation of attitudes and policies toward European Jewry had come to be regarded by several intellectuals as the most inspiring test of the reach of the Enlightenment, and the means by which this philosophical movement could most powerfully signal the transformation of society as a whole.

Toleration and Cosmopolitanism: Lessing, Mendelssohn and the Jew as Enlightenment Ideal

The young Voltaire, exiled in England in the late 1720s, believed that he was seeing a vision of the future. In his *Letters Concerning the English Nation* (1733), he praised the rationalism, productivity and particularly the religious diversity of England, which he saw as enabling a pragmatic disinterest in the ceremonies and beliefs of others: 'If one religion only were allowed in England, the government would very possibly become arbitrary; if there were but two, the people would cut one another's throats; but as there are such a multitude, they all live happy and in peace.'[57] This mutually beneficial cosmopolitanism was, in his eyes, best exemplified by the London Stock Exchange, where Christians, Jews and Muslims transacted business with each other 'as though they all professed the same religion, and give the name of Infidel to none but bankrupts'.[58] Even while celebrating this indifference to private religious particularities, Voltaire simultaneously gave voice to his own hostility to Judaism, which he pointedly presented as the height of absurdity. Summarizing the after-hours dispersal of the traders, he drew an implied diametric contrast between Jewish religious worship and inclusive convivial drinking, noting that 'some withdraw to synagogue, others to take a glass'. His descriptions of the various religious ceremonies the traders attend present the eccentricities of Baptists and Quakers as much more readily comprehensible than the Jewish circumcision ritual, which he summarizes with particular derision.[59] Voltaire's repeated ridiculing of Judaism here undercuts his own attempt to extol the equanimity of English cosmopolitan-ism. However, in a sense it also underscores it: the capaciousness of English tolerance is all the more admirable because, he suggests, it can even encompass Judaism. The Jewish case serves to stake out the extent of Voltaire's cosmopoli-tan ideal, even while simultaneously exposing its exclusionary underside.

Toleration was a central theme of the early Enlightenment. There was, though, considerable confusion over the optimum extent and essential mean-ing of this ideal—and this muddle was highlighted by the Jewish case. In the toleration debates of the late seventeenth century, Jews wereconsidered not so much as serious candidates for toleration, as rather a conceptually challenging and illuminating limit case. Both John Locke (1632–1704) and Pierre Bayle spe-cifically affirmed that Jews should have freedom of worship, but neither gave the matter close attention.[60] The Jewish example, however, highlighted ambi-guities and difficulties in the thinking of both men. Locke swiftly rowed back to safer theological territory when a critic, Jonas Proast, objected to his exten-sion of toleration to Jews in his *Letter Concerning Toleration* (1689): in response to Proast's allegation that this would undermine 'true religion', Locke argued that Jews should be tolerated precisely in order to establish a cordial environ-ment in which to further their conversion to Christianity.[61] The first explicit call for the extension of civic rights to Jews—John Toland's *Reasons for Naturalizing the Jews in Great Britain and Ireland* (1714)—was also more of an experimental than an earnest argument. Toland had been a strong supporter of the recent Naturalization Act passed by the Whig administration in 1709, which had fa-cilitated the migration to England of over ten thousand Protestant refugees from Germany (the 'Poor Palatines'). His proposal of 1714 extended these principles, which had become a key focus of contention between Whigs and Tories, to their limit of conceivability, by arguing that Jews should also be allowed to become property-owning subjects not only in Ireland (as James Harrington had argued six decades earlier), but across Britain. Toland was aware, however, that this policy stood no chance of adoption. His more profound aim was philosophi-cal: to advance a case for religious toleration which, as it was for Voltaire, was based on a public realm distinct from and indifferent to the private religious ritu-als of its diverse participants.[62]

Unlike Voltaire, however, Toland's attitude to Jews as prospective civic par-ticipants was overwhelmingly positive. As we have seen, his view of Judaism was complicated: while dismissive of the rituals of rabbinic Judaism he ideal-ized Moses as the supreme philosophical lawgiver. In his 1714 essay, he reart-iculated this distinction, finding support for it from his primary source, an essay

published in 1638 by the Italian rabbi Simone Luzzatto in opposition to a threatened expulsion of the Jews from Venice. Luzzatto, Toland claimed, had explained that the rituals of Judaism were a supplement for Jews alone, who with
respect to the non-Jewish world were simply 'enjoin'd to magnify . . . divine
goodness, wisdom, and power, with those duties of men, and other attributes
of God, which constitute natural religion'.[63] This was a broadly accurate summary of Luzzatto's argument, couched in Toland's own deist terminology: the
rabbi had placed considerable emphasis on the seven Noachide laws (discussed
in the previous chapter) as the universalistic principles at the core of Judaism.
Luzzatto's central theme, however, was the economic utility of the Jews for the
city of Venice. Toland here also echoed his Jewish source, praising the excellence of Jews as brokers of trade, and adding that as naturalized landowners they
would deepen and broaden their economic contribution.[64] Both Voltaire and
Toland, as well as many others in the early eighteenth century, saw the inclusion of Jews and the harnessing of their commercial prowess as a key aspect of
social and political progress. Whereas Voltaire's embrace of Jewish inclusion was
soaked in unease, for Toland, despite his critique of rabbinic Judaism and the
convolutions of his interpretation of Jewish history, this aspiration was a rallying call for his vision of the future. His eager anticipation both of Jewish naturalization in Britain and of Jewish restoration in Palestine has been aptly described as a form of secularized messianism, transposing the radical
millenarianism of the mid-seventeenth century into an Enlightenment key.[65]
Renewing the association between the transformation of the Jews and the advance of human history, Toland enshrined the inclusion of Jews as symbolically central to the agenda of Enlightenment.

In both France and Britain the social and legal status of Jews remained largely
a notional issue until the late eighteenth century. The fate of the British 'Jew Bill'
of 1753, which was swiftly repealed following a public outcry, underscored this,
as the panic it engendered, with the spectre raised of Jews taking control of parliament and forcibly circumcising the indigenous male population, bore almost no relation to the content of the legislation, which enabled an expensive
route to naturalization for a tiny number of wealthy foreign-born Jews. This
outburst was a popular expression of British Protestant identity, which was rhetorically shaped above all in contrast with French Catholicism. Jews, however,
stood in 1753 as a particularly resonant proxy for radical otherness.[66]

In Berlin, however, Jews by this time no longer figured primarily as an abstraction. Processes of change both in Prussian politics and in the Jewish world
combined to establish the status of Jews as, for the first time, a matter of serious

public consideration. Within months of his succession to the Prussian throne in 1740, Frederick II moved to annex Silesia, and the incorporation of this territory into Prussia in 1742 brought large numbers of Jews under his rule. The king's energetic plans to make his new territories more productive, and also to make his mark as a 'philosopher king', placed a review of policies toward Jews high on his political agenda. Berlin was also emerging in the 1740s as the main centre of the early *Haskalah*—'Jewish Enlightenment'—movement. Pioneering *maskilim* (exponents of *Haskalah*) in the city were engaging with current scientific and philosophical issues in a Jewish context, absorbing the core ideas of the mainstream Enlightenment and seeking to disseminate them as a force for moral uplift within the Jewish community.[67] In this environment of accelerating change, the local Jewish community presented an enticing opportunity for the social and political application of the ideals of the Enlightenment. Frederick's detailed revision of the Prussian Jewry law in 1750, although still very restrictive in its provisions, reflected this mood of rationalization and reform.[68]

It was in this context that the philosopher and dramatist Gotthold Ephraim Lessing (1729–81) embarked on his writing career in the Prussian capital. Soon after his arrival in the city in the late 1740s, Lessing became acquainted with Aaron Solomon Gumpertz, who was the first Berlin Jew to circulate in non-Jewish intellectual circles. It was through Gumpertz, in 1754, that Lessing met and established an intimate friendship with Moses Mendelssohn, the first Jew to make a major impact in the world of the German Enlightenment.[69] Whereas in Paris, Amsterdam and London those few Jews who found their way into non-Jewish intellectual life were highly assimilated, in Gumpertz and Mendelssohn Lessing encountered Jews who were religiously observant and actively engaged with the intellectual uplift of their own cultural tradition. It is not surprising, given the Prussian political conjuncture at the time, that Lessing was fascinated by them.[70] These friendships provided the model for him to depict Jews in highly positive terms in his writings, and to place their inclusion at the heart of his dramatization of the ideals of the Enlightenment.

Lessing's early play *The Jews* (1749) enthusiastically captured the winds of change in Berlin, critiquing prevalent prejudices toward Jews in order to advance a universalist argument for religious toleration. This drama revolves around a travelling baron's robbery, seemingly by highwaymen who are at first assumed to be Jews. The baron's Christian servants are later unmasked as his true assailants, and their crime is foiled by an anonymous and virtuous fellow traveller, who in the play's denouement is revealed to be himself a Jew. Lessing presents and celebrates the traveller as an ethical universalist, unmarked by any ethnic particularity, and moved to rescue the baron by his unrestricted love of humanity (*Menschenliebe*).[71] The figure of the Jew here stands, once again, as an ethical limit case. By presenting an idealized image of a member of the group most commonly linked with the opposing negative traits of inward-looking separatism and money-grubbing materialism, Lessing succinctly suggested that we are all capable of rising to the highest ethical standards of selfless love for our fellow-humans.

Lessing's Jewish traveller also carried more specific symbolic significance, as a figure whose humanistic universalism appeared as a perfect transcendence and full inversion of the particularism with which Judaism was traditionally associated. Soon after the play's publication in 1754, Lessing brought this implication to the fore, in response to a critical review by a prominent Hebraist at the University of Göttingen, Johann David Michaelis. Refuting Michaelis's argument that the Jewish traveller of Lessing's imagination could never exist in reality, Lessing invoked his friendship with Mendelssohn. Without naming him, Lessing praised his Jewish friend in the highest terms, declaring that his ethical integrity and philosophical acumen 'leads me to see him as the anticipation of a second Spinoza, with whom he is identical apart from the absence of his errors'.[72] This association of his fictional heroic traveller with both Mendelssohn and Spinoza places *The Jews* clearly in the tradition of the idealization of the post-Jewish Jew. For Lessing, as for many of Spinoza's admirers in the mid-seventeenth century and since, the pathway to the eagerly anticipated universalism of the future was most significantly and powerfully signposted by the Christ-like embodiment of universalist ethics and philosophy by Jewish figures of exceptional intellectual nobility.

Lessing's much more famous play *Nathan the Wise* (1779) focused once again on an ethically idealized and radically counter-stereotypical virtuous Jew. Like the hero of *The Jews*, the eponymous Nathan is presented in pointed contrast to the conventional Christian image of the Jewish religious scholar. We learn from his adopted daughter, Recha, that he 'has no love for cold book learning, which merely stamps dead letters into the brain'.[73] Lessing also elaborately inverts the tribal particularism associated with Judaism: a familial web emerges over the course of the play, connecting all its characters except for Nathan. Set in Jerusalem at the time of the Second Crusade, the drama opens just after Recha has been rescued from a fire by a Knight Templar, who in turn owes his own life to the mercy of his captor, the Sultan Saladin. When Recha thanks the Templar for his gallantry, he falls in love with her, but assumes that Nathan will never allow him to marry her, as he is not a Jew. In the play's final scene, however, Nathan reveals that he had been a friend of the Templar's father, who was also Recha's biological father and was neither a Jew nor, as the Templar had believed, a German, but in fact the lost brother of Saladin.[74] The love between the Templar and Recha—between a Christian man and a Jewess in cultural though not in racial terms—is thus transformed into a sibling bond, while the friendship between the Templar and the Sultan—a Christian and a Muslim—is reinforced by the discovery that they are nephew and uncle. Only Nathan stands outside this familial resolution. His Jewishness is presented as a radical inversion of the textual legalism and the clannish insularity with which Judaism was generally associated. An exemplary friend to everybody in the play, Nathan appears as a true universalist, exceptionally able to transcend the boundaries between religious communities and the squabbles and partisanships of ordinary human relationships.[75]

Nathan's uniqueness closely resembles that of Spinoza, who, as we have seen, was widely cast as implicitly the messiah of the Enlightenment: a Jew who, in rejecting and transcending his Jewishness, had become the perfect embodiment of universalism, serenely detached from the limiting emotions and attachments of normal human existence. As an argument for religious pluralism, then, *Nathan the Wise* is limited, as the play does not represent Jewish difference, or indeed any meaningful substance of religious difference, in a recognizable form.[76] In the famous 'ring parable' at the heart of the play, Nathan obliquely voices Lessing's view that all religions offer similarly useful, though imperfect, ethical guidance. More profoundly, however, this parable puts forward the Spinozist suggestion that universal reason offers the only true basis for human understanding. By conveying this message through Nathan, Lessing powerfully connected his own philosophy with the long-standing messianic tradition of ascribing to Jews unique agency in the emergence of a utopian future. This aspect of the play has seldom been explicitly recognized, even though it has been widely, if often subliminally, diffused over the past two centuries, almost throughout which *Nathan the Wise* has retained prime status, among both Jews and non-Jews, in the canon of morally didactic German letters.[77]

In his final publication, *The Education of the Human Race* (1780), Lessing contemplated the historical purpose of the Jews in a different register. He opens this essay by posing the question of why God, in his original revelation, chose the Jews for special education, despite the fact that this people was so uncouth and 'still so completely immersed in its childhood'. His answer is that God's intention was to use individual Jews to educate the rest of humanity: 'In this

people he was educating the future educators of the human race.'[78] Making use
of the theological principle of divine 'accommodation', as had Spinoza, Lessing
argued that the Mosaic revelation had been an appropriate moral 'primer' for
the intellectually infantile ancient Hebrews. Once subjected to the strained and
fantastical interpretations of rabbis, however, its influence on the Jews became
profoundly destructive, producing in them 'a petty, warped and hairsplitting
understanding', and making them 'secretive, superstitious, and full of contempt
for everything comprehensible and straightforward'.[79] Lessing's disdain for traditional Judaism, in absolute conformity with the conventional view in intellectual circles of his day, is here very clear. The historical role that he ascribes
to the Jews in the education of humanity, however, is profound, encompassing
but extending beyond the figure of Jesus.

Lessing does not explicitly ascribe any future role to Jews in the *The Education*, and, in a manner loosely reminiscent of Bayle, appears at times baffled by
the inscrutability of the divine plan for human progress. He leaves his intellectual explorations in this text unresolved and open.[80] However, he states that
the New Testament is a 'better primer', suited for the 'boyhood of the human
race' just as the Old Testament had been appropriate for its infancy. He also
looks forward to a 'new eternal gospel', which, he suggests, the followers of the
twelfth-century mystic Joachim of Fiore were the first to anticipate.[81] Joachim
was the first medieval Christian to place a strong emphasis on the peaceful and
harmonious conversion of the Jews, and on their restoration to divine favour
in the culminating phase of human history.[82] Lessing renewed this Joachimite
tradition in his own Enlightenment idiom. Alongside his denigration of rabbinic Judaism, he influentially projected, above all through the culturally enduring figure of Nathan, the positive association of exceptional, post-Jewish Jews
with universalist cosmopolitanism, which he presented as the loftiest expression of philosophical wisdom and benevolence.

This semi-secular reconfiguration of the idea of Jewish purpose, casting Jews
as the pre-eminent moral teachers of humanity, became much more prominent
in the nineteenth century, when, as we shall see, it was proudly asserted by many
Jewish intellectuals and community leaders. Lessing's simultaneous denigration of normative Judaism and idealization of the transformative potential of
Jews was shared with many other thinkers of his own time. His enshrining of
this split attitude within his celebrated tolerationist drama, however, has left a
mixed and often confused legacy. In the wake of *Nathan the Wise*, Jews were
widely positioned as both the primary recipients and the ideal teachers of toleration and cosmopolitanism. This freighted them with special significance in

two contrary senses within the very discourse that seemed to offer a path toward their normalization in European society.

Lessing's intense signification of Jews and Judaism posed particular challenges for his close Jewish friend Moses Mendelssohn. The fictional Nathan was immediately and universally associated with the living Mendelssohn, and the lofty rhetoric of friendship in the play echoed the intense expressions of intimacy that punctuate the correspondence between the two men, which is the primary testament to their much vaunted relationship.[83] Theirs was not, however, either an equal or a purely personal friendship. Lessing's association with Mendelssohn was of great public significance for the dramatist: it enabled him visibly to enact in his personal life the values of tolerance and inclusion that he set on the stage. For Mendelssohn, Lessing was an indispensable intellectual sponsor, without whom, particularly at the start of his career, he would have found it much more difficult to establish himself and gain respect in the world of the Berlin Enlightenment. The public perception of their friendship was shaped by Lessing, and by his idealized presentation of Mendelssohn as a 'second Spinoza' or a living Nathan. Unlike both these figures, though, Mendelssohn was a religiously observant Jew, closely involved in the life of his community. His own aspiration was to gain recognition as an incidentally Jewish philosopher, in the context of which his religious affiliation would be seen as insignificant. Despite his hopes, however, the goal proved to be unobtainable. This was due not only to the irresistible cultural significance of Mendelssohn's Jewishness for Lessing and many others, but also to the difficulties Mendelssohn encountered when he attempted to harmonize his view of Judaism with his Enlightenment philosophy.

In his first published work, his *Philosophical Dialogues* [*Philosophische Gespräche*] (1755), Mendelssohn indirectly responded to Lessing's characterization of him as 'second Spinoza', by offering his own interpretation of his supposed intellectual antecedent. While agreeing with Lessing that Spinoza's thought was brilliant but fundamentally flawed, Mendelssohn offered an independent view on the nature of those errors, and repositioned Spinoza from the radical margins to the central developmental trajectory of European philosophy.[84] Spinoza's fundamental mistake, Mendelssohn argued, was not that he had reduced God to the level of matter, and thus strayed into atheism, but rather the opposite: his equation of all nature with God was, if anything, excessively divine.[85] This was, though, a tragic error, and one that stemmed from Spinoza's over-ambitious attempt to leap from the Cartesian outlook of his time to the Leibnizian philosophy of the early eighteenth century, to which, in the form developed by Leibniz's follower Christian Wolff, Mendelssohn himself subscribed. For this advance to take place, 'someone had to plunge into the huge abyss' that lay between Descartes and Leibniz, and 'it was Spinoza who met this unhappy fate'. Spinoza's error, then, should not be scorned, but instead respected as a 'sacrifice for human understanding', and also as a notable reminder that 'a non-German, and moreover a non-Christian, has played a notable role in the advancement of knowledge'.[86]

Mendelssohn's aim was to strip Spinoza's philosophy of the exceptionalist aura it had acquired, approaching him instead as an important participant in the advancement of mainstream European thought, whose Jewishness, while irrelevant to his thought, was nonetheless worthy of note as a corrective to assumptions of German or Christian intellectual superiority. To his non-Jewish readership, however, Mendelssohn's emotionally dramatic account of the sacrificial historical role of Spinoza almost certainly bore a Christological resonance. It is possible that Mendelssohn absorbed this Christian inflection from Lessing, as the Dialogues may well reflect actual conversations between the two men.[87] Mendelssohn's suggestion was that Spinoza's conflation of God with nature, far from being atheistic (which was at the time generally assumed to be a key feature of 'Spinozism'), in essence implied the very opposite. His interpretation also fuelled, rather than deflected, exceptionalist and Judaic readings of Spinoza's philosophy. A similar idea had been put forward over fifty years earlier by the enigmatic German radical Georg Wachter, who, in his Spinozism in Judaism (1699), argued that Spinoza had drawn this dangerous conflation from the Jewish mystical tradition, the Kabbalah. Seven years later, writing in Latin for a more exclusive audience, Wachter crucially modified his thesis. Declaring himself a devotee of Spinoza's philosophy, he no longer critiqued, but rather celebrated the pantheism of the Jewish mystical tradition as the source of Spinoza's philosophical brilliance.[88] The echo of these ideas in Mendelssohn's arguments suggested, for some readers, a possible harmony between Spinoza and the perspectives of early modern Christian Hebraism, within which the Kabbalah had attracted fascination as the purest source of philosophical truth, and a crucial signpost toward a utopian future of universal wisdom.

Mendelssohn's reputation as the 'German Socrates' was established above all by his Phaedon (1767), in which he put forward a widely admired argument for the immortality and rationality of the human soul.[89] For many of his readers, however, this essay heightened the puzzle of Mendelssohn's continued Jewish observance, as in it he seemed to endorse a deistic theology, based simply on the acceptance of a minimal core of universal and rational truths. In

Enlightenment circles in the mid-eighteenth century, it was widely believed that these deistic beliefs, cased within a minimal Christian framework, would form the basis for the overcoming of divisions between all religious groups.

The dissolution of Jewish difference, however, retained a special messianic significance. It was a combination of messianic enthusiasm and a belief in the demonstrable unity of philosophy, science and Christianity that led the Swiss pastor Johann Caspar Lavater, in 1769, to challenge Mendelssohn either to refute the arguments he presented to him or to convert to Christianity. Although Lavater's challenge was widely viewed as highly discourteous, the ensuing controversy focused attention on Mendelssohn's Jewishness. Mendelssohn's religious beliefs remained under philosophical scrutiny for the rest of his life.[90] Thirteen years later, in 1782, he was once again publicly challenged, in an anonymous open letter written by August Friedrich Cranz, a deist and eager admirer of the philosopher, who believed that Mendelssohn's recent rejection of the right of rabbis to expel heretics from the community signalled that he had already abandoned a fundamental tenet of Judaism.[91] In response, Mendelssohn decided finally to write and publish a defence of Judaism in the terms of the Enlightenment: his *Jerusalem* (1783).

Mendelssohn here rejected the suggestion in Cranz's letter that it would be in the interest of all Jews also to abandon other religious laws that impeded their interaction with Christians, such as their dietary regulations and Sabbath restrictions. Christianity, Mendelssohn pointed out, was constructed upon Judaism, so conversion from the older to the younger religion could not provide any sturdier rational grounding for religion: it would be like moving from the lower to the upper floor of a collapsing building.[92] In contrast with Cranz's vision of a universally shared religion, Mendelssohn argued for religious pluralism. A union of faiths, he emphasized in his final paragraph, is not true tolerance, but its opposite: 'diversity is evidently the plan and purpose of Providence'.[93] The universal truths of reason were fully compatible with Judaism, and equally accessible to all. Judaism, he argued, was simply a particular supplement to these truths. The divine law revealed to Jews through Moses contained no beliefs or doctrines, but rather a set of prescribed actions. Judaism is thus not a 'revealed religion', but a 'revealed legislation', consisting of instructions, for Jews alone and carrying authority due to their transmission through the Jewish tradition, on how to act in this world 'in order to attain temporal and eternal felicity'.[94]

Whether or not Mendelssohn succeeded in providing an intellectually convincing harmonization of Judaism with the Enlightenment continues to be a keenly debated topic.[95] It is clear, though, that he did not defuse the complexities surrounding the exceptionality of Judaism and its special purpose in the world. Viewed at a distance, his argument seems to normalize Judaism, presenting it as one pathway among many for the living of a virtuous and dignified life. However, in his detailed explanation of the purpose of the ceremonial law, Mendelssohn places Judaism on a higher level than other religious systems, and relates this to the Jews' status as God's chosen people. The Jews, he argues, were singled out to be a 'priestly nation', with the responsibility 'continually to call attention to sound and unadulterated ideas of God'.[96] For this reason, he speculates, God provided them with a law based on actions, which are transitory, rather than beliefs, which are conveyed through the fixed signs of written language. These fixed signs can readily become confused with what they signify, and thus become the focus of idolatry. The genius of Judaism, he argues, is that it mandates only actions, and thus preserves a purer conception of the divine, offering the best possible protection from the eternal human tendency to sink into idolatrous worship.[97]

This lofty understanding of Jewish worship stood in diametric contrast to the prevalent stereotype of Judaism as a religion of unthinking legalism. Despite important differences, it also to some extent echoed Lessing's association of Jewishness with pure wisdom in *Nathan the Wise*. For Mendelssohn, this purity resided in the religious particularity of Judaism, whereas for Lessing it was associated with a post-Jewish universalism attained through the inversion of normative Judaism. However, as we have noted, Lessing nonetheless associated this philosophical loftiness with Mendelssohn, and in the nineteenth century, as we shall see, the idealization of Jews as teachers of moral purity resonated in both secular and religious terms. Mendelssohn also obliquely echoed the messianic allusions of Lessing's *The Education of the Human Race*. The references to a future messianic age in *Jerusalem* are discreet, perhaps because the supposed hope of Jews to return to Palestine was at this time being cited as an argument against the extension of civil rights to them. To an attentive reader, however, they are unmistakable, and the book's title itself alludes to a messianic future in which, as Mendelssohn underscores in his closing paragraph, the divine plan for the embrace of diversity and universal tolerance will finally be fulfilled.[98] This stirring rhetoric injected an element of visionary utopianism into Mendelssohn's political demands, casting a messianic inflection over the issue of Jewish civil rights, which was in the early 1780s for the first time attracting serious consideration.

Soon after the publication of *Jerusalem*, Mendelssohn was drawn into the most acrimonious quarrel of his intellectual life: his so-called *Spinozastreit* ('Spinoza Quarrel', or 'Pantheism Quarrel') with Friedrich Heinrich Jacobi (1743–1819). This ostensibly centred on the purported 'Spinozism' of Lessing, which Jacobi claimed the dramatist had divulged to him not long before his death in 1781.[99] The polemical edge of Jacobi's argument, however, was sharply directed against Mendelssohn, challenging both the authenticity of his friendship with Lessing and whether, more profoundly, it was possible for him, as a Jew, to occupy a respectable place in the German intellectual tradition. For Jacobi—a leading critic of Enlightenment rationalism—'Spinozism' was indeed synonymous with atheism, which he regarded as the inescapable and fatalistic terminus of all philosophy, from which the only possible escape was a transcendental leap into religious faith.[100] The perilous 'spirit of Spinozism', he argued, was both philosophically eternal and specifically Jewish: reviving Wachter's argument, to which Mendelssohn had also alluded in his *Philosophical Conversations*, Jacobi claimed that Spinoza and his followers had merely re-expressed the 'emanating *En-Sof*' ('Endless One') of the 'philosophizing kabbalists'.[101] Jacobi thus cast the Enlightenment as a whole as implicitly Jewish, and doubly implicated both Spinoza and Mendelssohn, as philosophers and as Jews, in what he regarded as the pernicious sterility of rationalism. As an alternative to reason, Jacobi asserted the primacy of faith, and against the cosmopolitan ideal, of which the friendship between Lessing and Mendelssohn had become emblematic, he suggested that true intimacy was possible only within a shared community of faith. Jacobi's argument nonetheless ascribed immense historical importance to Jews, presenting them as nothing less than the originators of modernity. This accusatory association of Jews with reason and cosmopolitanism formed the core of a highly influential negative version of the idea of Jewish purpose over the subsequent two centuries.

In the short term, however, Jacobi's attack backfired. Respectful attention to Spinoza's thought became, in reaction against Jacobi's violent rejection of him, a totem of reasonableness and sensitivity for most later German idealists. Several of these writers broadly endorsed Mendelssohn's interpretation of Spinoza, imbuing it with reverential romanticism: this is memorably captured in the summary of Spinoza, widely attributed to the Romantic poet Novalis, as a 'God-intoxicated man'.[102] In his *God: Some Conversations* [*Gott: einige Gespräche*] (1787), Johann Gottfried Herder bitingly satirized the second-hand dismissal of Spinoza by intolerant conservatives. Aggressive dismissal, in the manner of Jacobi, was for Herder the mark of bad conduct and bad philosophy; in contrast, open-minded and sensitive reading, attuned to the subtlety and wisdom of a thinker such as Spinoza, characterized the true philosopher. Herder's admiring approach was characteristic of the romantic spirit of the German 'Spinoza Renaissance' that followed in the wake of the quarrel between Jacobi and Mendelssohn, and which also encompassed Novalis, Goethe, Heine and others.[103] Despite their rejection of Jacobi's arguments, these thinkers shared his association of Spinoza with enlightened cosmopolitanism, and implicitly also his broader association of some aspect of Jewishness, or a derivative of it, with the highest form of reason. In the 1780s, when the political reform of Jewish status was only just beginning to be caught in the winds of change, there was a very wide perception of the special meaningfulness, as an indicator of modernity, of the position of Jews, and of attitudes toward them. The line of division, which was to deepen greatly in the following century, was over whether the Jewish role in the advent of the modern era was positive or malign.

Regeneration and Emancipation: Jewish Transformation as Enlightenment Fulfilment

The intense debates into which Mendelssohn was drawn in the early 1780s occurred simultaneously with, and were stimulated by, the sudden emergence in the Germanic world of government policies that aimed to change profoundly the social and political position of Jews. Following the death in 1780 of the Habsburg ruler Maria Theresa, her son and heir Joseph II, strongly influenced by the ideals of the Enlightenment, immediately introduced a new approach to the religious minorities under his rule. In his 'Edict of Tolerance' of January 1782, Joseph accorded to Jews, initially only in and around Vienna but later across the Habsburg Empire, the freedom to enter any educational institution and to pursue any trade. In exchange, the Jews were expected to abandon their 'customary distinguishing marks', use German rather than Yiddish in their business records, and cooperate in a range of ways with the cultural and economic policies of the regime, in order to become 'useful and serviceable to the state'.[104] Joseph II's edict gave renewed expression to the idea, expressed early in the century by John Toland and by others even earlier, that the proper harnessing of the economic prowess of Jews could be of great general advantage. The Habsburg emperor's attempt to activate these hopes through a dramatic change of policy toward his Jewish subjects placed the transformation of the Jews at the heart of his wider agenda of Enlightenment reformism.

At the same time, a major upheaval was occurring in Alsace, where, in the late 1770s, thousands of petty debtors had refused to continue their repayments to local Jewish moneylenders. In response, community leaders had asked Moses Mendelssohn to intercede. Seeking to secure a prominent Christian voice as an advocate for the Jews, Mendelssohn had passed on this request to Christian Wilhelm von Dohm, a reform-minded Prussian diplomat and scholar. This led to the publication, in summer 1781, of Dohm's *On the Civic Improvement of the Jews*: the first substantial and prominent European argument in support of Jewish civil rights.[105] On both the eastern and the western fringes of Germanic Europe, the status of Jews had suddenly leapt to the fore, no longer as a matter of merely notional thought experiments, but as the focus of concrete reformist proposals and ambitious legal changes.

These developments exposed to an unprecedented degree profound internal divisions within the Jewish world. Mendelssohn and other proponents of the *Haskalah* movement for Jewish cultural uplift played an important role both in working with Dohm and in seeking to promote Jewish support for Joseph II's edict. Leading rabbis, however, took a very different view, regarding both the *Haskalah* and these new reformist policies as a dire threat to traditional Jewish observance and to their own communal authority. At the end of the 1770s, the announcement of Mendelssohn's collaborative project to translate the Torah into German had already been met with rabbinical threats of expulsion from the community; in 1782, the same threat was issued to Mendelssohn's close associate Naphtali Herz Wessely, who had published a Hebrew pamphlet ardently supportive of Joseph II's edict. In response, and also in order to distance himself from Dohm's endorsement of the right of rabbis to expel individuals from the community, Mendelssohn declared his opposition to this sanction. It was this declaration that prompted Cranz to issue his anonymous challenge to Mendelssohn. In Cranz's eyes, Mendelssohn's declaration constituted a clear break with traditional Jewish law, and therefore invited the question of why he would not move further in the direction of reform.[106]

At stake in this debate was the issue of what conceptual and legal form Jewish communities should take in an enlightened polity. For both Cranz and Dohm—and also for at least one Jew at the time, the radical thinker Solomon Maimon—Judaism should be considered as a voluntary religious affiliation, and should therefore hold the right, like any voluntary association, to determine its own rules of inclusion or exclusion. Mendelssohn, however, saw things differently. For him, Jewish belonging was essentially familial in nature, and therefore both socially and ethically inviolable.[107] Although this might seem a minor matter, it cut to the core of the question of how Jewish particularism could be made compatible with a universalist political framework. For Cranz and Dohm, and many others, it was precisely the overcoming of Jewish difference that paradoxically rendered their transformation so emblematic of Enlightenment reformism. For Mendelssohn, however, this issue forced a confrontation with the limits of his desire for the normalization of the social and political position of Jews. Despite this aspiration, he nonetheless remained wedded to a notion both of Judaism and of Jewish peoplehood as special, and therefore not readily assimilable to the liberal norms that were taking shape in the late Enlightenment era.

Notwithstanding his close collaboration with Mendelssohn, Dohm shared the consensus view among educated Germans that the Jews of his day were, in general, a physically, culturally and morally impoverished people. In his treatise, he repeatedly described the Jews as dishonest, hostile to others and theologically mired in legalistic pettiness.[108] However, he argued that this was not their natural state: they had, rather, degenerated as a result of the discriminatory and hostile treatment they had suffered for centuries at the hands of Christians. Dohm confidently believed that, once embraced by the broader political society, the Jews would rapidly regenerate themselves. Their interests would before too long align with those of the states in which they lived, and they would return to the spirit of their noble 'ancient Mosaic constitution', suitably altered to fit 'changed times and circumstances'.[109]

The enduringly influential notion of racial degeneration had recently emerged in the work of the biological and anthropological thinker Johann Friedrich Blumenbach, who in his *De generis humani varietate nativa* [On the Natural Varieties of Mankind] (1775) had divided humanity into five races, coining the term 'Caucasian' for the original and most beautiful human type, of which the other races were a degenerated form.[110] The associated idea of regeneration had acquired a number of medical, biological and intellectual associations in recent Enlightenment writings; only in the 1780s, however, did its use in a political context become widespread.[111] In applying this vogue term to Jews, Dohm powerfully connected current reformist and scholarly thought with long-standing notions of Jewish exceptionalism and world historical purpose. The notion of regeneration had strong theological overtones, evoking resurrection and also the restoration of the Jews as God's chosen people. Dohm's references to the ancient Mosaic polity and to the revival of the Jews' moral 'spirit' echoed the political Hebraism of the seventeenth century and the strand of ethical idealization linking Spinoza, Mendelssohn and Nathan the Wise. Rather than presenting the civic improvement of the Jews as simply one potential project of benevolent and enlightened governance alongside many, Dohm imbued his subject with multiple and deep resonances, recasting the idea of Jewish purpose in the political language of the moment.

Dohm's treatise stimulated extensive debate. One of the most significant critiques it elicited was by Johann David Michaelis (1717–91), a colleague of Blumenbach at the University of Göttingen and the leading Hebraist of late eighteenth-century Germany. Michaelis regarded the ancient Hebrew texts he studied as reflective of the true and unchanging essence of Judaism. In the 1760s, he had been the key intellectual sponsor of a pioneering and catastrophically unsuccessful ethnographic expedition to the Near East (of the six members of the exploratory party, only the leader, Carsten Niebuhr, survived): improved knowledge of the nomads of Arabia, he had argued, would be of much greater value for the elucidation of the Bible than the observation of contemporary European Jews, whose original and inner nature had been distorted by the alien influences to which they had been exposed.[112] Against Dohm's argument that an extension of civic rights to Jews would lead to their integration, Michaelis insisted that this goal was unattainable, because the very purpose of the Mosaic law was to preserve the Jews as a separate people. In making his case for Jewish immutability, Michaelis melded biblical, cultural and biological arguments, all of which, in his view, were aspects of a single, essential Jewish nature. His most emphatic rejection of Jewish civic inclusion was on military grounds: the Jews could never serve modern states as loyal and emphatic fighters, because their religion forbade them from eating with other soldiers and from fighting on the Sabbath, and because they were in any case too short.[113] Jewish exceptionality, for Michaelis, was rooted in the biblical past, which held the Jews outside the normal flow of history. Their religious purpose as underwriters of the truth of Christianity precluded, in his view, their transformation under enlightened tutelage into model citizens.

Dohm's progressive reformism would seem at first sight to have little in common with Michaelis's biblicist fundamentalism. However, in his treatise, Dohm cited and praised Michaelis a number of times, and to a considerable extent also viewed contemporary Jews through the prism of the Bible. The disagreement between them hinged on the possibility of imminent and radical change. It was precisely at this time, at the dawn of the age of revolutions, that a transformed sense of temporal movement and of living within history was entering European consciousness.[114] This changing intellectual mood had influenced both men. In his early work on the nature and origin of language,

Michaelis had treated Hebrew as a uniquely immutable tongue, but in his later writings he revised this view, incorporating Hebrew into his overarching and influential theory of linguistic evolution.[115] Johann Gottfried Herder—another leading German writer on language—was also at this time grappling with how to integrate his idealized view of ancient Hebrew with his wider interest in processes of change. In his *On the Spirit of Hebrew Poetry* (1782), he lauded the intensity of this 'most simple, perhaps . . . most truly heart-felt poetry in the world', reflecting the uncorrupted purity of 'the infancy of the human race'.[116] Like Michaelis, however, he was fascinated by the question of how human language emerged and evolved.[117] Herder, Michaelis and Dohm shared a broadly similar intellectual outlook, and yet they each reached very different, though equally intensely expressed standpoints on the immediate historical significance of the Jews and their texts. These differences reflected the compelling nature of this question at this time, and the multiple directions in which it could be pulled. The exceptionality and importance of the Jewish case was not in contest. However, as a people associated both with a deep and unchanging past and with a messianic or visionary future, their place in history at this moment of rumbling but not yet dramatic change was a matter of fascination but also of great uncertainty.

In France too, the 1780s was a decade of intensifying discussion of the Jews as a social and political problem. Dohm's text was swiftly published in French translation in 1782, and three years later, in response to public interest in the topic, the Royal Academy of Sciences and Arts in Metz—the main Jewish urban centre in eastern France—announced an essay competition on the question 'Are there ways of making the Jews more useful and happier in France?' This title succinctly captured the widespread aspiration at the time for the improvement of Jewish lives to stand as a vivid test case for the ameliorative reach of enlightened governance, simultaneously promoting rational utility and general happiness. The broad social reach of this idea was reflected in the diversity of the competition winners. In 1788, the prize committee announced three joint victors: Zalkind Hourwitz, a Polish-born Jew resident in Paris; Claude-Antoine Thiéry, a barrister from Lorraine; and the abbé Henri Grégoire, for his *Essay on the Physical, Moral and Political Regeneration of the Jews*.[118] The arguments of Grégoire—by far the most influential winner—were in many respects similar to those of Dohm, and were even more emphatically based on the twin notions of degeneration and regeneration. Grégoire expressed his admiration for Jewish family life, charitable institutions and respect for elders and for education. However, he also regarded Jews as generally dirty, economically rapacious and culturally, sexually and physically degenerate. The total regeneration of them that he envisaged had at its core a moral reawakening that was strongly tinged with Christian conversionist millenarianism. He endorsed strong measures of surveillance and control until that regeneration had been achieved, including a prohibition on Jewish moneylending.[119]

Grégoire believed that humanity was on the brink of a new historical era of universal fraternity, for which the overcoming of the division between Jews and Christians was a key preparatory step. The fervent excitement with which he anticipated this imminent future, captured in the epigraph at the opening of this chapter, reflects the centrality of the role of the Jews in his millenarian historical schema. Whereas for Dohm and Lessing the religious resonance of the transformation of the Jews was relatively muted (though unmistakably present), in Grégoire's essay it was explicit: his fusion of practical and theological arguments for the regeneration of Jews echoed the case advanced for Jewish readmission in England in the 1650s. The evaluation of Grégoire's arguments has been a subject of long-standing debate. Patriotic nineteenth-century French Jews revered him as the father of their political emancipation, while in recent decades there has been increasing criticism of his denigratory attitudes toward Jews of his time, and of his conversionist expectancy.[120] It is misplaced, however, to reduce Grégoire either to a straightforward 'friend' of Jews or to an intolerant figure whose hopes for the dissolution of Jewish difference foreshadowed the eliminationist antisemitism of the Nazis. His passionate espousal of Jewish regeneration was not primarily animated by a direct concern with their plight, but rather by his belief, both as a millenarian Christian and as a man of the Enlightenment, that to promote this transformation was to advance the fulfilment of the Jews' crucial destiny in the messianic unfolding of human history.

The revolution of 1789 immensely heightened the sense of transformatory possibility in French political life. Elected to the Estates General that was convoked in Versailles in May 1789, Grégoire was outspoken, once this body had transformed itself into the National Assembly, in arguing for his proposed new approach toward the Jews of France. Despite the many urgent issues facing the new regime, the question of the status of the Jews was given an extraordinary amount of attention. It was discussed at no fewer than twenty-five Assembly sessions during the first year of the body's existence, several of them lengthy and notably passionate.[121] The Jews accounted for approximately 0.2% of the French population, and only a small proportion of them met the wealth qualification for the 'active citizenship' to which all Jews were finally deemed eligible by the decree of 27 September 1791.[122] Why, then, was this considered such a pressing and controversial issue? Clearly the Jews represented an important limit case for the expansiveness of French citizenship, and its requirements of similarity, morality and transparency.[123] Economic suspicion of Jews, particularly in eastern France, was a powerful factor motivating some to keep this minority outside the national community. Most significant, however, and ultimately decisive in the decision of the Assembly to extend citizenship rights to Jews, was the millenarian resonance of Jewish transformation, both in Christian terms and as a semi-secular imbuing of the Revolution with epochal meaning.

The extension of equal rights to Jews was exported across much of western Europe in the late 1790s by the conquering French armies of the Directory and Napoleonic periods. In these places, the liberation of Jewish communities from long-standing restrictions was seen as dramatically emblematic of the political transformations ushered in by the French forces. In Frankfurt and several cities in Italy, where the confining boundaries of Jewish ghettos were physically destroyed, this symbolism was particularly powerful. The anticipated 'regeneration' of Jews, however, did not proceed as swiftly as many had hoped. This was particularly apparent in Alsace, where the rural and traditional nature of both the Jewish and the non-Jewish population, the enduring tensions between them over moneylending, and the profound economic dislocation wrought by the Revolution itself all contributed to the retrenchment of long-standing economic and cultural habits.[124] These problems came to the fore in 1806, when complaints over Jewish moneylending were brought to Napoleon's attention in Strasbourg. In response, later that year in Paris, Napoleon convoked an 'Assembly of Jewish Notables', charged with answering a battery of questions concerning whether the Jews were or were not both willing and able to integrate into the French nation as patriotic and loyal citizens.

The members of the Assembly did their best to supply the emperor with the affirmative answers that he clearly wanted, and in order to seal the authority of their pronouncements, Napoleon had them ratified by a 'Great Sanhedrin', convened by him on the model of the supreme Jewish court during the Second Temple period.[125] This gesture underscored the fixity, in Napoleon's mind, of the Jews' association with their ancient past, even at this moment of their anticipated transformation. It was also an extraordinary act of theological intervention, through which Napoleon cast himself as the presiding authority in blasting the Jewish people into the modern era. The high political theatre of the Sanhedrin flattered the lawgiving emperor as a latter-day Moses—and it also flattered the Jews, who were uniquely able to bestow this status on their ruler.[126]

The exceptional significance of the Jews was thus dramatically brought to the fore in the very rituals that supposedly ratified their acceptance of their regeneration and normalization. This tension was also apparent in a set of decrees issued by Napoleon in March 1808, which established special measures of state oversight in the refashioning of its Jewish subjects. A consistorial structure of internal organization was imposed on French Jewry, modelled on the one created for French Protestants in 1802, but charged with particular responsibilities of surveillance and civic education; additionally, for the next decade, exceptional and discriminatory restrictions were imposed on the mobility and moneylending of the Jews of Alsace.[127] These measures have often been interpreted as revealing the half-heartedness of the French commitment to extending equal rights to Jews. Napoleon's approach was certainly considerably shaped by a willingness to give ground to the widespread anti-Jewish sentiment in Alsace. However, in the minds of many at this time there was no contradiction between imposing special regulation on Jews while simultaneously vaunting the principle of their inclusion under the revolutionary ideals of liberty, equality and fraternity. Jewish normalization was itself regarded as uniquely significant. It therefore warranted special attention and celebration, and special measures to monitor and ensure its success.

Across Europe during the Napoleonic period, the political status and socio-economic role of Jews was animatedly debated and variably reformed. In the Jewish demographic heartland of Poland, Jews briefly enjoyed legal equality for just over year, following the establishment by Napoleon in 1807 of the short-lived Duchy of Warsaw. Here and elsewhere, liberal intellectual values were closely allied with proposals for Jewish uplift and integration. However, the question of how to make sense of the significance and distinctiveness of Jews in relation to the abstract ideals and the practical policies embraced by these progressive political movements remained an area of considerable controversy and confusion for both Jewish and non-Jewish intellectuals.[128]

The boldest proposal to resolve these issues emerged in Berlin. In 1799, David Friedländer, the most prominent figure in the Berlin Jewish community, proposed in an open letter to the leading Lutheran cleric in the city that the Jews be offered a 'dry baptism', abandoning the rituals of Judaism and converting to Lutheranism, but with an exemption from its dogmatic and ritual aspects, such as the recognition of Jesus Christ as the son of God.[129] Friedländer's deistic proposal, which was in essence similar to Cranz's suggestion that Moses Mendelssohn had so emphatically rejected seventeen years earlier, may not have been entirely serious. He certainly cannot have been surprised that it was firmly rejected from all directions.

Friedländer's proposition nonetheless stimulated serious debate. The most thoughtful response to it came from the young Protestant theologian Friedrich Schleiermacher, who saw Friedländer's proposal as further undermining the central religious importance of sincere belief. With its pews already populated by plenty of nominal believers, the Church needed, Schleiermacher believed, to reassert the importance of authentic religious commitment, rather than diluting this further by admitting superficially converted Jews, who might well be inward deists adopting Christianity for purely practical reasons.[130] For Friedländer, in contrast, the detachment of private beliefs from collective religious participation was unproblematic. Taking further Mendelssohn's argument in *Jerusalem* that Judaism was not a religion of beliefs, but of legally prescribed actions, Friedländer declared himself ready to dispense with those behavioural laws and rituals, leaving simply its core of universal moral truths, of which Mendelssohn had declared the Jewish ceremonial law to be simply a supplement. This argument implicitly placed Jews, once again, at the vanguard of enlightened modernity. The future Jewish Christians envisaged in Friedländer's proposal shared the core distinctiveness of Spinoza and of Lessing's fictional Nathan. Abandoning their ancient traditions, leapfrogging over the dogmatic particularities of their newly adopted religion, and committing themselves only to the philosophical purity of universal morals, they looked very much like a precociously rationalist cell within Christianity.

Friedländer's radical vision of Jewish transformation was at the outer edge of what was imaginable at the turn of the century. However, in the heady environment of unprecedented political upheaval at that time, there was a widespread sense, among both Jews and non-Jews inspired by the ideals of the French Revolution, that the profound attenuation of Jewish separateness and difference, if not its absolute disappearance, was both desirable and likely in the near future. In Berlin, a number of salons hosted by Jewish women and infused with the values of the Romantic movement provided a new milieu in which Jews and Christians could interact socially and intellectually. Several of these women married Christian men they met at the salons, converting from Judaism in order to do so. However, the Napoleonic occupation of Berlin in 1806 led indirectly to a cooling of relations between Jews and non-Jews in the city. The rise of German nationalist sentiments in response to the occupation led to a more constricted and chauvinistic atmosphere: the salons waned, and the passing of legislation in 1812 which established virtual civil equality for the Jews of Prussia did not stem the popularity of conversion among the Berlin Jewish elite.[131] Following the fall of Napoleon, the issue of Jewish civil rights was discussed extensively at the Congress of Vienna, but the assembled diplomats ultimately decided, in June 1815, not to protect the reforms imposed by the French. This moment was the first major setback, repeated following the defeat of the revolutions of 1848, in what has been described by one historian as the 'tortuous and thorny' journey toward legal equality for European Jewry.[132]

It was not until the late 1820s that this process became known by the term still in general use today: 'Jewish emancipation'. This phrase was adopted as a rallying cry from the movement for 'Catholic emancipation' in Britain, which in turn had borrowed its rhetorical self-description from the anti-slavery campaign.[133] While of course important, the extension of equal rights of political participation to Jews—or, more correctly, to the limited number of prosperous Jewish men to whom these rights were in the main only applicable—was not of equivalent human significance to the actual emancipation of slaves. However, the resonance of the idea that the transformation of the status of Jews marked the fulfilment of the ideals of the Enlightenment enabled the term to acquire and maintain popular currency. The association of Jewish political rights with anti-slavery was particularly potent in Britain, where abolitionists presented their campaign as a cause on which a principled stand would legitimate the nation's claim to act as in international moral arbiter, in effect underwriting British economic imperialism with humanitarian credentials. With the final abolition of slavery in the British Empire in 1834, the plight of Jews moved increasingly to the fore as an alternative focus for the linking of religious, ethical and economic dimensions in the self-congratulatory rhetoric of British imperialism.[134]

The 'Damascus Affair' of 1840—a blood libel case in which several members of the Jewish community of Damascus were arrested and tortured for the alleged ritual murder of a Capuchin monk—was a key moment in the renewal, within the framework of nineteenth-century internationalism and competitive imperialism, of the protection of Jewish rights as a prominent aspect of European programmes for the transformative improvement of the rest of the world. Jewish leaders and communities in Britain, France and beyond mobilized energetically in response to the alarming news from Syria, and the cause of the unjustly imprisoned Jews drew widespread Christian support. The British foreign secretary Lord Palmerston vigorously condemned the assault on the Jews of Damascus. In France, the lawyer and community leader Alphonse Crémieux, who alongside the British leader Moses Montefiore spearheaded the Jewish response to the affair, invoked the legacy of the abbé Grégoire, at whose funeral nine years previously he had given a eulogy. Linking the causes of Jews and slaves, Crémieux presented the protection of Jews as a key element of the French 'civilizing mission' to advance the causes of equality, tolerance and justice.[135] In 1840, Jews still had not attained full legal and political equality in most of Europe, and credence was still given in some quarters to lurid and mythic accusations of ritual murder. However, for many western Europeans at this time— particularly liberals and evangelical or nonconformist Christians—the righteousness and importance of the cause of Jewish amelioration was clear. For many, the front line in this battle was no longer at home, where Jews were already firmly established in bourgeois society, but around the periphery of the continent, where Jewish communities were perceived to need and deserve imperial protection. This proved to be a crucial shift in the modern development of the Jewish purpose question.

———

Lurking behind David Friedländer's 'dry baptism' proposal, Friedrich Schleiermacher believed, was a more profound threat to Christianity: Kantianism. At least a quarter of the younger, educated Jewish householders in Berlin were already devotees of Kant, he commented, alleging that it was only Friedländer's arrogance that had led him to omit any mention of the Kantian inspiration of his suggested collective Jewish conversion.[136] Schleiermacher's statistic is unreliable, but it was certainly the case that, for the first post-Mendelssohn generation of Berlin *maskilim*, the philosophy of Immanuel Kant (1724–1804) was almost a second religion. In the 1790s, Solomon Maimon was widely recognized as one of Kant's sharpest early interpreters, and several other Jewish intellectuals were enthusiastic adopters and advocates of his philosophical outlook. Kantianism was attractive to so many Jews, from the late eighteenth through to the early twentieth century, because it was grounded in a universalist, nondogmatic approach to metaphysics that seemed to open up precisely the intellectual terrain that Mendelssohn had sought but failed to find: a neutral space where questions of philosophy and ethics could be explored without regard to differences of background or outward religion.[137] At the close of the eighteenth century, Kant's magisterial synthesis of Enlightenment philosophy was seen both by its adherents and by many of its critics as pointing the way to the philosophical and universalistic overpowering of religious dogmas and differences.

The future of Judaism was a particularly prominent and resonant theme in this debate.

Kant put forward his thoughts on this precise subject in response to a text by one of his most ardent Jewish admirers, Lazarus Bendavid (1762–1832), who spent much of the 1790s lecturing, tutoring and publishing primers on Kant's philosophy. In his *Notes on the Characteristics of Jews* (1793), Bendavid offered a searing critique of the Berlin Jewish community, which he depicted as polarized between an irreligious and amoral elite and the ignorant and superstitious masses. Only a radical return to the ethical core of Judaism, centred on the love of one's neighbour, along with a transformation of Jewish education, economic activity and participation in the public sphere, could in his view haul the Jews into living good and happy lives.[138] In *The Conflict of the Faculties* (1798), Kant referred directly to this essay, praising Bendavid's intelligence, welcoming his proposal for the Jews' public acceptance of 'the religion of Jesus', and connecting this to his own enthusiastic anticipation of the distillation of their religion purely to a system of morality: a transformation he famously describes as 'the euthanasia of Judaism'.[139]

Bendavid did not in fact mention Christianity in his text, nor explicitly argue that Jews should abandon Judaism. However, Kant equated 'the religion of Jesus', itself distilled to its moral essence, with the moral teachings identified by Bendavid as the core of Judaism. His hope for the 'euthanasia of Judaism' was thus at odds with the views of his Jewish disciple, but it was Kant's different vantage point, rather than a wilful misunderstanding, that led him to believe that Bendavid was in accord with him. Kant's choice of words suggests a voluntary realization on the part of Jews that their historical role as a distinct people was complete. Their fusion into the mainstream was for Kant a key step toward a philosophically fulfilled future of human universalism, 'in which there will be only one shepherd and one flock'.[140] In his earlier *Religion within the Boundaries of Mere Reason* (1793), he put forward a more detailed account of the historical progression from the statutory laws and tribal particularism of Judaism to the moral religion of Christianity, and ultimately to the true universalism that would be ushered in by the embrace of rational philosophy: '[t]he appearance of the Antichrist, the millennium, the announcement of the proximity of the end of the world, all take on their proper symbolic meaning before reason'.[141] In stating that 'the euthanasia of Judaism is pure moral religion', Kant meant that this self-extinguishing transformation would invert Judaism into its opposite: from legalistic particularism into the purest possible form of ethical universalism. He here echoed the familiar eighteenth-century understanding of Judaism, channelled above all through the figures of Spinoza, Mendelssohn and Lessing's fictional Nathan, as the particularist negative of philosophical universalism, but also the source of philosophy's ultimate and most perfect realization.

The genocidal denouement of German Jewish history has cast an inescapable chill of infamy over Kant's phrase. These historical overtones make it hard to read his envisioning of the end of Judaism in the spirit in which it was understood at the time. Placed alongside some casual derogatory remarks about Jews elsewhere in his writings, this comment has led to Kant being charged by some scholars as fundamentally antisemitic.[142] However, these anachronistic readings miss the embeddedness of Kant's philosophy in the deeper history of Western thought on the historical purpose of the Jews. For Kant, as for so many others, Jews were associated with both the past and the future, with both tribal particularism and utopian universalism, and both with the antithesis of reason and ethics and with their ultimate fulfilment. Amid the political upheavals of the final decade of the eighteenth century, Kant perceived, again like so many others, the emergence of a better future in which the transformation of Jews and Judaism was to play a crucial emblematic role.

Even among Kantians, however, there was by no means unanimity on whether the positive transformation of Jews was possible. In 1793, in an essay defending the French Revolution, the radical Kantian philosopher Johann Gottlieb Fichte (1762–1814) launched a fierce attack on the insularity and mercantile ruthlessness of the Jews. While expressing some sympathy for their poverty and suffering, Fichte argued that Jews would always form an unacceptable 'state within a state', and commented that they could never be granted civil rights, unless 'in one night we chop off their heads and replace them with new ones, in which there would not be one single Jewish idea'.[143] Fichte's outburst revealed a profound anxiety over Jewish petty commerce, which he saw as entrenched within a particularist mindset that was inherently exploitative of others. Hostility toward the economic activity of Jews was by no means a new phenomenon, but the intensity of Fichte's condemnation, and the prominence in it of his view of Jews as eternally and perniciously exclusive and self-interested, reflected an important development in the history of thinking on Jewish purpose. In the nineteenth century, these debates increasingly focused on social and practical matters. In the aftermath of the age of revolutions, the epochal and possibly millenarian change that over the previous two centuries had been firmly moored in the imaginary future was now widely felt to be already underway. With respect to Jews this was particularly the case, as their social and cultural transformation in early nineteenth-century western Europe was more profound than that of any other group, and very closely connected with the commercial and industrial transformations of the period. The role of Jews in the economy was to become one of the central strands of nineteenth-century thinking, both critical and celebratory, on the distinctive purpose of Jews in the world.

Fichte's anti-Jewish polemic was swiftly and trenchantly critiqued by another Berlin Jewish Kantian: Saul Ascher (1767–1822). In his *Eisenmenger the Second* (1794), Ascher drew parallels between Fichte's prejudices and those of a notoriously anti-Jewish German Hebraist active at the beginning of the eighteenth century. Ascher challenged Fichte's assumptions about Jewish dishonesty and amorality, and, also taking on Kant himself, insisted that Judaism was not simply a legal and political system, but in essence a religion of moral beliefs in its own right.[144] Ascher's arguments presaged another aspect of the development of the Jewish purpose question in the subsequent century. Increasingly prominent and widely assimilated in the bourgeois milieux of urban life, and yet still a culturally, socially and generally also religiously distinct group, Jews in the nineteenth century needed to articulate new understandings of the ethical and historical purpose of Judaism for the wider world. These arguments, following Ascher's lead, served to fortify Jewish pride, to parry anti-Jewish attitudes and to explain and justify Jewish distinctiveness to others.

In some ways, however, Jews were already in the late eighteenth century at the forefront of the transformations of the era. The most intriguingly 'modern' Jews in this period were the followers of the mercurial messianic leader Jacob Frank (1726–91), who, after making contact with the Dönme—the outwardly Muslim Sabbatian sect—in Salonika, in 1755 declared himself the messianic heir of Sabbatai Zevi himself. Expelled by local rabbis in the eastern Polish borderlands for engaging in highly transgressive sexual rituals, Frank and approximately three thousand others converted with much fanfare to Catholicism. In the 1770s and 1780s, Frank had repeated audiences with Habsburg empress Maria Theresa and her son Joseph II, and his enigmatic sect, which blurred the boundaries between Jewishness and Christianity and between religion and secularism, inspired widespread fascination. After Frank's death, the movement was led by his daughter Eve, who also assumed his messianic mantle. In the early nineteenth century, the Frankists were widely perceived as a quasi-secular secret society, broadly akin to Freemasonry, and were a distinct presence in the bourgeois life of a number of central European cities.[145] In some respects, particularly with regard to gender equality, the Frankists and other Sabbatian groups were close to the political vanguard in this period. They attracted attention, however, not directly because of this but because of the special symbolic significance of their embrace, as Jews, both of a nominal Christianity and of the ideas and collective practices that were associated with the emergence of a universalist future. The Frankists readily appeared as a living example of the abstract ideal evoked in representations of Spinoza, Mendelssohn and Nathan the Wise: an actual collective embodiment of post-Jewish cosmopolitanism.

Despite their perceived 'modernity', the Frankists tested the boundaries of reason, and in this sense they stood within the tradition of Judaism serving as a limit case and testing ground for Enlightenment thought. Jacob Frank has been described as a notable example of a late eighteenth-century charlatan, similar to the famed Italians Casanova and Cagliostro: like them, Frank dabbled in alchemy, as did some other Jews linked with Sabbatianism, such as 'the Baal Shem of London', the rabbi and kabbalist Samuel Jacob Falk.[146] The Frankists, and these other Jewish eccentrics, highlighted in a particularly concentrated way the contrary dynamics of the late Enlightenment. The Frankists seemed in some ways strikingly cosmopolitan, but they also maintained a highly exclusive sense of their separateness from all others. Their messianism also clearly disrupts any attempt to align developments in the Jewish world in this period with the supposedly inexorable rise of secularism.[147] In the nineteenth century, despite many challenges to the authority and worldviews of mainstream religion, the messianic underpinning of Western thought about the future retained its vitality, as did the special association of Jews within this final denouement of history. Both during and after the revolutionary era it was widely believed, in various different ways, that the early tremors of this climactic moment were readily detectable. As the social, economic and political controversies of the nineteenth century brought to the fore a new set of associations with Jews, these accreted upon the enduringly significant and repeatedly reimagined messianic bedrock of the Jewish purpose question.

3

Teachers and Traders

JEWS AND SOCIAL PURPOSE

We will point out to our children the world-redeeming power, the ever-
widening significance of the Sinaitic teaching which is ever-enduring; the
changeable character of its outward forms; . . . [t]he unparalleled sacrifices its
preservation has cost; the wonderful vitality with which it has marched on,
unscathed, amid the crash of worlds. We will also point out the universal
union of the nations in God, the end for which Israel was set apart from the
rest of mankind; and, finally, the mission of our scattered people to carry the
Law of God to all peoples and all climes.[1]

—RABBI DAVID EINHORN (1855)

AROUND THE END of the eighteenth century, the understanding of most Europeans of their place in time was profoundly transformed. Before the French
Revolution, the present generally seemed to unfold in gentle continuity with
the past. The convulsions unleashed by the events of 1789 ruptured this familiar sense of continuity. Change was now accelerated and unpredictable, creat-
ing a new sense of living amid the forging of history, dislocated from the recent
past and in continual transition toward an uncertain future.[2] The transformation of Jews—a people who had been regarded during the early modern period
as quintessentially unchanging—was emblematic of both the hopes and the
fears associated with this historical drama. Political inclusion was extended to
them on a *quid pro quo* basis: the revolutionary rights exported across Europe
by the forces of Napoleon were expected to catalyse the 'regeneration' of Jews
that had been envisaged by Dohm, Grégoire and others.

This exchange was eagerly embraced by many early nineteenth-century Jewish leaders, who exhorted their communities to elevate themselves by embracing secular high culture and universal morality, and reorienting their economic activity away from commerce and toward 'productive' artisanal and agricultural occupations.[3] However, although western European Jewry was more dramatically transformed than any other ethnic group in the half-century following the French Revolution, this process did not follow the trajectory that the ideologues of regeneration had envisaged. Significant numbers of Jews entered the ranks of the urban bourgeoisie and adopted the fashions and tastes of their non-Jewish neighbours. They did not, though, dissolve as a distinct social grouping, and they retained their long-standing concentration in the rapidly developing economic sectors of trade and finance.[4] The expectations of transformation that had been dominant at the end of the Enlightenment period, it soon became clear, had not been fulfilled. The significance and purpose of Jews in the nineteenth-century world therefore needed to be profoundly rethought.

The messianic transformations associated with the unfolding of Jewish world-historical destiny had, until approximately 1800, been clearly located in the future. Even at times when these transformations seemed to some to be underway, such as during the mid-seventeenth-century upheavals surrounding the readmission of Jews to England and the surge of Sabbatian millenarianism, the most crucial changes were anticipated in the imminent future, and were expected to mark an epochal break with the past. The French Revolution gave rise to another wave of anticipatory fervour: in England, the self-proclaimed prophets Joanna Southcott and Richard Brothers attracted rival bands of supporters in the 1790s for their competing claims to be the appointed leader of the return of the Jews to Zion.[5] In the nineteenth century, however, past and future no longer seemed so neatly separate. The future was now: urbanization, industrialization and changing forms of both political and religious affiliation were all experienced as forces of profound transformation already active in the present. The future-oriented significance of Judaism and Jews therefore became enmeshed with these current processes of social transformation, and with the political, cultural and economic debates that raged over them.

Most currents of historicist thinking in the early nineteenth century, influenced above all by the philosophy of Hegel, viewed Judaism—often along with all other religions—as obsolete, and worthy of analysis only in order to understand its past role in the forward march of history. At first a significant number of Jewish intellectuals shared this view, believing that the rise of universal values had brought to an end any historical role for Judaism. However, the idea of Jewish purpose was soon reasserted with new vitality and vigour. The rapid growth of Reform Judaism, which first emerged in Germany soon after the Congress of Vienna, signalled a widespread commitment to a renewed sense of proud and edifying Jewish distinctiveness in the modern world. Far from being a relic from the past, the leaders of the Reform movement argued, Judaism continued to serve a vital purpose in the present and for the future. Inverting the widespread claim of many Hegelians that Judaism was particularly mired in the material, and was devoid of 'spirit'—a claim that echoed Jacobi's conflation of Enlightenment rationalism with Jewishness, and a long lineage of earlier juxtapositions stretching back to Paul's opposition of Christian love to Jewish law—the reformers asserted that Jews were in fact the guardians of the spiritually purest form of religion and ethics. The 'mission of Israel', they argued, was to disseminate these ideas to all peoples. This lofty vision imbued the continuation of Jewish identity and observance with a powerfully universalist purpose. It gained wide currency within nineteenth-century Jewry, particularly but not only on the reformist wing, and not only in Europe but also in America, where it resonated with the optimism and sense of unique destiny of this burgeoning centre of Jewish life. For the rabbi David Einhorn (1809–79), who began his career in Germany and later became one of the leading figures of Reform Judaism in the United States, the Jews' unique mission was central to their sense of pride and purpose. In the quotation at the head of this chapter, from his inaugural sermon at his first American pulpit in Baltimore, Einhorn powerfully expressed his renewed understanding of Jewish messianism. The Jews, he proclaimed, were charged with a unique and indispensable divine mission to disseminate true ethical universalism through all humanity.

This idea of mission brought the long-standing messianic focus of Jewish purpose into the present. Breaking with the loose consensus among both Jews and Christians since the time of their theological divergence, the world-historical purpose of Jews was no longer understood as becoming manifest only at the dawn of the messianic age. Rather, it was already active, in the ethical exemplarity and pedagogical role of the Jews in their diasporic dispersion. The casting of Jews as teachers was the central nineteenth-century answer to the Jewish purpose question. This frequently shaded beyond the domain of religion and ethics, moving into more clearly political or cultural territory. Jews had long been contrasted with Greeks: this binary stretches back to the juxtaposition of Athens and Jerusalem by the early Christian moralist Tertullian in the third century CE. In the eighteenth century, Greek reason was opposed to Jewish law, and while Mendelssohn's identification as the 'German Socrates' disrupted this opposition, it was precisely this disruption that intensified pressure on him to convert to Christianity, in accordance with the dominant Enlightenment view of Judaism as immaturely pre-rational.[6] The nineteenth-century endurance of Judaism and Jewish difference prompted a reframing of this relationship, not in developmental terms, but as a simultaneous binary, with 'Hebraic' virtues of asceticism, spirituality and moral earnestness balancing 'Hellenic' this-worldly values of pleasure and creativity. This contrast was influentially advanced both by Jews (Heinrich Heine) and Christians (Matthew Arnold). Other social virtues, such as energy, resilience and collective and familial cohesion, were associated with Jews by figures ranging from Benjamin Disraeli to Friedrich Nietzsche. These various associations were often inchoate, mobile or tinged with ambivalence or outright hostility. However, they also figured prominently in the various attempts by both Jews and non-Jews to make sense of the meaning and function of Jews in the dynamic and disputatious societies in which they lived.

The social force that was subject to the greatest controversy in the nineteenth century was also the one with which Jews were increasingly most associated: money. Resentment of Jews as non-productive traders and moneylenders had been widespread in the early modern period and earlier, and remained in evidence in the early nineteenth century. The linkage of Jews with money was, however, taken to a new level by Karl Marx, who in his *On the Jewish Question* (1844) attempted to shift the entire debate on Jewish emancipation to the necessary liberation of the world from the dehumanizing impact of 'Jewish' commerce. This text, and its legacy to mass politics in the late nineteenth and twentieth centuries, has rightly figured prominently in histories of antisemitism.[7] The relationship of Jews to the development of capitalism was not, however, always perceived in negative terms. In the decades around the turn of the twentieth century, the newly emerging objective social sciences attempted to analyse Jewish distinctiveness through a self-consciously objective lens. Leading sociologists such as Georg Simmel (1858–1918) and Werner Sombart (1863–1941) ascribed to Jews a central role in not only the economic, but also the intellectual and cultural aspects of modernity.

Sombart's work before the First World War on Jews and capitalism was interpreted by many people, including some Jews, as a flattering appreciation of Jewish economic acumen. Two decades later, however, it was appropriated by the Nazis, from whom the elderly scholar made no clear attempt to distance himself.[8] After 1945, this taint led to the disappearance of the entirety of Sombart's work from the sociological canon, amid a wider and enduring cultural recoil from the topic of Jews and money. The depiction of Jews as exploitative capitalists featured prominently in the prelude to their genocide; it is therefore not surprising that historians have tended to give a wide berth to any material bearing a similarity to that stereotype. The economic history of Jews in the modern era remains today a quiet and cautious field, often focused more on representations than realities.[9] An odour of antisemitism is today often perceived also to linger over the Victorian discourse of Hebraic virtues, while the idea of the mission of Israel (as we shall see in later chapters) has fallen from favour, but retained an awkward intellectual presence.

The broader idea that Jews are different from others—'allosemitism'—has also been linked to the Nazi genocide. According to this argument, the seemingly anomalous nature of Jews, even when their distinctive features were not necessarily in themselves viewed negatively, disrupted the ordering logic of the modern era. Their perceived difference therefore readily became the primary lightning-rod for angry discontentment with modernity.[10] The complex set of associations with Jews, and their straddling of the nation- and class-based divisions of modern society, were undoubtedly important factors in fuelling the rise of political antisemitism in Europe from the 1870s onwards, and its calamitous twentieth-century denouement. Antisemitism was by no means the only channel, though, into which ideas of Jewish difference and purpose flowed. If we are to grasp the diversity and energy of nineteenth-century thinking on this subject, we need to resist being overwhelmed by the historical backshadow of the Holocaust. It is only in the terms of the period itself that we can understand the importance of Jewish purpose in the varied attempts by both Jews and non-Jews to find sense and meaning in history, amid the unprecedentedly bewildering and contested forces of social change that shaped their lives.

From the Spirit of Judaism to the Mission of Israel: Jews as Universal Teachers

In the 1790s, in the immediate aftermath of the French Revolution, there was a broad consensus among European intellectuals that the time of Judaism was over. Immanuel Kant, in his late writings during this decade, influentially set the philosophical agenda for approaching Judaism in a historicist fashion, as a relic from a past era. This historicist perspective was developed much further by G.W.F. Hegel (1770–1831), whose work in turn exerted enormous influence on the nineteenth-century development of the Jewish purpose question. In his early writings, Hegel was already preoccupied by his central philosophical notion, *Geist* ('spirit'), and its role in the religious and ethical advance of humanity. His *On the Spirit of Christianity and its Fate* (1799)—one of his first attempts to set out his historicist insistence on the interpretation of ideas as a product of their political and social context—opened, in accordance with this logic, with a chapter on 'the spirit of Judaism'.[11] This spirit, he declared, was above all 'slavish' in character. The Mosaic law was shaped in accordance with the mental limits of the Jewish people: as they could not exercise 'reason and freedom', their law simply demanded unthinking obedience, underpinned by 'the terror of physical force'.[12] Hegel's argument echoed the long-standing Pauline trope contrasting the immaturity of Jewish law to the plenitude of Christian faith. It also made use of the established theological concept of divine 'accommodation', which Spinoza had deployed to explain the unphilosophical legalism through which God addressed the 'childlike' ancient Hebrews. For the young Hegel, however, the spiritual infancy of the Jews represented a crucial first step in the development of humanity toward ever-increasing understanding and wisdom. Hegel shared with many of his contemporaries a conviction that this process was nearing fulfilment, and that a higher, millennial spirit of cultural unification was about to sweep the European continent.[13]

After the fall of Napoleon, such straightforward optimism was no longer tenable. Established from 1818 onwards at the pinnacle of the philosophical profession at the University of Berlin, Hegel in his late work developed a more intricately historicist understanding of philosophy. His dialectical explanation of the forward movement of history through the resolution of opposites aspired to ascribe a place and a purpose to everything. With respect to Judaism, however, it was far from straightforward for him to integrate this ancient but enduring religion into his schema. In his hierarchical view of world civilizations, Hegel grouped the Jews, alongside Indians and Arabs, as 'Orientals', lacking the sense of individuality necessary for the 'hard European understanding' of true philosophy. Even Spinoza's thought, despite its important place in Hegel's account of the historical pathway from Descartes's dualism to his own philosophical synthesis, was cast as 'an echo from Eastern lands'.[14] However, despite Hegel's insistence on the non-European otherness of the Jewish spirit, he ascribed to it a crucial importance at the junction of Eastern and Western thought. This distinction between Eastern and Western, he argues, is marked by an insight that the Jews were the first to attain: the separation of spirit from nature, and its divine abstraction as 'the pure product of thought'. Despite their many limitations, Hegel regarded the ancient Hebrews as having taken a vital step in the forward movement of history, by exalting God as the distinct, abstract and supreme creator of the natural world.[15]

Hegel also imbued new life into another long-standing strain of the Jewish purpose question, extending back to the book of Isaiah and figuring prominently in medieval 'witness people' theology: the association of Jews with suffering. The 'world-historical importance and weight' of the Jewish people, he argued, lay in their painful consciousness of the 'wretchedness' of the isolated self, and their 'longing to transcend this condition of soul'. This was a crucial advance in human self-consciousness, which Hegel saw manifested in the beautiful and pure feeling of the psalms of David and the biblical prophets, expressing 'the thirst of the soul after God, its profound sorrow for its transgressions, and the desire for righteousness and holiness'.[16] After the destruction of their Second Temple in 70 CE, the Jews were left without comfort, in a state of 'misery and failure', their surviving hope in God nonetheless animating them with 'a boundless energy of longing'.[17] The overcoming of this suffering, meanwhile, came with Christianity, which reconciled God, man and spirit in the Trinity, and found its ultimate realization in the 'German spirit'.[18]

Hegel's historical positioning of Judaism transposed into his own philosophical idiom the key features of the traditional Christian view of Jews as both distant and similar, and both backward and yet crucial in the forward motion of history. However, even in the 1790s, when it was widely believed that what Kant had termed 'the euthanasia of Judaism' would herald the imminent triumph of ethical universalism, Hegel did not directly ascribe millenarian agency to the Jews. In his mature work, this role was very clearly in the hands of the Germans, whose fulfilment of the philosophical destiny of history was the culminating theme of his late writings. These texts and lecture series placed in clear relief his understanding of the crucial historical purpose that the Jews had fulfilled in the past. Their significance for the present and future, however, was less clear. By so decisively displacing them from their traditional millenarian centrality, Hegel shifted attention to the social characteristics with which he associated them. All three of his distinct characterizations—Jews as abstract intellectuals; as eternal sufferers; and as possessors of unusual energy—found prominence in later articulations of the continuing purpose of Jews in the social unfolding of history.

For German Jews also, the years following the Congress of Vienna were a watershed. The outcome of that diplomatic assembly led to the removal of some of the civil rights they had gained during the revolutionary era, while the political radicalism of German students and others took a nationalist turn. At the

Wartburgfest gathering in 1817 marking the three-hundredth anniversary of the Reformation, books of those that the nationalists considered their enemies were ceremonially burned. These included Saul Ascher's *Germanomania* (1815): a trenchant attack on the Gallophobia and Judaeophobia of the nationalists, in which Ascher reiterated the argument he had advanced against Fichte and Kant in the 1790s, insisting on the ethical, authentically religious and enduringly valid essence of Judaism.[19] By this time, however, Ascher was a rare voice sustaining the once widespread commitment to Kantian ethical universalism in the Berlin Jewish community. The younger generation of Jewish intellectuals had been seduced by the dominance of Hegelianism, and sought to integrate their own inner understandings of Judaism with that philosophical perspective. In 1819, they formed a society that grappled with that challenge, while also seeking to address the predicament of German Jewry at this moment of setback and uncertainty. The Verein für Cultur und Wissenschaft der Juden [Association for the Culture and Science of the Jews] involved only a handful of individuals in Berlin and Hamburg, and lasted less than five years. However, its innovative focus on the Jewish past injected new and bold socio-historical perspectives into the idea of Jewish purpose.

The agenda of the Verein was set out in a programmatic essay by Immanuel Wolf (1799–1847) in the inaugural 1822 issue of its journal. Objectivity, Wolf insisted, was the most essential attribute of the association's scientific and scholarly approach. This explicitly foreclosed any instrumental notion of purpose: Judaism must be studied 'in and for itself, for its own sake, and not for any special purpose or definite intention'.[20] This declaration, which sought to pre-empt any suspicion that the members of the association were partisan defenders of Judaism, also signalled their intention to harmonize their work with the wider scholarly projects of their day. Foremost among these was the Hegelian effort to produce an integrated philosophical understanding of human history. The grandeur of this integrative ambition runs through much of this early *Wissenschaft des Judentums* scholarship, which sought to set aside questions of faith and group affiliation, and to establish a place for the objective study of the Jewish past and present within the state-oriented framework of late Hegelian thought.[21]

Despite his claim to objectivity, Wolf nonetheless unhesitatingly echoed in his essay the sweepingly negative judgments of traditional Judaism that were widely held at the time. Most contemporary Jews, he asserted, lived in 'hollow isolation', mired in 'the weeds of a ceremonial that a thousand years of habit have made mechanical and lifeless'. Their impoverished state, however, should be understood as a consequence of their oppression by medieval Christians, while the new spirit of science must be mustered to lift the Jews into the modern age and to overcome their alienation from the outside world. In this optimistic vision of a better future, with which his essay culminates, Wolf gave expression to the sense of purpose that imbued his understanding of the *Wissenschaft* project, despite his claims to the contrary. The advancement of objectively scientific inquiry offered the prospect of the unification of all people in 'the bond of pure reason [and] truth'; the Jews must therefore join others in working doughtily toward this 'common task of mankind'.[22]

Alongside this broad embrace of scientific purpose, according to which the role of the Jews is simply to labour alongside others to further the advancement of universal understanding, Wolf also put forward a specific conception of Jewish world-historical importance. The inner 'idea of Judaism', he argued, was a purely spiritual understanding of God, conceived only in abstract terms and in clear distinction from the natural world. As possessors of this theological clarity and purity, the Jewish people were marked apart as 'guardians of the idea of God'.[23] This claim resonated with the conception of Judaism that Hegel was developing at this time, which also emphasized the abstraction and purity of the Jewish notion of the divine. However, unlike Hegel, Wolf argued that Judaism had continued to nurture this idea beyond the emergence of Christianity. The practical laws of the Talmud had woven into the everyday life of the Jews a mindfulness of this pure idea of God; only in the face of medieval persecution and exclusion did Judaism lose its spiritual vitality.[24]

Wolf's argument echoed that of Moses Mendelssohn, who in his *Jerusalem* had argued that the biblical designation of the Jews as a 'priestly nation' signified that they were entrusted with protecting the conceptual purity of the divine from the temptations of idolatry. Mendelssohn, however, emphasized the central importance of traditional Jewish observance in sustaining this spiritual consciousness. For Wolf, this was no longer true after medieval European Jewry had been driven into 'a debilitating lethargy'. The idea of Judaism nonetheless then found expression, he claimed, in its highest, most purely rational form: the philosophical system of Spinoza. Wolf's heroizing association of Spinoza simultaneously with reason, spirituality and the positive distillation of Jewishness integrated the outlook of the German Romantic 'Spinoza Renaissance' into his broader notion of Jewish purpose. His account of the 'idea of Judaism' was only lightly sketched, muted by its insertion into his wider Hegelian framework, and in the main impatiently dismissive of contemporary Jewry. His essay nonetheless set out the key conceptual and historical underpinning of the 'mission of

Israel' argument that would soon resound from synagogue pulpits in Germany and beyond.[25]

The main driving force behind the Verein was Eduard Gans (1797–1839), who was its president from 1821. One of Hegel's most lauded students, Gans was a leading figure in bringing his teacher's philosophy into closer engagement with political economy.[26] Despite his practical and even proto-materialist orientation, however, Gans shared with other members of the Verein a firm belief that the Jews possessed a unique spiritual role in human history. His central emphasis was on the idea of unity. The Jews, he declared in his second presidential address to the society, had been 'appointed to guard the idea of the oneness of God'. The special relationship of the Jews with unity had, he argued, unfortunately been sustained through history not in intellectual or political but in economic terms. After the loss of their ancient political independence, the Jews had become isolated as a distinct commercial class, replacing their former constitutional unity with an artificial and suffocating economic unity. The task of the present, Gans proclaimed, was to bring to an end the isolation of the Jews, so that they could join the increasing tide of unification in Europe.[27]

What would this union mean for the future of European Jewry? On this question Gans is delicately ambiguous:

> The wealth of its particularities is the very source of Europe's strength, and it can neither scorn it nor have too much of it. No particularity will ever harm Europe; only the autonomous rule of this particularity and its exclusive law must be abolished; it must become a dependent particle among the many. They who see no third alternative between destruction and conspicuous separation . . . have neither understood their age nor the question at hand. This, however, properly understood, is the consoling lesson of history: that everything passes without perishing, and everything remains even though it has long been consigned to the past. That is why neither can the Jews perish nor Judaism dissolve; in the larger movement of the whole they will seem to have disappeared, and yet they will live on, as the river current [*Strom*] lives on in the ocean.[28]

Addressing his peers less than three years after the anti-Jewish 'Hep! Hep! riots' in many German towns in 1819, to which he alludes directly in this lecture and perhaps indirectly in this quotation, Gans is clearly mindful of the destructive threat to Jewish existence, and keen to speak out against it. He nonetheless here suggests, in keeping with his wider hostility to all religiosity, that the time of Judaism was emphatically in the past. Judaism will not 'dissolve', however, but endure 'as the river lives on in the ocean'. Gans's fluvial metaphor has long been intensively debated.[29] When a river flows into an ocean it seems precisely to dissolve, losing any trace of its separateness. Gans associates the Jews, though, with the current of the river—its motive force—which diffuses, he suggests, throughout the ocean. Echoing and extending Hegel's ascription of 'boundless energy' to Jews, Gans imbues his vision of the universalist future with an invisible but nonetheless pervasive Jewish animating presence.

The members of the early *Wissenschaft* circle challenged the lack of serious historical attention given to Judaism in German intellectual culture in the 1820s. However, they assented to the dominant view that the time of Judaism had passed, and that its religious rituals were now obsolete. For traditionally religious Jews, such a dismissal could not be accepted. It is therefore perhaps not so surprising that the most assertively Jewish engagement with Hegelian thought on this point came from the more culturally conservative demographic heartlands of eastern Europe. The philosophical autodidact Nachman Krochmal (1785–1840) wrote his *Guide for the Perplexed of Our Time* in the 1830s in Galicia: a region beyond which he never travelled, and where the large local Jewish communities were riven by the rivalries between Hasidic, maskilic and traditionally observant camps. Krochmal responded to this local mood of crisis and 'perplexity' by seeking to establish a sense of meaning and unity in Jewish history.[30] Seduced by Hegel's historicism, which he had studied in detail, Krochmal profoundly rejected Hegel's view of Judaism as obsolescent. History, he argued, in Hegelian fashion, was shaped by the rise and fall of successive civilizations and nations. Israel, however, was an exception to this rule, as it alone was eternal, living through not just one but repeated cycles of growth, flourishing and decay. The history of the Jews, chosen by God as guardians of the 'absolute spirit', and promised in return eternal life and divine protection, is the history of this supreme idea: 'through it we have become teachers of the great multitude of nations; through it we continue to exist to this day; and with it we shall arise and be forever redeemed'.[31]

Krochmal's opus was written in Hebrew, and remained incomplete and unpublished during his lifetime. It finally appeared in 1851, thanks to the editorial efforts of Leopold Zunz, the most committed scholar of the Berlin *Wissenschaft* circle.[32] The influence of Krochmal was therefore limited. However, a simultaneous religious turn to history was also afoot in Germany, under the aegis of the Reform movement. Reformed services were first held in Berlin, from 1815 to 1823, and more enduringly in Hamburg, where worship at the 'New Israelite Temple Association' commenced in 1818. At first these innovations spread only gradually, but by the beginning of the 1840s a self-conscious Reform movement had emerged, engaged in intense battle with their traditionalist adversaries (who became known as the 'Orthodox'), and developing new arguments for the continued significance of Judaism in the modern world.[33] Unlike Krochmal, the early thinkers associated with German Reform Judaism were oriented outward as much as inward. They sought to imbue Jews with a sense of pride and purposiveness as adherents of a minority religion living alongside Christians in harmony and mutual respect. They shared with Krochmal, however, an insistence on the fundamental purity of Judaism, and an emphasis on of the wider purpose of Jews as spiritual teachers of others.

The early scholar-rabbis of German Reform continued the attempt, initiated by the essentially secularly oriented members of the Verein, to reclaim for Judaism an unambiguously positive and enduring association with the key Hegelian notion of 'spirit'. This aspiration was immediately evident from the title of the first major historical tome in this tradition, by Salomon Formstecher (1808–89). In his *Religion of the Spirit* (1841), Formstecher argued that Judaism was the religion of the self-consciousness of spirit. Whereas Hegel had argued that only through Christianity could the preliminary Jewish understanding of spirit be taken forward in history, Formstecher cast Judaism and Christianity, as well as Islam, as allied religions in the advance of the spirit over pagan idolatry. It was in Judaism, however, that the purest understanding of spirit was preserved. In the final chapter of his book, Formstecher elaborated at length on 'the mission of Judaism to humanity', which was to spread this understanding throughout the world. While the inward life of Judaism guarded the purity of this truth, Christianity and Islam, 'the northern and the southern missions of Judaism to pagan humanity', engaged at the frontline of this spiritual dissemination.[34] Formstecher thus repositioned Judaism in the Hegelian understanding of history, presenting the older religion as the spiritual power behind Christianity rather than its obsolete prelude. Judaism on this account was necessarily aloof from the missionary labour of spreading higher religious insight, while remaining the indispensible origin and inspiring exemplar of this central dynamic of human progress.

For Formstecher's rabbinical colleague Samuel Hirsch (1815–89), the most crucial element in this process of spiritual advancement was recognition of the idea of freedom. This, he argued, was the kernel of the truth that God had entrusted to the Jews. In his *Religious Philosophy of the Jews* (1842), Hirsch offered his own revision of the Hegelian historical schema, in which, like Formstecher, he contrasted Judaism, in association with Christianity, with the spiritual weakness of paganism. His central contrast was of 'active' Judaeo-Christian versus 'passive' pagan religiosity. Abraham, he argued, was the first individual in human history to fully recognize and actively exercise human freedom, in his argument with God, almost immediately after the forging of the covenant, over the collective punishment of the people of Sodom. This established Abraham as 'the role model of true and absolute religiosity'.[35] God has created humanity for freedom—and it was the historical purpose of the Jews to sustain and disseminate this fundamental truth.

Hirsch cast the mission of the Jews in powerfully messianic terms. The final section of his book is devoted to the messianic era, when evil will finally be defeated, and 'absolute religiosity' will be attained. As 'the bearers of messianic truth', the mission and 'unique calling' of the Jews is to prepare the world for this ultimate era.[36] Hirsch repeatedly intoned from the pulpit that God had chosen the Jews, as a priestly nation, to bring all peoples ultimately to God.[37] This was, he stressed, a lonely and onerous task. The Jews' insistence on freedom and their rejection of evil inevitably provoked the resentment and even the hatred of others, who sought an easier accommodation with the imperfections of the present.[38] The status of Judaism in the messianic era was a point of disagreement and sometimes ambiguity among these early Reform thinkers. For Hirsch, the Jews would retain their distinct religious practice even though all peoples would be united in one religion; according to Formstecher—echoing Maimonides—at the end of times Judaism would dissolve into universalism, its mission having been fulfilled.[39] For both rabbis, though, and for the early Reform movement more broadly, Jews in the present should take pride in fulfilling their purpose in history, which they should approach in a spirit of collaboration, rather than of rivalry or antagonism, with Christians.

As the challenge of the Reform movement to Jewish identity became increasingly controversial over the course of the 1840s and 50s, these disputes focused on the question and symbolism of Jewish separateness. The practice of circumcision proved particularly divisive. The 1844 intervention on this topic by Samuel Holdheim (1806–60)—one of the most radical early Reform rabbis—provoked widespread disquiet, as he counselled the communal acceptance (though not the endorsement) of the small number of parents at the time who refused to circumcise their sons but nonetheless sought continued inclusion in the religious Jewish world.[40] This dispute highlighted the most delicate tension negotiated by the Reform theology of Jewish mission. Reform leaders sought to emphasize the universalism of Judaism's core values, but they also stressed the importance of sustaining the particularity of the Jewish people as the guardians and teachers of those values.

The political energies unleashed by the revolutions of 1848 reinforced the idealism of Jewish mission theology. Linking this outlook to the emancipatory political hopes of the era, Holdheim proclaimed, in a noted sermon of 1853, that it was the 'destiny of Judaism . . . to pour the light of its thoughts, the fire of its sentiments, and the fervour of its feelings upon all the souls and hearts on earth'. Through the inspiration of its teachings Judaism would thus be 'the seed-bed of the nations', enabling the fulfilment of the 'messianic task of Israel to make knowledge of God and the pure law of morality of Judaism the common possession and blessing of all the peoples of the earth'. Simultaneously, however, the Jews must safeguard their own Torah. This implied a dual mission, involving two distinct understandings of Judaism: 'this, then, is our task: to maintain Judaism within the Jewish people, and at the same time to spread Judaism amongst the nations'.[41] The Jews, for Holdheim, were above all spiritual teachers and moral exemplars for the world. However, they could only fulfil this mission if they sustained their own internal rituals and traditions, while revising them in accordance with the rational and universalist insights of the modern era.

No individual did more to propagate this distinctively Reform sense of Jewish purpose than Abraham Geiger (1810–74). The most prominent early leader of the Reform movement, Geiger knitted together the various strands of thought developed by his rabbinical colleagues. He powerfully communicated a proud and detailed account of the place of the Jews in history, and a moral understanding of their significance in the present, in which he sought to renew the contemporary relevance of the biblical prophets.[42] Geiger is particularly noted for his close engagement with Christianity. The publication of David Friedrich Strauss's *Life of Jesus* (1835), which applied a historically sceptical approach to the biblical account of Jesus and interpreted his miracles as myths, provoked immense controversy in the Christian world. Strauss also destabilized conventional understandings of the relationship between Christianity and Judaism: his essentially non-historical, spiritualized approach to the New Testament distanced Jesus from the Jewish context of his life.[43] Geiger regarded Strauss's account of Jesus as profoundly flawed, but nonetheless was inspired by him to develop from a Jewish perspective a similarly source-critical approach to the past.

Using Strauss's methods of textual analysis against his conclusions, Geiger argued that Jesus was a Jewish Pharisee, preaching ideas that were entirely characteristic of his Jewish milieu in first-century Palestine. In his widely read *Judaism and its History* (1865), Geiger engaged closely with current Christian scholarship, taking on not only Strauss, who had published a revised version of his text the previous year, but also the leading French intellectual Ernest Renan (1823–92), whose bestselling *Life of Jesus* (1863) had portrayed the Christian messiah as a pioneering spiritual visionary whose teachings were in explicit contrast to the dogmatic harshness of Judaism.[44] Geiger's work has been interpreted as a Jewish reversal of the dominant vector of interpretive power, anticipating postcolonial challenges to other forms of Christian and European intellectual hegemony.[45] In insisting on the Jewishness of Jesus, however, Geiger aimed not to do battle with Christianity, but rather to renew the close association between the two religions, and to explore the roots of what he regarded as their closely allied roles in human history.

Geiger's historical reappraisal of Jesus was only a small part of the material he covered in this historical survey, which offered a commanding and detailed sweep of the entirety of the Jewish past. Although richer in detail than either Hirsch or Formstecher, and freed of their grandiloquent Hegelian rhetoric, Geiger's interpretation of Jewish history echoed the core perspectives of his Reform antecedents. Geiger also contrasted the spiritual and moral purity of Judaism to the coarseness of paganism.[46] Favourably citing Judah Halevi's analogy between the relationship of Jews to other nations and that of the heart to the other bodily organs, he declared that Judaism was 'a religion of truth', and its revelation an animating spirit for all peoples. Its message is universal, but it required a particular, tightly-knit nation, endowed with a special 'religious genius', to introduce it to the world.[47] Nonetheless, Geiger repeatedly insisted that the purpose of Judaism was extensive and for everybody: it had come into existence not simply to bring forth a new understanding of God, but 'to transfigure and enoble all human relationships'.[48] Across his historical work, Geiger described how Jews had engaged energetically with their surroundings, absorbing the best features of neighbouring cultures such as that of the Greeks, and inspiring the fundamental features not only of Christianity but also of Islam.[49]

Although the messianic dimension of Geiger's understanding of Jewish purpose is not as pronounced as for some other early Reform rabbis, this idea was unmistakably significant for him. In his enthusiastic discussion of Spinoza, in which he ascribed to him foundational importance in almost all the key intellectual advances of the modern era, he hinted that this messianic universalization of the insights of Judaism was already afoot. Spinoza, Geiger misleadingly claimed, had never abandoned Judaism, although he was not, the scholar-rabbi admitted, an 'intimate adherent' of it. Spinoza's Jewishness was connected, Geiger suggested, to his indisputable status as 'the father of a new spiritual life', who had laid the transformatory groundwork for modern philosophy and had freed humanity from many fears and superstitions.[50] Concluding the first volume of *Judaism and its History* with a look to the future, Geiger insisted that the mission of Judaism had not yet reached its conclusion. This time would ultimately come, but meanwhile the religion will continue to play its vital part in history: 'it walks with humanity on its triumphant path, and transfigures it with mild rays'.[51] Like his rabbinic peers, Geiger was stirringly optimistic, perceiving a deep harmony between the progressive spirit of the age and the forward-looking spirit of Reform Judaism. Guardians and teachers of the purest spiritual truths, the active mission of the Jews was unique and supremely important. This special role did not isolate them from others, but rather intimately allied them with the ever-strengthening forces of enlightenment and progress.

The idea of Jewish mission was not the sole preserve of Reform Judaism. Indeed, one of its earliest and most sharply focused formulations came from the foundational thinker of modern Orthodox Judaism in Germany, Samson Raphael Hirsch (1809–88). In Hirsch's most noted work, *Nineteen Letters on Judaism* (1836)—written before the intense rabbinical quarrels of the 1840s and 1850s in which he confronted his Reform adversaries (including his contemporary namesake Samuel Hirsch)—a central theme is the mission of Israel to proclaim and exemplify devotion to God. This was, Hirsch declared, an arduous mission, requiring the renunciation of the worldly temptations to which the rest of humanity had largely succumbed. Tested, tempted and thereby strengthened in exile, the Jews brought the truths of true religion to all the peoples of the world: 'it is written with Israel's heart-blood upon all the pages of history that there is but One God, and that there are higher and better things for mankind than wealth and pleasure'. Ultimately, however, the noble suffering of Israel will come to an end, having achieved its purpose. Citing at length the irenic prophecies of Isaiah, Hirsch looked forward to a utopian future when all humanity, 'refined and purified by Israel's teachings and Israel's example', will turn to God, and Israel's mission will have been accomplished.[52]

In Hirsch's later writings, the idea of universal Jewish mission receded in prominence, as he focused more on his intra-Jewish defence, in response to the challenge of the Reform movement, of the unmodified observance of Jewish law. Nonetheless, the mission of Israel remained a cornerstone of his thought, and of his participation in those debates. True Judaism, Hirsch argued, could not be restricted to the sphere of religion, because its proper observance penetrated all aspects of life. This lived unity was vital in enabling Jews to fully inhabit, as Jews, the universalism of their mission to mankind. In Reform Judaism, Hirsch argued, the idea of 'allying' religion to progress—which was indeed central to the worldview of Geiger and others—was based on a division between these two realms, and on a false demand for the validation of the former by the latter. In Hirsch's vision, however, Judaism already encompassed universalism, and therefore required neither adjustment nor justification in order to thrive in the modern era.[53] Although he echoed the Reform movement's insistence on the compatibility between Judaism and the modern era, his approach bequeathed to modern Orthodoxy a greater emphasis on continuity rather than change, and on Jewish intellectual self-sufficiency rather than alliance with other like-minded spiritual and political movements.

The mission of Israel was also asserted beyond Germany. The idea occupied a particularly important place in the eccentric but influential thinking of Elijah Benamozegh (1822–1900), rabbi of the major Italian Jewish community of Livorno. Benamozegh developed an elaborate theory of the universalism of Judaism, which he sought to harmonize with a positive appreciation of global religious pluralism, considering not only paganism, Christianity and Islam but also Hinduism and Buddhism. While respecting and valuing this pluralism, Benamozegh, like Geiger and others, claimed for Jews a special 'religious genius', and cast their priestly mission as consisting not only in adhering to the purity of their religious understanding, but also in crucially holding together the deeper unity between the particular and the universal, or, as he expressed it, between 'Israel and Humanity'.[54]

Benamozegh, however, was an unusual case. Also a learned kabbalist, he wrote extensively on the harmony between the Jewish mystical tradition and his wider philosophical outlook. He was severely criticized by other leading Italian rabbis, while his leading disciple was a French non-Jew, Aimé Pallière.[55] He was also a fervent patriot, asserting the exceptionality of Italy, just as nineteenth-century German, British and French Jewish leaders trumpeted their devotion to the nations in which they lived. These various attempts to insert the Jews into the various European ideologies of national purpose and cultural superiority were, however, inevitably somewhat strained, as Jews could only claim a subsidiary importance to the dominant national cultures of their home nations. In the United States of America this was not the case. It is not surprising, therefore, that it was across the Atlantic that the idea of Jewish mission flourished most readily.

In mid-nineteenth-century America the idea of national mission was extremely potent, but its meanings were both much more open and much more contested than in any European country. In this young nation, a sense of divine chosenness was a fundamental underpinning of a widely held collective belief in American exceptionalism, universalism and historical destiny. The Jews' uniquely venerable notion of their own designated mission, particularly when articulated in the German Reform tradition as devoted to the diffusion of universal truths to all humanity, therefore nested extremely comfortably within this broader national sense of divine election.[56] The early leaders of American Reform clearly recognized the hospitality of this environment for their project, which they were able to develop much more boldly than in Europe. For David Einhorn, who like most Reform rabbis until the late nineteenth century was born and trained in Germany, America was 'the land of the future', and the ideal ground for the advancement of the Jews' divine mission.[57] This optimism is evident in the epigraph of this chapter, from his inaugural American sermon in 1855. The immense and ever-increasing significance of the mission of Israel, Einhorn told his new Baltimore congregation, should be confidently taught to children, and its divinity further confirmed by its flourishing advancement in the freedom of the American environment.

Einhorn soon discovered, however, that the embrace of American freedom was not so straightforward. Like Samuel Hirsch—who later also crossed the Atlantic and joined him as a leading figure in American radical Reform—Einhorn placed great emphasis on freedom as a core value of Judaism. In 1861, at the moment of the outbreak of the American Civil War, Einhorn preached powerfully against slavery, identifying it with Israel's implacable enemy, Amalek. A riot broke out in response to his sermon, forcing him to flee from Maryland, which was bitterly divided between the Union and Confederate camps, to the firmly anti-slavery city of Philadelphia. There Einhorn continued to rail against slavery, both in its literal form and as metaphor for the wider perils—materialist 'enslavement of conscience' and Christian supremacist 'enslavement of spirit'—that in his opinion threatened America at the time. Einhorn's political courage, however, did not become the rabbinical norm. After the Civil War, appeals to the moral loftiness of Israel's pedagogical mission remained a stock theme in Reform sermons, but rabbis tended to avoid associating this with political specifics that might divide their congregations.[58]

As in Germany, in America also the Reform movement struggled to find agreement on the appropriate extent and means of maintaining Jewish separateness alongside its commitment to the universalism of the Jewish mission.

At the 1869 conference of Reform rabbis in Philadelphia, Einhorn and Samuel Hirsch clashed on the issue of mixed marriages: Hirsch supported blessing them, while Einhorn did not, on the grounds that this would jeopardize the cohesion and strength of the Jewish people, which needed to be sustained in order for them to fulfil their mission.[59] Defending separateness while simultaneously affirming universalism was by this time emerging as the central challenge for American Reform Judaism, particularly because it operated in an environment that seemed to many perilously conducive to complete assimilation. This careful balancing was evident in the seven agreed principles that emerged from the conference, which centrally affirmed the distinct messianic mission of Israel while rejecting Jewish separation from others. 'The messianic aim of Judaism', the rabbis affirmed, 'is not the restoration of the old Jewish state', which would suggest 'a second separation' of the Jewish people. The aim of their priestly mission was, on the contrary, 'the union of all men as children of God', and their dispersal around the world was not a punishment but a necessary enabler of their divine purpose 'to lead the nations to the true knowledge and worship of God'.[60]

The idea of the mission of Israel retained its vital force for the remainder of the nineteenth century and beyond. Einhorn and Samuel Hirsch both sought to relate the idea not only to Christianity and Islam, but also to scholarship on Buddhism, Hinduism and other non-Western religions.[61] At the Chicago 'World's Parliament of Religions' in 1893, the idea figured prominently in Reform Jewish contributions to this landmark event of religious encounter between East and West.[62] Over the second half of the nineteenth century, however, the cultural authority of all religions was profoundly buffeted by numerous challenges, not least those arising from the impact of Darwin. This religious conception of Jewish purpose in the world therefore increasingly competed and also cross-fertilized with other notions of Jewish purpose that were rooted, to varying degrees, in a secular understanding of the dynamics of society.

The Virtues of Hebraism

In his final years, Hegel increasingly appeared as a Christian philosopher, presenting his ideas not so much as the eclipse of religion but rather as its culmination: a revelation of the most fundamental truths of ethical life (*Sittlichkeit*) that underlay the harmony between Protestantism and the Prussian state. However, in the decade following Hegel's death in 1831, the status of religion became the central terrain of controversy among his varied intellectual disciples in Germany. Strauss's *Life of Jesus* profoundly challenged the theological assumptions of the day—but although Strauss threw into question the historicity of the New Testament, he did not seek to displace the cultural and moral authority of the biblical text. A considerably more profound challenge came from arguments that pointed in precisely that direction. The key pioneer of this 'Left Hegelian' critique was Ludwig Feuerbach (1804–72), who had already, in a famous letter to Hegel in 1828, asserted the need for a secular, this-worldly radicalization of the abstractions of Hegelian philosophy. In his *The Essence of Christianity* (1841), to much acclaim from his peers, Feuerbach fleshed out this argument. The notion of God, he here argued, should be understood as the externalization of human needs, and religion therefore ought to be interpreted in these same human terms, as 'an unconscious esoteric pathology, anthropology and psychology'.[63]

This humanist rejection of the authority of religion undercut the premises on which all accounts of Jewish purpose had hitherto been based. For as long as history was understood in relation to a biblical framework, Jews were almost inescapably regarded as of past significance, and they readily maintained a messianic importance for the future also. The Christian historicism of Hegel's thought had therefore provided a hospitable philosophical idiom for nineteenth-century Jewish 'mission of Israel' theology. At the same time as these arguments were taking shape, however, another current of Hegelianism was gathering strength, which took direct aim at the biblical basis for Jewish distinctiveness and purpose. For these 'Left Hegelians', the religious terms in which Jewish difference had conventionally been understood no longer had any meaning. In what new framework, then, should Jews and Judaism be understood? Only two years after the publication of Feuerbach's foundational book of 1841, this question was addressed in detail by the most radical Left Hegelian critic of conventional religious thought: Bruno Bauer (1809–82).

Bauer started his career as a theologian, but his encounter with Hegelianism swiftly led him to an even more trenchant critique of Christianity than that of Feuerbach. The forward march of history, Bauer drew from Hegel, was toward a perfect universalization of thought. Christianity, however, *contra* Hegel, did not herald the completion of this process, but rather entrenched yet more deeply a divided human consciousness. In a sequence of works culminating in his *Christianity Exposed* (1843), which was immediately suppressed by the authorities, Bauer argued that all religions asserted their truth claims in opposition to those of others. The Christian aspiration toward universalism represented a historical step forward; however, its betrayal of that aspiration made it the worst religion of all. The ethical claims of the New Testament were not universal, but simply exclusive assertions of superiority over others: the precept from the gospel of Matthew to 'love your enemies', for example, was merely a polemical attack on the supposed ethical inferiority of the Jewish scriptures. The freedom of true universalism could only be embraced, Bauer argued, when humans fully liberated themselves from all traces of 'religious consciousness', and from the artificial and exclusionary divisions with which all religions were inescapably associated.[64]

Religion and the state were for Bauer, as for Hegel, intimately associated. Whereas Hegel saw the Prussian state as the highest expression of Christianity, Bauer argued that modern states reproduced in the political realm the exclusionary structures of religion. It was his desire to elucidate this nexus that led him to the topic of what is today his most noted and infamous text: *The Jewish Question* (1843). Bauer here rejected the terms in which the vigorous debate in Germany at the time on the civil inclusion of Jews was being conducted. The bestowal of rights to Jews as a religious minority community was not, he argued, a progressive step, as this maintained the presence of religious divisions within society. At the core of Judaism he saw a separation from others, and a sense of exclusivity, which he associated with the doctrine of divine chosenness and many aspects of Jewish religious observance.[65] True emancipation required the overcoming of all such exclusivity: Jews and Christians will only be able to consider and treat each other 'as men' when both groups abandon their separateness, and embrace 'the common essence of humanity as their true essence'.[66] The conversion of Jews to Christianity cannot achieve this, as Christianity is also a religion of exclusivity. Not only can Judaism and Christianity never be at peace with each other, because they both claim exclusive possession of religious truth, but the rituals of Christianity, such as baptism and the Eucharist, serve, just like the dietary laws of Judaism, to draw boundaries of exclusion and separation.[67] Jews thus cannot be emancipated as Jews, but only in the wider context of the overcoming of all the privileges and claims to exclusivity that divide humanity; an event to which, in conclusion, Bauer looks forward 'with the calm confidence of history'.[68]

Bauer's full-frontal critique of the campaign for Jewish emancipation provoked an immediate reaction, particularly from the leaders of the Jewish Reform movement, who were closely identified with that campaign. These rebuttals sought not only to defend the case for emancipation, but also to address Bauer's negative view of Judaism, and particularly his insistence that the Jews' devotion to their eternal law had placed them largely outside history, enslaved to outdated and arbitrary rules and resistant to the forces of change and progress.[69] Samuel Hirsch—the author of one of the swiftest and heftiest counterblasts to Bauer—had, in his *Religious Philosophy of the Jews* of the previous year, argued in a very similar Hegelian vein precisely the opposite: that Judaism represented the active force of freedom in human history. Hirsch's book was also, though, a critique of the static view of Judaism that was asserted at the time by traditionally observant Jews such as his namesake Samson Raphael Hirsch. The arguments of Hirsch and his Reform colleagues against this anti-historicist Orthodox position were structurally very similar to the critique that Bauer levelled against Judaism *in toto*. The relationship of Judaism to historical change was a deeply contentious issue in Jewish theological debate in the 1840s, and Bauer's text therefore posed an awkward challenge to Jewish Reform thinkers such as Samuel Hirsch.[70]

Some recent scholars, overlooking these debates, have cast Bauer as an antisemite, ranking among the first of many to transpose old tropes of Christian Judaeophobia into a secular key.[71] It is certainly true that Bauer's association of Judaism with unthinking legalism, unchanging rigidity and clannish exclusivity echoed not only Hegel's similar ideas, but a much more venerable intellectual lineage extending all the way back to Paul. Unlike both Hegel and Paul, though, Bauer subjected Christianity to a closely related critique. His grappling with Judaism can be properly understood only in the context of the wider mid-nineteenth-century debates, among Jews, Christians and secularists, on the significance of religion in general. Judaism made sense at this time in the context of a Bible-based religious historical framework. In rejecting that framework, Bauer also rejected the basis on which Jewish historical purpose was endowed with meaning. He therefore faced the challenge of developing an alternative account of the distinctiveness of Jews, and of their place in history.

The notion of a 'Jewish question' had been in vogue in Germany since the late 1830s. This phrase echoed the problematizing formulation used to refer to other debates over ethnic identities and rights, such as the 'Irish question' in Britain, and was part of the broader self-consciously interrogative fashion of the long nineteenth century, which has aptly been described as 'the age of questions'.[72] Bauer's essay, however, was the first major text to focus on this particular question, and also to do so in an influentially new way. The Jewish question, in his view, had been wrongly posed. The issue of Jewish emancipation was *not* the 'Jewish question', but a matter that needed to be subsumed within a wider 'emancipation question': the general necessity for the eradication of all forms of paternalism and privilege.[73] Although this was Bauer's primary political concern, his central focus in this essay was to reframe in specific terms a narrower 'Jewish question'. This question of definition is itself, in essence, his 'Jewish question'. The question cannot refer to Jewish minority rights (which he rejects as a concept) or to the notion of any Jewish messianic role in the unfolding of history (which he equally rejects). The question must therefore, Bauer insists, be understood in entirely different terms.

Despite promising to pose the question in its proper terms, Bauer does not clearly do so. The central chapters of his essay do, however, attempt to sketch out an alternative, non-political and non-theological approach to Jewish difference. Highlighting Jewish legalism and exclusivity as the hallmarks of a broader Jewish particularity, he gropes for an alternative explanation for this pronounced and persistent distinctiveness. While not explicitly defining his overarching approach to this issue, Bauer repeatedly falls back on the distinctive character of Jews. He refers repeatedly to their stubbornness and rigidity, and most of all to their tenacity (*Zähigkeit*), for which he notes they have been widely but wrongly praised. It is above all due to their tenacious clinging to their laws and traditions, he argues, that the Jewish collective spirit became so resistant to change, and the Jewish people therefore separated from the progressive unfolding of history.[74] Hegel himself, as we have seen, had over the course of his career shifted focus from the millenarian significance of Jews to the distinctive social characteristics that he associated with them. Bauer, in comprehensively rejecting any role for religion in the unfolding of human history, pushed this shift further. The only remaining possible frameworks for understanding Jewish difference within Bauer's schema were secular and social.

By the early 1840s, there was indeed an established European tradition of associating Jews with particular positive characteristics. Following the mid-eighteenth-century lead of Lessing's *The Jews*, a number of writers, such as the English novelist Maria Edgeworth in *Harrington* (1817), had presented self-consciously counter-stereotypical depictions of benevolent and virtuous Jews.[75] Under the influence of Romanticism, however, Jews were increasingly considered not only in relation to ethical abstractions, but also in sentimental terms. Both Herder and Hegel, among others, perceived a particular spiritual intensity in the poetry of the Hebrew psalms. Admiration for Jewish fortitude in the face of suffering was particularly widespread: this sentiment was also present in Hegel's writings, and was given considerable prominence by many Jewish thinkers influenced by him. These associations also shaped the enthusiasm of the German Romantics for Spinoza, whom they saw not as an icon of atheistic rationalism, but as a figure of noble virtue and divine feeling. In his *On the*

History of Religion and Philosophy in Germany (1835), Heinrich Heine (1797–1856), by that time a nominal convert to Protestantism but still ubiquitously perceived as a Jewish writer, placed Spinoza at the heart of his account of the German cultural tradition. The great philosopher became, in Heine's evocative historical narrative, the central emblem of the Jewish essence and origins of the Christian values of ethical purity and heroic suffering: 'It is known that Spinoza's life was utterly beyond reproach, as pure and unblemished as the life of his divine cousin, Jesus Christ. Like him, Spinoza suffered because of his teachings; like him he wore a crown of thorns. Wherever a great spirit articulates its thoughts, *there* is Golgotha.'[76]

The greatest early nineteenth-century influence on the representation of Jews, though, and indeed on the representation of the past in general, was Walter Scott (1771–1832). Effectively the inventor of the historical novel, Scott followed his pioneering early *Waverley* novels with his immensely successful *Ivanhoe* (1819), a vividly romantic portrayal of the internal conflicts of twelfth-century England, which played a major role in establishing the Victorian fascination with medievalism. Scott's readers responded with particular intensity to the novel's female protagonist: the beautiful Jewess Rebecca, who heals, consoles and wins the love of the eponymous knightly hero, but finally renounces that love. Her sacrifice enables Ivanhoe to marry the Saxon princess Rowena in a union that symbolically reconciles the Saxons with their Norman overlords, bringing unity and peace to the English realm.

Rebecca's apparent virtues are multiple: she is magnanimous, modest, peaceable and wise. Her most significant overarching characteristic, however, is precisely the one that Bauer strove to cast as a Jewish defect: her tenacity. This is exhibited in her withstanding of the lascivious attentions of a Norman Templar, and in her gentle rejection of the attempt by Rowena, at the end of the novel, to convert her to Christianity. Frustrated by Rebecca's resistance to his seduction, the Templar accuses her of being the personified concentration of the obstinacy of her race, but Scott's authorial voice presents this same racialized characteristic in positive terms, as 'passive fortitude'.[77] Rebecca's tenacious commitment to Judaism over Christianity is more emotionally complicated, injecting a disruptive note into the novel's otherwise happy resolution. Rebecca responds to Rowena's conversionist overture, made just after her wedding to Ivanhoe, with the announcement that she will that night leave with her father for Granada, where life under Muslim rule offers greater security for her people. The novel does not suggest any theological endorsement of her decision, but it is clearly presented as courageously loyal and also movingly sad. The separation of the two women is painful for both of them, and also serves as a reminder that England, even at this moment of newly established peace under 'Good King Richard', remained a country prone to intolerance and violence.[78]

The historical challenge faced by the Saxons in *Ivanhoe* mirrors that of the eighteenth-century Scots in Scott's *Waverley* (1814) and other novels. The Highland Scottish resistance to the dominance of the Lowlanders and to the Union with England was, in Scott's eyes, valiant and romantically seductive, but nonetheless wrong: the Union represented the positive and inexorable advance of progress. The Saxons of England were similarly divided in their response to the Norman invaders, but at the end of *Ivanhoe* they reach an acceptance of their necessary fusion with them. In this context, Rebecca's steadfast adherence to Judaism represents the road not taken: a refusal of progress, rather than its embrace. As an interpreter of history, Scott was in agreement with the view of Hegel, later advanced much more forcefully by Bauer, that Jews stood outside the current of human advancement. Unlike Hegel, however, he keenly felt that this advancement came at a price. Writing in the immediate aftermath of the revolutionary and Napoleonic eras, Scott gave expression to the new historical consciousness of the European bourgeoisie, for whom the present was experienced as unprecedentedly fast-changing and unstable, and the past as a seductive but irretrievable realm of sentimental nostalgia.[79] The Jewish resistance to these forces of change, tenaciously holding fast to traditions even in the face of great consequential suffering, therefore appeared to Scott as fascinatingly and tragically alluring, even if—or rather precisely because—he believed this was an impossible option within the grander scheme of history.

Rebecca's isolation at the end of *Ivanhoe* both echoes and transposes the position of Nathan at the end of Lessing's eighteenth-century drama. Like Rebecca, Nathan renounces his own love—in his case, for his adopted daughter—and so enables an amorous plot resolution from which he is excluded. Nathan's lonely isolation at the end of the play reflects the higher universalism of his Enlightenment wisdom, which Lessing portrays as loftily transcending the personal attachments and partisanships of everyday human life. Scott's *Ivanhoe* appeared only forty years later, but at a time when such faith in reason, even if it retained philosophical vitality, was no longer artistically or emotionally compelling. Rebecca is a figure of feeling, rather than of reason; of suffering, rather than of imperviousness to subjective experience; and of alluringly embodied beauty, rather than of impersonal intellectuality. However, both Nathan and Rebecca perform similar roles as didactic figures standing outside and in a sense above the web of normal human relationships. They both also similarly stand outside time, although Scott's understanding of Rebecca's timeless tenacity incorporates an element of ambivalence that is absent from Lessing's idealized vision of Nathan.

Scott's Rebecca was the first of many virtuous and movingly suffering Jewesses to populate the nineteenth-century novel and stage. She was followed, for example, by the highly popular French opera *The Jewess* [*La Juive*] (1835), and later by the melodramatic play *Deborah*, first performed in Vienna in 1849 and attaining immense international popularity in various adaptations in the third quarter of the century.[80] These dramas inherit from Scott the presentation of the Jewess as exotically beautiful, majestically tragic, sacrificially devoted and determinedly tenacious, both in belief and in love. The shift from the Enlightenment icons of Spinoza, Moses Mendelssohn and Nathan to the nineteenth-century literary Jewess reflects the profound difference between the rationalist optimism of the earlier period and the emotional uncertainty of the subsequent era. However, these figures nonetheless all stand in a closely connected lineage of Jewish purpose. Whether their hallmark is masculine universal wisdom or feminine tenacity and intensity of feeling, they represent the extremity and timelessness of Jewish exemplarity, projecting a vision of individual virtue that stands outside the bounds of normal possibility.

Jews were no less subject to pangs of nostalgia than their non-Jewish contemporaries, and possibly more so, given the exceptional rapidity with which many of them had moved from a Yiddish-speaking world of religious traditionalism into the bourgeois culture of the nineteenth-century metropolis. Whatever their actual feelings toward the world they had left behind, however, the association of Jews with attachment to the past placed them in prime position to narrate and retail this nostalgia to wider audiences.[81] The composer of *The Jewess*, Fromental Halévy, was Jewish, though not his librettist; so was the original author of *Deborah*, Salomon Mosenthal, though not most of its adapters: both the production and the consumption of the Jewish past were broadly shared cultural endeavours.

The popular literary genre of the 'village tale' was pioneered in the 1840s by two Jewish writers—Berthold Auerbach in Germany and Alexandre Weill in France—who depicted the fast-vanishing world of both Jews and non-Jews in the small rural communities either side of the Rhine.[82] The pioneering French Jewish novelist Eugénie Foa, most notably in her tragic historical romance *La Juive* (1835)—sharing both its title and its year of publication, but not its plot, with Halévy's opera—imitated Scott's lushly oriental depiction of Jewish womanhood, and its virtuous association with both religious and amorous commitment. Jewish tenacity is here presented both positively and negatively. The heroine's love for a Christian man is cruelly obstructed by her father, a coldly religious banker, who inflexibly insists that his daughter's contracted betrothal to a Jew must be honoured. However, in contrast to her father's stereotypical personification of legalistic Jewish obduracy, Foa's protagonist personifies a contrastingly positive version of Jewish tenacity, demonstrated above all in her unwavering commitment, despite the tragic ostracism and death to which it leads her, to her love.[83]

The most successful Anglo-Jewish exponent of the idealized virtue of the Jewess was Grace Aguilar (1816–47). Also heavily influenced by Scott, Aguilar's historical fictions focused on the suffering of the clandestine crypto-Jews under the oppression of the Iberian Inquisitions. Her emphasis, once again, was on the steadfast tenacity with which these Jews adhered to their religion, in the face of intense conversionist pressures and to the point of martyrdom. Aguilar was equally influenced, however, by the writing of English evangelical Protestants, many of whom were women and ranked among her most enthusiastic readers and supporters. The evangelical literature of the period frequently dissected Judaism in gendered terms, criticizing the unfeeling legalism of Jewish men, while regarding Jewish women, suffering under their oppression, as highly spiritual and much more amenable to sincere conversion. Aguilar's novels, although written in explicit opposition to Christian conversionism, presented a similar, quasi-Protestant image of Jewish female religiosity. Her portrayal of the domesticity and authentic piety of domestic crypto-Judaism, set in contrast to the ritualistic flamboyance of Spanish Catholicism, echoed the Evangelicals' self-image in contrast to High Church Anglicanism.[84] In their reading of Aguilar, and in their desired and imagined intimacies with Jewish women more broadly, these early Victorian Evangelicals in a sense reprised the enthusiasm of millenarian Protestants for the readmission of Jews to England two centuries earlier, with Aguilar in a similar role to Menasseh ben Israel.

In Aguilar's posthumous and extremely successful *Vale of Cedars* (1850), the plot of which echoes *Ivanhoe*, this cross-confessional affinity between feminine 'religions of the heart' is given expression above all through the intensity of female friendship. The passionate intimacy between the novel's crypto-Jewish heroine, Marie Morales, and Queen Isabella of Castile—inventively depicted by Aguilar as at heart an opponent of the Inquisition, and thus rendered an amenable figure of identification for her evangelical readers—repeats and surpasses the relationship between Rebecca and Rowena in *Ivanhoe*. Like Rowena, Isabella attempts to convert her cherished Jewess, but is politely though firmly rebuffed. Unable to protect Marie from the Inquisition, Isabella then arranges for her to flee from Spain. Before she reaches the border, Marie dies in the arms of her English Christian beloved, whom she has also spurned due to her steadfast commitment to her Jewish faith. At this moment, though, Isabella is at least as much in her thoughts. 'Her creed condemns, but her heart loves me', Marie murmurs in almost her final words, beseeching her beloved to tell the Queen 'that we shall meet again, where Jew and Gentile worship the same God'.[85] This quasi-millenarian reminder of the universal truth ultimately under-lying both Christianity and Judaism underscored the connection between the loving bond of these two women and the deeper universal significance of Juda-ism. Both for Aguilar and for her Protestant readers, Marie's tenacious and unwavering loyalty—to her ancient religion, and to the spirit of love that lay at its heart—represented the unchanging core truth that lay also at the heart of Christianity and of the universal credo that would ultimately unify all humanity.

The feminization of Jewish virtue reflected the prominence and even pre-dominance of women as both writers and readers of the novel, which was the primary medium through which this ideal was developed and transmitted. The genre of philosophical history was, by contrast, almost exclusively male. While men argued in a Hegelian idiom over the significance of Jews in the unfolding of human history, women were mostly much more interested in the moral and emotional resonance of Jewishness. In the post-Napoleonic period, it became increasingly clear that there would not be a swift or straightforward fulfilment of the quasi-millenarian transformatory expectations of the revolutionary era, or of the attenuation or even dissolution of Jewish difference that had been widely seen as emblematic of that transformation. Against this background, the ideal of Judaic virtuous tenacity provided a powerful alternative configuration for Jewish purpose, particularly appealing because of its imagined timelessness, and readily amenable to fictional representation. For many women, still largely restricted to the sidelines of the drama of historical change, this non-historical, intimate and domestic vision of Jewish purpose resonated with their own lives and concerns. The figure of the valiantly stoical, intensely feeling and spiritu-ally tenacious Jewess implicitly connected all women with the unchanging val-ues of loyalty and love, underscoring the venerable roots of these values in the Old Testament and linking them directly to an irenic ecumenical vision of fe-male harmony in the present and future.

For some male writers, however, and particularly for Jewish male writers, the exclusion of Jews from history was a more vexed matter.[86] Victorian masculinity was necessarily 'active', and any rehabilitation of the Jewish man therefore required his reinsertion into the thrust of historical change. By far the most vivid early Victorian attempt to do this was by Benjamin Disraeli (1804–81). Despite his baptism at the age of twelve, Disraeli was intensely proud of his Jewish ancestry, and embraced the public perception of him as a Jew in British political and cultural life. In his 'Young England' trilogy—*Coningsby* (1844), *Sybil* (1845) and *Tancred* (1847)—Disraeli gave novelistic expression to his political vision of neo-feudal traditionalism combined with socio-economic reform: a fusion he achieved in large part through the binding agent of Jewish male intellect and energy.[87] In *Coningsby*, a *Bildungsroman* tracing the youth and entry into politics of a reform-minded aristocrat, the main influence over the novel's eponymous hero is Sidonia, a mysteriously charismatic and supremely successful Sephardic Jew. 'The greatest capitalist in the kingdom', Sidonia is also an intellectual genius with a vast network of international contacts, and a unique sharpness of insight: guests at an elite gathering at Coningsby's family seat concur that 'Sidonia is the only man who tells one anything new'.[88]

Sidonia returns in *Tancred*, in which he is again a crucial formative influence over that novel's youthful and aristocratic eponymous hero. Sidonia facilitates and finances Tancred's visit to the Holy Land, where in the romantic setting of Jerusalem by moonlight the young hero grasps the indomitable strength of Judaism, and the triumph of its message through its descendant religion, Christianity: despite the destruction of the Jewish Temple by Titus, 'the God of Abraham, of Isaac, and of Jacob is now worshipped before every altar in Rome'.[89] In relation to politics in *Coningsby* and religion in *Tancred*, Sidonia dispenses a unique clarity and profundity of insight. Disraeli's thoroughly masculine and homosocial representation of Jewish brilliance and insight is outwardly the diametric opposite of the literary figure of the virtuous and loving Jewess: Sidonia's heart is unmoved by individuals, and the only human quality that interests him is intellect.[90] However, at the core of his character there lies, once again, an unyielding and awe-inspiring tenacity. The loyalty and devotion of Scott's Rebecca and Aguilar's Marie is transposed by Disraeli into the toughness, unwavering self-confidence and all-conquering genius of Sidonia—but all three characters are similarly compelling representations of the invincible and inspiring strength of the timeless values that these authors sought to associate with the Judaic root and essence of European civilization.

A rather different attempt to write historical fiction incorporating a dynamic understanding of the place of Jews in history was made by another prominent baptised Jew of the same generation: Heinrich Heine. In his *Rabbi of Bacherach*

(1840)—conceived and begun in the early 1820s, before his conversion and in-spired by his involvement with the *Wissenschaft des Judentums* association—Heine attempted to apply Scott's literary approach to the late medieval history of Rhineland Jewry. In 1840, Heine found himself unable to complete the work, and published it as a fragment.[91] His Romantic evocation of Jewish steadfastness in the face of persecution and suffering was not lacking in emo-tional power, but it sat uneasily alongside his own uncertain relationship to the Jewish past. Heine's fictional forays into Jewish history had little impact; much more influential was his analytical approach to Jewish distinctiveness and signifi-cance. Also in 1840, in his memorial essay for yet another baptised Jew, Ludwig Börne (1786–1837), Heine introduced a new paradigm for thinking about Jewish virtues: the dichotomy between 'Jews' and 'Hellenes'. Conflating Christians with Jews, and often using the term 'Nazarene' to cover them both, he divided the world into two personality types: 'all men are either Jews or Hellenes; men with ascetic drives, hostile to images, and addicted to spiritualization, or men with a realistic nature, with a cheerful view of life, and proud of evolving'.[92]

Heine and Börne were both political radicals from prominent German Jew-ish banking families, but their relationship was more one of rivalry than friend-ship. Drawn to Paris by the July Revolution of 1830, and then remaining there in political exile, Börne established himself as a leading communicator of French political radicalism to German readers. Assuming the mantle of a Jewish apos-tle of true freedom and cosmopolitanism, he responded defiantly to the ethnic chauvinisim of German nationalists. Evoking his childhood confinement within the Jewish ghetto in Frankfurt, he proudly declared that 'because I was born into servitude, I love freedom more than you do . . . [and] because I was born with-out a fatherland, I yearn for a fatherland more fervently than you'.[93] Heine was disdainful of Börne's increasing radicalism in the 1830s, and was also discom-fited by Börne's unabashed association of his distinctive Jewish perspective with a purer political consciousness. In his memorial essay, Heine cast Börne's relentless political earnestness as an expression of his 'Nazarene' asceti-cism. Heine's own self-identification, meanwhile, was with the life-affirming sensuality of Hellenism.

Heine's dichotomy to a considerable extent unshackled the 'Jewish' category from actual Jews. 'Jews', he declared, could be Athenian-born descendants of Theseus, while the 'republican virtue' of Börne and his ilk was akin to the 'thirst for martydom' of the early Christians.[94] Heine repeated, however, the familiar Hegelian contrast between the ahistorical rigidity of Judaism and the more posi-tive, and fundamentally un-Jewish, embrace of human progress. His playfully semi-ironic schema cast not only Judaism but also Christianity as negatively resistant to both beauty and the unfolding of historical change, while an idealized Hellenism stood for human-centred pleasure and progress. In the mid-1830s Heine had, as we have noted, placed a Christianized Spinoza at the heart of his account of German philosophical and religious history. This analysis, which was also provocatively semi-ironic, aligns rather than conflicts with the philhellenism of his *Börne* essay: Heine admired Spinoza as a pantheist, and enlisted him to his pagan mythologization of German thought and culture.[95] Heine was most deeply hostile to religious enthusiasm, in any form, and it was his detection of this in Börne that prompted his most scornful comments.

Börne's late writing had indeed been characterized by a quasi-messianic future-oriented militancy, most trenchantly in his translation into German of the prophetic call to arms of the socialist French Catholic Félicité de Lamennais.[96] Alluding to this, Heine commented that only Börne's death had saved him from the disgrace of converting to Catholicism.[97] Börne's messianism was, however, at least as readily associated with the prophetic tradition in Judaism—as Heine's dichotomy indeed suggested. Rather than rejecting this long-standing messianic current of Jewish political purpose, Heine sought to disassociate himself from it, and to deflect it onto others.

Almost three decades later, Heine's pairing was influentially reworked, as 'Hebraism and Hellenism', by the English poet and cultural critic Matthew Arnold (1822–88). Unlike Heine, Arnold accorded equal value to these two cultural forces, behind which, he argued in his *Culture and Anarchy* (1869), lay the fundamental activities of 'doing' and 'thinking'. Echoing Moses Mendelssohn's *Jerusalem*, Arnold defined Hebraism as above all concerned with action, particularly through the careful observation of enduring religious precepts. Hellenism aspired, in contrast, 'to see things as they really are', seeking a full and mobile understanding of the universe; it was governed by a 'spontaneity of conscience', and Hebraism by a 'strictness of conscience'.[98] Since the sixteenth-century triumph of Protestantism, England had been dominated, Arnold argued, by the Hebraic moral earnestness of Puritanism. This had stunted the diffusion of the traditions of human-centred inquiry arising from the Renaissance, to which he urged a greater and more Hellenic openness. This did not, however, imply any denigration of the virtues associated with Hebraism, which Arnold praised fulsomely, and identified in time-honoured terms as residing above all in an uncompromising moral seriousness and tenacity. This 'strength and prominence of the moral fibre' was in Arnold's view an important link between the 'genius' of the English and that of the ancient Hebrews. The English race, he declared, inherited 'a strong share of the assuredness, the tenacity, the intensity of the Hebrews'.[99]

Between Heine and Arnold stood Charles Darwin. The publication of Darwin's *The Origin of Species* in 1859 had ushered in the 'Victorian Crisis of Faith', with which Arnold was closely associated. It is in the context of the rising challenge of scientific inquiry that we should interpret the cultural significance of notions of Hebraic virtue in the third quarter of the nineteenth century. In the preceding quarter-century the ideal of Hebraic moral tenacity had provided a compelling alternative, particularly when cast in Romantic terms as an unwavering feminine commitment to love and duty, to the Hegelian insistence on the embrace of progress. In the wake of Darwin, the biblical basis for the significance of Jewish distinctiveness was cast more deeply into question, as alternative explanations for the development of human difference, rooted in philology as well as biology, moved to the fore. The idea of Jewish ethical purpose in history, as invoked by 'mission of Israel' theology and other broadly messianic currents of thought, was also challenged by the very different temporalities suggested by advances in geological and biological knowledge. However, the timeless virtues associated with Judaism did not become any less compelling. Arnold's vision of Hebraism closely resembles that of Walter Scott. For both men, the Hebraic quality of moral steadfastness was all the more compelling because it stood at odds with the relentless and unsettling forward movement of the scientific conception of time.

Arnold's binarism shadowed a closely related pairing of 'Aryans' and 'Semites', which in this period was most prominently associated with the philological arguments of Ernest Renan. The realization that Sanskrit was closely related to the major European languages—perceived since the 1780s, and firmly established within the field of comparative philology by the 1820s—in a sense anticipated the shock-waves later created by Darwinism. For Renan, who as a Breton youth had been destined for the Catholic priesthood, it was the philological study of the Hebrew Bible that led him to lose his faith in the mid-1840s, and to devote himself to the study of the Semitic languages that were the contrasting analytical foil for the 'Indo-European'—or in alternative parlance 'Japhetic' or 'Aryan'—language family.[100] In his first major philological study, published in 1855, Renan characterized the Semitic languages—with Hebrew above all in mind—as rigidly unchanging, in contrast with the constant adaptation of Indo-European languages. He explicitly related this to the religious importance of the Hebrews, and their associated mentality, which had been moulded by their language. The Hebrews were the guardians of the unchanging and basic truths of monotheism, but were incapable of developing this beyond its infant stage.[101]

In his *Life of Jesus* (1863), Renan sought to explain how Christianity became in spirit an 'Aryan' religion, arguing that the fertility of Jesus's Galilee contrasted with the characteristically Hebraic aridity of Judea to the south, and that in any case Jesus was a profoundly unique and individual thinker, able to transcend his Jewish origins. Nonetheless, Judaism remained for Renan the indispensable, even if in some ways profoundly alien, origin of Christianity: 'Jesus proceeded from Judaism; . . . a man is of his age and his race even when he reacts against his age and his race'.[102]

Nineteenth-century philology exerted a powerful influence on other subjects, and stimulated increasing interest, particularly from the 1850s, in broader racial differences that were widely assumed to parallel those of language. Renan contributed extensively to this, and has rightly been identified as a key figure in the consolidation of the condescending assumptions of European orientalism.[103] However, while his scholarly work centred on the study of Hebrew and the Old Testament, the Jewish people were for him in important respects exceptions to the Semitic rule. In 1881, when anti-Jewish pogroms broke out in Russia, Renan joined with Victor Hugo in organizing a Parisian committee of support for Russian Jewry, and it was at this late stage in his career that he retreated, particularly in relation to Jews, from his earlier racial arguments.[104]

In his famous 'What is a Nation?' lecture (1882), Renan stressed that nations were based not on ethnicity but on a 'daily plebiscite' of willed collective destiny, and that religion was irrelevant to the matter, with Catholics, Protestants, Jews or secularists equally able to be French, English or German.[105] Most Ashkenazic Jews were in any case, he believed, probably descendants of much earlier converts to the religion, such as the Khazars. In an 1883 lecture, he expressed in detail his deep admiration for the Hebrew prophets, especially Isaiah, who had transformed Judaism from a self-interested local creed into the first truly universal religion, with the moral ideal of justice at its core. Judaism in this form became 'a banner for humanity', providing a vision for a happy future for all peoples. As a proselytizing religion for much of its history, Judaism had diffused this message.[106] And the special role of the Jews continued in the present:

> The Israelite race has rendered the world the greatest services. Assimilated to different nations, in harmony with diverse national units, it will continue to do in the future what it has done in the past. By its collaboration with all the liberal forces of Europe, it will make an eminent contribution to the social progress of humanity.[107]

The purpose of the Jews, for Renan, retained its classic messianic underlay. However, its culminating moment, marked as in so many earlier iterations of this idea by the final dissolution of Jewish separateness itself, is not deferred to the future, but is located in the Jewish alliance with progressive liberalism in the European present.

There is no figure whose attitudes to Jews and Judaism has generated more confusion and controversy than Friedrich Nietzsche (1844–1900).[108] Like Renan, Nietzsche in his early writings was casually uncritical of mid-nineteenth-century racial thinking, but in the 1880s trenchantly critiqued the emergence of populist antisemitism. The negative sentiment of *ressentiment*—vengeful and envious hostility—was, he repeatedly noted in his mature writings of this decade, most frequently and crudely directed against Jews, both in the foundational era of early Christianity and in the nationalist demagoguery of the day.[109] Jews were, however, in Nietzsche's eyes centrally responsible for the introduction of *ressentiment* into Western culture, as a consequence of the 'slave rebellion in morals' initiated by the Hebrew prophets' valorization of meekness and poverty over nobility and strength.[110] Nietzsche was thus most critical of precisely the phase of Jewish history that Renan most admired, and for precisely the same reason that Renan admired it: because it paved the way for Christianity. Nietzsche expressed admiration, however, both for pre-prophetic Judaism, with its ennobling emphasis on the divine strength of Yahweh, and for the Jews of the modern era, whom he associated with his own core values of intelligence, resilience and resourcefulness. The central virtue of the Jews for Nietzsche was, once again, their tenacity, manifested in their indomitable self-preservation even in the most extreme circumstances.[111]

Nietzsche shared Renan's hope that the Jews would continue to assimilate into European society, and also imbued this with a quasi-millenarian, albeit secular, significance. The Jews' superior qualities, he hoped, would contribute to the dilution of nationalism and to the unity, uplift and redemption of the continent.[112] Nietzsche's most detailed discussion of the place of the Jews in history is in a gnomic, and in the light of later history ominously prophetic, extended aphorism in *Daybreak* (1881):

> Among the spectacles to which the coming century invites us is the decision as to the destiny of the Jews of Europe. That their die is cast, that they have crossed their Rubicon, is now palpably obvious: all that is left for them is either to become the masters of Europe or to lose Europe as they once a long time ago lost Egypt . . . For two millennia an attempt was made to render

them contemptible by treating them with contempt, . . . and it is true that they did not grow cleaner in the process. But . . . they have never ceased to believe themselves called to the highest things, and the virtues which pertain to all who suffer have likewise never ceased to adorn them. . . . In addition, they have known how to create for themselves a feeling of power and of eternal revenge out of the very occupations left to them . . . one has to say in extenuation even of their usury that without this occasional pleasant and useful torturing of those who despised them it would have been difficult for them to have preserved their self-respect for so long. . . . They themselves know best that a conquest of Europe . . . on their part is not to be thought of; but they also know that at some future time Europe may fall into their hands like a ripe fruit . . . : then there will arrive the seventh day on which the ancient Jewish God may *rejoice* in himself, his creation and his chosen people, and let us all, all of us, rejoice with him![113]

Nietzsche's admiration for the tenacity, intellectual loftiness, self-belief and dignified suffering of the Jews integrates all the central themes of their nineteenth-century ethical heroization. In *Daybreak*, he expresses this in candidly material terms, saluting not only their inner strength but also their shrewdly targeted vengeance on their enemies. Nietzsche was keenly aware that political tensions in Europe were in the 1880s reaching a crescendo, and that this was closely related to the mobilization of animosity toward the perceived financial power of Jews. Economics was of little interest to him, but he saw very clearly that the prominence of Jews in the workings of capitalism was of crucial importance, both for their future and for that of the world as a whole. The topic of the Jews and capitalism had been attracting considerable attention since the 1840s. In the final decades of the nineteenth century, against this backdrop of political agitation, it emerged as itself one of the most prominent terrains on which the idea of Jewish purpose was rearticulated and contested.

The Jewish Ethic and the Spirit of Capitalism

In his essay of 1843, Bruno Bauer had redefined the terms of the 'Jewish question', insisting that true political emancipation did not lie in extending rights to religious minorities, but rather in liberating politics from all forms of privilege and division, including and especially those of religion. While Bauer's argument incensed liberal proponents of Jewish political inclusion, other Left Hegelian thinkers were interested in it for a different reason: as a challenge to further refine the true meaning of human emancipation. This was the ambition of by far the most famous response to Bauer: Karl Marx's *On the Jewish Question* (1844). At the outset of this essay, the young Marx (1818–83) admiringly endorsed Bauer's focus on the reformulation of this issue, declaring that 'the critique of the Jewish question is the answer to the Jewish question'.[114] Bauer's demand for the elimination of religion from the political sphere was, however, in Marx's view, inadequate. In the United States, he pointed out, this had largely been achieved, but religion, as a private matter, was if anything even more vigorous there. This demonstrated, Marx argued, that religion was a symptom and not a cause of the most fundamental social ills, which must be remedied within civil society itself, rather than at the political level of state policy. The most fundamental requirement, therefore, is not political emancipation, but 'human emancipation', necessarily defined not in political or theological but in social and practical terms.[115]

This led Marx to one of the most infamous and intensely debated pronouncements of his entire *oeuvre*:

> Let us consider the actual secular Jew, not the sabbath Jew, as Bauer does, but rather the everyday Jew. Let us not look for the secret of the Jew in his religion, but rather the secret of the religion in the actual Jew. What is the secular basis of Jewry? Practical need, self-interest. What is the secular cult of the Jew? Haggling. What is his secular God? Money. Now then! Emancipation from haggling and from money, thus from practical, real Jewishness, would be the self-emancipation of our times. . . . The *social* emancipation of the Jew is the *emancipation of society from Judaism*.[116]

Human emancipation, Marx argued, required liberation not from religion, but from the forces of social atomization that divided people and drove them into competition with each other, preventing them from sensing their natural 'species ties'. This ruthless spirit of commercialism and competition was a social phenomenon, independent from and stronger than both religion and state politics. Marx clinched this point by pointing once again to the United States, where religion had itself become a business. Bauer's attempt to explain the distinctiveness of the Jewish character in relation to their religion was therefore beside the point, as the truly significant differences between people lay in their actions in civil society. Marx used exactly the same term as Bauer to describe the central characteristic of the Jews, but offered a different explanation of it: 'The tenacity of the Jew is not to be explained by his religion, but much rather by the human basis of his religion—by practical need and egoism'.[117] It was from this egoism, and not from religion, that humanity most fundamentally needed emancipation.

Marx presents his argument as a radical secularization of the idea of emancipation. The historical account he sketches of the relationship between Judaism, Christianity and the state—which as a Young Hegelian thinker he felt instinctively compelled to provide—nonetheless draws him back to theology, and also to the familiar themes of Jewish purpose. Driving his disagreement with Bauer to its fullest possible extent, Marx argues that the withdrawal of the state from religious matters, far from being an emancipatory triumph, in fact constitutes the ultimate fulfilment of Christianity. In the United States, where this has already happened, religion serves only to alienate people both from each other and from the state. This brings about the absolute domination of human self-estrangement, and renders Christianity in practical terms indistinguishable from Judaism. At this point, however, the 'anti-social' nature of civil society 'must necessarily be dissolved': this final triumph of the egoistic essence of Judaism, through the privatization of Christianity, also heralds the collapse of the old order and the advent of true human emancipation.[118]

Marx here clearly echoes the classic Pauline oppositions of the literal to the figural and the material to the spiritual. Jewish difference, for Marx as for Paul, represents the quintessence of particularity. It retains its significance as a marker of particularist extremity even when historically eclipsed by Christianity, its final erasure occurring only at the moment of transition to a new humanist order. Beneath his secularizing rallying call, then, Marx rearticulated the messianic logic that had structured the thinking of so many earlier thinkers, in casting the Jews, once again, in the crucial purposive role of agents and indicators of the approaching transition to a better world. The Jews, for Marx, represent the egoistic kernel most fundamentally resistant to universality; but they also signal, through the diametric transformation of their self-interested particularism into its very opposite, the route to the inexorable ultimate triumph of utopian universal harmony.

On the Jewish Question has been extensively critiqued, and is widely regarded as a key text in the canon of modern antisemitism.[119] This argument is complicated by the fact that Marx was himself of Jewish descent: his attitudes to Judaism have been ascribed to his background in terms ranging from 'Jewish self-hatred' to messianic inspiration from the biblical prophets.[120] According to Karl Löwith—the most sophisticated twentieth-century exponent of a 'Jewish' reading of Marx—the redemption-oriented historical theory of Marxism (only visible in embryo in this early essay) corresponded closely with the messianic historical teleology of both Judaism and Christianity.[121] Although the interpretation of Marxism and communism as akin to a religion has become a commonplace, the more specific implications of Löwith's insight have generally been overlooked. The Jews, Marx implies, retain in his theoretical interpretation of history a special status, the key features of which are closely related to their traditional 'chosen people' designation.

Rejecting Bauer's excision of them from the forward thrust of progress, Marx restores the Jews to a position of central historical purpose. For him—as for so many earlier thinkers, from Paul to Lessing and Grégoire—the Jews stood as representatives of the fundamental essence of particularist existence, the inversion of which would mark the passage of humanity to its higher universalistic state. Christianity, as represented by Marx in his *Jewish Question* essay, was not a more sophisticated elaboration of Judaism, but rather a failed attempt to overcome the practical reality of egoistic materialism that was represented by the older religion.[122] As such, though, Judaism represented the distilled truth of unemancipated human existence, which, as Marx elaborated in his later work, could only be overthrown once it had reached full domination, when it would inevitably collapse under the weight of its own contradictions. It makes little sense, then, to ascribe the fundamental structures of Marx's view of Judaism to suppositions either of his attenuated Jewish sensibility or of his internalized anti-Jewish prejudice. The argument of *On the Jewish Question* stands directly within the long-standing common tradition of Jewish and Christian thinking on the purpose of the Jews in human history.

Marx's interpretation of Judaism was heavily indebted to Feuerbach, who in his *Essence of Christianity* three years earlier had declared that 'egoism' was the ancient religion's foundational principle. Developing Hegel's argument that Jews had been the first to perceive a clear distinction between God and nature, and linking this to his own argument that God was simply an externalization of human needs and desires, Feuerbach argued that the Jewish idea of divine providence enabled the Jews to justify the subjection of nature to their own egoistic instrumental use.[123] The concept of egoism was, however, a controversial subject among the Young Hegelians in the early 1840s. Max Stirner, in his *The Ego and Its Own* (1845), put forward a powerful critique of Feuerbach, arguing that his avowedly anti-theological rejection of individual self-interest was ungrounded, and therefore collapsed back into its own form of theological dogmatism. For Stirner, to focus on one's own personal interests was the only true escape from the gloomy and fantastical spirit-worship of religion. He therefore regarded the worldly Jews, with their imperviousness to the spiritual delusions of Christianity, as admirably close to his own unabashedly egoist philosophy.[124]

Stirner's book provoked an intense and confused reaction from Marx's intellectual circle. Engels was initially impressed, but Marx took it as an attack on his own Feuerbachian conception of human emancipation, and devoted several months to writing an extremely lengthy satirical polemic against it.[125] This excess of adversarial energy, even by Marx's standards, reflected the profound difficulties he and his associates faced as they struggled to escape from theology and to focus attention firmly on the material realities of contemporary society. The wide-ranging arguments and heated emotions generated by this issue were to a considerable extent channelled through the figure of the Jew, who—as the icon of materiality in Christian theology—most intensely embodied the challenge of separating the material and the theological realms.

Western European Jewry was at this time becoming more broadly associated with the materiality of economic forces and relations. This shift was most clearly evident in France, where, in the Restoration period from the fall of Napoleon to the July Revolution of 1830, public rhetoric concerning the Jews had been dominated by the theological insistence of the Catholic Church that they could only be incorporated into French society if they converted to Christianity.[126] Already in the 1820s, however, Jews played a significant role in envisioning the economic future of France. They were notably numerous in the Saint-Simonian movement, which put forward an alternative theology based on human love and emancipation, to be driven by a meritocratic state investing in industry, infrastructure and accessible credit institutions. A number of the leading Saint-Simonians were from Jewish banking families, and drew a connection between the legislation of the ancient Hebrews and the sophistication and philanthropic spirit of Saint-Simonian practices of commerce and credit; a similar argument was advanced by the prominent French Jewish scholar Joseph Salvador (1796–1873) in his monumental *History of the Institutions of Moses* (1828).[127] By the 1840s, Saint-Simonianism was no more, but rapid industrial and infrastructural development was in full swing, and the dislocations they caused were widely blamed on the pre-eminent banking family of the day, the Rothschilds. In the rhetoric of several French radical leaders, this spilled over into a generalized railing against the exploitative cunning and avaricious spirit of the Jews in general, who were described in one popular polemic as 'the kings of the era.'[128]

The financial might of the Rothschilds shortly before the outbreak of the revolutions of 1848 was indeed immense, as leading investors in the European railway network and creditors of rulers and regimes across the continent.[129] In the second half of the nineteenth century, as increasing numbers of Jews established themselves in western European bourgeois society, general economic development and the dramatic economic advancement of the Jews were closely connected. In Germany, where Jews constituted approximately 1% of the population, they played a prominent role in some of the most conspicuous economic transformations in this period, such as the emergence of the department store and the growth of the press, while also owning and operating well over a third of the country's banks.[130] For those who felt excluded and disoriented by the transformations of the era, Jewish prosperity, and its association with the little-understood but all-important workings of the stock market, was an obvious focus of resentment. The dramatic crash of 1873, which began in Vienna and rippled across Europe and North America, was widely blamed on Jews, fuelling a wave of hostility that by the end of the decade had consolidated into a new popular movement of political antisemitism.

The roots of modern political antisemitism have been intensively debated, and clearly lie both in deep-seated traditions of anti-Jewish prejudice and in the specific economic context of the late nineteenth century. The ideology of antisemitism was also a variant, in inverted form, of the idea of Jewish purpose. According to the German journalist and agitator Wilhelm Marr (1819–1904)—who in 1879 formed the first explicitly antisemitic political party, the 'League of Antisemites', through which this neologism was popularized—the essence of modern history was the struggle of the peoples of the West against the 'corrosive mission of Judaism', the aim of which was to bring Germany and the rest of Europe to its knees. Marr perceived the usual set of mental and cultural traits as characteristically Jewish. In his bestselling *The Victory of Jewry over Germandom* (1879), he noted the tenacity, intelligence and familial intimacy of the Jews, and ascribed to these collective qualities their current triumph over the indolent and stingy Germans. He echoed Marx, however, in arguing that the 'Jewish question' was most fundamentally socio-political in character. It was against the material power of the Jews, and particularly their alleged control of banking and the press, that he urged the Germans to fight back.[131]

Marr drew together all three of the main strands of nineteenth-century thinking on Jewish purpose: he ascribed to Jews a position of central importance in his loosely post-Hegelian schema of history, recognized in them a uniquely potent distinctiveness and toughness of character, and viewed their present significance above all in terms of their economic power. All of these, however, he cast in decisively negative terms: although he appeared more admiring of the typical personal characteristics of Jews than those of Germans, he believed that these were self-interestedly used by Jews to the detriment of the German people. The sense of German historical purpose that Marr sought to rally was defined in direct opposition to the allegedly domineering and alarmingly successful mission of the Jews.

Over the next three decades numerous other antisemitic polemicists and politicians successfully secured a popular audience by evoking the spectre of Jewish economic domination. In Austria, Karl Lueger was elected as mayor of Vienna in the late 1890s on a platform of populist opposition to the corruption of 'Jewish' liberalism and laissez-faire capitalism. In France, Édouard Drumont's *Jewish France* [*La France juive*] (1886), a major bestseller, revived the 1840s image of French Jewish bankers and business operators as deviously manipulative and ruthlessly self-interested.[132] In the terms of their own anti-Jewish objectives, these antisemitic movements were unsuccessful: neither the civic inclusion nor the economic prosperity of Jews were rolled back anywhere in western Europe. However, Jews became firmly established as the lightning rod of economic discontent and the pre-eminent symbol for the resentments, temptations, frustrations and confusions generated by the intensification of commerce and capitalism.

Bewilderment over the nature of money itself, as the immaterial and unstable repository of material wealth, was a widespread reaction to the economic fluctuations of the nineteenth century. Heinrich Heine, in his essay on Börne, had praised the Rothschilds—semi-ironically, as ever—as among the great 'levellers of Europe', because their money undermined the power of the old landed aristocracy, and replaced it with a much flimsier and therefore less pernicious financial elite: 'Money is more fluid than water, breezier than air, and we can forgive the impertinences of today's financial nobility when we consider its transience.'[133] In the wake of the crash of 1873, however, the immateriality and uncertainty of money typically bore more ominous associations, which were widely projected onto the figure of the Jew. The most suggestive example of this is perhaps the larger-than-life character of Augustus Melmotte in Anthony Trollope's *The Way We Live Now* (1875). A cosmopolitan financier of uncertain origins, reputedly able to make or break companies at will through his stock trading, and to 'make money dear or cheap as he pleased', Melmotte is uncertainty incarnate. It is not even certain whether he is a Jew, although he is a vivid embodiment of the Jewish stereotype of the day. Trollope's novel both reflected and interrogated the assumptions and anxieties behind this stereotype. His narrative highlights the fascination at this time with the immaterial unfixity of

money, and the readiness with which this could be projected onto the seemingly similarly uncertain idea of the Jew.[134] Long associated with the boundary
between the material and the spiritual, by the 1870s Jews had attained full political rights in western Europe, and their social advance and integration into
mainstream society also further blurred the boundaries between linguistic, religious, national and ethnic identities in this period of intense international
rivalry and self-conscious patriotism. Multiple uncertainties flowed together
in the antisemitic image of the Jewish financier, held together by an underlying
uncertainty over materiality and fixity itself.

For many Jewish intellectuals at this time, meanwhile, a materialist focus on
economic matters seemed to offer a promising ground for rethinking the place
of Jews in European society and history. This was particularly the case in eastern Europe and Russia, where the vast majority of European Jews lived, mostly
in modest economic circumstances. Early eastern European Jewish Marxists
such as Aaron Lieberman (1843–80) sought to marry Marx's economic analysis with the messianic and mystical traditions in Judaism. This blending of Marxism with the Kabbalah would, they hoped, draw religious Jews toward a materialist understanding of the need for a concrete transformation of the economic
relations not only between Jews and non-Jews, but also between all people.[135]
The contrastingly immaterial figure of the *luftmensch*—the 'airy' Jew, lacking
a properly grounded connection to labour and the land—became associated
by these radicals with the unhealthiness and fragility of the condition of the Jews
in Russia.[136] After the wave of anti-Jewish pogroms in Russia in 1881, these early
currents of Jewish philosophical materialism developed in various ways, flowing into Zionist thought and also into the later development of Russian and
early Soviet Marxism. Spinoza—who had long been associated, along with the
Kabbalah, with a putatively Jewish materialist philosophy—was frequently admired in this tradition as an early forerunner of Marxian 'dialectical materialism', and even repeatedly described as 'Marx without a beard'.[137]

In western Europe, however, left-wing leaders were unable to embrace a
straightforwardly materialist response to the 'Jewish question', because this had
been firmly appropriated by the antisemitic right. The scapegoating of Jews offered an alluringly simple diagnosis of the ills of modernity, which threatened
to draw away from the Left a significant tranche of their natural working-class
support base. Antisemitism was commonly described by German Social Democrats in the 1890s as 'the socialism of fools'. This phrase encapsulates why these
leftist leaders found it so difficult to articulate a powerful response to political
antisemitism: they hoped to persuade these 'fools' to redirect their hostility

against the capitalist class rather than against Jews, and therefore did not wish
to alienate them by dismissing and deriding their anti-Jewish prejudices. Many
leading German Social Democrats broadly shared the position of the influential writer Franz Mehring (1846–1919), who in 1891 staked out a position of equal
opposition to antisemitism and to 'philosemitism', which he defined as a smoke-
screen for the defence of capitalism.[138] Mehring was a strong promoter of a
'materialist' interpretation of Marxism, which he believed guaranteed its objectivity. Only true socialism, with its clear-sighted and objective analysis of the
material basis of class relations, Mehring claimed, could step clear of the ob-
fuscatory partisanships of both philo- and antisemitism.

Whereas some early Russian Marxists incorporated Jewish perspectives into
their understanding of materialism, or even implicitly placed them at its root,
for Mehring and others true materialism transcended the relatively trivial concerns of religion and ethnicity that the Jewish case brought to the fore. This
supposed escape from the 'Jewish question' was widely presented as a demonstration of the superior objectivity of socialism. However, the cultural strength
and exceptionalist logic of the idea of Jewish purpose could not be eluded so
easily. Protracted debates over antisemitism led to the issue of the relationship
of Jews to capitalism becoming a prominent testing ground for competing
claims to objectivity. Far from stemming disproportionate attention to the subject, this added an additional twist to the question of the economic role and
purpose of Jews, as it became intertwined with the more abstract issue of the
nature and purpose of objectivity itself.

The 1890s also witnessed the emergence in both France and Germany of the
new academic field of sociology, dedicated to the objective analysis and applied
mitigation of the social dislocations of modern life. The possibility of an objective, 'value free' and genuinely scientific form of social science was a central
tenet of the founders of the discipline. In Germany the leading sociologists Max
Weber (1864–1920) and Werner Sombart (1863–1941) were key protagonists in
the 'value judgments dispute' (*Werturteilsstreit*) that led to the foundation in
1909 of the separate German Sociological Association, jointly led by Weber,
Sombart and the two other 'founding fathers' of German sociology, Ferdinand
Tönnies (1855–1936) and Georg Simmel (1858–1918). All four men were, alongside their commitment to objectivity, centrally concerned with the threat
posed to human relationships by the encroachments of modern commerce.[139]
Their approach was strongly influenced by Marx, and followed the lead of Tönnies' *Community and Society* [*Gemeinschaft und Gesellschaft*] (1887), which had
posited a dichotomy between the personal interactions of community life and

the impersonality and instrumentality of modern monetary interactions. This led them to a special interest in the relationship between religion and the development of capitalism. The extended debate on this subject between Weber and Sombart highlighted the particular complexity and sensitivity of this topic with regard to the Jewish case.[140]

The starting-point of this exploration was Sombart's two-volume *Modern Capitalism* (1902): an analysis of the advance of capitalist industry in which he placed great emphasis on the rise of a new 'spirit' (*Geist*) of economic calculation, promoted by the emergence of more sophisticated monetary instruments of valuation and exchange, and driven no longer by simple need-satisfaction, but by the 'acquisitive principle'. Weber's *The Protestant Ethic and the Spirit of Capitalism* (1905) developed Sombart's analysis of the capitalist 'spirit', associating it specifically with Protestant asceticism.[141] Sombart in turn responded with his *The Jews and Modern Capitalism* (1911), which he presented as a corrective to his esteemed colleague, arguing that the traits Weber had identified with the most austere strains of Protestantism should more correctly be assigned to Judaism: he declared in summary that 'Puritanism *is* Judaism'.[142] In structural terms, however, these two texts were broadly similar, and after the First World War Weber (though not Sombart) returned to their debate, continuing to insist on the primary role of Puritans rather than Jews in the advent of industrial capitalism, but emphasizing the important contribution of Jewish asceticism and rationalism to the 'disenchantment of the world'.[143] Today, however, Weber's *Protestant Ethic* remains a central, if controversial, text of the sociological canon, whereas Sombart's text has acquired an aura of infamy. Read today, if at all, largely as an artefact in the history of antisemitism, the recoil from *The Jews and Modern Capitalism* is largely responsible for Sombart's broader disappearance from the historical consciousness of the discipline.[144]

Sombart's descent into virtual scholarly oblivion has much to do with his relationship to later events. In old age, he accommodated himself without difficulty to the rise of Nazism, and by the time of his death in May 1941 had made no clear attempt to distance himself from the regime or from its antisemitic use of his arguments.[145] The extermination taking place by then makes it impossible for us to read *The Jews and Modern Capitalism* in the same unencumbered spirit as that in which we still approach Weber's thesis. Sombart is today associated above all with the trafficking of the stereotype of the Jewish arch-capitalist, which clearly abetted the Nazi genocide. At the time of its publication, however, his study was read by many as a pro-Jewish work, despite his strenuous presentation of it as a model of the professional standards of value neutrality to which he, no less than Weber, was deeply committed. Sombart was a critic of capitalism, and so his ascription to the Jews of a key role in this economic system was in this overarching sense certainly not complimentary. However, like so many earlier writers, he repeatedly noted the tenacious single-mindedness, intellectual prowess and family-oriented sobriety of the Jews. Statements such as 'Israel passes over Europe like the sun: at its coming new life bursts forth; at its going all falls into decay' were readily cited both by Jews who welcomed Sombart's admiration and by antisemites who were fiercely critical of what they regarded as his errant philosemitic streak.[146]

While Sombart's evaluative judgment of the traits he identified as characteristic of the Jews was deliberately unclear, there was no doubt that he regarded them as exerting a hugely disproportionate historical impact. *The Jews and Modern Capitalism* stands in a long tradition of European exaggeration of the importance of Jews in finance, and in particular the inaccurate ascription to them of the invention of the crucial credit instrument, the bill of exchange.[147] It is notable, however, that Sombart drew a great deal of his material from recent Jewish historical research, which over the previous three decades had undergone a boom. His footnotes contain frequent citations to articles by Jewish amateur historians in the various European and American journals of Jewish history that had been founded in the 1880s and 1890s, as well as to works by the leading late nineteenth-century German Jewish historians Heinrich Graetz and Meyer Kayserling, and to the monumental twelve-volume *Jewish Encyclopedia* published in New York between 1901 and 1906, which he praised highly. Some of Sombart's most inflated claims for the economic importance of the Jews reflect prevalent Jewish preoccupations and perspectives. He makes much, for example, of the Jewish role in the discovery of America, writing that 'it is as though the New World came onto the horizon by their aid and for them alone, as though Columbus and the rest were but managing directors for Israel.'[148] An egregiously preposterous claim, to be sure—but one that Sombart based on the effusively celebratory literature on the Jewish contribution to the colonization of America that had emerged as part of the enthusiastic American Jewish commemorations of the 400th anniversary, in 1892, of Columbus's voyage, and the 250th anniversary, in 1904, of Jewish settlement in America.

There was a particular affinity between Sombart's work and the intensifying attempt at this time by Zionists to marshal social scientific evidence in support of their Jewish nationalist project. Sombart found a particularly rich seam of material in the recently founded journal of the leading institution of the new Jewish social science, the Berlin-based Bureau für jüdische Statistik. Arthur

Ruppin (1876–1943), the driving force behind this movement and later the early architect of Jewish settlement in Palestine, was delighted by Sombart's book, rushing out a revised version of his own *The Jews of Today* [*Die Juden der Gegenwart*] (1904), incorporating what he regarded as the considerable reinforcing evidence and authority it provided for his own 'scientific' argument for Zionism.[149]

The Jews and Modern Capitalism met with immense interest from the German Jewish community, and exposed the depth of its internal division. Sombart's promotional lecture tour drew an enthusiastic audience of younger Zionist Jews, while the mainstream community organization dedicated to opposing antisemitism, the Centralverein, discouraged attendance. Significant intra-Jewish violence erupted at at least one of these events.[150] The turn to the 'objective' study of the economic role of the Jews thus dramatically failed to establish the calm empirical consensus to which its advocates, whether Marxist activists or professional sociologists, aspired. The search for a materialist analysis of the Jews' historical function led instead to the opposite outcome, drawing the topic into the heart of the most highly contentious debates of the period over class, race, nationalism and economic justice. In the febrile intellectual atmosphere in Europe shortly before the outbreak of the First World War, the multiple stakes on the question of Jewish purpose could scarcely have been higher or more confused.

The first sociologist to ascribe to the Jews a notably distinctive place in the development of the mentality of modern capitalism was neither Sombart nor Weber, but Georg Simmel, who in his *Philosophy of Money* (1900) described them as the quintessential 'stranger' people. When the Jews first dispersed across Europe, according to Simmel's speculative history, they found all agrarian and artisanal niches in the European economy already occupied by others, and so they had no option other than to establish themselves as traders. This was an isolating role, in which their relations with others were overwhelmingly mediated by money. The vulnerability of their position, outside the more organic bonds of community, was compounded by their lack of real estate. This led them to require a 'higher risk premium' in their business dealings, in the form of higher interest rates than were generally considered acceptable in the medieval world. These monetary relations, he argued, shaped the mentality of the Jews, sharpening their logical faculties at the expense of their creative ones.[151]

In the final chapter of his book, Simmel focused on the role of money in promoting calculating, intellectual and 'supra-personal' modes of thought, which in modern society increasingly displaced more affective and emotional approaches to life. Because money and intellect are both supra-personal, he argued, they operated in tandem to bring to the fore a distanced and objective perspective on the world. The 'most brilliant example of this', he wrote, was Spinoza, whose philosophy gave expression to the most perfect objectivity of outlook: 'nowhere are the incalculabilities of individuality allowed to break through the logical-mathematical structure of the unity of the world'.[152] Simmel, like Spinoza, was a Jew who had exited the Jewish community, but was nonetheless almost universally perceived as Jewish. (In Simmel's case, both his parents had been baptised before his birth, but there are numerous recorded references to his Jewishness, and he believed that antisemitism had hindered his career.[153]) It is clear that, like many other Jewish intellectuals of the period, such as the prominent Danish critic Georg Brandes, Simmel identified with Spinoza and regarded him as a distinctively Jewish model of cosmopolitan secular modernity.[154] This reverential representation of the philosopher echoes the established Enlightenment association of him, along with Moses Mendelssohn and Lessing's fictional Nathan, with the attainment of perfect philosophical universalism.

In his influential essay on 'The Stranger' (1908), Simmel further developed his analysis of the distinctive outlook of the stranger-trader. The stranger, he here argues, is typically a trader, whose relationships with others are primarily transactional, mediated by money rather than true social intimacy. The outlook of the stranger-trader therefore becomes more rational and intellectual, which further heightens the outsider's exclusion from the affective bonds of the wider society. The Jews are for Simmel 'the classic example' of the stranger, although the commercial bustle of the modern metropolis promotes a similar outlook in all city-dwellers. His view of this social type is double-edged: their outsider perspective is valuable and intellectually impressive, but this comes at the price of a rather lonely exclusion from the connective fabric of their host society. As an outsider, he noted, the stranger 'is not bound by ties which could prejudice his perception, his understanding, and his perception of data'.[155] This objectivity of perspective aligns perfectly with Simmel's own professional commitment to 'value free' social science. His argument subtly suggests that Jews are likely to make the best sociologists—and perhaps particularly baptised Jews such as Simmel, who were outsiders among both Jews and Christians.

In Simmel's figure of the Jew as stranger-trader, two of the main strands of nineteenth-century thinking on Jewish purpose are brought together. His Jewish trader is an economic figure, whose social importance is defined in terms of this material function. However, the trader readily becomes a teacher, because this economic role fosters the mental outlook of rationalism and objectivity that enables the clear-sighted explanation to others of the workings of society. Despite its apparent absolute secularism, Simmel's argument also rearticulates the fundamental messianic structure of the idea of Jewish purpose. The objective Jew—epitomized by Spinoza or by Simmel himself—transcends through this precise quality any trace of the insular particularism with which the Jewish collective had long been associated, and which was central to the antisemitic perception of Jews at this time as clannishly self-interested. The possibility of a perfectly objective understanding of society underpinned the hopes of Simmel and his sociologist colleagues for a better human future. It was, in effect, their messianic vision. Its prophets, on Simmel's account, were the stranger-trader-intellectual Jews, whose rationalism and objectivity marked their absolute overcoming of the diametrically contrasting characteristics of superstition and partisanship that were associated with their religious past, and their transformation into inspirational exemplars of the universalistic values of the future.

———

For Hermann Cohen (1842–1918), the leading German Jewish philosopher of his generation, the figure of the stranger was in an entirely different sense fundamental to the relationship of Jews to others. In his magnum opus *Religion of Reason out of the Sources of Judaism* (published posthumously in 1919), Cohen emphasized the loving and decent treatment of the stranger as the cornerstone of Jewish ethics. Critiquing the Christian interpretive tradition of the biblical exhortation to 'love your neighbour as yourself' (Leviticus 19:17–18), he argued that the translation of the Hebrew word *rea* as 'neighbour' introduced a privileging of proximity that was not only incorrect, but also undermined the ethical imperative of love being directed toward 'the other' in general, whether familiar or alien, and near or distant. Cohen reframed love of the neighbour as love of the stranger, stressing the biblical commandment that 'the stranger who sojourns with you shall be unto you as the homeborn among you, and you shall love him as yourself' (Leviticus 19:33–4). Love of the stranger, he argues, is the foundation for love of the fellow human.[156] From this flows the feeling of pity in response to the suffering of humanity, which gives rise to the ethical demand for social action, most powerfully expressed by the Hebrew prophets: 'The prophet becomes the practical moralist, the politician and jurist, because he intends to end the suffering of the poor.'[157] Rather than seeing the Jews themselves as strangers, Cohen saw them as an integral part of European and especially German society, perceiving a profound affinity between Judaism and German Protestantism. The Jews' distinctive ethical contribution, though, is in their insistence on the extension of human fellowship toward the stranger. This encompassing fellowship points the way to the overcoming of all human divisions. This is the universalist ethical mission of the Jews: they are, he argues, a 'signpost' to the messianic goal of the unity of mankind.[158]

Like Simmel, though, Cohen cast the Jews in a crucially important pedagogical role, as teachers of rational objectivity—as a committed Kantian, Cohen interpreted Judaism as the 'religion of reason' *par excellence*—and also of the theological grounding of applied ethics. Jewish law, he argued, should be considered as a 'teaching', and as its guardians the Jews were charged with diffusing the monotheistic ideal, which underpinned the universalist humanity of European culture and morality.[159] Cohen also echoed Simmel's depiction of the place of Jews in the world as a lonely and vulnerable niche. Glossing Isaiah's 'songs of the suffering servant', he describes the historical suffering of the Jews as an inescapable aspect of their 'tragic calling': their 'freely assumed suffering' demonstrates their dignity and their 'heartfelt desire for the conversion of the other peoples', and will only cease in the messianic future, when everyone 'will worship the unique God'.[160] This emphasis on tragic and dignified suffering was a familiar theme in nineteenth-century thinking on Jewish purpose, from Hegel to Nietzsche, and Cohen's association of it with the fulfilment of their pedagogic moral mission is very similar to the formulation of modern Orthodox rabbi Samson Raphael Hirsch in the 1830s.

The recounting of the Jewish past as a moving narrative of suffering was ubiquitous in the nineteenth century, but is most closely associated with the German Jewish popular historian Heinrich Graetz (1817–91), whose eleven-volume *History of the Jews* (1853–76), and its even more popular later distillations and translations, disseminated an assertively proud and passionate account of Jewish 'suffering and learning' across the ages. Graetz was a strong believer in the Jews' unique and sacred historical mission, which he, like Cohen and many others, located in their maintenance and teaching of pure monotheistic worship.[161] However, when in 1880 Cohen was stirred to defend Judaism against the antisemitic attacks of the Prussian nationalist historian Heinrich von Treitschke, he simultaneously attacked Graetz, who had been one of Treitschke's primary targets. While defending Jews in general from Treitschke's accusations of anti-German and anti-Christian chauvinism, Cohen agreed that Graetz exhibited these ugly attitudes. He condemned Graetz's historical sensibility as

'Palestinian' in character, by which he meant to capture its parochial focus on the tribal narrative and material interests of the Jews, in stark contrast to the ethical universalism of Cohen's own understanding of the meaning and purpose of Jewish history.[162]

Cohen's critique of Graetz highlights the complex entanglement of Judaism in debates on politics, national identity and ethical reasoning in the decades around 1900. Graetz's quasi-nationalist interpretation of the Jewish past reduced it, in Cohen's eyes, to a partisan account of the worldly struggles and rivalries through which the Jews had navigated their survival and material flourishing. Cohen's own non-Marxist socialist politics, based on his neo-Kantian ethical philosophy, were distinctly to the left of Graetz. Social justice, in Cohen's heart-felt opinion, was not an optional concern extraneous to Jewish communal life, but rather the outward manifestation of the ethical essence and purpose of Judaism.

Since the extermination of European Jewry, the acceptance of suffering as an intrinsic component of the Jewish mission has become almost impossible to countenance. Cohen's pronouncements on this topic in *Religion of Reason* can scarcely be read today without a shudder. The broader emphasis on suffering in Jewish history was influentially critiqued in the 1920s by the pioneer of professional Jewish history in the United States, Salo Baron, as 'lachrymose'. In recent decades, academic historians have tended strenuously to avoid the romanticization of Jewish victimhood associated with Graetz in particular.[163] Already in the late nineteenth century, however, many Jews firmly rejected the inevitability of their victimization, and adjusted their wider outlook accordingly. Over the long twentieth century, the most energetic and transformatory expression of this rejection was Zionism, which among many other things also led to profound alterations and intensifications of the idea of Jewish purpose in the world.

4

Light unto the Nations

JEWS AND NATIONAL PURPOSE

Today, as we renew our independence, our first concern must be to build up the land, and to foster its economy, security and international status. But these are the means, not the end. The end is a state that will fulfill prophecies, and bring salvation, being a guide and example to all humanity. In the words of the prophet, for us an eternal truth: 'I will make you a light unto the nations, that my salvation may reach the ends of the earth.'[1]

—DAVID BEN-GURION (1951)

NATIONALISM IS A CHILD of the nineteenth century. The term was coined in the late 1790s, and it was during the upheavals of that revolutionary period that the two main currents of modern nationalist thought took shape. The first, 'civic nationalism', emerged in France, and identified the nation state with the emancipatory values of the French Revolution: membership of the national community was in principle open to whoever was prepared to accept its founding principles. The second, 'ethnic nationalism', first took shape in Germany, where, in part in response to the humiliation of initial defeat by the Napoleonic armies, the distinctiveness and superiority of German language and culture was increasingly asserted. In his *Addresses to the German Nation* (1808), Johann Gottlieb Fichte influentially argued that the German people were crucially different from other Europeans, and exhorted them to embrace their collective identity as a nation.[2] Over the course of the nineteenth century, the burgeoning fields of linguistics, archaeology and ethnography bolstered the development of a nation-based understanding of history, which was promulgated through the educational systems of Europe's existing nations, and spurred the development of nationalist movements among stateless cultural groups such as Poles, Czechs and Finns.[3] Modern Jewish nationalism was a belated addition to this cluster. The term 'Zionism' did not appear in print until 1890, and its dramatic historical impact is a twentieth-century story.

The underlying template for European thinking on peoplehood, however, was the account of Jewish collective identity provided by the Hebrew Bible.[4] In the seventeenth century, as we have already noted, the newly Protestant nations of the Dutch Republic and England identified strongly with the ancient Hebrews, both regarding themselves as a divinely chosen 'new Israel'. This religious fervour and sense of election fuelled the intensification of British national identity in the eighteenth century, in which a vivid anti-Catholic Francophobia played an important role.[5] The Hebraic political theology of the seventeenth century also continued to resonate as an intellectual model for the formation of nation states: Jean-Jacques Rousseau, for example, in his *Considerations on the Government of Poland* (1772), echoed Machiavelli's admiration for Moses as a supremely inspired lawgiver.[6] The political guidance offered by the Hebrew Bible, however, was extremely ambiguous. The first biblical covenant, forged between God and Abraham, appears clearly 'ethnic' in character; but the second, Mosaic covenant encompasses not only Abraham's descendants, but also the 'mixed multitude' (*erev rav*), seemingly of varied ethnicity, who fled with them from Egypt. This covenant—which is also more reciprocal, setting out divine expectations as well as promises—suggests a more 'civic' notion of nationhood. The chosenness of the Jews was also intimately associated with their divine purpose. The early modern Dutch and English, in assuming this sense of divine purpose, sought to express it through their efforts to sustain and diffuse their Protestant piety. This mantle of religious purposiveness was generally less obviously incorporated into modern nationalist ideologies, but the idea of Jewish collective purpose remained the most venerable and resonant reference point for attempts to valorize any nation in terms of its contribution to humanity as a whole.

The ingathering of the Jews in the Holy Land had long been understood by both Jews and Christians as the key event heralding the imminence of the messianic age. According to Augustine's 'witness people' doctrine, the dispersal of the Jews was their punishment for failing to recognize the divinity of Jesus, and their return to Zion would thus signal their restoration to divine favour. As we have already seen, in the 1660s Sabbatian enthusiasts across Europe excitedly prepared to travel to Palestine, while in the Christian world figures as different as the deist philosopher John Toland in the 1710s and the charismatic prophet

Joanna Southcott in the 1790s sought to contribute to the return of the Jews to their imagined territory of origin. Southcott died in 1814, believing, as did her followers, that she was pregnant with the messiah who would lead the Jews to Zion. The millenarian movement she founded nonetheless retained its popularity into the 1830s.[7]

From the 1830s, evangelical Christians in England, led by the social reformer Lord Shaftesbury, vigorously promoted the idea of the 'restoration' of the Jews to the Holy Land. In 1840, at the time of the Damascus Affair, Shaftesbury successfully persuaded the foreign secretary Lord Palmerston to consider extending British protection of the existing Jews in Palestine and to support in principle further Jewish settlement there.[8] There were other concerns that also drove British interest in this region. The eastern Mediterranean was a crucial area of international competition, where British imperial purpose and the restorationist understanding of Jewish purpose dovetailed extremely neatly. The nineteenth-century temporal foreshortening of the messianic significance of the Jews was accompanied by an associated geographical compression: the land on which this messianic destiny was expected to unfold was no longer remote from a European perspective, but now 'the gateway to the East', and therefore of an important terrain of rivalry between the competing imperial powers.

Jews before the late nineteenth century were generally much more circumspect about the establishment of their own polity in Palestine. In 1770, Moses Mendelssohn received an anonymous letter from an admiring 'man of rank', proposing the establishment of a Jewish state in Israel. He politely parried the idea, describing the 'character of his people' as focused on 'monkish piety' rather than political activity. Twelve years later, in his contribution to the debate over Dohm's call for the 'civic improvement' of Jewry, Mendelssohn foreclosed this idea more forcefully: the idea of a return to Palestine was purely religious, he argued, and it was prohibited both in the Bible and the Talmud for Jews to do anything to force this divinely determined messianic event.[9] Mendelssohn sought to stress that Jews were absolutely committed to civic participation in their European states of residence, and were in no sense distracted from this by hopes of migration and political autonomy.

Most nineteenth-century rabbis and communal leaders continued strenuously to advance this argument, which was reinforced by the emphasis of the Reform movement in particular on the pedagogical 'mission of Israel'. As teachers of spiritual loftiness to others, Jews could only perform their historical purpose in diaspora. For more religiously traditionalist Jews, the injunction on 'forcing the end' cited by Mendelssohn in 1770 was decisive:

seeking to intervene in messianic matters risked, in their eyes, lapsing into sectarianism—as the Sabbatian episode had demonstrated—or compromising the full divine redemption that was ultimately promised to Israel. In the middle decades of the nineteenth century, influenced by the activist nationalism of the non-Jewish world around them, a few Orthodox figures in eastern and central Europe initiated modest steps toward the Jewish resettlement of Palestine. These steps were strongly condemned by most Orthodox and Hasidic leaders, sometimes citing talmudic and midrashic references to the 'three oaths' by which the people of Israel foreswore political intervention in their destiny, and particularly any action to 'force the end'.[10]

Nationalist movements remember their histories as autonomous endeavours. Long subjugated, the people finally found their authentic voice, and through their heroic liberation struggle won their freedom: this is the archetypal self-narrative of nationalist triumph. The Zionist movement is no exception to this. The first manifesto for a self-governing Jewish homeland to capture the imagination of other Jews—Leo Pinsker's *Auto-Emancipation!* (1882)—decisively proclaimed this emphasis in its title. After witnessing in Odessa the anti-Jewish pogroms of 1881, Pinsker was convinced that civic inclusion—the 'emancipation' bestowed on western European Jews by their governments—was no remedy for the antisemitism of the moment. A new, and less craven, approach was required, in which Jews themselves took responsibility for their own security and freedom. Pinsker's pamphlet is often taken as a key founding document of modern Zionism, anticipating the much more influential arguments in the following decade of the movement's primary founder, Theodor Herzl (1860–1904).[11]

The elaboration and actualization of the Zionist idea over the past two centuries must nonetheless be understood as a further chapter in the shared Jewish and non-Jewish history of the idea of Jewish purpose. The profound millenarian significance for Christians of the restoration of the Jews in Palestine was indisputably of immense importance for the development and success of Zionism, and it remains a key factor behind international support for Israel today. In the nineteenth and early twentieth centuries the nature of the national community was a fundamental question in public debate, and the case of the Jews, as a uniquely overdetermined collectivity, also played a very prominent role in its exploration, across literature, politics and social thought.

Since its emergence as a political movement in the 1890s, Zionism has been characterized by intense internal disagreements over its philosophy, strategy and identity, beneath which lies the profound and persistent tension within Zionist thought over the project's overarching purpose. Does Zionism seek to normal-ize the place of the Jews in the world, by securing for them a state like those of other national groups? Or is it a continued expression, in nation-state form, of the exceptionality of the Jewish mission in the world: as a 'light unto the na-tions', a formulation repeatedly used, as in the opening quotation above, by Israel's first prime minister, David Ben-Gurion (1886–1973)? This question cuts to the heart of the Jewish purpose question, and its confused but potent significance, for Jews and for non-Jews, throughout the long twentieth century. All modern states, in some sense, claim exceptionality: it is hard to conceive of a sustainable basis of national identity without some form of grounding in a no-tion of meaningful and at least potentially positive distinctiveness. In its na-tionalist iteration, then, the Jewish purpose question poses with particular in-tensity the fundamental questions of collective identity and role in the world that are faced by all of us, as citizens of states and members of nation-based and state-sponsored cultural communities.

Jewish Purpose and the Emergence of the Zionist Idea

In the middle decades of the nineteenth century Jewish internationalist poli-tics became increasingly identified with both the rhetoric and the authority of the two leading European imperial powers. The Damascus Affair of 1840, as we have noted, was a key moment in the identification of the rights and security of Jews with the self-justifying arguments of both French and British global pro-jection. In invoking their rival 'civilizing missions' in support of their authority over non-Europeans, both nations to some extent implicitly assumed the man-tle of chosenness and higher purpose that was traditionally associated with the Jews. These imperial missions were therefore particularly readily burnished through association with Jewish causes, and also through support from Jewish leaders, which Alphonse Crémieux in France and Moses Montefiore in Britain enthusiastically provided. Both these communal leaders played a prominent role in response to the 'Mortara Affair': the abduction by the authorities of the Papal States in 1858 of the six-year-old son of a Jewish merchant in Bologna, who had been baptised by a family housemaid, and therefore, according to papal law, was irrevocably a Catholic and needed to be removed from his family in order to be raised as a Christian.[12] Whereas similar earlier incidents had stirred little reaction, in 1858 the established British and French rhetoric asserting their civi-lized liberalism in contrast to the fanatical barbarism of outdated theocratic regimes—first articulated in defence of Jews in 1840—was again powerfully mobilized. Although the campaign to return the young Edgardo Mortara to his family was unsuccessful, it retrenched the alliance between Jewish internationalism and the humanitarian self-image of both British and French imperialism. Across the British Empire, small but dynamic Jewish communities filled important economic niches and proudly asserted their imperial loyalty, while in Paris in 1860, Crémieux and others founded the Alliance Israélite Universelle, an organization dedicated to promoting French culture and education among the Jews of North Africa and beyond.[13]

European Jewish intellectuals participated alongside community leaders in this imperial turn, and connected it more elaborately to the theme of Jewish purpose. The French scholar Joseph Salvador, in a sequence of monumental works from the early 1820s onwards, repeatedly emphasized the world-historical importance of Judaism: we have already taken note of his 1828 celebration of the economic sophistication of the ancient Hebrews. In his last major work, *Paris, Rome and Jerusalem, or the Religious Question in the Nineteenth Century* (1860), Salvador put forward his most elaborate and most optimistically messianic account of his theory of history. Each of his three titular cities simultaneously represents a spirit, a temporality and a period of history since the French Revolution. 'Paris' stands for the spirit of revolutionary change, the present and the years from 1789 to 1815 in which progress was dominant; 'Rome' signifies the spirit of reaction, the past since the era of the Roman empire and the emergence of Christianity and, in recent history, the 'Throne and Altar' years from 1815 to 1840. 'Jerusalem' represents 're-edification' and renewal, and its dual temporality is of the pre-Roman era of ancient Judaism and of the future already emerging in the present. The essence of the Jewish mission, for Salvador, is the link the Jews provide, as a distinct people, between the deep past and the universalism of destiny. Both a particular and a universal people, the Jews have been preserved 'as the repository of a seed for the future'.[14]

Although expressed more convolutedly than most, this core idea of *Paris, Rome and Jerusalem* is similar to many earlier nineteenth-century articulations of the mission of the Jewish people. Salvador's anchoring of this mission in space and time, however, is noteworthy. The moment of 'Jerusalem' begins in 1840: a year that Salvador identifies as significant above all because of the Damascus Affair, which both highlighted the plight of Jews and brought the 'Eastern question' to the fore.[15] This year marks the beginning both of the era of the future and of 'the movement of Europe into Asia', reaching its first culmination with the concluding peace of the Crimean War in 1856, with which he ends his historical narrative. Salvador's 'Jerusalem' is predominantly an abstraction—a utopian city of the messianic future. His messianic expectancy, however, is extremely ripe, and is couched in a strikingly specific geopolitical language that reflected the interventionist western European mood at the time. Without explicitly declaring any proto-Zionist strategy or intent, Salvador unmistakably narrowed the conceptual distance between the theological ideal of 'Jerusalem' and the anticipated future of the actual city of Jerusalem.

Others at this time directly rejected this ambiguity. Also in 1860, Ernest Laharanne—a liberal Catholic civil servant, possibly attached to the secretariat of Emperor Napoleon III—published a pamphlet titled *The New Eastern Question: The Egyptian and Arabian Empires—Reconstitution of the Jewish Nation*, in which he called for the Ottoman Empire to be replaced by a European-sponsored Jewish state, extending from Suez to Smyrna. Laharanne's envisioned this state both as the fulfilment of the mission of the Jews and as the guarantor of future world peace and prosperity. It was due their subjugation at the hands of Christians that the Jews were not 'master of their own home'.[16] With European encouragement, though, particularly from their French emancipators, they would surely fulfil their holiest of missions, and establish the most successful and harmonious of states:

> You will be intermediaries between Europe and the extremities of Asia, and you will open up the great routes that lead to India and China, and to archipelagos still unknown . . . You will be a moral compass of the worlds in the East . . . You will be the triumphal arch of the future era of peace, and under this huge portico great pacts will come to be sealed, witnessed by the shadows of the past and the hopes of the future.[17]

Laharanne was an ardent admirer of Jews, associating them with civilization, progress and the French revolutionary tradition. His vision of their future state was intensely liberal, profoundly linked to the French imperial civilizing mission and also firmly rooted in the pedagogic, universalist and messianic understanding of Jewish purpose. Once gathered in their own nation, the Jews would become teachers to the peoples of Africa and Arabia, purifying them of all superstition and fanaticism, and unifying the world in common belief in 'the principles of emancipation, love, charity, alliance and peace'.[18]

Although a few isolated Jews had since the 1830s promoted Jewish settlement in Palestine, it was not until two years after Salvador's and Laharanne's publications that the first clear Jewish call for the establishment of a Jewish state there appeared. In his *Rome and Jerusalem* (1862), Moses Hess translated into German lengthy passages from Laharanne, and cited Salvador, whose title he partially borrowed, as evidence for wider Jewish support for the restoration of Jerusalem. He critiqued Salvador's religious vision, however, as 'fusionist', emphasizing in contrast his own advocacy for an enduringly Jewish national state in Palestine.[19] Moses Hess (1812–1875) had been raised in a pious environment in the small Rhineland city of Bonn. Loathing his traditional Jewish education, as a young adult he declared himself an atheist and joined the colony of German radicals in Paris, drawn there by the heady political atmosphere following the July Revolution of 1830. Forced by destitution to return to Germany and accept a clerical job at his father's sugar refinery in Cologne, Hess threw his youthful energies into radical politics, becoming a close associate of Karl Marx in the 1840s.[20] In *Rome and Jerusalem*, however, he declared that 'the race struggle is the primal one, and the class struggle secondary', and asserted in the book's first sentence his newly found sense of national belonging: 'After an estrangement of twenty years, I am back with my people.'[21]

The argument of *Rome and Jerusalem* was underpinned by Hess's conception of Jewish purpose, which preoccupied him throughout his life. He explored this idea most fully in his early socialist writings, and particularly in his first book, *The Holy History of Humanity* (1837), in which he set out his theory of history. Hess here divided time into three eras: the early 'plant kingdom', which was the era of Judaism; the 'animal kingdom', in which Christianity was dominant; and the 'human kingdom', which began to emerge in the late seventeenth century. Both the latter two eras were initiated by messianic Jewish individuals: Jesus Christ and Spinoza. Hess's greatest interest, however, was not in the past but in the future. In the *Holy History* he provides a lengthy account, in a pseudo-biblical prophetic tone, of the transformations heralded by Spinoza, which would soon give rise to a 'New Jerusalem', governed by a 'new holy constitution' of equality and social justice. The Jews, he emphasizes, will play a key role in this process. Finally reawakening, after a long slumber, to 'a higher consciousness', the Jewish people is on the brink of fulfilling its primordial calling to 'conquer the world, not, like pagan Rome, by force of arms, but through the inner virtue of its spirit.'[22] In the late 1830s, Hess was immersed in Young Hegelian debates about the shape and meaning of history. Despite his avowed secularism and his complete alienation from the German Jewish community, he filtered these concerns through the religious template that dominated his schooling, and through a core fascination with Jewish historical significance and destiny.

At the time of the 1843 publication of Bruno Bauer's *The Jewish Question*, Hess was in close contact with Karl Marx, in whose circles he was reputedly nicknamed 'the communist rabbi'.[23] Hess's sharp essay *On Money* (1844) puts forward a similar argument to Marx's approximately simultaneous response to Bauer, and there is no clear scholarly consensus on the primary direction of influence between these two texts. As in Marx's *On the Jewish Question*, Hess here linked Jews with parasitic economic exploitation. Retaining the tripartite historical schema of his *Holy History*, he emphasized the determining historical role of the Jews, not as heralds of the enlightened 'human' epoch, but as the fiscal predators driving the preceding 'animal' epoch to its final collapse:

> The Jews, who in the natural history of the social animal-world had the world-historical mission to turn humans into predatory animals, have now finally accomplished their appointed task . . . In the fiscal state, where free competition reigns, all privileges and distinctions of rank come to an end; . . . there reigns the poetry-less freedom of the predator, based on the equality of death. In the face of money, kings . . . and priests . . . preserve their authority only by virtue of . . . their shared qualities as predators, as bloodsuckers, as Jews, as money-wolves.[24]

The fully monetized nineteenth-century world has, according to Hess, turned everybody into 'Jews', or ruthless predators—but actual Jews have played a central role in bringing this harsh reality into being. The fiscal power of the Jews is brutalizing; but it is also, he argues, progressively transformative in the Hegelian sense, because it is uniquely corrosive of the old hierarchies of feudal and clerical rule. Heinrich Heine had made a similar argument with respect to the Rothschilds in his *Börne* essay of 1840, but Hess's net was wider, equating Jewishness with money in considerably harsher terms than in Marx's response to Bauer.

Both Marx and Hess closely linked Jews with the socially atomizing forces of relentless economic competition. They both also saw this destructive process as ultimately redemptive, leading to the inevitable collapse of the oppressive commercial order and the final attainment of genuine human emancipation. The messianic framework of this argument, which is unmistakably implicit in *On the Jewish Question*, is in Hess's thinking both explicit and profoundly Judaic. The classic duality of the idea of Jewish purpose—the imbuing of Jews with significance first as particularists and then as midwives to universalism—is recast by him in only superficially secular terms. Crucial first as fiscal materialists, and then, above all through his hero Spinoza, as the heralds of the dawning utopianism of the final epoch, the Jews are for Hess the primary agents of both negative and positive historical change.

The nationalism of *Rome and Jerusalem* seems at first sight to set it sharply apart from Hess's earlier writings. However, Hess himself insisted on his continued adherence to the schema of his *Holy History*, and appended to his later volume a lengthy epilogue titled 'Christ and Spinoza', in which he re-rehearsed it.[25] He quietly dropped the harshly critical assessment of Jewish economic activity in *On Money*, commenting in stark contrast that among Jews 'solidarity and social responsibility were always the fundamental principles of life and conduct'.[26] However, the underlying argument of his earlier analysis remained discreetly in evidence. The Jews need their own homeland, he argued, because 'the social man . . . needs for his growth and development a wide, free soil; without it, he sinks to the status of a parasite, which feeds at the expense of others'. The Jews of Europe, he protested, were particularly deprived of access to land, leaving unstated but unmistakable the critical implication that followed from this.[27] The positive aspect of his view of Jewish historical agency and purpose, however, is repeatedly and fulsomely reasserted in *Rome and Jerusalem*. Judaism, he insists, is the root of civilization and humanitarianism, and the establishment of a Jewish state in Palestine will bring about the regeneration of all humanity.[28]

In what sense, though, would this Jewish state remain distinctively Jewish? Hess addressed this issue in detail, through an engagement with the mid-nineteenth-century rabbinical debate on the universal mission of the Jews. The two poles of this argument were represented by the two Hirsches: the Reform rabbi Samuel Hirsch, who believed that the Jews would lead the world into a messianic age of universal religion, in which Jewish difference would become irrelevant, and the Orthodox rabbi Samson Raphael Hirsch, who, according to Hess, continued to insist on the exclusive truth of Judaism.[29] Hess's universalistic vision of the future had much in common with the Reform perspective, but he was determined to distance himself from the 'fusionism' of which he accused both Samuel Hirsch and Joseph Salvador. In order to account for the continuing significance of Jewish distinctiveness even after the establishment of universal harmony that would follow the establishment of a Jewish homeland, Hess developed an elaborate biological metaphor for the relations between the leading nations of the world. Each nation, he argued, performed a particular role as a unique 'organ' in the living body of humanity. England, France, Germany and America each made their specialist contributions to the whole: the industry of England 'regulates the alimentary system of mankind'; France deals with the 'general motion' of society; Germany 'discharges the function of thinking'; and America represents the 'regenerating power' of the assimilation of diverse peoples. The role of the Jewish people is the most transcendentally mystical: they are 'the living, creative force in universal history, namely, the organ of unifying and sanctifying love'.[30] It is likely, given Hess's religious upbringing, that he consciously adopted this image from Judah Halevi, who in his twelfth-century *Kuzari*, as we have noted, used a similar metaphor, describing Israel as the heart among the nations.

The metaphor appears again in George Eliot's final novel *Daniel Deronda* (1876), in which Mordecai, the intellectual inspiration of the eponymous hero, declares, citing Halevi, that 'Israel is the heart of mankind'.[31] He makes this pronouncement at a working-men's 'Philosophers' Club' meeting to which he has brought Deronda, where the wide-ranging discussion moves from how ideas and societies progress to a focus on the question of nationality. A Jewish watchmaker argues that 'the sentiment of nationality' is being swept away by the 'current of progress'; another Jew asserts that there is no reason, now that his brethren have political equality, for them not to 'melt gradually into the populations we live among'.[32] Mordecai, however, awes the group into silence with his passionate advocacy for Jewish national renewal. Through his voice, Eliot (1819–1880) remoulded the classic features of Victorian thinking on Jewish purpose into a highly textured Zionist argument. Jewish history is here once again encapsulated as a tale of remarkable tenacity in the face of suffering. Mordecai insists on the active energy of the Jews in history, diffusing knowledge and virtue as well as material goods across the nations of the world, and repeatedly renewing their religious life and their economic dynamism in the face of waves of hatred and oppression.[33] Their purpose in the world, however, will be fulfilled only with the establishment of their own homeland. Eliot, through Mordecai, imbues this Jewish seizing of their own destiny with immense spiritual and historical significance, not only for Jews but for the world as a whole:

> The Messianic time is the time when Israel shall will the planting of the national ensign. . . . The divine principle of our race is action, choice, resolved memory. Let us . . . help to will our own better future and the better future of the world—not renounce our higher gift . . . but choose our full heritage, claim the brotherhood of our nation, and carry into it a new brotherhood with the nations of the Gentiles. The vision is there; it will be fulfilled.[34]

The Jewish polity envisioned by Mordecai will, as for Laharanne and Hess, both reinforce European colonialism, projecting Western values in the East, and simultaneously transcend this division: it will be 'a new Judea, poised between

East and West—a covenant of reconciliation'.[35] This irenic internationalism
captures the extent of the universalistic hopes that Eliot linked to the fulfilment
of the Jews' particular national destiny.

At this point in the novel Daniel Deronda is unaware of his ancestry, believing himself to be the illegitimate son of an English gentleman. Nonetheless,
Mordecai's arguments make a great impression on him. Precisely because of the
uncertainty of his own identity, Eliot tells us, 'he had a yearning . . . after the
obligation of avowed filial and social ties'.[36] At the end of the novel, having discovered the he is in fact Jewish, Deronda prepares to travel to 'the East', and to
devote his life to turning Mordecai's vision into a reality. Through Deronda's
journey of self-discovery, Eliot presents nationalism as a natural form of human
belonging, and Jewish nationalism as the most historically and emotionally rich
form of this instinctive desire to be part of a collectivity, and of the positive value
of these collectivities for humanity as a whole. Deronda's narrative and outlook
also draw together the themes of Jewish and English nationhood: at the novel's
close he states, for example, his desire to establish for the Jews 'a national centre such as the English have', serving a similar role beyond its borders because
both the English and the Jews are 'scattered over the face of the globe'.[37] The
purpose of the Jewish nation, as presented in Daniel Deronda, lies not only in
the messianic significance of the establishment of their own polity, but in the
model they provide to others of the nobility and virtue of devoted commitment
to the national group.

In 'The Modern Hep! Hep! Hep!' (1879), the final essay of her final work,
Eliot focused specifically on relating the Jewish case to the broader question
of national identity and sentiment. The wellspring of anti-Jewish hatred, such
as in the 'Hep! Hep! riots' in Germany in 1819, she suggests through her fictional
authorial voice of the English bachelor Theophrastus Such, lies in the long-
standing European tendency 'to consider the Jews as altogether exceptional'.
While there is indeed a great deal that is particularly remarkable about the Jews,
all nations are distinctive, the essay argues, each in its own way. The 'superlative
peculiarity' of the Jews should be recognized by the English and others, but appreciated in a spirit of affinity with them, as one might appreciate 'the distinctive note of each bird-species' while recognizing their communality as birds.[38]
On this foundation, Eliot elaborates her defence of 'the spirit of separateness',
which is rooted in the distinct memories and characters of different peoples,
and has created the healthy diversity of humanity: the 'varying genius of nations'.[39] Citing John Stuart Mill's argument in On Liberty (1859) in praise of
the enriching idiosyncrasies enabled by individual liberties, Eliot extends his

argument to the national plane. Why, she asks, in the light of Mill's insight, should we look forward to the 'complete fusion' of the Jews into the various nations of Europe? Jews should, on the contrary, feel bound to sustain their exceptionally rich heritage. Like her fictional creation Daniel Deronda, they should remain 'steadfast in their separateness', and aim 'to constitute a new beneficent individuality among the nations'.[40]

The liberal pluralism of Eliot's vision of Jewish national renewal proved politically fragile. This was exposed by the wider confusion and controversy at this time, in Britain and beyond, over the relationship between national identity, cosmopolitanism and international power politics. In 1877, Britain hovered on the brink of military involvement in the Balkans, while hostility toward the two powers whose confrontation animated the 'Eastern question'—Russia and the Ottoman Empire—competed in the national public sphere. Reports of massacres of Bulgarian Christians by Turkish militia in the summer of 1876 inflamed public opinion. This mood was stoked by the Liberal Party leader William Gladstone, who accused Disraeli, prime minister at the time, of insufficient concern for these Christian victims. Disraeli's foreign policy at the time aimed to contain Russia, and was therefore more supportive of the Ottoman regime. This position was won support from the Anglo-Jewish leadership, as well as from George Eliot, due to concerns over the plight of Jews in Romania, which had worsened significantly following the removal of that territory from Ottoman suzerainty in 1877, with Russian assistance. The instability in the Balkans brought the question of the place of the Jews in Europe to the fore, highlighting the precariousness of their diasporic existence in a continent increasingly shaped by nationalism. Gladstone's opportunistic rhetoric, which played on Disraeli's ethnic origins to portray him as more sympathetic with 'alien' Jewish and Muslim interests than with the suffering of Christians, drew this tension into British political debate. Whereas Eliot, as well as others with instinctive liberal sympathies, regarded Jewish and British exceptionalism as fully compatible and naturally allied forces in the world, Gladstone's populist nationalism pitted British Christian identity against the perceived otherness of the Judaeo-Islamic Orient.[41]

In the same year as the publication of Eliot's 'Hep! Hep!' essay, Wilhelm Marr founded his 'League of Antisemites' in Germany. Two years later, in 1881, anti-Jewish pogroms swept across Russia, leading to a shift of Jewish political energies from the ideal of legal emancipation to other options: socialism, emigration and Zionism. The new thinking of Pinsker and some others rapidly attracted attention among the Jews of eastern Europe, although the large majority were at first indifferent if not hostile. It was not until Theodor Herzl published his pamphlet *The Jewish State* [*Der Judenstaat*] (1896) that a Jewish Zionist movement truly came into existence. Herzl developed his arguments largely independently: at the time of writing *The Jewish State* he had not read either Hess or Pinsker.[42] Nonetheless, the earlier circulation of these ideas undoubtedly prepared the ground for the Jewish Zionist movement, which would also have been scarcely conceivable without Christian receptivity to the idea. Herzl's great impact was due to his success in convincing Jews that he had conceived of a practical remedy for the hardships they faced in Europe. However, his proposal was also dependent on the resonance of both old and new conceptions of Jewish usefulness and purpose.

Unlike the eastern European Jews who were most receptive to Zionism, Herzl was from an assimilated, bourgeois and German-speaking background. Born in Budapest, he became in 1892 the Paris correspondent of the leading Viennese newspaper, and it was the antisemitism he encountered there that changed his thinking. Herzl witnessed the increasing influence of Édouard Drumont, who in that year launched his antisemitic newspaper *La Libre Parole*. Two years later, Herzl was reporting on the Dreyfus Affair: the scandal over the framing of a Jewish captain in the French army, Alfred Dreyfus, as a German spy. In January 1895, despite overwhelming evidence of his innocence, Dreyfus was humiliatingly stripped of his military status and sentenced to life imprisonment. The intensity of the anti-Jewish prejudices exposed by the Dreyfus Affair convinced Herzl that the Jews did not have a secure future in Europe.

In *The Jewish State*, published just over a year after Dreyfus's degradation, Herzl put forward his strategic and organizational proposals for the establishment of an independent Jewish polity under the protection of the European powers. Despite this practical orientation, his pamphlet also echoed the exceptionalist ideals that earlier writers had associated with the Zionist idea. While open to alternative locations, such as Argentina, Herzl was particularly drawn to Palestine as the site for Jewish settlement and autonomy. Palestine, he wrote, was 'our unforgettable historic homeland', where a Jewish state would form 'a rampart of Europe against Asia, an outpost of civilization as opposed to barbarism', and would safeguard the holy sites of Christianity as 'the great symbol of the solution of the Jewish question after eighteen centuries of Jewish suffering'.[43] Although he did not explicitly couch his proposal in messianic terms, he clearly imbued it with deep universal significance. A Jewish state would not only secure the welfare of Jews but also, he confidently concluded, unfailingly benefit humanity as a whole: 'The world will be freed by our liberty, enriched by our wealth, magnified by our greatness.'[44]

Herzl's vision swiftly attracted support from two prominent intellectuals who in different ways saw Zionism as the remedy not only for antisemitism, but also for their broader diagnosis of the ills of Western society. The First Zionist Congress, held in Basel in 1897, was organized by the physician and writer Max Nordau (1849–1923), Herzl's close ally and also a Budapest-born Jew thoroughly assimilated into Germanic culture. A leading exponent of late nineteenth-century medicalized social critique, in his *Degeneration* (1892), Nordau had argued that the culture of the time had subsided into decadence, mysticism and self-absorption, undermining the progress of civilization and contributing to the rise of debilitating diseases of nervous exhaustion. Although in this work he only briefly mentioned antisemitism—as an aspect of the Germanic hysteria of the Richard Wagner cult—in his speech to the 1897 Congress he hailed Zionism as the cure for Jewish degeneracy.[45] In the following years, Nordau became the principal advocate for the cultivation of a new 'muscular Jewry' (*Muskeljudentum*), promoting an emphasis on gymnastics and physicality in order to regenerate the enfeebled and unhealthy Jewish male body. The new Jewish masculinity, which became an important strand of early Zionist culture, bore similarities with various other attempts to foster manly vigour in opposition to *fin-de-siècle* urban decadence. For Nordau and his supporters, though, the Jewish case was uniquely dramatic, because of the extremity both of the immiseration and degeneration of the Jewish masses and of the great contribution that a regenerated Jewry, with its own homeland, would make to civilization.[46] Echoing the language of the abbé Grégoire and others a century earlier, the regeneration of the Jews once again resonated as emblematic of an anticipated wider transition to a better world.

Herzl's most prominent early supporter in France was the Jewish radical journalist Bernard Lazare (1865–1903), who, like Herzl and also Nordau, was jolted into Zionism by closely witnessing the Dreyfus Affair. Shortly before that scandal erupted, Lazare had published his *Antisemitism: Its History and Causes* (1894), in which he both critiqued anti-Jewish prejudices and ascribed them to a considerable extent to the reality of Jewish difference from others. The separateness of the Jews, he argued, had profoundly marked their character, heightening both their mystical intellectuality and their worldly commercialism.[47] These traits provoked antisemitism, which in turn reinforced Jewish separateness and distinctiveness. Most significant for Lazare, however, was 'the revolutionary spirit in Judaism', which stemmed from its emphasis on justice in this world (rather than, as for Christianity, in the afterlife), and engendered in Jews an intellectual and political restlessness that placed them at the fore of social and intellectual progress. Marx, with his 'clear Talmudic mind', was for Lazare only the most recent prominent example of Jewish progressive leadership.[48] Ultimately, though, both antisemitism and the distinctiveness of the Jews themselves were destined for oblivion. Antisemitism, Lazare declared, self-undermining: hatred for Jewish capitalists strengthened hatred for capital in general and thus hastened the advent of socialism, which would bring with it the overcoming of all prejudices. Judaism was also, he believed, in a process of dissolution, and would ultimately be superseded by a new international spirit of 'cosmopolitanism [and] universal altruism'.[49] Lazare's analysis of antisemitism was principally based on his understanding of Jewish world historical purpose, which drew together the pedagogical, ethical and economic strands of nineteenth-century thinking on this topic, and was framed by a prophetic messianism modulated into a secular socialist key.

The venom unleashed by the Dreyfus Affair led Lazare to abandon his optimistic predictions. However, while embracing Zionism almost immediately after the publication of Herzl's pamphlet, he did not renounce either his socialism or his proud conception of the ethical loftiness of the Jewish spirit and role in the world. Jewish nationalism, he insisted, was in no sense incompatible with internationalism. Jewish nationalism was necessary so that Jews could restore their dignity and 'be themselves'. However, their project was not one of pure self-interest, but was imbued with profound moral importance for the world. Citing Ernst Renan's scholarship in support of his argument, Lazare exhorted the Zionist movement never to forget that 'you were the people who introduced justice to the world', and always to be 'soldiers for justice and human fraternity'.[50] The socialist universalism of Lazare's Zionism, and its fusion with his unflinchingly critical analysis of Jewish capitalism and religious insularity, was similar in many respects to the earlier arguments of Moses Hess. His idealism was not easily integrated, however, with Herzl's more pragmatic focus on diplomatic and economic efforts to advance the Zionist cause. In 1899, Lazare parted ways with Herzl over these issues, presaging the contentious role that the strain between outward- and inward-oriented aspects of the Zionist vision were to play in the twentieth-century history of the movement.

Messianism, Normalization and the Contest of Zionisms

The primary alternative to Herzl's political Zionism was advanced most powerfully by the Russian Jewish intellectual Asher Ginsberg, better known by his Hebrew pen-name Ahad Ha'am ('one of the people') (1856–1927). The son of a rabbi in a small town near Kiev, this passionate essayist lost his religious faith in his youth, but remained throughout his life deeply committed to the spiritual uplift of the Jewish people, through what came to be described as 'cultural Zionism'.[51] Ahad Ha'am was from his earliest writings dismissive of what he regarded as the craven tendency of western European Jews to express their Judaism in terms designed to impress their non-Jewish neighbours. He was particularly critical of the usual formulation, particularly but not only within the western Reform movement, of the 'mission of Israel' idea, which he viewed as an unnatural subordination of the self-fulfilment of Jews to the interests of others. Accusing the self-satisfied western proponents of this idea of spiritually enslaving themselves in exchange for their political emancipation, he insisted on the assertion of Jewish cultural pride in its own terms and for its own sake:

> Do I envy these fellow-Jews of mine their emancipation? . . . No! A thousand times No! . . . I may not be emancipated, but at least I have not sold my soul for emancipation. . . . I at least have no need to exalt my people to Heaven, to trumpet its superiority above all nations, in order to find a justification for its existence. I at least know "why I remain a Jew"—or, rather, I can find no meaning in such a question, any more than if I were asked why I remain my father's son.[52]

The notion of a Jewish mission to others, Ahad Ha'am argued, was invented after the French Revolution, when some Jews felt ashamed that the idea of the election of Israel was at odds with the new political spirit of universal equality and fraternity. They therefore adapted the idea, recasting the chosenness of the Jews as an instrument for the diffusion of general human wellbeing.[53]

Ahad Ha'am did not, however, dispense altogether with the idea of a Jewish mission. The Jews were indeed chosen by God for a purpose: 'to give concrete expression in every generation to the highest type of morality'. However, their moral election was an end in itself, and exclusively concerned the Jews, 'without any regard to the gain or loss of the rest of mankind'.[54] Ahad Ha'am was sharply critical not only of the assimilated western European Jewish elite, but also of eastern European Jewish intellectuals who were seduced by Nietzsche's notions of the 'superman' and the 'transvaluation of values'. There was no need, he argued, to turn to Nietzsche for an inspiring basis on which to conceptualize the inner significance of Jewish existence. Alluding approvingly to Judah Halevi's twelfth-century assertion of the essential difference and superiority of the Jews, he declared that the essence of Nietzsche's ideas, as they usefully pertained to Jews, had already been explicated eight centuries earlier.[55] Nor did

Ahad Ha'am entirely reject messianism, although he conceived of this utopian horizon in extremely distant and mystical terms. The prophetic mission of the Jews was, he argued, different from the western European notion of the 'mission of Israel', because the Jewish prophetic devotion to righteousness was eternal, and demanded the concentration and self-direction of the Jewish nation, rather than its dispersal among the nations.[56] While rejecting the outward-oriented, pedagogic interpretation of the Jews' ethical mission, Ahad Ha'am retained this lofty notion of Jewish purpose, and enshrined it as the moral core of his inwardly-directed vision of cultural Zionism.

The difference between Ahad Ha'am and Herzl was highlighted most starkly by the controversy over Herzl's novel *Old New Land* [*Altneuland*] (1902). Herzl here described a thriving Jewish homeland in Palestine in the near future, where religion is minimal, and Jews communicate mostly in German, enjoy the best of western European culture, and radiate civilization and progress to the rest of humanity. In a scathing review, Ahad Ha'am condemned Herzl's vision as both utterly unrealistic and repugnantly assimilationist, devoid of any authentically Jewish character.[57] Ahad Ha'am perceived in the novel, quite reasonably, a highly disdainful attitude to eastern European Jewish culture. He was also repelled by Herzl's insistence on the contribution to the wider world of his envisaged Jewish polity.

It was, however, Ahad Ha'am's emphasis on the integrity of Jewish spiritual values that sustained his insistence, in contrast to many other early Zionists, on the importance of decency toward the Arab inhabitants of Palestine. In 1922, soon after leaving Europe and settling in Tel Aviv, he was dismayed by reports of a revenge killing by Jews of a Palestinian youth, and by the forgiving response to this by other Zionist settlers. In a letter to the *Haaretz* newspaper condemning this, Ahad Ha'am invoked the 'great ethical teachings' that Jews 'were obliged to follow even at the risk of our lives, until they become the possession of the human race'. Without those principles, he argued, the Zionist project would be almost worthless, reduced simply to one small vengeful nation morally indistinguishable from its neighbours and rivals.[58] Despite his hostility to any justification of Jewish existence in terms of the interests of others, Ahad Ha'am fervently believed that Jewish values demanded fair treatment of others. In the setting of Palestine, he was willing to insist on this by appealing powerfully to the traditional idea of Jewish moral purpose, even reinstating the pedagogical element that in Herzl's hands he saw as so cravenly assimilationist.

Ahad Ha'am's cultural ideals were most concretely advanced by the project to establish a Jewish university in Jerusalem, which bore fruit in 1925 with the opening of the Hebrew University campus on Mount Scopus. Its founding chancellor, the American-born Reform rabbi Judah Magnes (1877–1948), envisioned the institution as a beacon of learning and reconciliation for the entire world. Magnes shared Ahad Ha'am's vision of Jewish settlement in Palestine as a source of strength for diasporic Jewish life, rather than as a replacement for it. He also embraced the idea of Jewish mission, fusing the outward-looking perspective of the Reform movement with the cultural Zionist tradition inherited from Ahad Ha'am. The Jewish people, he argued in 1930, was 'a wondrous and paradoxical organism', and unlike all other nations. Its dispersion enabled 'the fulfilment of its function as a teacher', spreading 'light and learning'. By providing a centre for the renewal and deepening of Jewish philosophy and religion, settlement in Palestine 'can help this people perform its great ethical mission as a national-international entity'.[59] Like Ahad Ha'am, Magnes believed that it was therefore essential that these ethical principles were not compromised for the Zionist cause. The establishment of a Jewish homeland without regard for the interests and assent of the local Arab population would, he warned, undermine the values of the Jewish people and their respect in the eyes of others. Magnes's commitment to a binational political settlement, ensuring equal rights for Jews and Arabs, was grounded in his belief that only a just and peace-loving Zionism was compatible with the exceptional ethical purpose borne by Jews across the world.[60]

The early 'Jerusalem scholars' of the Hebrew University also attempted in other ways to underscore the connection between universalist principles and the Zionist project. This was the underlying purpose of the major event held on Mount Scopus in February 1927 to mark the 250th anniversary of the death of Spinoza, at which the eminent scholar Joseph Klausner symbolically lifted the ban imposed on the renegade philosopher by the Sephardic community of Amsterdam in 1656. Identifying Spinoza as a proto-Zionist on the strength of his elliptical comments on the election of the Jews in his *Tractatus theologico-politicus*, and declaring him among the greatest of Jewish thinkers, Klausner concluded his speech by intoning the repeated rabbinical formula used to rescind a communal ban: 'Baruch Spinoza: . . . you are our brother, you are our brother, you are our brother!'[61] Klausner's gesture, which was derided by some as meaningless in religious terms, echoed Heine, Geiger, Hess and many other nineteenth-century Jews in insisting on the essential Jewishness of Spinoza's genius, and in associating it with a specifically Jewish messianism of modernity. In 1927, however, this perspective pushed against the philosophical grain of the era. Multiple claims on Spinoza were advanced in this widely commemorated anniversary year, but he was predominantly associated with a cosmopolitan universalism, and celebrated as a hero of humanity precisely because he belonged to all and none.[62] In claiming Spinoza for Zionism, Klausner struck to the core of the tangled and controversial relationships between the secular identity of the Zionist movement, its tinge of religious messianism and the values of universalism and cosmopolitanism.

For Klausner's colleague Gershom Scholem (1897–1982), of much greater interest was the other leading seventeenth-century source of Jewish messianic energy: Sabbatai Zevi. Raised in a highly assimilated bourgeois environment in Berlin, Scholem's youthful search for meaning had led him to Zionism, and he was one of Magnes's key academic appointments at the time of the opening of the Mount Scopus campus. Scholem largely ignored the Spinoza festivities of 1927, embarking instead on his detailed study of the Sabbatian movement, which came to form a central component of his rethinking of the history of Jewish messianism. The messianic strand of Judaism, Scholem argued, was inherently dangerous. It encompassed two contrasting poles of catastrophic and utopian apocalypticism, which could not be imagined independently from each other: any transition to the messianic future was necessarily revolutionary and cataclysmic.[63] The Sabbatean upheaval was in his view a vivid example of this, culminating in Sabbatai's outward apostasy, and in the syncretic antinomianism of the Dönme and the Frankist movement. Scholem described Jacob Frank as 'one of the most frightening phenomena in the whole of Jewish history': a corrupt, degenerate and self-absorbed nihilist. However, he recognized in Frank's teachings a compelling authenticity, giving mythic form to a radical vision of a different and better way of living. Scholem also perceived this popular energy in Sabbatai's teachings, which he lauded as a liberatory blasting open of the traditionally elitist kabbalistic tradition, enabling the Jewish masses to access a sense of 'inner freedom'. These utopian impulses, he argued, prepared the ground for the embrace by some Frankists of the radical ideals of the French Revolution.[64]

Through the history of Jewish mysticism, Scholem gave expression, in a different idiom, to the long-standing association of Jews and Judaism with the envisioning of the utopian destination of history, and also with the inversions of the existing order that arrival at that destination must entail. This was for him the essence of the messianic idea, with which the place of the Jews in human history was inextricably bound. Like Ahad Ha'am, who was an important influence on him, Scholem preferred to focus on the internal dynamics of Jewish history, rather than to explain or justify it in relation to the historical whole.

Nonetheless, he also adopted the notion that the messianic idea was the fundamental Jewish contribution to humanity, and was intimately linked to the historical suffering of European Jewry and to the ultimate overcoming of that suffering. As the bearers of messianic hope, the Jews were restricted to powerlessness, and to 'a life lived in deferment', morally grand but existentially unreal and provisional. This was 'the price which the Jewish people has had to pay out of its own substance for this idea which it handed over to the world'. Zionism, Scholem argued, was the redemption from this price. By assuming collective agency and rejecting the absolute deferral of messianic realization into the future, the Jewish people were finally entering into the 'concrete realm' of history. This was, as with any conjuring with messianism, a dangerous transition. Scholem was nonetheless convinced that it was an invigorating, bold and, after the horror of the Holocaust, undoubtedly essential task.[65]

In a sense, then, Scholem regarded Zionism as a political normalization of Jewish life. No longer would Jews live in deferment: they would instead work together, just like other nationalities in their own nation-states, to build a better future for themselves in the present. However, as a movement that was at its core messianic—the final phase, in his view, of the history of Jewish 'activist messianism' that Sabbatai had unleashed—Zionism was for Scholem by no means merely of parochial significance for Jews alone. In his earlier writings, he tended to emphasize the autonomy of the Jewish mystical tradition, underplaying the considerable importance of syncretic influences from Christianity and Islam in shaping Sabbatianism.[66] This approach suggested a preference for an internalist approach to Jewish history—although he did not hesitate to point to the outward influence of Jewish messianism and radicalism on others. However, after the establishment of the state of Israel in 1948, and even more so after the Arab–Israeli Six-Day War of 1967, Scholem was more outspoken in his rejection of the idea of Jewish normalization, and in his call for the Jewish state to serve as a moral beacon in the world. In a 1974 essay, he declared that he had never accepted the slogan 'like all the nations' as a vision for Zionism. Its realization, he argued, could only lead to 'the decline or even the disappearance of the Jewish people'. His own Zionism, in contrast, was grounded on 'an unshakeable belief in a specific moral centre, which bestows meaning in world history on the Jewish people'.[67]

In public conversation in California in 1973, quoted in the epigraph to the introductory chapter of this book, Scholem offered perhaps the most candid expression of his complex attitude toward the idea of Jewish purpose. On the one hand, he rejected any Jewish obligation 'to justify our existence by working for the world'. This expectation, which, he notes, is only ever made of Jews, is seen by some as 'scandalous'. This is not, though, Scholem's own reaction. Rather, he speculates that this expectation might 'come to fruition one day', finally resolving 'the enigma of being the chosen people'.[68] These gnomic comments reflect Scholem's belief in the burden but also the inescapability of Jewish purpose, which for him was the kernel of the wider historical significance of the Jewish messianic idea. After the 1967 war, Scholem perceived in Israeli politics a serious threat to the principles of peace and justice that lay at the core of that vision. The pursuit of peaceful coexistence with Arabs was, he argued, an absolute imperative, and one that would, in quasi-messianic fashion, in the end inexorably triumph: 'The great enterprise of the land of Israel . . . is also a great experiment in human alchemy, one which shall in the future change hatred and animosity to understanding and respect.'[69]

The early Zionist movement was for the most part vehemently opposed by Jewish religious traditionalists, who saw it as an attempt to 'force the end', heretically trespassing on divine sovereignty over the advent of the messianic era. Most religious supporters of Zionism sought to distance it from messianism, arguing that the goal of a Jewish homeland was simply a practical measure to alleviate the suffering of eastern European Jewry. For this group, the proposal for Jewish settlement in British East Africa—the 'Uganda Plan' supported by Herzl but rejected by the movement, after much consideration and debate, in 1905—was particularly attractive, as it avoided all confusion with religious matters.[70] After the Balfour Declaration of 1917, in which the British pledged their support for 'a Jewish homeland in Palestine', these alternative 'territorialist' visions of Zionism were effectively abandoned, and there was a hardening of the division within religious orthodoxy between those who were willing to cooperate with the Zionist movement and those who were most stridently opposed to it.

The most vehement criticism of Zionism came from those within the ultra-Orthodox camp who saw the Zionist blurring of the political and the religious domains as dangerous in the extreme. Zionism, in their view, threatened to undermine the spiritual purity of Judaism, which they regarded as a religion uniquely detached from the worldly contamination of politics. Gershom Scholem similarly recognized the entry of Jewish messianism into human history as theologically transformatory and dangerous. Whereas he embraced this risk, the most influential voices of Jewish orthodoxy until after the establishment of the Jewish state in 1948 uncompromisingly rejected it, insisting instead on the sharp separation between the profane and the holy, and between the human present and the messianic future. From this perspective, the exceptionalism of the Jews was marked above all by their detachment from the worldly sphere. These traditionalist leaders therefore thoroughly rejected what they saw as the impudent and inadmissible pulling of Jewish purpose into the corrupted realm of the political present.[71]

A long-standing tradition within religious orthodoxy, however, saw things differently. Already in the 1830s, two rabbis—Yehudah Alkalai in Serbia and Zvi Hirsch Kalischer in the German–Polish border region of Posen—had begun independently to propose Jewish settlement in Palestine as a step toward national and human redemption. Both rabbis were influenced by the mood of nationalist enthusiasm that was particularly widespread in the linguistically mixed imperial borderland regions in which they lived.[72] In the early twentieth century, a similar sense that the destiny of the Jews was intimately bound up with the restless spirit of the age shaped the thinking of the leading theologian of religious Zionism: rabbi Abraham Isaac Kook (1865–1935). Born in Latvia—another area of notable nationalist tension, within the Russian Empire—Kook migrated to Palestine in 1904, becoming rabbi to the Jewish community of Jaffa. The upheaval of the First World War, the establishment of the Soviet Union (to which he was vehemently opposed) and a more general sense of global instability convinced Kook that the world had entered a period of epochal transformation, in which the fulfilment of the Zionist vision would play a crucial role: 'The securing of the structure of the world, which is now tottering in the bloody tempests of war, demands the upbuilding of the Jewish nation.'[73] Like Scholem, Kook was fascinated by the Lurianic Kabbalah, and its emphasis on *tikkun olam* ('repair of the world'). The contemporary world was disordered, he believed, because the Jews were not in their allotted place. Their ingathering would bring with it universal redemption and human unity: 'All religions will don new and precious raiment, casting off whatever is soiled, abominable and unclean; they will unite in imbibing of the dew of the Holy Lights, that were made ready for all mankind at the beginning of time in the well of Israel.'[74]

Kook's activist messianism was based on a firm belief that the renaissance of the Jews in Zion was central to the divine plan for all humanity. Like Judah Halevi, he believed that Jews were categorically superior to others: 'We are not only different from all the nations, . . . but we are also of a much higher and greater spiritual order.'[75] The purpose of the Jews, however, was for the world as a whole. Like so many earlier thinkers, such as the nineteenth-century Reform advocates of the 'mission of Israel', Kook expressed this in lofty moral and pedagogical terms: 'We have made many great moral contributions to the world, and we are now ready to become its teacher of joyous and vibrant living.'[76] However, in opposition to those who continued to argue that this mission required the dispersal of Jews among the nations, for Kook the Jewish people would fulfil their purpose only through their messianic ingathering in the Holy Land. This event was for him inseparable from the redemptive transformation of the entire world. Kook shared the concern of anti-Zionist rabbis that the holy perfection of the messianic era must not be profaned by the corruption of the unredeemed world. Precisely for this reason, Kook argued, a Jewish polity could be established only as part of a wider transformation of all human politics, bringing an end to the violence and the nationalist animosities of the era.[77]

The events of the 1940s—the Holocaust and the establishment of the state of Israel—transformed the context in which the meaning of Zionism was considered. For the radical religious wing of the anti-Zionist camp, the Nazi extermination of European Jewry was interpreted as a divine punishment for the Zionists' sinful violation of the oaths forbidding the 'forcing of the end', and the state of Israel was rejected as illegitimate. These views are now extremely marginal, but the continued anti-Zionism of the ultra-Orthodox Satmar and Neturei Karta communities has exerted wider influence in the traditionalist Jewish world, as a position that maintains an uncompromising separation between the spiritual purity of messianism and the profanity of the secular sphere.[78] For the followers of Kook, these compromises were at first extremely challenging. The Holocaust was not readily harmonized with his messianic optimism, to say the least, and further difficulty was posed by the borders of Israel as demarcated in 1949, which excluded the Old City of Jerusalem and other key biblical sites in the West Bank.

After those territories came under Israeli control in 1967, however, messianic religious Zionism was vigorously renewed. This revival was spearheaded by Kook's son, Zvi Yehudah Kook (1891–1992), who recast his father's teachings in a more activist form. For the younger Kook, the catastrophes and triumphs of the Jews were of apocalyptic significance, signalling the irreversible unfolding of the messianic climax of history. This was therefore the time for Jews to settle across the newly occupied territories. The younger Kook and his supporters provided the theological underpinning for the post-1967 religious settler movement, which grew slowly until the early 1980s, and then much more rapidly. This settler project has for the past fifty years been a central point of contention in the conflict between Israel and the Palestinians. In stark contrast with his father's irenic Zionist vision, which echoed the expectation of many other earlier thinkers that a Jewish polity would be an anchor of international peace, the settler Zionism supported by the messianism of the younger Kook and his more recent intellectual heirs has been closely associated with the more belligerent and uncompromising wing of Israeli politics. This outlook is also at odds with the Zionism of the older Kook, and indeed with almost all earlier thinking on Jewish purpose, in its inward-looking emphasis on the perceived interests of the Jews themselves. Followers of the younger Kook have preferred to regard his particularism as simply a shift of emphasis. It seems clear, however, that since 1967 universalistic and irenic conceptions of Zionism have increasingly been pushed to the margins of Israeli and wider Jewish politics, despite the protestations of Scholem and many others. In recent decades, these previously dominant perspectives have across much of the Jewish world been supplanted by a predominantly inward-looking and self-interested understanding of Jewish purpose, espoused most assertively by contemporary messianic religious Zionism.[79]

Religious Zionism in the mid-twentieth century was pitted against two contrasting Zionist currents that nonetheless shared a strong emphasis on the political and cultural normalization of the Jews, and rejected the notion of a unique Jewish purpose in the world at large. The first of these was socialist Zionism, which coalesced as a movement in the first decade of the twentieth century. According to Ber Borochov (1881–1917), the foundational Marxist theoretician of the movement, the primary cause of antisemitism was the anomalous class position of European Jewry. Excluded from the peasantry, concentrated in the petty bourgeoisie and disproportionately present in the capitalist elite, the Jews served as a lightning-rod for the economic resentments of the proletariat. This popular antisemitism distracted from the class struggle, and created an unnatural alliance among its victims: Jews of all social classes. The solution, Borochov argued, was for Jews to form a society of their own, in Palestine, where they would necessarily occupy all class positions. Only there could normal class antagonisms emerge within Jewish society, enabling the full development of a Jewish proletariat able to participate as part of the international working-class struggle against capitalism.[80]

This ideology exerted a major influence on labour Zionism, which was dominant in the wider movement and in Israeli politics until the 1970s. Even when it diverged from its socialist roots, labour Zionism placed great emphasis on the dignity and organization of the workforce.[81] Jewish trade unionism, both before and after 1948, was widely regarded as the means through which a normal class structure among the Jews would be established. This would finally overcome their historical association with commerce, which socialist Zionists regarded as a somewhat embarrassing anomaly that was pernicious for both Jews and others. The idea that a Jewish polity would transform the Jews' economic role was of long-standing pedigree, and was advanced most vividly in the nineteenth century by Moses Hess. However, Hess had couched this transformation in messianic and exceptionalist terms. Most twentieth-century socialist and labour Zionists were in contrast firmly secular. The diversification of Jewish economic activity in Palestine was generally regarded by them as the overcoming of all such exceptionalism, and also of the antisemitism that it drew in response, through the normalization of the place of Jews in the world.[82] Nonetheless, the vision of a future socialist utopia was strongly tinged with messianism. Although socialist Zionists did not formally consider that Jews would play a special role in the attainment of this utopia, their movement fostered a notably intense idealism, instantiated above all through the numerous collectivist *kibbutz* communities they established across Palestine.

The other normalizing current within Zionism was Revisionism, which was established in 1925 by Vladimir Jabotinsky (1880–1940) as the opposing wing to the Left within the wider Zionist movement. Jabotinsky, like Abraham Kook, was intensely opposed to socialism and communism, and deeply struck by the political ferment in Europe in the aftermath of the First World War. He interpreted this as a struggle between races, in which resilience and strength were crucial. Nations, he believed, were based on racial differences, and were the key unit of social organization. The influence of European fascist models on Revisionism was particularly apparent in its paramilitary youth movement, Betar, which focused on instilling discipline and Jewish national pride. This outlook was clearly based to some extent on a belief in Jewish superiority, particularly over Arabs, whom Jabotinsky denigrated as fatalistic and passive. However, despite some inconsistency on this subject, he generally regarded a chauvinistic belief in one's own national superiority, and a xenophobic attitude toward others, as a normal and healthy human attitude. This led him to express a certain respect and admiration for other right-wing nationalist movements, even when, as in the case of Ukraine, they were heavily inflected with antisemitism. Nationalism, for Jabotinsky, was the sovereign ideology of the era. A robustly assertive Zionism, emulating the equivalent movements of other national groups, was therefore essential if Jews were to overcome their anomalous diasporic condition and thrive amid the ruthless nationalist competition of the international order.[83]

Revisionism also absorbed a messianic tinge, however, despite the secular and normalizing nature of its overarching outlook. The right-wing Hebrew newspaper edited by Jabotinsky played a significant role in fomenting tensions between Jews and Muslims over the Western Wall in Jerusalem, which erupted into violence across Palestine in August 1929, in which over a hundred people on either side lost their lives. This spurred the emergence of a more radically combative wing within Revisionism, which at times embraced a secularized rhetoric of apocalyptic messianism. One of the paramilitary leaders, Abraham Stern—whose Lehi organization carried out terror attacks against British, Palestinian and international targets in the 1940s—even appropriated and inverted the rabbinic injunction on 'forcing the end', poetically describing himself as a messianic soldier fighting for precisely that goal.[84] Despite their secular and normalizing ideology, the Revisionists were increasingly influenced by the heady religious environment of the Holy Land, particularly in the heat of intensifying conflict from 1929 onwards. In some ways echoing the earlier Frankist and Dönme movements, they proved able to combine their secular impulse toward normalization with an antinomian and particularist sense of millenarian expectancy. From 1977, when the recently founded Likud Party was swept to power under the leadership of the former Revisionist paramilitary leader Menachem Begin, this combination took on a renewed significance in Israeli politics.[85]

The brand of messianism that most formatively stamped the Zionist movement, however, was that of David Ben-Gurion. A labour Zionist and leading trade unionist before serving almost uninterruptedly as Israel's prime minister from 1948 to 1963, Ben-Gurion's eloquent rhetoric projected a lofty image of the Jewish state, both to Jews and non-Jews. His political vision drew together a 'red messianism', inspired in particular by the early achievements of the Soviet Union, with a semi-secular fascination with the biblical resonance of the Zionist project. Drawing on the long-standing idea, extending back to Salvador and Laharanne in 1860, that a Jewish state would be a nodal point of connection between Europe and Asia, Ben-Gurion presented Israel as a 'living bridge' between those two continents, and more broadly as a mediator between the West and the Third World, relaying development aid and, even more importantly, ethical principles of peace and justice. He communicated this idealism through many channels, such as his regular essays in the *Israeli Government Year Book*, in which he particularly emphasized the importance of Israel's exceptional role as 'a light unto the nations'. Isaiah's prophetic formulation signalled for Ben-Gurion the profound distinctiveness of the Jewish people, rooted above all in the tenacity of their commitment to ethical virtue. All nations, he wrote, regarded themselves as different from others—but no other nation had the same quality or strength of difference as the Jews, which stemmed from the 'unique spiritual and moral quality' that they possessed.[86]

Ben-Gurion did not abandon the labour Zionist valorization of normalizing the class structure of Jewish society. The Jews, he proudly asserted in 1952, were becoming 'a people of workers', as in other autonomous nations. This did not mean, however, that they were becoming normal overall: despite their modest collective size and strength, the Jews remained absolutely exceptional 'by standards of ethics and culture'.[87] He was in no doubt that this exceptionality was rooted in their status as a chosen people, with a messianic destiny. Welcoming international scholars of Judaism to Jerusalem for an international congress in 1961, Ben-Gurion requested them to focus their future attention on 'the messianic vision of the prophets of Israel concerning the redemption of their people and of all the peoples of the world'. The dual nature of this vision of redemption, oriented both inwardly to the Jewish people and outwardly to all humanity, was for him of crucial importance. In loosely similar terms to the older Kook, Ben-Gurion insisted on the interdependence between these two aspects, and the indispensability of universal redemptive transformation: 'the redemption of one nation is inconceivable without the redemption of all humanity'.[88] Belief in the realization of this vision was, he claimed, a shared commitment of the Jewish Israeli population as a whole. In his afterword to a celebratory book on Israel nominally edited by him in retirement in 1966, he declared that Israelis regarded their reborn statehood as inseparable from the inexorable advancement of all mankind toward 'a world of freedom, of justice and peace, of human partnership'.[89]

Only one year later, the relationship of the Israeli state to global peace became, and has since remained, much more fraught. Messianism has remained a powerful and highly contested force in Israel since 1967, but its focus has shifted inward, with the universalistic rhetoric of Ben-Gurion present as a cultural trace memory, but seldom as a continuing current in political life. Internationally, however, messianic Zionism has assumed unprecedented strength, above all due to the rise of millenarian evangelical Christianity. Israel's lightning victory in 1967 had an extremely dramatic impact on evangelical Christians, many of whom regarded the unification of the holy sites of Jerusalem under Jewish control as a clear sign that a messianic unfolding was afoot. Evangelical support for Israel has played an important political role since then, above all in the United States since the Reagan presidency.[90] This has culminated, most recently, with President Trump's transfer in May 2018 of the United States embassy in Israel from Tel Aviv to Jerusalem: a decision almost certainly primarily motivated by his desire to enthuse his evangelical domestic support base.

Despite the continued emphasis in Israeli and Jewish Zionist political discourse on the central guiding principles of Jewish self-reliance and self-
determination, it may well be the case that the political mobilization of Christian messianic expectancy is now of greater importance in shaping the destiny
of the Zionist project.[91]

The intertwinement of Jewish and Christian thinking on Jewish purpose is
certainly nowhere more intensely and consequentially evident than in relation
to Zionism. From its eighteenth-century anticipation by figures such as John
Toland, through its promotion by Lord Shaftesbury and other British evangelical Christians from the 1830s, to Laharanne's blueprint of 1860, Christian Zionism had a lengthy history well before the emergence Herzl's Jewish movement.
The British motivations behind the 1917 Balfour Declaration were complex and
multiple, but a sense of Christian identification with the Jews and with the biblical resonance of the Zionist idea undoubtedly figured prominently among
them, and also in the articulation of American Christian support for Zionism
prior to 1948.[92] These resonances, however, were significant not only in instilling Christians with an outward-oriented sympathy for Jews, but also in the
shaping of Christian understandings of themselves. Various quasi-ethnic forms
of Christianity in the nineteenth and twentieth centuries, such as British Is-
raelism and Mormonism, as well as some Black Christian counter-theologies,
were based on claims of Hebraic identification or appropriation.[93] More broadly,
and beyond the terrain of religion, the idea of Jewish nationhood has been
throughout the twentieth century a central intellectual test case for defining the
nature of nationhood in general. In this respect, the Jewish purpose question
has been, and remains, highly relevant to the meaning of national identity and
purpose for everyone.

Nationhood and Jewish Exemplarity

After several decades of intensifying nationalism in Europe, the outbreak of the
First World War was widely welcomed as an invigorating opportunity for the
fortification of patriotism and valour. Western and central European Jews fully
participated in this mood, in some cases with particular enthusiasm, as support
for the war effort enabled them to affirm their identification with their states
of residence, which the rise of antisemitism, and to some extent also Zionism,
had cast into question.[94] In Germany, where the war was initially embraced by
almost all Jews except those on the radical Left, the neo-Kantian philosopher
Hermann Cohen patriotically asserted the deep affinity between Jewish and

German culture. In his *Germanism and Judaism* (1915), he emphasized the profound resonance between Judaism and German Protestantism, and their commonality of purpose in promoting moral responsibility and the betterment of the world. Central to this endeavour was the messianic prophetic vision of the Israelite prophets, which Cohen regarded as the core of Judaism, and barely of lesser importance in the German ethical tradition, from the idealism of Kant to the social democratic movement in politics, in which he proudly noted that Jews had played a prominent role. The mission of Judaism, for Cohen, was profoundly universal in character, and Germany provided the most hospitable environment for its development. Jewish prophetic messianism was the indispensable 'lodestar of perpetual peace', given political substance in the contemporary world through socialist internationalism and in the bond between the cosmopolitan essences of the German and the Jewish spirit.[95]

Cohen was therefore firmly opposed to Zionism. In 1916, he participated in an extended public debate with the leading German cultural Zionist Martin Buber (1878–1965), in which he emphasized the necessity of the dispersion of the Jews for the fulfilment of their messianic purpose. Citing the prophet Micah—'The remnant of Jacob shall be in the midst of the many peoples, like dew from the Lord'—he argued that Jews were required to live among and for the nations of the world, diffusing the humanistic and universal moral teachings that were divinely entrusted to them as their universal mission.[96] Cohen interpreted Jewish suffering as part of this moral mission: analogously to the atonement of individual Jews at Yom Kippur for the collective sins of the congregation, the Jews in a sense collectively atoned through their historical travails for the sins of all humanity. This was not, though, their eternal fate. Cohen's messianic vision was not eschatological, but rather a political vision of a new universal dawn that was to be attained in this world.[97] The structures of politics, and of the German philosophical and socialist traditions in particular, were therefore essential to his understanding of messianism. Jews could only fulfil their mission as participants in the political life of the state. They must therefore embrace the nation states in which they lived, and recognize their ethical obligation to them. Cohen rejected the Jewish particularism of Zionism, and instead cast Judaism as the universalist strand of other, particular nationalisms. In Germany—and potentially in other nations too, though Cohen did not believe they had attained the same ethical heights—the Jews played a special role in sustaining the ethical and cosmopolitan core of collective patriotic pride in the modern state.

Martin Buber disagreed. The lesson of history, he believed, was that as long as the Jews were fully dispersed across the states of Europe they would be denied the possibility of collective self-definition and self-realization. They would therefore remain unable truly to flourish, as this required the ability to act as a group. A Zionist spiritual centre in Palestine was essential, Buber believed, in order to enable the Jews to move from passivity to activity. In opposition to Cohen's affirmation of the importance of the state, he regarded the nurturing of Judaism as a living religion as a higher Jewish calling.[98] He agreed with Cohen, however, that the purpose of the Jews was messianic and universal, amounting to nothing less than the salvation of humanity as a whole. An admirer of Ahad Ha'am, Buber believed that a centre of Jewish spiritual regeneration would enable the renewal of Judaism across the diaspora, and therefore also the fulfilment of its transformative role for all humanity.[99] The centrality of ethics in Buber's understanding of Judaism led him to play a leading role in seeking peaceful and cooperative coexistence with the Palestinian Arab population, particularly through the Brit Shalom movement that he established, with Gershom Scholem and others, in 1925. Although his vision of cultural Zionism sought to transcend the horizons of state-bound politics, he shared with Cohen a strong progressive commitment to Jewish ethical exemplarity in the political sphere.[100]

The ethical and dialogical philosophy of Judaism that Buber developed in the 1920s, most notably in his *I and Thou* (1922), bore similarities to the simultaneous work of his friend and collaborator Franz Rosenzweig (1886–1929). In the febrile cultural environment of Weimar Germany, both Buber and Rosenzweig sought to capture the experiential essence of living a meaningfully Jewish life. Rosenzweig shared with both Cohen and Buber a profound sense of the crucial purpose of Judaism for humanity as a whole. In his elusive but nonetheless extremely influential *The Star of Redemption* (1921), he put forward his own philosophical understanding of the meaning of religion, and Judaism in particular, in human life. Unlike Buber—but following Cohen, who was a major influence on him—Rosenzweig rejected Zionism. However, he also rejected Cohen's politically engaged socialism. The unique significance of the Jews as God's chosen people required them, he believed, to stand apart from politics, and aloof from the national structures and affiliations of the world. Rosenzweig's view of Jewish peoplehood, as a rejection of the normal structures of human existence, nonetheless strongly connected Jews to others, as an exemplary model in the present and a signpost to the messianic future. In presenting them as the loftiest possible exemplar of collective being, he cast the Jews as a philosophical ideal, fusing the intimacy of peoplehood with a universality of ethical purpose. In possessing this harmony, the Jewish people was in his view 'already at the goal toward which the peoples of the world are just setting out'.[101]

Rosenzweig's thought was shaped by a close engagement with Christianity. Close relatives and friends of his had converted to Protestantism, and in 1913 he came to the brink of doing so himself. His experience of active service in the First World War was equally crucial, and also pushed him to search for the clearest possible understanding of the inner meaning of Judaism and of its significance in the world. Jewish separateness from others, he argued, was different in kind from the separations between the other peoples of the world. 'Every border has two sides'—but this does not apply in the case of the Jewish people, which does not enclose itself within borders, but 'must include the borders within itself', absorbing inwardly all sense of separation while living dispersed among the peoples of the world.[102] This understanding of the unique nature of Jewish particularity was intimately bound up with Rosenzweig's theology of Jewish election, which is central to the *Star*. The Jews' particular possession of revelation attunes them to the necessity and ineluctability of universal redemption. Their particular marking apart by God thus binds them to awaiting the universal future, when they, the patiently faithful 'remnant of Israel', will receive the messiah, and their distinctiveness will lose its significance in this final attainment of redemption for all humanity.[103] Although Rosenzweig's manner of expressing these ideas is highly distinctive, his core argument aligns with the long tradition of European thinking on Jewish purpose. Jewish particularity is once again presented as unique in both its nature and its significance, because it constitutes an anticipation, in microcosm, of the messianic fulfilment of all the peoples of the earth.

Rosenzweig repeatedly described the Jews as 'waiting'. Standing outside worldly affairs, the intensity of their religious consciousness centres upon the eternity of redemption, the waiting for which is encoded in the annual cycle of Jewish life, with its culmination at Yom Kippur (the liturgical structure of which is shadowed by the structure of Rosenzweig's *Star*).[104] Whereas Judaism inhabits an eternal realm, continually waiting for the messiah, Christianity performs a complementary role within history of actively diffusing religious truth. Rosenzweig contrasted the inward and timeless focus of Judaism with the outward and historical orientation of Christianity: Judaism is the 'fire' while Christianity is the 'rays'; Christianity is rooted in a historical faith in Jesus, while Judaism is centred in an eternal sense of messianic hope. Rosenzweig's notion of the complementarity of Judaism and Christianity has been praised for its ecumenical spirit, while also criticized for, among other things, its cursory and glib discussion of Islam. Notwithstanding his respect for Christianity, it is also important to note that Jews alone, in his view, possess an intimacy with redemption in the present. The existence of the Jews, with their sense of eternity and divine election, reminds Christians of what they lack, and that they remain only 'on the way'. This, he writes, 'is the deepest ground of Christian hatred of the Jews'. Although the two religions point together toward a messianic and universalist future, their relationship in the present necessarily encompasses tension and conflict.[105]

Zionists such as Buber and Scholem believed that Jews needed to escape from these fraught conditions of existence in Christian Europe, by abandoning their passivity and seizing collective empowerment through political action in history. Rosenzweig insisted, in contrast, that the eternality of Israel, standing outside the contingencies and tussles of historical time, was fundamental to Jewish meaning and purpose.[106] Reinforcing his argument for the uniquely unenclosed nature of Jewish being in the world, he asserted that Jewish nationhood was also uniquely constituted. Whereas other peoples grounded their sense of community in both blood and land, the Jews alone 'have put our trust in the blood and parted with the land'.

The racial overtones of Rosenzweig's definition of Judaism as a 'community of blood' have provoked considerable unease among commentators. This aspect of the *Star* should however rather be seen primarily as a Judaic repudiation of the nationalist violence in the midst of which the book was drafted. The peril of land-and-blood peoplehood, he writes, is that love of life can be overwhelmed by love of the soil, to the extent that 'the very life of the people pours out on it'. Serving in the German army on the Balkan front during the First World War, Rosenzweig must have felt that he had witnessed precisely this. In stark opposition to Zionism, he argued that an aloofness from struggles over land was fundamental to Judaism: the biblical narrative opens not with assertions of indigeneity but with a narrative of migration, and ascribes meaning to land only in a holy sense, as 'land of longing'. He thus cast Jewish peoplehood as an exemplary rejection of land-based nationalism, and of the enmity and violence that accompanied it.[107]

Rosenzweig's quasi-biological grounding of Jewish distinctiveness nonetheless brings him close to the long-standing tradition, from Judah Halevi to Abraham Kook, of regarding Jews as ontologically different from non-Jews. Rosenzweig was particularly drawn to Halevi: he published his own commentaries on a selection of Halevi's poems in 1924, and prominently cited in the

Star his image of the Jews as transformative 'seed', generating a tree the fruit of which will be the messiah who will be recognized by all humanity. He connects this account from Halevi's *Kuzari* with the 'suffering servant' of Isaiah 53. The vicarious suffering of the servants of God will continue until this moment of fruition, when all nations will recognize the Jewish root of the messianic tree, and 'venerate the root that they once despised'.[108]

It was also in response to Halevi that Rosenzweig put forward his most politically salient comments on Jewish purpose. Every Jewish generation, he wrote, has been divided between those whose 'strength of faith' has led them to be deluded by 'false messiahs', and those whose 'strength of hope' has enabled them to resist this delusion. An openness to messianic faith in this world is essential: without this possibility of delusion and disappointment, messianic waiting in hope is itself not authentic. Rosenzweig's attitude to Jewish followers of false messiahs is deeply respectful: he says that they are 'better', while those who remain in hope are 'stronger', and that the shedding of these deluded Jews is part of the process of the intensification and inward retreat of the Jewish 'remnant', until the ultimate moment of the true messianic arrival.[109] He clearly recognizes the virtuous, socially engaged passion of the 'deluded', holding in mind not only the past followers of Sabbatai Zevi and Jacob Frank, but also almost certainly the Jewish socialism of Hermann Cohen and many others, and probably also the Zionism of Buber and Scholem. The highest Jewish virtue for Rosenzweig, however, is patience. In relation to the nineteenth-century traditions of Jewish purpose, he largely rejects the 'mission of Israel' theology associated with the Reform movement, delegating instead to Christianity this pedagogical role as diffusers of true ethical values. He stands in continuity, though, with the more literary tradition of emphasizing Jewish virtue as a timeless quality closely associated with the withstanding of suffering, and above all with tenacity, which he recasts as the patient waiting of the Jews of strongest hope for the time of universal human redemption.

The Nazi seizure of power and extermination of European Jewry placed under immense strain the idealization of Jewish non-nationalist exemplarity of both Cohen and Rosenzweig. Their ascription of moral meaning to Jewish suffering, and their confidence in the symbiotic harmony of purpose of Jewish and German Christian culture, seemed in the light of these events almost inescapably discredited. After the establishment of Israel in 1948, the non-national exceptionality of the Jews also came to an end, and the young state rapidly developed its own nationalist mythology. Until the end of the 1950s, this was largely normalizing in character, placing little emphasis on the memory of the

Holocaust and focusing instead on Israeli versions of generic international tropes of patriotic valour and heroic sacrifice.[110]

For many European Jewish intellectuals, however, the horror of Nazism deepened the necessity of affirming the opposition between Jewishness and the myths of modern nationalism. This was the view of Ernst Cassirer (1874–1945), student of Cohen and inheritor of his mantle as the leading Jewish neo-Kantian of his generation, who had famously defended the universalistic validity of this philosophical tradition, so popular among German Jews since Kant's own time, in debate with Martin Heidegger in 1929 at Davos. In 1944, exiled in New York, Cassirer strongly asserted his belief in the moral mission of the Jews, writing that the struggle for Jewish survival was also a struggle for the 'ethical ideals' that had been bequeathed by Judaism to 'all civilized nations'. Prominent among these was the rejection of nationalism: 'If Judaism has contributed to break the power of the modern political myths, it has . . . once more fulfilled its historical and religious mission.'[111]

For Theodor Adorno and Max Horkheimer, leading figures in the overwhelmingly Jewish Frankfurt School of Marxist critical theory, the relationship of Judaism and reason to myth was more complicated. In their *Dialectic of Enlightenment* (1947), written in wartime American exile, they argued that the Enlightenment had become self-destructive: in crushing the remnants of myth, it had led to human alienation and defencelessness against economic domination, from which the delusion of mass antisemitism was a seductive decoy. The Jews were a focus of envy because they had first and most successfully incorporated a stable system of myth into their own collective identity, traditions and ethical codes: 'They are declared guilty of something that they were the first to overcome: the lure of base instincts, reversion to animality and to the ground, the service of images.'[112] Adorno and Horkheimer were critics of what they saw as the totalizing instrumental reason of the Enlightenment— but they nonetheless saw no alternative to the use of reason to renew the critical potential of the Enlightenment tradition. Despite their absolute secularism and their resistance to avowed Jewish identification, they clearly positioned their own quietly Jewish intellectual tradition, and also their portrayal of Judaism as a successful mastery of myth, in stark opposition to the chauvinism and demagoguery of modern nationalism.

In France, in the immediate postwar years, the existentialist philosopher Jean-Paul Sartre (1905–80) turned to the Jewish case in order to do battle against French exclusionary nationalism. The idea of the Jew, he argued in his essay *Anti-Semite and Jew* (1946), was a fantasy of the antisemite, who projects onto the Jew a mix of social and personal fears that have nothing to do with Jews themselves. It was therefore the responsibility of non-Jews—following Sartre's lead—to confront antisemitism, most fundamentally by working toward a socialist France in which bonds of solidarity would embrace everybody without differentiation.[113] Over three decades later, in *Hope Now* (1980), Sartre returned to Jewish themes in a different register, showing much more interest in the substantive content of Judaism itself. He was particularly fascinated by Jewish messianism, which he saw as fundamental to the Jews' sense of metaphysical destiny: a looking forward to a historical finality 'which must ultimately reunite humanity', and which provides inspiration to non-Jews for the secular project of political revolution. Taking issue with Hegel's ascription to the Jews of a subordinate and preparatory place in world history, Sartre's strong association of them with the central thrust of political transformation echoed the long-standing tradition among both Jews and non-Jews of ascribing crucial importance to the Jewish messianic idea in sustaining hope in the radical transformation of the world. In both his early and his late writing on the topic, Sartre also valorized the idea of the Jew as stranger, challenging the exclusionary tendencies of the national community and pushing it toward a more capacious and progressive future.[114]

The figure of the Jew as outsider, and as the unique purveyor of key universal values to all humanity, is also of central importance in the thought of Emmanuel Levinas (1906–95). For Levinas, the fundamental truth of Judaism lay in the recognition of unconditional responsibility for the Other. This tenet of interpersonal ethics was, he acknowledged, by no means exclusive to Judaism, but the 'incomparable prophetic excellence' of the Jewish Bible offered privileged access to it. The Jews were also special bearers of this universal ethical responsibility. In their particularity as a chosen people, and the persecution to which this has exposed them, the Jewish people have been uniquely bound, through their suffering, to this responsibility for the Other. Levinas described this sacrificial ethical commitment as 'the ultimate essence of Israel', and its 'invisible universality', shining a light of moral exemplarity for all the peoples of the world.[115] Levinas's account of Jewish purpose, notwithstanding his intricate elaboration of it, is deeply rooted in the long history of this idea. Grounded upon the time-honoured notion, in both Jewish and Christian thought, that it was precisely through their particularity that the Jews were most intimately tied to the universal, he linked this to a familiar set of Jewish traits and experiences: their ethical intensity, prophetic inspiration, historical suffering, noble selflessness and geographical mobility and dispersion.

Some critics have contrasted Levinas's Jewish embrace of rootlessness with the 'appropriation' of this idea by Sartre and other non-Jewish celebrants of Jewishness as a chimerical signifier of non-nationalist universalism.[116] Both men, however, were drawing on the same pool of associations with Jewish purpose, as Levinas acknowledged in his appreciations of Sartre shortly after his death in 1980. He then highlighted for special approval Sartre's solidarity with the state of Israel: a striking choice, in the light of the importance of Jewish dispersal as a repudiation of nationalism in the work of both thinkers. Levinas's support for Zionism was at first couched in idealistic and universalistic rhetoric, but became more overtly partisan in his later writings, in alignment with the broader rise of Zionist loyalism within French Jewry following the 1967 war.[117]

In a widely noted early discussion of Levinas, Jacques Derrida (1930–2004) dissected his attempt to present a philosophical argument for the disruptive externality of Jewish religious ethics to philosophy itself. This opposition was unstable, Derrida argued, because it could itself be articulated only through the language of philosophical reasoning. In opposition to a tendency in some of Levinas's writing to position a Jewish ethics of alterity as fully outside the history of philosophy, Derrida suggested that both traditions were inescapably intertwined within the historicity of Western thought. The practice of philosophy, as Heidegger had, for Derrida, already shown, entailed both an engagement and an embattlement with its Greek origins. The idea of an alternative to its reasoned logic—the transcendental authority of a religious ethics—was itself part of the history of philosophy. Derrida thus disrupted the juxtaposition of 'Greek' and 'Jewish' modes of thought. He acknowledged, however, the seductive power of this binarism, in which the latter represents an alternative point of origin to the former, its ethical imperatives lying in some sense beyond the procedural norms of European philosophy while always operating in intimate connection with it. Opening his essay by quoting Matthew Arnold on Hebraism and Hellenism as the 'two points of influence' over the world, and ending with James Joyce's famous declaration in his *Ulysses* (1922) that 'jewgreek is greekjew', Derrida linked Levinas's thought to the earlier history of this binary opposition.[118] Arnold, Heine and Renan, in distinct but related ways, had each regarded the Hebraic or the Semitic as resistant to the flux of historical time. In highlighting and problematizing Levinas's renewal of this idea, which could be traced back further to Pierre Bayle at the end of the seventeenth century, Derrida did not offer an exit from it. His aim was rather to prompt reflection on the inevitable interpenetration of the contingencies and complexities of historicity with the anti-historicist yearning for timelessness and transcendence.

Derrida was also concerned to probe the relationships between Jewish particularity, universal purpose and the historical formation of national identities. All humans, he argued, find themselves marked by particularity, through which they access and exemplify the universal. This condition is, though, represented with unique symbolic eloquence by the mark of circumcision: the intimate bodily cut through which the Jewish male, Derrida included, finds himself already scored and opened up by the particularity of ethnic belonging, and by the theology of covenantal chosenness—and thus of divinely determined universal purpose—that this ritual recalls and inscribes. This symbolic wound represents the stamp of language and culture, inescapably prior to the thought and choices of the individual; it also represents a vulnerable opening to responsibility for the Other, and for humanity as a whole. It encodes, enigmatically, the meaning of being Jewish, which Derrida paraphrases as 'testifying to the humanity of human beings, to universality, to responsibility for universality', and of Jewish chosenness, understood as the claim that 'we are par excellence, and in an exemplary way, witnesses to what a people can be'.[119] Such exemplarity is by no means straightforwardly associated with actual Jews. Rather, it is linked to this ideal of being Jewish, which contains with it, in its embrace of universality, a measure of disavowal of its own particularity.[120] It is this paradoxical Jewishness that is, for Derrida, exemplary of collective exemplarity.

The claim to universal significance and exemplarity is, Derrida argued, a ubiquitous feature of modern national identities. Nationalism is not alien to philosophy, but is itself philosophical. In the 1980s, Derrida conducted a sequence of seminars on 'philosophical nationality', which he opened with a close reading of the seventh of Fichte's *Addresses to the German Nation* (1808). True 'Germanness', Fichte here claimed, is rooted in the affirmation of life and universal freedom. In contrast to other political approaches, which Fichte collectively termed as 'foreignism', authentic German nationhood 'will be imbued by a spirit not narrow-minded and exclusive, but universal and cosmopolitan'.[121] Derrida describes Fichte's nationalism as 'archaeo-teleological', rooted in quasi-timeless origins and a future horizon, and thus only minimally associated with actually existing Germans: he quotes Fichte's explicit declaration that whoever does not share this conception of the national spirit should not be considered as a German, 'wherever they were born and whichever language they speak'.[122] This exclusionary rhetoric draws attention to the potential for an 'essentialist universalism' to be philosophically enlisted in the name of national exemplarity, and used to combat the 'false' claims to national belonging of those deemed as enemies within.[123] It was Fichte, as we have noted, who in 1793 had forcefully argued that the Jews were precisely such enemies, and could never be incorporated into the German polity, unless 'we chop off their heads and replace them with new ones'.

In another essay arising from his 'philosophical nationality' project, Derrida focused attention on Hermann Cohen's *Germanism and Judaism* (1915). This wartime text, Derrida observed, put forward 'a sort of German hypernationalism', and was addressed above all to American Jews, whom Cohen aimed to mobilize in opposition to the entry of the United States into the First World War alongside Britain and France. Cohen's claim that the German spirit stands at the centre of world history is explicitly indebted to Fichte, whom he places, along with Kant, at the summit of that spirit. While Cohen praises Kant for, among other things, his profound affinity with Judaism, he credits Fichte with the crucial realization of the necessarily social nature of the national collectivity. Citing Fichte's characterization of the German spirit as 'universal and cosmopolitan', Cohen interprets this as an *avant la lettre* identification of Germanism with socialism, which, as we have already noted, he in turn identifies with the universal mission of Jewish prophetic messianism. For this reason, and also because of their linguistic bond through Yiddish, the Jews of America—including those from the Yiddish heartlands far to the east of Germany—should identify with the German side of the war then raging in Europe.[124]

Derrida reconstructs Cohen's argument in patient detail, demonstrating the proximity between Fichte's German nationalism, forged during the Napoleonic wars, and Cohen's Jewish endorsement of this tradition at another moment of traumatic military conflict, over a century later. Not only was the idea of collective exemplarity by no means unique to Jews, but in this case the idea was deployed by Cohen, despite regarding himself as a pacifist, to coat the Great War with a patina of moral idealism. Derrida also carefully presented the evasions that enabled Cohen to sustain this position. Cohen bracketed from consideration the question of the purpose of the war, on the grounds that this was a historical rather than a philosophical question. Jewish messianism, meanwhile, would remain the 'lodestar of perpetual peace' under the hegemonic protection of a victorious Germany.[125] In salutary contrast to the ethical loftiness linked with Jewish diasporic cosmopolitanism by so many thinkers, including Levinas, Rosenzweig and Cohen himself, Derrida here sharply exposed how easily, particularly at times of war, these ideals could slip into practical support for exclusionary nationalism and militaristic violence.

In this essay, titled 'Interpretations at War', Derrida also held in mind a third conflict: the first Palestinian Intifada, which had broken out in 1987, the year before he first presented the piece orally at a conference in Jerusalem. In his opening comments, Derrida explicitly addressed this context, calling, among other things, for a 'withdrawal of Israeli troops from the occupied territories', and declaring both his 'concern for justice' and his 'respect for a certain image of Israel and . . . hope for its future'. It is perhaps with regard to that hope that he ends the essay on a quietly optimistic and with respect to Cohen surprisingly exonerating note. He here turns to the Kantian argument for the 'federation of free states' as a necessary foundation for perpetual peace. Noting that 'confederation is everywhere a pressing matter of the moment', Derrida finds this argument also in Cohen's statement in *Germanism and Judaism* that 'confederation is the end that the state must pursue'.[126] It isn't entirely clear what resonance with the present Derrida had in mind here, but he seems to imply that some sort of federal arrangement with a Palestinian polity was the Israeli future that he then desired and advocated.

Derrida would at that time have been keenly aware of the earlier controversy, still today to some extent unabated, over Levinas's seemingly permissive response to Israel's role in the Sabra and Chatila massacres in Lebanon in 1982.[127] Derrida's tendency in response to Levinas's Zionism, as with his final comments on Cohen in 'Interpretations at War', was not only to critique the dangers of enlisting the idea of Jewish exemplarity and universal mission in the name of nationalist military power, but also to soften these arguments by highlighting the contrasting insistence of both these thinkers on hospitality and fellowship toward the Other. Despite his repeated disavowals of any easy adoption of Jewish identity, this generosity of approach signals Derrida's desire to excavate and renew the positive political resources of the tradition of Jewish exemplarity and purpose. In the spirit of hope that has been so persistently associated with Jewish messianism, his thought endeavours to sustain the exemplary potential of Jewish nationhood without occluding the ethical perils and injustices with which it has been implicated.

———

In the irenic Zionist vision put forward by George Eliot through the voice of Mordecai in *Daniel Deronda*, a Jewish polity in Palestine would be 'a halting-place of enmities, a neutral ground for the East as Belgium is for the West'.[128] (Eliot's exaltation of Belgium, created as a neutral buffer state in 1830, is with hindsight sharply jarring. In 1876, the publication year of her novel, King Leopold II of Belgium hosted the Brussels conference at which the 'International African Association' was founded: a purportedly philanthropic organization through which Leopold initiated his brutally violent and rapacious colonization of the Congo.[129]) Herzl also glanced at existing models for a Jewish state. Dismissing the possibility of communication in Hebrew, he held up the example of Switzerland as a 'federation of tongues'.[130] Claims to exemplarity and uniqueness of contribution or purpose in the world have been central to the formation of modern national identities, and they have also shaped the ways in which national groups have compared themselves to others and at times appreciated and sought to learn from each other.

The biblical paradigm of Jewish election and universal purpose has undoubtedly been of exceptional influence on other national identities. In the modern era, and particularly since 1948, it has resonated most powerfully in the United States, where a profound sense of identification with Israel continues to play an extremely important political role. The strength of Protestant religiosity in America, a sense of divinely bestowed entitlement to the land (trumping the claims of its indigenous inhabitants) and a strong tradition of asserting a universal mission in the world have provided the theological and emotional basis for the intense bond between the 'chosen peoples' of Israel and America.[131] Despite and indeed because of the rhetorical intensity and inspirational power of the idea of Jewish national purpose, its significance remains a highly contested and mobile resource in contemporary political debate.

For much of the twentieth century the idea of the nation was shaped alongside vigorous debates over the nature and role of transnational structures in the organization of the world. The interwar League of Nations—the first modern institution of supranational governance—instituted and oversaw a new system of protection of minorities in the states of eastern Europe, underwritten by international treaties. The Jews were the primary case in point, and Jewish lobbying groups played a significant role in placing minority rights on the international agenda in the wake of the First World War.[132] The dominant ideology among early twentieth-century eastern European Jews was socialism, the internationalism of which was elaborated with particular sophistication by the Yiddish-speaking Bundist movement, which was founded in Vilnius in 1897 and attained its greatest popularity in interwar Poland. In stark contrast to their rival socialist Zionists, the Bundists stressed the principle of *doikayt* ('hereness'), and argued that the Jews were a transnational nation entitled to cultural autonomy and collective rights in their states of residence.[133]

The close engagement of Jewish international politics with European imperialism, and the blending of Jewish concerns with the rival British and French 'civilizing missions', first established at the time of the Damascus Affair in 1840, continued into the following century. In the British case, this was sealed with the securing of the Balfour Declaration in 1917, while in France prominent Jewish figures such as René Cassin played an important role in articulating the continued meaningfulness of the French imperial project, up to the time of the Algerian Revolution. Within Europe, Jews were the most ardent supporters of the transnationalism of the Austro-Hungarian Empire, and its most eloquent nostalgics after its demise in 1918.[134] In all these contexts, Jews occupied a special position in Western thinking about transnationalism, particularly in relation to attempts to manage or resist the rise of insular nationalist sentiments.

In the second half of the twentieth century, this association between Jews and transnationalism became more muddled and muddied. Jewish international lawyers—most notably Cassin and the Galician-born Hersch Lauterpacht—played a prominent role in shaping the postwar framework of human rights law. It was not until the 1970s, however, that the idea of human rights moved to the centre of international debate and activism. At this time anti-colonialism—largely excluded from the human rights agenda of the newly formed United Nations in the late 1940s—was finally recognized as a leading human rights cause. Whereas in the early years of its existence Israel was able to project itself as an exemplar and a solidaristic 'light' to other young nations freeing themselves from European imperialism, after 1967 it became increasingly seen outside the West as itself a colonial and oppressive state, and therefore essentially on the wrong side of the human rights agenda of the era.[135] Over the past fifty years, as the lines of conflict entrenched in 1967 have hardened, along with those of the international political debate over their legacy, Jews and Judaism have come to be increasingly associated with Israeli nationalist particularism and assertiveness rather than with internationalist cosmopolitanism. Before 1948, a future-oriented temporality of Jewish national restoration could readily coexist with the idealization of Jewish cosmopolitanism, within a wide range of overarching conceptions of Jewish world historical purpose. Since that time, however, these two poles of meaning have increasingly strained against each other.

This has rendered the relationship of Jewishness to nationhood an extremely confused and charged terrain.

In a speech to her party in October 2016, the Conservative British prime minister Theresa May made a comment of uncharacteristic philosophical interest. 'If you believe you are a citizen of the world,' she declared, 'you are a citizen of nowhere. You don't understand what the very word "citizenship" means.' This pronouncement prompted much controversy, and was condemned by some as implicitly antisemitic. For the leading Liberal Democrat Vince Cable, May's pronouncement was 'quite evil', and 'could have been taken out of *Mein Kampf*'.[136] The Nazis did indeed promote a disdainful perception of Jews as rootlessly and unpatriotically internationalist, though the use of term 'rootless cosmopolitans' as a criticism of Jews did not originate with Hitler, as Cable erroneously believed, but in Stalin's purge of Jewish intellectuals after the Second World War. The Brexit vote of June 2016 raised the stakes on cosmopolitanism in Britain, intensifying the attachment among anti-Brexiteers to the ideals of world citizenship that have long been associated with Jews. Although virtually nobody in Britain in 2016 had any knowledge of the German 'Spinoza Quarrel' of the 1780s, the argument over May's speech nonetheless echoed its essential structure. 'Remainer' opponents of Brexit identified with the ethical universalism and cosmopolitanism that were symbolically represented in Enlightenment thought by Spinoza, Lessing and his fictional creation Nathan the Wise, and Moses Mendelssohn. May's suggestion that true belonging was necessarily rooted in place, and implicitly also the particular shared values of that place, bore an affinity with the view of Mendelssohn's adversary in the Spinoza Quarrel, Friedrich Jacobi, who was sceptical of the vaunted cosmopolitan friendship between Lessing and Mendelssohn, and believed that human relations could only truly flourish within a common community of faith.

The necessity of rootedness in both community and soil has, though, also been asserted by many Jews. The Zionist movement has in various ways sought to convince Jews of this need. While many strands of Zionism have incorporated an ideal of universalist Jewish purpose, this is by no means ubiquitous: Jabotinsky, for example, as we have noted, believed in the single-minded pursuit of the nationalist cause, and regarded collective self-interest and xenophobia as a normal and healthy human attitudes, among Jews just as among others. Jabotinsky's normalizing vision of Zionism, with its concomitant rejection of the idea of Jewish purpose, sits uncomfortably within Western thought on Jews, in which the notion of purpose is so pervasive as to seem almost axiomatic. In the twentieth century, the rise of the human sciences and the increasing integration and standardization of social life have combined to place the question of normality itself at the heart of cultural debate. What does it mean to be normal, and to what extent is it desirable? The Jewish aspects of this question overflow far beyond Zionism and the issue of nationhood. The meanings and limits of normality must themselves be considered as a major and multi-faceted terrain of Jewish purpose in the modern era.

5

Normalization and Its Discontents

JEWS AND CULTURAL PURPOSE

Civilization has to use its utmost efforts in order to set limits to man's
aggressive instincts and to hold the manifestations of them in check by
psychical reaction-formations. . . . The advantage which a comparatively small
cultural group offers of allowing this instinct an outlet in the form of hostility
against intruders is not to be despised. It is always possible to bind together a
considerable number of people in love, so long as there are other people left
over to receive the manifestations of their aggressiveness. . . . In this respect
the Jewish people, scattered everywhere, have rendered most useful services to
the civilizations of the countries that have been their hosts; but unfortunately
all the massacres of the Jews in the Middle Ages did not suffice to make that
period more peaceful and secure for their Christian fellows.[1]

—SIGMUND FREUD (1930)

THE RUSSIAN POGROMS of 1881 spurred a new dynamism in Jewish political
life. Increasingly unwilling to accept the hostility, violence and economic hardship of their current existence, the eastern European Jewish masses turned to
competing alternative visions of their future: socialism, Zionism and emigration. These new perspectives jostled alongside long-standing Jewish aspirations
for social and economic integration and assimilation. The still unfulfilled goal
of full political and legal equality remained a prominent concern in late imperial Russia. Meanwhile, the mass migration of over two million Yiddish-speaking
Jews, mostly to the United States but also to western Europe, Canada, Argentina, South Africa and elsewhere, diffused the restlessness of the 'new Jewish
politics' across the Jewish world.[2] This provoked considerable unease within

the existing Jewish communities alongside which these new arrivals settled. More affluent and assimilated Jews—particularly in major centres of Jewish immigration such as London, New York and Vienna—often felt that their social integration was endangered by the arrival of large numbers of Jewish immigrants who were widely associated with poverty, ritualism and foreignness: the very traits from which these established communities had long laboured to distance themselves. The rise of political antisemitism in Europe heightened this concern.[3] The question of 'fitting in' therefore assumed unprecedented importance for western Jewish community leaders in this period.

With the process of legal and political emancipation in western Europe now complete, Jewish communities there and in North America faced a new set of challenges. There were no longer any formal barriers to the full integration of Jews into their surrounding societies, though this was nonetheless impeded by widespread prejudices toward Jews, drawn further to the fore by the increased visibility, due to immigration, of Jewish cultural difference. To what extent, though, was integration desirable? How could it best be managed, defended and promoted? And once it was to a significant extent achieved within certain bourgeois public and professional spheres, what was the meaning and value of continued Jewish religious observance and cultural affiliation? Many western Jews firmly asserted their patriotic commitment to their states of residence, sometimes pointedly presenting their Jewishness as secondary to their identity as citizens. This is reflected in the full name of the organization formed in 1893 to combat antisemitism in Germany: the Central Association of German Citizens of Jewish Faith (the Centralverein). In the United States, antisemitism was a much lesser concern, but the entwinement of Jewish self-expression and associativity with the patriotic assertion of national belonging was equally if not more firmly established there. The fraternal order B'nai B'rith, founded in New York in 1843, grew rapidly in the second half of the nineteenth century, placing civic involvement in American life at the heart of its activity, and in 1913 establishing the Anti-Defamation League, specifically charged with ensuring fair treatment for Jews.[4] Whereas the Zionist movement sought to normalize the Jewish people by furthering their own nationalist cause, the primary concern of most bourgeois Jews around the turn of the century was to establish a secure sense of normalcy and belonging for themselves within their home nations and cultures.

What, though, did normalcy mean in this context? From a Zionist perspective, Jewish efforts to integrate readily appeared both craven and futile. Integrationists, meanwhile, typically and often vociferously rejected Zionism, seeing it as undermining their efforts to demonstrate their patriotic loyalty to their non-Jewish fellow citizens. The philosophical arguments of Hermann Cohen and Franz Rosenzweig exemplify this response. The question of Jewish purpose in the twentieth century was not, however, always overshadowed by the issue of nationhood. The pluralism internal to nations and cutting across them—along multiple axes of race, religion, gender, sexuality, class and other categories and identities—has over the past century grown increasingly prominent in Western political debates and cultural conversations, and the Jewish case has figured with particular significance in this domain also. Grappling over the meaning of Jewish difference in the past and present, and its prospects in the future, has in various different guises provided an important gateway to the wider question of the relationship of human diversity to the idea of normality itself.

This has been particularly notable in the United States, where the challenges arising from diversity and inequality have fundamentally shaped the nation's law, politics and culture from its inception. The importance of Jews in America derives in part from their privileged position in the Protestant theology of the early and formative European settlers, and in part from the disproportionate Jewish impact on certain key aspects of American social and economic life. In the final four decades of unrestricted migration to the United States, there was a more than eightfold increase in the number of Jews in America, from about 250,000 in 1880 to over three million by 1920. These Jewish immigrants embraced the consumer culture of their new homeland with particular enthusiasm, acculturating through consumerism and adapting and extending American patterns of consumption in the process.[5] The integration of Jews into American society has by no means been an unthinking or purely material process, however. As a community with a notably intense tradition of reflecting on its identity and purpose, and freighted with particular significance for the Christians who constitute the large majority of their fellow Americans, Jews have been a central reference point for the relationship of particularity, in all its forms, to the wider American whole. The primary guiding metaphors for imagining American diversity—Israel Zangwill's 'melting pot' and Horace Kallen's pluralistic 'orchestra'—were first formulated by Jews, and above all with respect to Jews. The idea of multiculturalism, within and beyond the United States, remains today highly indebted to these early twentieth-century attempts to reimagine the place and significance of Jews in America.

The most influential and probing interrogator of normality in the twentieth century was also a Jew: Sigmund Freud (1856–1939). The functioning of civilization, he argued, placed a heavy burden on the individual. We are, according to Freud, driven by powerful instinctual urges of aggression and desire, which the regulating norms of society require us to restrict or renounce. He developed this argument most fully in his *Civilization and Its Discontents* (1930), in which he posited the existence of a 'cultural super-ego', imposing on the individual psychically impossible demands such as the requirement to 'love your neighbour'.[6] This ideal of universal love, established by Paul as a cornerstone of Christianity, led inevitably to the channelling of instinctual aggression toward those outside the community of faith. This, according to Freud, was the explanation for antisemitism. In the opening quotation above, he deploys dark irony in describing the purpose of the Jews as a cultural lightning-rod for the aggression of the majority. In this role they performed 'most useful services', but even the repeated massacring of them during the Middle Ages 'unfortunately . . . did not suffice' to exhaust the violent urges of their Christian neighbours. As fascism and antisemitism advanced during the 1930s, Freud devoted much more serious consideration to the social and psychological significance of Jewish difference. He only felt able to complete and publish his elaborate thinking on the subject, as *Moses and Monotheism* (1938), when he was exiled in London following the annexation of Austria into Nazi Germany.

The enormity of the Holocaust, unimaginable before its occurrence, cast a chill over the entire topic of Jewish purpose. This applied particularly to theories such as Freud's that seemed to consider Jewish victimization and suffering as inevitable. In the years of reconstruction following the Second World War, there was a strong desire almost everywhere to forget the bitter hatreds of the past, memories of which were to a large extent buried beneath the new and all-consuming antagonism of the Cold War. Gradually, however—starting in the 1960s and intensifying in the 1980s and 1990s—the Holocaust rose to prominence in Western and global consciousness, and with this there emerged a renewed understanding of Jewish suffering as uniquely meaningful in public debate. In recent decades, the Holocaust has become the touchstone of horror and of political ethics, and the primary marker of Jewish exceptionalism. Other traditions of thought on Jewish purpose have nonetheless retained their vitality. This applies in particular to the deeply rooted association of Jewishness with cosmopolitan universalism. This link played a very important though often semi-concealed role in the development of left-wing thought and activism in the first half of the twentieth century. Since then, the ethnic sociology of political radicalism has changed, but the complex significance of Jewish intellectual traditions and of the status of Jewish distinctiveness in left-wing thought has by no means dissipated. In recent debates on Jews and the Left, the competing political attractions of normalization and difference have strained against each other with particular confusion and intensity.

Integration and Jewish Purpose in Britain and America

In various locations around the Atlantic, large segments of the Jewish economic elite had already become highly integrated into mainstream Gentile society before the beginning of large-scale Jewish immigration from eastern Europe. This process was particularly pronounced in Britain. Significant numbers of upwardly mobile Jews assimilated during the Victorian period, drifting toward religious indifference or converting to Anglicanism or more universalistic denominations such as Unitarianism or Theism. It was in order to stem this widespread disaffection with Judaism within the established community that, around the turn of the twentieth century, Claude Montefiore (1858–1938) and Lily Montagu (1873–1963) initiated a new organization, the Jewish Religious Union, which in 1909 developed into Liberal Judaism.[7]

Both Montefiore and Montagu were born into affluent and prominent Anglo-Jewish families, and they both had a strong sense of belonging in England. As an undergraduate at Oxford, matriculating only seven years after the University Tests Act of 1871 fully equalized the position of non-Anglicans at English universities, Montefiore was strongly influenced by the liberal theologian and classicist Benjamin Jowett, who encouraged him to focus his energies on the spiritual uplift of the Jewish people.[8] Montefiore developed a strong interest in Christianity and in constructive engagement with Christians, shaped both by his encounters with Jowett and other Christians and by the earlier work of Jewish scholars such as Abraham Geiger. Like Geiger, Montefiore placed Jesus within his Jewish context, arguing that he stood squarely within the Jewish prophetic tradition, preaching a message that was imbued with the moral essence of Judaism. He recognized, however, a noteworthy distinctiveness in the style of Jesus's teachings, and in his emphasis on the redemption of all sinners. Both Jews and Christians, Montefiore argued, could and should learn from each other—but there was no incompatibility between 'the spirit of the Gospel' and the observance of liberal Judaism.[9]

Montefiore was not simply concerned to defend and burnish Judaism in the eyes of his non-Jewish peers. He sought most fundamentally to reanimate the spiritual energies of his fellow Jews, and their sense of religious meaning and collective purpose. He also adopted from the German Reform tradition a passionate commitment to the idea of Jewish mission, to which he returned in many of his writings. The proposal of one of his most enthusiastic supporters, Oswald John Simon, that this mission should be interpreted in a proselytizing sense—with religiously disengaged non-Jews as well as Jews being invited to join a new, liberal form of Judaism—was a step too far for him: in a round-table article in the *Jewish Quarterly Review* devoted to this suggestion, Montefiore saluted Simon's 'grand prophetic faith in Judaism', but expressed scepticism as to the current feasibility of his vision.[10] The outward-oriented essence of Jewish election was, however, central to Montefiore's theology. The Jews were 'a chosen people, not chosen for themselves, but for others'. Rather than being oriented toward their own material success, political power or cultural flowering, they had been chosen to learn, and to share their learning with humanity as a whole: 'to help in diffusing true doctrine and true experience about God and righteousness'.[11]

Lily Montagu's outlook was also grounded on a firm belief in Jewish mission, which she, much more than Montefiore, vigorously endeavoured to put into ecumenical social and practice. In the 1899 article in which she set out the initial rallying call for what became Liberal Judaism, she diagnosed a profound spiritual lethargy among both unthinkingly traditionalist 'East End Jews' and religiously indifferent and materialistic 'West End Jews'. For both groups, a concerted renewal of the prophetic purposefulness of Judaism was urgently needed: 'If . . . we are able by a strongly organised religious movement to arrest our own spiritual degeneration and to revive our faith, that mission of the Lord's Servant unto the nations, which was the highest aspiration of the Second Isaiah, may even yet be turned from a vision into reality.'[12] Daughter of the banker and Liberal politician Samuel Montagu, who raised his children in an environment of both religious orthodoxy and practical commitment to the uplift of the poor, Lily regarded her social engagement as part of her familial inheritance. Her father's unyielding opposition to Liberal Judaism, which she believed was in the spirit of the ethical values according to which he had raised her, caused her much pain. In her fictional writing, she introduced a strain of anguished intergenerational conflict to the Victorian trope, from the novels of Grace Aguilar and others, of the virtuous, spiritual and suffering Jewess.[13]

In Montagu's fiction (as in Aguilar's), and also in her life, intimacy across the confessional divide played a prominent role. In social work, which started with her establishment in 1893 of a pioneering club for Jewish girls working in the retail and garment industries, she collaborated with her close friend Margaret

Ethel MacDonald, wife of the Labour politician Ramsay MacDonald. Through the Jewish League for Woman Suffrage, in which she and her sisters were leading activists, she forged alliances with analogous organizations across the Christian denominations. In 1914, when these activities were suspended, she became a leading organiser of a Jewish voice within the wider peace movement, and in the 1920s she was the driving force behind the creation of the interfaith Society of Jews and Christians.[14] This tireless activity, and also the broader history of the role of early twentieth-century Jewish women in the furtherance of universalist and ecumenical causes, has not been accorded the same status in the annals of progressive Judaism as the more theoretical labour of men such as Claude Montefiore. In these endeavours, however, she imbued the idea of Jewish mission with new energy and distinctive concreteness. This concept, which since the early nineteenth century had been so often abstractly invoked in relation to ministry to others and to Isaiah's 'suffering servant', was put into practice in her work as hands-on assistance to the socially marginalized and the active advancement of causes of justice and peace.

Until the 1930s, British Liberal Judaism was almost entirely opposed to Zionism. Montefiore was particularly firm in his hostility: the Zionist movement in his view undermined the universalist mission of the Jews, and was not a solution but a stimulus to antisemitism.[15] Rejecting the notion that the Jewish people constituted a nation, he put forward his alternative self-understanding as 'an Englishman of the Jewish persuasion'. Nationhood and religion, he argued, were entirely separate matters, while racial origins, often mixed in any case, were irrelevant to human affairs. The Jews had a distinctive mission to perform, in England and elsewhere, not as a nation but as a 'religious brotherhood'. It was the value of this mission for the wider world, and this alone, that provided compelling grounds for Jews to remain committed to their ancestral faith, rather than embracing intermarriage and joining the most universalistic denominations of Christianity.[16]

Montefiore's antipathy to Zionism was reciprocated. For Ahad Ha'am, Montefiore personified the craven desire of western European Jewish elites to ingratiate themselves with their Christian peers, against which his own Zionist vision of Jewish cultural self-assertion was most sharply defined. In a 1910 essay written expressly against Montefiore's positive appraisal of the gospels, Ahad Ha'am rejected as illogical the Christian (and Liberal Jewish) idealization of altruism, arguing for the superiority of the emphasis in Jewish ethics on justice. This more rational perspective was, he claimed, the essence of the Jewish 'genius', the sustaining of which required Jewish separateness: rather than embracing the wisdom of the gospels, as Montefiore exhorted, the Jews should accept their position 'in a corner', apart from the mainstream.[17] The disagreement between the two men hinged above all on their contrasting views on the relationship of Jews, and of their role in the world, to others. The bitterness stirred by this disagreement presaged the deepening of divisions among Jews on this issue over the subsequent century.

The openness and dynamism of the United States provided a much more hospitable environment for Jewish religious innovation. In the late nineteenth century, this was most vigorously pursued in Chicago, where in 1874, amid the frenetic rebuilding and growth of the city following the fire of 1871, the Sinai congregation took the radical step of introducing Sunday services.[18] For over four decades from 1880, the rabbi of this community, Emil Hirsch (1851–1923), was the boldest voice in the development of a distinctively American version of Reform Judaism. The son and son-in-law of the two most influential rabbinic importers of the Reform movement from Germany (Samuel Hirsch and David Einhorn), the younger Hirsch sustained their emphasis on the mission of Israel, and explicitly linked this to the social issues of the day. By the 1890s, he was drawing large numbers to his Sunday sermons, in which he spoke out on contemporary social justice issues, supporting campaigns against sweatshops and for unemployment insurance and a six-day working week. Hirsch's ecumenical approach also attracted large numbers of Christians to his temple, where prominent non-Jews, such as the social reformer Jane Addams, were regular guest speakers.[19]

The wider Reform movement, while mostly not as radical as Hirsch in Chicago, was strongly supportive of the Progressive Era reforms of President Theodore Roosevelt in the first decade of the twentieth century. Matching the widespread invocation by Protestant leaders of the 'social gospel' as the ethical basis for tackling the suffering and injustice within American society, Reform rabbis cited the ethical message of the prophets as the moral underpinning of this political agenda. In the early 1930s, in response to the soaring unemployment of the Great Depression, several rabbis and communities were outspoken in their critiques of capitalism, and energetic in mobilizing a practical volunteer response to homelessness and poverty. While some lay leaders were uneasy with messages from the pulpit that seemed very close to socialism, there was nonetheless a broad consensus in the movement, across the first third of the twentieth century, that the prophetic ideals of Judaism demanded both clear words and concrete social action.[20]

This outlook was clearly enshrined in the 'Pittsburgh Platform' of 1885: a crisp eight-point document that officially defined the essence of American Reform Judaism until the late 1930s. Revisiting the themes of their debate in Philadelphia sixteen years earlier, the rabbis assembled in Pittsburgh again affirmed the importance of the Jewish mission, but this time with greater self-confidence and breadth of vision. The platform opens with a clear restatement of the special significance of Judaism for all humanity: while respectfully acknowledging that all religions contain valuable 'consciousness of the indwelling of God in man', the text asserts that 'Judaism presents the highest conception of the God-idea', which it has preserved and defended through the tribulations of Jewish history 'as the central religious truth for the human race'. An optimistic spirit suffuses the document. The universalism, rationalism and progressivism of the modern age heralded 'the approaching of the realization of Israel's great messianic hope for the establishment of a kingdom of truth, justice and peace among all men'. Exhorting fellowship with all those who wish to work with Jews in 'the fulfilment of our mission', the document concludes with a commitment to strive for social justice in the spirit of the Mosaic law. Already capturing the spirit of the Progressive Era some years before its heyday, the Pittsburgh Platform emphatically fused theological and political reformism in its uninhibited declaration of Jewish purpose in the world.[21]

The confidence of this statement was forged, however, at a moment of widening division among American Jews over the question of their separateness in American society. On one flank, theological adjustments that facilitated the social integration of Jews came under attack from more traditionalist rabbis, such as the Italian-born Sabato Morais (1823–97) of Philadelphia, both on religious grounds and as a threat to communal cohesion. Morais shared the reformers' active commitment to social justice, and also espoused a belief in the universal and messianic mission of the Jews as ethical teachers to the world. He was nevertheless deeply alarmed by what he regarded as arrogant Reform tampering with Jewish law on matters such as ritual observance, mixed marriages and dietary restrictions. Intense arguments over these issues were sparked by a controversy over the serving of non-kosher food at a banquet to celebrate the first graduating cohort at the Reform rabbinical seminary in Cincinnati in 1883. The Pittsburgh Platform's declaration that the Jewish people should no longer be considered as a 'nation', but as a 'religious community' also outraged more traditionalist community leaders. These disputes led to the foundation in New York in 1886, under Morais's leadership, of the Jewish Theological Seminary, which in the early years of the twentieth century evolved into the leading institution of American Conservative Judaism.[22]

On the opposing flank, Felix Adler (1851–1933), the son of a leading New York Reform rabbi, had already in the previous decade challenged the validity of any continued Jewish separation in the modern world. Adler became disillusioned with the Reform approach during his student years in Germany, where, in the early 1870s, he studied with Abraham Geiger, intending to follow his father into the rabbinate. Embracing Charles Darwin's theory of natural selection and new historical approaches to the study of religion, both of which were having a profound impact in Germany at this time, Adler concluded that these advances in human knowledge undermined both the idea of a providential God and the notion of Jewish chosenness. In 1877, he established the New York Society for Ethical Culture, through which he called for a new 'practical religion', focused on human betterment rather than theological doctrines. This movement remained small, but soon spread to other cities, breaking decisively with conventional organized religion and posing a significant intellectual challenge to American Reform Judaism. For several decades it continued to attract an ethnically predominantly Jewish audience to its lectures and events.[23]

The wholehearted commitment of the American Reform movement in the decades around 1900 to the universality of the Jewish mission exposed the nature and purpose of Jewish distinctiveness to deeper questioning. In this unprecedentedly hospitable environment, where Jews were not unique in their minority status and where neither legal discrimination nor shared experiences of widespread antisemitism held them together as a community, the continuation of Jewish separateness could no longer simply be assumed. For many of those drawn to Felix Adler's movement—both Jews and non-Jews—the logic of the Jewish mission itself implied that in the modern era, Jewish separateness should dissolve into the final universalism that had been so widely understood as its ultimate goal. Despite his firm rejection of the chosen people idea, Adler echoed the Reform tradition in regarding the ethical vision of prophetic Judaism as a fundamental contribution to humanity. He referred on occasion to Jewish 'genius', and even, in 1878, to his early, mostly Jewish, followers as a new 'chosen people'.[24] In a broad sense, the Ethical Culture movement was a reprise, in its restrained key of moral rationalism, of the universalistic messianism that swept Europe in the third quarter of the seventeenth century, and of the hope around the time of the French Revolution that the ending of the political exclusion of Jews would also bring to an end their religious separateness, ushering in an era of fully enlightened universalism. The radical wing of the Reform movement marked its distance from this perspective only through its affirmation of the continued meaningfulness of a distinct Jewish mission, which provided justification for continued Jewish communal affiliation and religious observance.

For almost all the eastern European Jewish immigrants flocking into America in this period, however, the notion of the imminent dissolution of Jewish distinctiveness was scarcely imaginable. Heavily concentrated in predominantly Yiddish-speaking neighbourhoods in New York, Philadelphia, Chicago and other urban centres, networks and bonds of Jewish ethnicity both enabled collective economic advancement and were reinforced by those gains.[25] Many of these recent arrivals were nonetheless strongly drawn to the universalism of left-wing politics. A Jewish labour movement burgeoned in the first two decades of the twentieth century, and played an important role in the rise of American socialism to its historical high point in this period. In New York in particular, Jews were so numerous in socialist and organized labour circles that these movements were broadly imbued with the cultural flavour of Yiddish secularism.[26] The rise of socialism among recent immigrants, and the accompanying rapid decline in their religious observance, alarmed mainstream community leaders and rabbis even more than the challenge from radical Reform and ethical secularism. A desire to stem this trend was a leading factor in the re-establishment of Morais's institution in 1902 as the Jewish Theological Seminary of America, with the eminent scholar and rabbi Solomon Schechter lured from Cambridge University to serve as its new president.[27]

The most vigorous rethinking of Jewish identity and purpose in America came from an early student and then teacher at that seminary: Mordecai Kaplan (1881–1983). Born in Lithuania, Kaplan arrived in America at the age of eight, and came of age in the bustling Jewish environment of New York's Lower East Side. He remained intensely committed to a vibrant and creative Jewish community spirit—an ideal that set him apart from the more genteel and assimilated German Jewish 'uptown Jews' who predominated in the Reform movement. Kaplan soon came to believe, however, that the inclusivity of American democracy, which had proved so enabling for these immigrants in material terms, nonetheless posed a threat to Jewish communal life. A 'new nationalism', he argued in 1916, was increasingly eclipsing religion in commanding the loyalty and energy of the citizenry across the West. In America, a national 'religion of democracy' was emerging, the rise of which would inexorably lure Jews away from their own religion. It was therefore essential to recognize that Jews were not simply a religious collectivity: they constituted a 'social organism with a self-conscious soul', sustained by energetic participation in a wide range of cultural, intellectual and welfare activities. Jewish life in America could thrive only through a regeneration of the synagogue as a centre of community activity: the synagogue needed to become 'the Jew's second home ... his club, his theatre and his forum'.[28] Whereas Reform rabbis emphasized the affinity between Jewish and American values, Kaplan prioritized the need to develop forms of Jewish community organization that were compatible with American life. America was a composite of religion-based communities, and it was therefore around the structures of religion that American Jews needed to build the richness of their wider shared existence.

Kaplan developed this core argument in numerous books and essays across his long career, but most influentially in his *Judaism as a Civilization* (1934). By this time, he perceived a 'crisis' in American Judaism. In the 1920s, Jews encountered a range of discriminatory barriers to their upward mobility, in housing, employment and higher education, and the onset of the Great Depression at the end of the decade further exacerbated anti-Jewish sentiments. Before the nineteenth century, Kaplan argued, Jews had endured suffering and persecution without difficulty, because they had firmly believed that their Jewishness was a privilege that would bring them salvation in the world to come. In the modern era, Jews lost this belief, and therefore readily regarded being Jewish as an unwelcome social and economic burden.[29] Kaplan confronted this loss of belief directly, and indeed to a considerable extent shared it. In his student days at Columbia University, he had been taught philosophy by Felix Adler. He was strongly and enduringly drawn to Adler's ethical universalism, noting in his journal in 1916 that he had often thought that 'I ought to join the Ethical Culture Movement'.[30] Like Adler, Kaplan recognized that the holy texts of Judaism could in the modern era only be understood as shaped by historical circumstances and cross-cultural borrowings, and therefore could not be considered as unique, infallible or timeless.[31] Unlike Adler, however, he did not conclude that the basis for a separate Jewish collectivity was therefore undermined. Jewish life needed, rather, to be grounded on a different basis: not on any claim that the Jews possessed distinctive or superior beliefs, but on the straightforward sociological reality of their existence as a community. The challenge of the moment, Kaplan argued, was to invigorate the synagogues and other organizations of Jewish life in order to better nurture all the diverse areas of activity encompassed by his capacious concept of Judaism as a 'civilization'.[32]

The Reform assertion that the Jews were not a nation was firmly repudiated by Kaplan. In his view, this denial etherealized Jewish life to the brink of meaninglessness, and was tantamount to collective suicide. Divorcing Judaism from the secular dimensions of Jewish life reduced it to 'a way of speaking rather than a way of living'; once so distilled to 'a medley of anemic platitudes', it was no surprise that many Jews abandoned it all together for secularism.[33] Kaplan's understanding of Jewish peoplehood, and his associated commitment to cultural Zionism, was indebted above all to Ahad Ha'am. He shared Ahad Ha'am's belief in the self-validating nature of Jewish existence, and in the craven redundancy of the efforts by figures such as Montefiore to justify it in terms of its contribution to wider society. He nonetheless also believed, as did Ahad Ha'am, that Jewish nationalism needed to be of the loftiest kind, linking the land of Israel to the invigoration of the Jewish diaspora. He envisioned Jewish cultural nationalism as 'the call of the spirit': a model of nationhood that was not tied to state power, and would therefore serve as a beneficent force in human society.[34]

Kaplan was disdainful of the Reform emphasis on the idea of the Jews as a chosen people. In his *The Meaning of God in Modern Jewish Religion* (1937), written under the shadow of Nazism, he declared that this idea bore 'a kinship and resemblance to the similar claims of other national groups which have been advanced to justify oppression and exploitation', mentioning in particular the Third Reich's persecution of Jews. He also diagnosed the appeal of the idea among American Jews as a compensating mechanism for their inferiority complex with respect to the dominant culture. The Jewish covenant, he argued, should be interpreted as a commitment among Jews to preserve their spiritual heritage, just as all other nations should preserve theirs, 'as a contribution to human knowledge and experience'. An ideal of the holiness of Israel could thus be preserved without any suggestion that the Jews were superior to others, or charged with a mission different from that of 'any nation that chooses to live its life on a high ethical plane'.[35] Kaplan regarded the claim of uniqueness, which underpinned the doctrines of Jewish chosenness and mission, as historically untenable. He aspired to normalize the place of Jews in American and world society, by liberating them as much as possible of their inherited baggage of exceptionalism. The grotesquely exceptional treatment facing European Jewry in the late 1930s prompted him to his most unequivocal rejection of these tenets.

The idea of chosenness proved difficult for him to elude, however—as it had been for Felix Adler, Ahad Ha'am and many others. In putting forward his interpretation of the spiritual and cultural meaningfulness of Judaism, Kaplan repeatedly vaunted the uniqueness and great significance of its gifts to human civilization. This was manifested in their transformation of seasonal festivals, marked in all cultures since the earliest times as a religious expression of gratitude for the fertility of nature, into rituals of historical commemoration. Through this elevation the Jews had 'directed the human mind to the consciousness of history as an ethical and spiritual influence in human life'. This historical awareness, he argued, had been 'given to the world' by the Jews, and was exemplified in the entwinement into the Jewish nature festivals of an emphasis on the ideals of justice, freedom and ethical striving in human history.[36] The Jewish idea of God thus moved beyond metaphysics and into human experience, as a meaningful and ethical presence in Jewish life. Kaplan asserted unequivocally that this was a loftier conception of 'godhood' that that of any other civilization.[37] Concluding this argument, he returned, despite his rejection of Jewish chosenness, to the 'mission of the Jew', drawing on many familiar hallmarks of the language of Jewish purpose over the previous century and beyond. The Jews' mission, he declared, should be to draw on their creative genius to contribute to the cultural and spiritual advancement of the world. They should embrace the suffering that their minority status has brought them as itself a source of their spiritual resilience and ethical virtue. They should proclaim with pride their commitment to the lofty ideals with which they were associated in negative terms: intellectuality and education, social justice and equality of opportunity, and cosmopolitan cooperation rather than chauvinist nationalism.[38]

Reconstructionist Judaism, inspired directly by Kaplan's thought, did not emerge as a separate movement in American Judaism until the 1960s. His ideas were, however, extremely influential much earlier. The emergence of the 'synagogue center' pre-dated Kaplan's major work: the semi-ironic phrase 'shul with a pool' was coined in the 1920s to describe this new phenomenon. Nonetheless, his emphasis on the wider social and civilizational significance of collective Jewish life provided the most eloquent support for the expansion of the scope of Jewish life in the era of suburbanization.[39] The Reform 'Columbus Platform' of 1937—the first comprehensive revision of the Pittsburgh document of 1885—also bore the trace of Kaplan's influence. The platform reaffirmed the universal and irenic values of 'Israel's mission' and the 'messianic goal' of the Jewish people. This was expressed more modestly than it had been fifty-two years earlier, though, and without any mention of Jewish chosenness.[40]

Kaplan grappled throughout his career with the tension between embracing American Jews' desire for social integration and normalcy, and sustaining and renewing their particular cultural vitality and cohesiveness. In the late 1940s, he put forward the idea of 'vocation', or 'calling', as an alternative to both Jewish election and mission. Seeking to displace the apparent claim to Jewish superiority of both those concepts, he offered a new formulation that emphasized the similarity between the social and spiritual commitments of Jews and of others: both his suggested alternative terms were more familiar in relation to Christianity. The notion of a Jewish 'vocation' did not, however, find resonance.[41] In his *The Purpose and Meaning of Jewish Existence* (1964), Kaplan focused explicitly on the answer to the question, 'Why remain a Jew?', which he argued required continual revision in order to remain in harmony with 'the most advanced thought and the most progressive social aspiration'.[42] Although he continued to avoid the explicitly exceptionalist language of chosenness, Kaplan's final extensive account of Jewish purpose strongly resembled many earlier articulations of the special significance of Jews in the world. He referred repeatedly, as he had since the 1930s, to the importance of Jewish exemplarity in the 'art of living'. Even without the label of 'the mission of Israel', he echoed the classic formulations of that idea in his concluding summary of Jewish purpose: 'to be a people in the image of God ... [and] to foster in ourselves as Jews, and to awaken in the rest of the world, a sense of moral responsibility in action'.[43] In 1960s America for Kaplan, as in nineteenth-century Germany for the early Reform rabbis and others, Jews found their purpose above all as disseminators and teachers of universal values to others.

The enduringly central metaphor for the integration of immigrants in America was vaulted to prominence by another tireless grappler with the opposing forces and impulses shaping modern Jewish identity: Israel Zangwill (1864–1926). Born in London to parents from eastern Europe, Zangwill's first and greatest success was his novel *Children of the Ghetto* (1892), which combined a realist representation of Jewish immigrant life in London's East End, biting satire of the assimilated Jews of the 'West End', and a probing literary exploration of the sentiments and ideas of reflective Jews caught between those two worlds. He followed this novel with a sequence of writings on the ghetto theme, describing and sentimentalizing the emotional and intellectual vitality of Jewish life. In his *Dreamers of the Ghetto* (1898), he idealized this environment as the source of successive visions of a better future, from Spinoza's philosophy— which he declared was profoundly Jewish both in its underlying unity and in its focus not on metaphysical abstraction but on ethical conduct—and the messianic hope of Sabbatai Zevi, to the poetic brilliance of Heine and the socialism of the 'people's saviour', the German Jewish radical activist Ferdinand Lassalle.[44] Zangwill is most remembered, however, for his play *The Melting Pot* (1908), which focused not on the Old World history of Jewish ghetto life, but on a vision of Jewish universalism and integration in the New World of America. His portrayal of America as a 'melting pot' of ethnic differences and antagonisms has been intensely debated since the drama's opening performance in Washington, DC, when President Theodore Roosevelt himself reportedly exclaimed, as the playwright took his bow, 'That's a great play, Mr. Zangwill!'[45]

In this drama, Zangwill put forward an image of America as 'God's crucible', in which 'all the races of Europe are melting and re-forming', purging the rivalries, feuds and vendettas from new arrivals as they are transformed into Americans.[46] The historical and rhetorical resonance of his presentation of this idea, however, was specifically Jewish. The visionary hero of *The Melting Pot* is David Quixano, a Jewish immigrant who has fled from Kishinev in the Russian Empire following the bloody pogrom there in 1903, in which he was injured and his parents and sisters killed. In New York, he falls in love with Vera, a Russian radical of aristocratic descent—but then recognizes her father as the commander of the soldiers who had opened fire on his community. His faith in the healing power of America falters, but, fortified by Vera's unwavering love, it soon returns, and at the end of the play the two affirm their union, accompanied by the imagined roaring and bubbling of the great American melting pot. The one hatred that we witness this cauldron eradicating is antisemitism: primarily through the symbolic reconciliation of David and Vera, but also in the shift from ignorant contempt to empathic understanding in David's grandparents' Irish housekeeper's attitude toward her religiously observant employers. David's passionate evocation of the potential of America is prophetic and quasi-biblical in tone. The word 'prophet' is associated with him repeatedly in the play, and David himself, while struggling with his continued hatred for Vera's family, interprets this as God's 'supremest test' of his prophetic mission and dream.[47] Like Lessing's Nathan the Wise, Zangwill's David is a fictional prophet of a post-Jewish universalism, in which the divisions of the past will be overcome through cosmopolitan familial blending. He is himself a 'dreamer of the ghetto', echoing the Jewish idealism that Zangwill identified in Heine, Spinoza and implicitly also in Jesus, who is mentioned sympathetically and described as a Jew in the prefatory poem to that earlier work.[48]

Zangwill was not, however, unambiguously eager for the erasure of Jewish distinctiveness. In *The Melting Pot*, David's grandfather puts forward the pessimistic view that Jews are hated also in America.[49] In his *Children of the Ghetto*, Zangwill had presented this debate more equivocally. At the end of this novel, its heroine sets sail for America, with an idealistic Russian former rabbi who is travelling there to preach 'universal Judaism'. Her intention, though, is to return to London to marry her betrothed, who is committed to sustaining the cohesion and welfare of the Jewish people through the promotion of 'intellectual orthodoxy'.[50] An early advocate for Zionism, Zangwill broke with the mainstream movement in 1905 over its decision to reject the 'Uganda Plan' and aim exclusively for a Jewish homeland in Palestine. Standing against the majority, he argued that Palestine was already populated, and that an alternative settlement location should therefore be sought. He was the key figure in the 'territorialist' movement that worked toward this goal, exploring multiple possibilities including Mesopotamia, Cyrenaica (today's eastern coastal Libya) and in 1912 opening serious discussions with the Portuguese government over Jewish colonization in Angola.[51]

Zangwill's espousal of radical assimilation in *The Melting Point* is not obviously compatible with his simultaneous territorialist activism. He was both a pragmatist and an idealist, and it is the different temporality of these two agendas—rather than any inner confusion or ambivalence on Zangwill's part—that explains the contrast between them. The renewed wave of pogroms in the Russian Empire between 1903 and 1906, and increasing obstacles to Jewish migration—particularly the British Aliens Act of 1905—convinced him that a practical Zionist solution was urgently needed. His vision of America as a utopian melting pot stood in a different category. America for Zangwill, both in *Children of the Ghetto* and in his famous play, figured as the semi-secular realization of his own ghetto dream, which was also his idealized understanding of the fulfilment of Jewish purpose in the world. Writing in the *Jewish Chronicle* in 1898, he celebrated the Jewish 'spiritual consciousness' of this sense of collective purpose: 'a burning conviction of some great world-part to play, some great world-end to serve'. The fulfilment of this purpose would bring Jewish meaning, and thus Jewish difference, to an end: 'the disappearance of Jews in the success of Judaism would be no deplorable end of the great dream'.[52] This, however, even if it was moving toward realization in America, was a utopian vision of the future. The politics of the Jewish present meanwhile required a more practical response, both in seeking genuinely vacant territories for settlement and in ministering to the immediate exigencies and aspirations of ghetto life.

The most significant response to *The Melting Pot* came from another Jewish intellectual: Horace Kallen (1882–1974). Like Mordecai Kaplan, Kallen was born into a traditional rabbinical household in Europe, and migrated to America—in his case from Silesia to Boston—as a young child in the late 1880s. Educated at Harvard, Kallen's thinking was shaped by the distinctively American outlook of philosophical pragmatism that he encountered there. Also like Kaplan, he was centrally concerned throughout his life with reconciling the continuation of Jewish communal vitality and cultural distinctiveness with the integrative power of American society. Kallen turned away from religion as a young man, however, and he also rejected Zangwill's idealized vision of cosmopolitan fusion as a desirable Jewish future. Whereas America for Zangwill was in large measure a screen onto which an imagined utopia could be projected, Kallen was keenly aware of his country's tensions and fault-lines, and in particular the increasing hostility toward immigrants in the early twentieth century. Among his colleagues at the University of Wisconsin, where he taught philosophy from 1911 to 1918, was the prominent sociologist Edward Alsworth Ross, who influentially argued that continued immigration, particularly of physically unimpressive Jews and southern Europeans, would undermine the cultural cohesion, political functioning and rugged good looks of the American people. Taking aim at both Ross and Zangwill, in 1915 Kallen published a landmark essay in *The Nation*, America's leading progressive magazine, in which he argued that the strength of American democracy was based upon the abiding diversity and vigour of the country's immigrant communities.[53]

Kallen offered an alternative metaphor to Zangwill's melting pot: America as a harmonious orchestra, in which each ethnic group represented a distinctive instrument, with its own 'timbre and tonality'. Far from erasing difference, the musicality of the American orchestra was dependent on it. Culturally and linguistically pluralistic societies in Europe, such as Switzerland and the four-nation Great Britain and Ireland with its wider empire, offered earlier models of this, but America, with its potential to overcome 'the waste, the squalor and the distress of Europe', held out the promise of perfecting the cooperative possibilities of humanity, becoming 'a multiplicity in a unity, an orchestration of mankind'.[54] Each European immigrant group offered its own distinctive contribution to this 'symphony of civilization': Kallen admiringly surveyed the institutional and cultural vigour of the Norwegians in Minnesota and the Germans in Wisconsin, and the indomitable cultural pride and national spirit of the Poles, Bohemians and Irish of America.[55] He was notably silent, however, about immigrants from Asia, and also made no attempt to incorporate into his argument Native Americans or Black descendants of slaves.

Jews, on the other hand, received particularly close and positive attention. They are, Kallen argued, like other European immigrants, but more so. Their eargerness to embrace America—unlike other European arrivals, they have no native land to which they retain an attachment—is matched by the exceptional density and energy of their religious, educational, literary and welfare institutions. This autonomy of spirit and cultural self-consciousness is 'in tune with Americanism', and is indeed enabled by it: as the Jew becomes an American, 'he tends to become all the more a Jew'.[56] American Jewry thus most perfectly exemplifies Kallen's argument for pluralistic collective organization and cultural self-expression as both the epitome and the sustaining resource of American democracy. He presents his case in quasi-scientific and universalist terms: Zangwill's melting pot ideal, he argues, contradicts the natural biological tendency for the diversification of life.[57] By no means all cultures, however, are reconciled into Kallen's alternative ideal, while the Jews, with their uniquely intense sense of collective identity, offer the musical keynote on which the harmonies of his American orchestra are based.

The identification of a profound harmony between Jewish and American values had been a staple of rabbinical rhetoric since the late nineteenth century.[58] Kallen's reformulation of this affinity was distinctive, however, in its avowed secularism. At Harvard, he had become a disciple of William James, and a committed adherent of his pragmatist philosophy, which emphasized the practical consequences of ideas and beliefs rather than their abstract content. Kallen applied this approach to the ethnic and religious pluralism of America, arguing that these multiple subcultures enriched the nation as a whole, and were almost invariably more edifying than the generic and banal alternative of American mass culture.[59] In 1906, he co-founded the Harvard Menorah Society, which over the next two decades grew into a flourishing movement—the Intercollegiate Menorah Assocation—across American campuses, aimed at encouraging Jewish students to take a proud interest in the richness of their heritage. This movement was to some degree modelled on the Verein für Cultur und Wissenschaft der Juden, established in Berlin in 1819 also in order to sustain a positive interest in Jewish matters in an environment that was widely hostile to cultural difference. The intellectual underpinning of pragmatist philosophy, however, imbued the Menorah Association with a distinctively American self-confidence. The anti-theoretical, down-to-earth orientation of pragmatism was seen by James and others as deeply in harmony with the American spirit. In connecting the new movement with this philosophical outlook, Kallen and his supporters underscored the Americanness of Jewish cultural uplift.[60]

Kallen used the term 'Hebraism' to capture his secular understanding of Jewish distinctiveness. He offered his own decisively pragmatist definition of this term, in direct contrast to Matthew Arnold's influential formulations: 'Hellenism is not concerned with "seeing things as they really are," but with seeing things as they *ought to be*; Hebraism is not concerned with conduct and obedience, it is concerned with making the best of a bad job.'[61] Even more pugnaciously, he rejected Arnold's conception of the symbiosis and broad parity of esteem between these two outlooks. In Kallen's view, the idealized and static worldview of Hellenism, epitomized by the eternal forms of Plato, had been decisively challenged by the revolutionary realization by Darwin of the decisive role of unpredictable flux in the evolutionary shaping of the universe. The embrace of change, and the prioritization of practical consequences over metaphysical abstraction were, Kallen argued, the core features of Hebraism. With the rise to dominance of Darwinian thought, the Hebraist outlook with which it was in harmony would also ascend to supremacy. The pragmatism of William James, alongside the related work of the French secular Jewish philosopher Henri Bergson, essentially rearticulated this ancient wisdom, in the form of 'purified philosophic Hebraism.'[62] The Jewish tradition, according to Kallen, did not simply exemplify the spirit of the modern era and its American instantiation. It foreshadowed this worldview, and was its most enduring and resilient expression.

Kallen was intensely hostile to the 'mission of Israel' theology of American Reform Judaism. The idea of 'universal Judaism' was, he asserted in response to a paper in support of the notion at the Harvard Menorah Society in 1909, both self-contradictory and vacuous. Universalism, he argued, was a Greek idea alien to Judaism, and imperialistically aspiring to an all-encompassing scope that erased the specificity of Jewish beliefs, laws and practices.[63] He also accused proponents of a Jewish mission of betraying an underlying insecurity, in implicitly accepting that Jewish existence was in some way problematic, and in need of justification: there was, he pointed out, no talk of an English or Japanese mission, or of a 'problem' or 'question' associated with those nations. The Jewish contribution to society should, rather, be evaluated in pragmatic terms, through an appreciation of the particular 'note' added by their 'Hebraism' to the harmony of human culture.[64] His own assessment of this historical contribution placed the Jews at the centre of the philosophical, moral and economic heritage of humanity:

The historic content of Hebraism was in metaphysics the vision of reality in flux; in morals, the conception of the value of the individual; in religion, the conception of Yahweh as moral arbiter. That the national life in Palestine, expressed in the Scriptures, is the source of a considerable portion of the moral and religious ideas of the western world is, of course, a commonplace. What is not so clearly apprehended is the fact that the Jews, as an *ethnic group*, were the great middlemen of medieval times, and that what they disseminated was as much the wisdom of the ancients as the commodities of commerce.[65]

Fusing together the Sombartian tradition of admiration for Jewish economic prowess with the familiar nineteenth-century idealization of Jews as teachers of ethics, justice and clarity of thought, Kallen's view of the place of the Jews in human history strongly resembled the rabbinic rhetoric he sought to reject. The Jews, in his mind, were undoubtedly long-standing bearers of purpose for others, and they remained in the present privileged exemplifiers and disseminators of ethnic pragmatism. Despite his protestations against the idea of Jewish mission, Kallen simply transposed it into his own key.

The persistence of Jewish purpose in Kallen's thought resembled the protracted wrestling with the idea in the work of one of his most important influences: Ahad Ha'am. Kallen concluded his most trenchant attack on Reform mission theology with an anticipation of his orchestra metaphor, but set in an international rather than a national context, as an expression of his vision of Zionism. The 'sectarian' nature of Reform Judaism, he argued, had thinned the vitality of the Jewish people as a national group. Zionism was the antidote to this: in a Jewish national home 'that unique note which is designated in Hebraism has a chance to assume a more sustained, a clearer and truer tone in the concert of human cultures, and may genuinely enrich the harmony of civilization'.[66] In 1913, Kallen sent this essay to the eminent jurist Louis Brandeis (1856–1941), who had recently become interested in his Jewish heritage and adopted the Zionist cause. Kallen's arguments strongly influenced Brandeis's idealistic and self-consciously American Zionism, according to which Jewish settlement in Palestine was envisioned as historically analogous to the morally earnest seventeenth-century Puritan settlement of New England.[67] Kallen's cultural Zionism was also idealistic: in 1918, he expressly rejected the claim to 'national self-determination', which had just been endorsed in the Balfour Declaration of the previous year, arguing instead that the Zionist project should herald the emergence of a new form of nationalism that was hospitable to pluralism and not based on the nation-state model.[68] Like Mordecai Kaplan, he reworked Ahad Ha'am's thought from an American perspective. In Kallen's vision of a Jewish homeland as a beacon both of 'Hebraism' and of the American embrace of difference, Jewish and American exceptionalism and moral purpose were closely entwined.

In 1924—the year in which nativist sentiments finally prevailed, with the introduction by the US Congress of formal quotas on immigration from most of Europe—Kallen introduced the term 'cultural pluralism' to denote his riposte to the defence of privilege and hatred of diversity epitomized by the Ku Klux Klan.[69] He continued to develop this idea into the 1970s, placing interaction across boundaries of difference at the heart both of American Jewish identity and of American life as a whole.[70] In the early postwar decades of suburbanization and the new homogenizing influence of television, the idea of pluralism proved less popular than Zangwill's vivid image of the America as a melting pot. Ethnic difference, however, remained a powerful force in American society. Even though the melting pot idea remained prominent in national debate in the 1960s, it was generally conceived as accommodating these enduring differences: up close, the melting pot looked more like a pluralistic orchestra. In content if not in rhetoric, therefore, Kallen's influence can be said to have outlasted Zangwill's.[71]

Jews, while continuing to stand out as a 'model minority' in their self-conscious celebration of the harmony between the ethno-religious and American aspects of their identity, also bore a particular significance in relation to the language of ethnic exclusion in the American city. The concept of the urban ghetto, which in Zangwill's writings had been stamped with Jewish ethnic nostalgia and political idealism, had moved by the late 1920s into the realm of social science: it provided the framework for pioneering sociological study of Jewish life on the Near West Side of Chicago influenced by the 'stranger trader' theory of Simmel.[72] By the 1940s, the term was almost exclusively associated, by sociologists and others, with impoverished and economically marginalized Black urban neighbourhoods. This association was forged at the same time as Jewish ghettos reappeared in Nazi-ruled Europe, establishing the idea of the ghetto as an irredeemably negative product of prejudice and hatred.[73] In the postwar period, as we shall see, the idea of Jewish purpose in America moved beyond the parameters of the early twentieth-century debate dominated by Kaplan, Zangwill and Kallen, and became profoundly entangled both with the fate of the Jews of Europe and with both domestic and global issues of racial justice.

Cultural Distinctiveness and Cultural Critique
in Austria and Germany

Jewish immigrants in America were able, in various ways, to regard the flourishing of their own cultural identity as an exemplary expression of the strength of the nation as a whole. This integration was much less readily conceivable in the cities of central Europe, to which eastern European Jews also migrated in very large numbers in the decades around 1900. In the capital cities of Berlin, Budapest and Vienna the Jewish population rose from a low base in 1880 to reach in each case between 150,000 and 200,000 by the early 1920s.[74] These Jewish communities were socio-economically diverse, but constituted a large proportion of the growing bourgeois class, and were particularly prominent in the commercial and cultural life of all three cities. The widespread enthusiasm of these bourgeois Jews for European secular high culture, often accompanied by an attenuation or abandonment of Jewish religious observance, superficially suggested a process of ardent assimilation. However, occupational distinctiveness, residential clustering and also the vocal rejection of Jewish integration by antisemitic individuals and organizations sustained a consciousness of Jewish separateness in these cities and elsewhere, even though the nature and significance of this social boundary was far from clear.

In Vienna, where Jews constituted almost 10% of the city's population in the decade preceding the First World War, their disproportionate impact on cultural life, and especially on the avant-garde experimentalism of the *fin-de-siècle*, was widely noted.[75] The degree of Jewish prominence in the intellectual and cultural spheres of Vienna in particular—as owners, consumers and producers—led to these domains being widely perceived as in themselves somewhat 'Jewish', despite in no sense being so in terms of their formal content. Bourgeois Jewish cultural assimilation thus paradoxically generated new forms of Jewish distinctiveness. Identifying the purpose of Jewish existence in this environment was, certainly when compared to America, an intricate and often fraught endeavour.

The pious religious ritualism and provincial habits of many of the newly arrived *Ostjuden* provoked unease and embarrassment among many established German-speaking Jews. This view was outspokenly expressed by Walther Rathenau (1867–1922), the son of a leading Berlin industrialist, a prominent member of that city's social elite, and after the First World War a leading liberal politician. In his essay 'Hear, O Israel!' (1897), Rathenau described the recent

Jewish arrivals in Berlin as 'an Asian horde', and exhorted them to cast off their 'tribal qualities' and transform themselves into 'Jews who are German by nature and education'.[76] Although thoroughly secular, Rathenau nonetheless retained a sense of pride in his Jewish roots, and firmly rejected baptism, which he regarded as a dishonourably weak and insincere act. In his most influential works, such as his *Critique of the Times* (1912), he argued that Germany needed to adopt rigorously meritocratic policies in order effectively to adapt to the new era of modernization and mechanization. The most talented Jews—and Rathenau undoubtedly had himself in mind as a prime example—had a prominent role to play in this process.[77] In a manner similar to Disraeli and his fictional creation Sidonia, Rathenau combined a fervent commitment to Jewish assimilation with a strong belief in the special forward-looking dynamism of an elite Jewish cadre.

The most pointed Jewish critic of Jewish assimilation in the Germanic world was the Viennese writer and satirical journalist Karl Kraus (1874–1936). From 1899 until his death the publisher and mostly the sole author of his own periodical *Die Fackel* [The Torch], Kraus relentlessly exposed and mocked what he regarded as the hypocrisy and corruption of the age, often singling out assimilated and influential Jews for particular scorn. The attempt by many bourgeois Jews to erase their Jewish distinctiveness constituted, for Kraus, a prime example of pretence and hypocrisy, as these Jews continued to cluster together as a distinct social group, often also with interlocking economic interests and habits of mutual support. Kraus relished drawing attention to aspects of Viennese life, such as the realities of prostitution and non-normative sexuality, that others preferred to veil. It was in this spirit that he spiced his writing with characterizations of Jews and Jewishness that violated conventions of politeness and often resembled familiar antisemitic stereotypes. He focused much of his critical energy on the liberal 'Jewish press', attacking the corruption, censoriousness and general intellectual and literary sloppiness of the established print media. Jews were closely associated with newspapers in Vienna and elsewhere in the Germanic world, as owners and as journalists, and also as enthusiastic readers. With the rise, around 1900, of populist and antisemitic newspapers, Jews became particularly avid consumers of the countervailing liberal press. Kraus regarded reverence for the journalistic commentary in these papers as corrosive of independent thought. He was particularly hostile to 'feuilleton' journalism: the airy mingling of facts, opinion and received wisdom that filled the inside feature pages of newspapers such as Vienna's leading liberal daily, the *Neue Freie Presse*.[78]

The editor of those pages, until he became the paper's Paris correspondent shortly before the eruption of the Dreyfus Affair, was none other than Theodor Herzl. In his pamphlet *A Crown for Zion* (1898), Kraus repeatedly referred belittlingly to Herzl's background as a feuilletonist.[79] Zionism, he here alleged, pushed the excesses of Jewish assimilation to their furthest limits, in accepting the arguments and goals of antisemitism. In response to the antisemitic cry 'Out with you Jews!', the Zionist replied, 'Yes indeed, out with us Jews!'[80] While mocking the attempts of bourgeois Zionists to overcome their cultural distance from their poorer and more religious allies from eastern Europe, Kraus was even more critical of the most ardently assimilationist and typically anti-Zionist members of the Jewish elite, who could be distinguished from their non-Jewish peers only by the absurdity of their over-zealous imitation of them.[81] While imagining itself as a rejection of this craven assimilationism, Zionism in Kraus's eyes merely reproduced it in a different register, and was tantamount to 'Jewish antisemitism'.

Beyond his mobile and piercing satirical critique Kraus offered occasional hints toward possible alternative visions of the place of Jews in society. He was not a consistent political thinker, but he criticized Zionism as an illusory distraction from the realities of Jewish economic hardship in eastern Europe, and concluded that a second Red Sea, social democracy, would block the Zionists' entry into their promised land.[82] Kraus also obliquely suggested how he himself reconciled the paradoxes of his own position, as a journalist critical of journalism and an assimilated Jew critical of Jewish assimilation:

> The irrefutable belief in the adaptability of the Jewish character is the best orthodoxy; one should let simply that become the credo of the tradition. Certainly, by staying insoluble while opening up into all surrounding cultures, and yet always remaining a ferment, the Jewish character proves itself more powerfully than its over-enthusiastic promoters.[83]

Kraus's career fitted this description. Fully immersed in the world of Germanic letters, he nonetheless did not seek to occlude his Jewishness, and relentlessly unmasked the attempts of other Jews to do so, while wielding his satire as a productively disruptive force in Viennese cultural and political life. In contrast to the attempts of thinkers such as Kallen and Kaplan to argue for the harmony between Jewish, national and universal collective aspirations and purpose, Kraus rejected this approach in all its available forms. He asserted instead the value of the dissenting individual, which he here identified in passing as in some sense the most authentically Jewish outlook.

In perhaps his most biting satirical essay, *Heine and the Consequences* (1910), Kraus iconoclastically attacked one of the most revered Jewish contributors to German literature, pithily summarizing his critique in a single phrase: 'Without Heine, no feuilleton.'[84] Heine's easily digestible, colourfully ornamented and pleasantly entertaining writing, Kraus alleged, had set German letters on its inexorable path toward the democratic banality of the pages of cultural and political comment that filled the daily newspapers a half-century after his death. Kraus's most vivid barbs in this essay have themselves ironically become some of the most quotable and chuckle-worthy phrases in the history of Germanic literary commentary. 'Heine so loosened the corset on the German language that today every salesclerk can finger her breasts'; 'today every Itzak Wisecrack can probably outdo him when it comes to making an aesthetic anaesthetic and using rhyme and rhythm to turn candied husks of thought into cherry bombs.'[85] Kraus persistently linked the Jewishness of Heine and of his journalistic successors to the vacuity of their output, and did so using imagery that often echoed the stereotypes of popular antisemitism. The name 'Itzak Wisecrack' [Itzig Witzig], for example, alluded mockingly to the attempts of Jews to adapt their names to sound less Jewish. Heine's own distancing from his Jewishness—his self-identification as a creative and sensual 'Hellene', contrasting himself, in his essay of 1840 in which he first introduced this dichotomy, to the Hebraic or 'Nazarene' asceticism of his rival Ludwig Börne—is trenchantly critiqued by Kraus. Attacking Heine's moralistic and crowd-pleasing deployment of homophobia in his own polemics, Kraus portrays him as falling far short both of uncensorious sensualism and of genuine linguistic creativity.[86]

The underlying target of *Heine and the Consequences*, and of Kraus's work more generally, was the narrowness of bourgeois culture in Vienna and elsewhere, which prized creativity but produced conformity. As the social ascent of Jews, in Vienna in particular, was closely associated with the rise of that culture, Kraus's attacks on Jewish superficiality, imitation and status anxiety cut to the core of his critique, and lent it additional transgressive spice. Jews, however, were even more disproportionately prominent among the modernist experimenters whose artistic work and intellectual innovation brought such sparkle to the Viennese *fin-de-siècle*. Particularly vulnerable to the anti-modernist and anti-bourgeois sentiments of populist politics, which were most potently articulated through antisemitism, creative Jews experienced with particular acuteness the brittle fragility of this cultural environment.[87] Alongside several other notable Viennese Jews of this period, Kraus himself rejected bourgeois conventionality, and was also a target of popular anti-modernist antisemitism.

In the pages of *Die Fackel*, Kraus inventively and incisively gave expression to his own independent perception of the darker truths of the world he inhabited. Only very occasionally did he present his cultural critique as itself in some sense Jewish, as for example in a 1913 essay in which he responded to questions from readers about his Jewishness by identifying himself, as an outsider among Jews, with both Jesus Christ and the biblical prophets.[88] It would have strained against his rejection of Jewish self-satisfaction and clannishness for him to represent his own journalistic role as a form of Jewish purpose. Nonetheless, as a Jewish individual expressing a universal ethical message, and standing outside the Jewish collectivity while remaining invariably identified as Jewish, Kraus's position bore similarities to Spinoza and Marx, and resonated more broadly with the long tradition, extending back to Paul, of the Jewish repudiator of the blinkers of the Jewish world being recognized as a privileged speaker of universal truths.

The malady of 'Jewish self-hatred' has in recent decades been ascribed by critics to numerous Jewish intellectuals, but particularly to Heine, Marx and Karl Kraus.[89] The self-hating Jew, according to this interpretation, is someone who has accepted and internalized the antisemitic prejudices of their surrounding environment. In Kraus's case, however, this is precisely what he accuses other Jews of doing, and himself most decisively rejects: he provocatively applies Jewish stereotypes to his satirical targets in order to undermine the assimilatory efforts of both Zionist and anti-Zionist Jews. The Holocaust has transformed the resonance of these stereotypes, making it difficult for later readers to register them in Kraus's intended tone. His writing was filled with paradoxes, and to a large extent drew its energy and wit from them. Kraus was knowingly steeped in the world that he satirized, as a journalistic anti-journalist and a bourgeois critic of bourgeois culture. He was also a Jewish critic of Jewish culture, though this final paradox was not the inner essence of, but rather the rhetorically vivid outer casing for, his act of satirical escapology.[90] Kraus relished his exceptionality: there is no sign in his writings of any form of self-hatred. His individualistic contrasting of himself to the conformist collective was the wellspring of his creative energy. In defiantly rejecting any form of comfortable assimilation, he stood against the dominant trends of Viennese Jewry, and affirmed instead his neo-prophetic role as a truth-telling outsider.

The notion of 'Jewish self-hatred' emerged in the interwar period, with connotations very different from those it carries today. Coined, it seems, in 1921 by the flamboyant Viennese Jewish writer Anton Kuh (1890–1941), the phrase was most influentially diffused by the prominent and prolific German Jewish essayist Theodor Lessing (1872–1933).[91] In his *Jewish Self-Hatred* (1930), Lessing developed his long-standing interest in Jewish collective psychology, which he argued was an extreme but not categorically unique case: 'The psychology of the Jews is only a particularly illuminating example of the psychology of the suffering minority.'[92] Jews have suffered, according to Lessing, because of their social and economic isolation: as a trading community, standing outside the social bonds of the majority, they became particularly watchful and critically self-aware. They also needed to find some meaning in their suffering, in order to withstand it. They therefore ascribed to themselves the blame for their predicament. Their fate was imbued with 'special purpose' through their belief that 'God chastises those that God loves', and that their historical travails were therefore a confirmation of their divine favour.[93]

Lessing's analysis of the psychological implications of the Jews' economic isolation was heavily indebted to the 'stranger' thesis of Georg Simmel, on whom he wrote a reverential essay.[94] His emphasis on the Jews' ascription of meaning to their historical suffering also built on his own earlier writings on the philosophy of history. The study of the past, Lessing had argued, was not a science, but a product of the human will—not *Wissenschaft* but *Willenschaft*—and its purpose was to give meaning to the objective meaninglessness of human existence.[95] The Jews' distinctive historical experience had made them notably precocious in this regard. Their condition had become universal: alienation was now the endemic condition of modern society. A tireless progressive, Lessing laboured in many ways against the forces of industrialization and human oppression that he saw as the underlying causes of misery: he was a committed feminist and anti-colonialist, and the founder of the first German noise abatement association.[96] In the culminating sections of *Jewish Self-Hatred*, he unveiled his boldest 'cure' for the suffering of humanity. The Jews, he argued, had discovered how to survive and even thrive through suffering, by embracing, loving and accepting responsibility for their fate. Their discovery was not for them alone: their 'pure spiritual mission for all nations' was to diffuse their insights for the benefit of all those who suffer.[97]

Lessing's text has been very aptly described by a recent critic as akin to a self-help book, ultimately conveying, despite the severity of its critique of modernity, a messianic message of hope.[98] Far from being a pathology to which Jews were uniquely vulnerable, 'self-hatred' for Lessing was a universal condition that the Jews had been the first to overcome. In their psychological resilience, turning their inward self-criticism into a source of strength, Lessing offered his own identification of the Jews' special gift to the future, the preservation and diffusion of which was their world-historical purpose.

Writing his essay in 1929, as violence between Jews and Muslims erupted in Palestine and the impact of the Wall Street Crash rippled across the world, Lessing's optimism was fragile. He was keenly aware of the danger that majority populations might choose not to learn from the Jews to take responsibility for their own destiny, but instead continue to cast them as scapegoats for the political and economic woes of the era.[99] In June 1922, months after becoming German foreign secretary, Walther Rathenau had been assassinated in Berlin. Eleven years later, Theodor Lessing met the same fate: fleeing to Marienbad, Czechoslovakia, soon after the Nazi seizure of power in January 1933, in August he was shot through the window of his study by Nazis from the Sudetenland.

In Vienna, Karl Kraus spent most of that year in self-imposed silence. A slender edition of *Die Fackel* appeared only in October, containing very little beyond a short poem, beginning with these lines: 'Let no one ask what I've been doing since I spoke. / I have nothing to say / and won't say why.' ['Ich bleibe stumm / und sage nicht warum.'].[100] Saved by his death soon after a heart attack in 1936 from a likely similar fate to Rathenau and Lessing, his final anti-Nazi polemic, written in 1933 but published in full only posthumously, opens with his most famous statement on the inadequacy of satire in the face of barbarism: 'On Hitler, nothing comes to my mind.'[101] Debates over Jewish integration, distinctiveness and mission now seemed utterly redundant, as persecution and then genocide was wrought indifferently on Jews of all classes and opinions. This previously inconceivable slaughter profoundly changed the resonance of the idea of Jewish purpose in European and global culture.

The Holocaust and the Lessons of Jewish Suffering

Karl Kraus was a persistent critic of psychoanalysis. He regarded psychoanalytic interpretations of works of art as dangerously reductive, and, in keeping with his general relish for highlighting rather than discreetly ignoring the distinctiveness of Jews in Viennese bourgeois society, attacked Freud's almost entirely Jewish circle in provocatively pseudo-antisemitic terms: 'They control the press; they control the stock exchange; and now they control the unconscious too!'[102] Nonetheless, Kraus and Freud were in amicable contact over the first decade of the twentieth century, and the later tension between them can to a considerable extent be ascribed to what Freud identified as 'the narcissism of minor differences'. They were the two boldest cultural critics of late Habsburg and interwar Vienna, which they both dissected from a self-consciously neutral outsider position that closely matched Simmel's model of the Jewish stranger intellectual.[103] They also both fundamentally rethought their critical approach in the light of Nazism.

Freud had briefly touched upon the causes of antisemitism a few years before 1933, in *Civilization and its Discontents*, which also marked his first sustained attempt to apply psychoanalytic concepts to society at a whole. For the final five years of his life, however, he was centrally concerned with the significance of Judaism and Jewish difference, as he repeatedly revised and extended his major work on this theme. He completed his first draft of this study in 1934, and entitled it *The Man Moses: A Historical Novel*.[104] This naming signalled the originality of the project, in which Freud delved far more deeply into historical and imaginative speculation than in any other of his texts. His protracted rethinking of the nature and value of Jewish distinctiveness in the world nonetheless reprised a number of the key features of nineteenth-century writing on Jewish purpose.

The plot of *Moses and Monotheism*, as the final (1938) version of Freud's study is known in English, is extremely intricate. Moses, Freud hypothesized, had been an Egyptian priest, and an adept of the short-lived monotheistic religion introduced by the pharaoh Akhenaten. In order to preserve this new religious outlook after Akhenaten's fall, Moses led the Jewish tribe out of Egypt and imposed it on them. Finding this religion too spiritually demanding, the Jews killed Moses, and repressed their memory of this crime. They later joined forces with other tribes, from whom they adopted the less intellectually exacting worship of a volcano God named Yahweh. Much later, however, the repressed memory of their original collective murder returned to their consciousness. This disturbing irruption of guilt was addressed through the emergence of Christianity, with was founded upon a symbolic ritual atonement for the murder through the narrative of Jesus's crucifixion and resurrection. This 'advance' in the psychic history of religion led to much hostility toward those Jews who rejected this new religion and the absolution from guilt that it offered. 'They were constantly met with the reproach "You killed our God!"', behind which, Freud, argued, there lay this more complex psychological reasoning: 'You will not *admit* that you murdered God. . . . We did the same thing, to be sure, but we have *admitted* it and since then we have been absolved.'[105]

Freud's final account of Jewish purpose did not, however, simply ascribe to his ethnic kin a functional role, as necessary victims of the safety-valve release mechanism for the pent-up violence of civilization. The Jewish claim to be 'the first-born, favourite child of God' generated among Christians an unconscious envy, of such intensity that 'it is as though they thought there was truth in the

claim'.[106] The resentment provoked by the Jews' separateness and distinctiveness was compounded by their indomitable success: they 'defy all oppression',
and 'show a capacity for . . . making valuable contributions to every form of cultural activity'.[107] The distinctiveness of the Jews, in Freud's eyes, was in itself
an impressive and significant phenomenon. He observed in them a special self-
assurance and mental strength, which he described in highly admiring terms:

> There is no doubt that they have a particularly high opinion of themselves,
> that they regard themselves as more distinguished, of higher standing, as su-
> perior to other peoples—from whom they are also distinguished by many
> of their customs. At the same time they are inspired by a peculiar confidence
> in life, such as is derived from the secret ownership of some precious pos-
> session, a kind of optimism: pious people would call it trust in God.[108]

The Jews owed their special self-esteem and 'tenacity for life' to Moses himself,
who had anchored in their religion the sense of separateness and divine chosenness that had been the source both of their intellectual and cultural strength
and of their suffering at the hands of others.[109]

Despite Freud's claim that Christianity marked a step forward in psychic
terms, as a means of overcoming the primal guilt for having murdered Moses,
it is clear that he viewed Judaism as the loftier religion, preserving within it the
intellectually rarefied monotheism of the Egyptian priestly elite. The phrase that
he uses to describe the superiority of Judaism—*Fortschritt in der Geistigkeit*—
has been much debated, and can be translated into English in two ways, neither of which is entirely satisfactory: as an advance in 'intellectuality' or in
'spirituality'.[110] Freud's use of the term *Geist* harks back to Hegel, and beyond
him to Paul. For both these men the idea of 'spirit' was central, and particularly
so in binary opposition to Judaism. For Paul, and for a long lineage of Christian thinkers down to Hegel, Jews had been too immaturely legalistic to grasp
the spiritual plenitude of Christianity. Hegel nonetheless attributed to the ancient Jews, as we have noted, the realization of the separateness of divine spirit
from material nature. He in a sense foreshadowed Freud in ascribing to them
an acutely unresolved sense of past transgressions, which in Hegel's view imbued them with 'a boundless energy'.[111] In claiming 'spirit' (*Geistigkeit*) firmly
for Judaism, Freud in essence reprised the core argument of nineteenth-
century Jewish Hegelians such as Nachman Krochmal and the early scholar-
rabbis of the German Reform movement, who cast the Jews as the guardians
of spirit in its purest, most rigorously monotheistic form. The distinctive features Freud associated with Judaism—tenacity, worldly success and an

optimistic vision of the future—also echoed the nineteenth-century rhetoric of Jewish purpose.

Freud did not explicitly endorse the idea, beloved of those nineteenth-century Reform rabbis, that the Jews were charged with a universal mission to diffuse the truths of ethical monotheism. His 'Egyptian Moses' thesis, however, placed the significance of Judaism firmly within a universalist lineage. He developed this thesis primarily on the basis of early twentieth-century archaeological and biblical scholarship. The core hypothesis of the Egyptian derivation of Moses's teachings had though been put forward much earlier: most notably by John Spencer and John Toland in the decades around 1700. While there is no direct evidence of Freud's indebtedness to those thinkers, he was drawn to this idea for the same reason as they had been: in order to place Moses, and Judaism in general, within a wider, and implicitly universal, historical framework.[112]

Freud's Moses ultimately stands beyond both the Jewish and the Egyptian realms. The Mosaic religion, in Freud's account, preserved the intellectual essence of putatively the most venerable priestly cult of human civilization. This religious outlook was only very briefly dominant in Egypt, and endured within Judaism only as a largely repressed intellectual counter-tradition to the more accessible current of Yahweh worship. This presentation of Mosaic Judaism bears a notable affinity to psychoanalysis: Freud's own effective religion. Psychoanalysis was also a highly intellectual theory of human existence and fulfilment, mediated by its own priestly elite. Although Freud developed his psychoanalytic concepts within a specific and essentially Jewish milieu, he claimed for them a universal reach. The demandingly rigorous wisdom within but also beyond Judaism that Freud associated with Moses is in this sense analogous to the truths that Freud saw himself as offering to the world. Entwined in Jewish worlds and traditions, but signalling toward a universalism beyond all particularities, psychoanalysis was the prophetic message that he believed himself entrusted to diffuse. For a brief period, he and others explored the idea of a Christ-like broadening of the psychoanalytic movement through the passing of the mantle of leadership to his non-Jewish Swiss disciple, Carl Jung. After his rift with Jung in 1913, Freud abandoned this fantasy, which had in any case never been for him wholehearted: he reasserted on numerous occasions the inextricable Jewishness of psychoanalysis.[113] The complexity of his interest in nonetheless reaching beyond these borders is illustrated by his relationship to Jung, as well as in his conception of Moses as both originator and transcender of Judaism. The truths of Mosaism and of psychoanalysis, for Freud, were preserved and transmitted by Jews, but in both cases their essence and destiny were universal.

Freud's attribution of the philosophical core of Judaism to 'Egypt' has struck some readers as a strangely unsolidaristic response to the crisis facing European Jewry in the 1930s. This charge was most eloquently made by the historian Yosef Yerushalmi (1932–2009), who in 1991 lamented that Freud had not unequivocally affirmed the particularity of Judaism, and that even in the face of Nazism he had continued to present psychoanalysis as loftily universal, in implicit contrast to the parochialism of Jewish identity.[114] In many respects, however, Freud in *Moses and Monotheism* strongly emphasized the intensity and particularity of Jewishness. His argument that the Jews had retained a memory of their murder of Moses was dependent on a quasi-Lamarckian theory of the hereditability of acquired characteristics, which in the 1930s was widely regarded as disproven: ignoring this prevalent view, he developed an account of Jewishness based on seemingly indelible traces of early collective memory.[115]

The roots of Jewish difference were for Freud extremely strong and deep. His vision of the future eclipse of that difference was at one level an aspect of his wider hope that the illusions of all religions would ultimately—'in a distant, distant future' according to his prediction in *The Future of an Illusion* (1927)—be displaced by the primacy of reason, intellect and science.[116] If, however, psychoanalysis is considered as a secularized version of Mosaic Judaism, maintaining the religion's philosophical core while inverting its cultural form from particularism to universalism, then Freud's orientation toward the future repeats the classic pattern of the idea of Jewish purpose. Psychoanalysis, the highest outcome of the superior intellectuality of the Jews, was in essence Freud's own version of the Jewish world-historical mission. Echoing the many earlier notions of the ultimate fulfilment of Jewish purpose, psychoanalysis held within its uncertain promise not only the erasure of Jewish difference, but the liberation of humanity from the illusions and divisions of all forms of religious and cultural particularism.

For Yerushalmi, Freud's failure to engage with the specific predicament of the Jews of Europe betrayed a markedly 'un-Jewish' failure of hope.[117] It is unsurprising, though, that in 1938 Freud's view of the Jewish future was bleak. In the penultimate paragraph of *Moses and Monotheism*, he repeated his account of the attack on Jews as God-murderers, adding Germans to his historical list of their accusers. He then noted darkly that in rejecting the Christian confession and ritual atonement for this murder, the Jews have 'taken a tragic load of guilt on themselves; they have been made to pay heavy penance for it'.[118] Freud, as we have noted, followed many earlier thinkers in regarding Jewish suffering as formative of Jewish resilience and tenacity, and thus finding positive meaning in their ordeals at the hands of others. His ascription of guilt to the Jews bears a close similarity to Theodor Lessing's conception of Jewish self-hatred as accepting responsibility for one's fate: there was an intellectually courageous integrity, Freud's argument suggests, in the choice not to flee this guilt by embracing the comforting but illusory atonement offered by Christianity. Writing in exile from the Nazis, however, Freud could not emulate even the extremely hesitant optimism of Lessing at the end of the 1920s. In this closure of his text, in contrast to the sections of *Moses and Monotheism* written earlier, he eschewed any identification of redemptive purpose in the suffering Jews then faced.

Freud died in September 1939, three weeks after the outbreak of the Second World War. The extermination of European Jewry during that war was on a scale that far exceeded even the most fearful predictions that circulated during Freud's lifetime. This mass murder of millions of Jews profoundly altered the place of Jewish suffering in European and global consciousness. In the nineteenth and early twentieth centuries, Jewish suffering had frequently been linked to Jewish purpose, but the enormity of the Holocaust seemed to make this association untenable or even obscene. The writer Stefan Zweig (1881–1942), another Jewish giant of the cultural life of interwar Vienna, had in his early play *Jeremias* (1917) vividly portrayed the Jews as inextricably both a people of suffering (*Leidensvolk*) and a people of God; in 1942, exiled in Brazil and in despair, he committed suicide.[119]

The eliminationist Nazi genocide was itself an inverted version of the prophetic and messianic ideas associated with the notion of Jewish purpose. Hitler repeatedly assumed a prophetic voice, including, in 1939, 'prophesying' the extermination of European Jewry, and scorning the laughter of Jews in response to his earlier prophecies that he would come to power and then 'achieve a solution to the Jewish question'.[120] The overcoming of Jewish difference marked for him the pathway to a new era: not, though, by transforming Jews into universalists, but by slaughtering and eradicating them. Historians have only since the late 1990s recognized 'redemptive antisemitism' as a fundamental driving force of Nazi ideology. It seems clear, though, that only the Nazis' quasi-messianic expectations of a new dawn of Aryan racial purity, in which Germans would conclusively displace Jews as the 'chosen' positive agents of history, can convincingly explain their obsessive, relentless and at the end of the war manifestly counterproductive implementation of the Holocaust.[121] This ideological distortion, and its relationship to the deep cultural and theological

traditions of the West, was barely graspable during the Nazi era and its immediate aftermath. The warped obsessiveness of Nazi antisemitism, though, was
glaringly evident. The most straightforward and ubiquitous response to this
was to recoil from anything that bore any possible relationship or proximity to
this obsession—including close interest in the Holocaust itself. In the immediate postwar years, across the world, both Jewish suffering and the idea of Jewish
purpose were largely shrouded in numbed silence.

There were also several further reasons for the initial postwar lack of interest
in the Nazi genocide. The nuclear-charged tensions of the Cold War focused
minds on the new lines of global division. On both sides of the Iron Curtain
the political mood was competitively forward-looking, focusing on brisk reconstruction and the ambitious development of national welfare provision. For
Jews in the West, the main concern in the 1950s was with 'fitting in'. There was
a general preference not to dwell on the violence and hatred of the past, which
in America in particular seemed to be dissipating amid the homogenizing prosperity of suburban life.[122] Seeking, and to an unprecedented degree attaining,
a sense of normality in mainstream society, American Jews were uncomfort-
able with anything that set them apart. This encompassed not only the raw
memory of the Holocaust, but also notions of Jewish chosenness and special
purpose. Reform and Conservative rabbis in this period moved discreetly away
from those ideas, and from emphasis on the Jewish mission to the world, which
had been such a cornerstone of Reform rhetoric up to the 1930s. Claims of Jewish exceptionality or exemplarity jarred with the integrationist ethos (among
white people) of American suburbia, and also, as Mordecai Kaplan had already
argued in 1937, could appear embarrassingly similar to the Teutonic supremacist ideology of the Nazis. Invocations of Jewish chosenness did not disappear
from American synagogue pulpits in the early postwar era, but they were typically couched in modest terms, emphasizing similarity and cooperation with
others.[123]

In Israel at this time, the memory of the Holocaust also jarred with the priorities of the present. Jewish powerlessness in the face of their slaughter in-
duced feelings of shame in the young state, where the collective focus was on
forging a very different future, in which Israeli Jews, in pointed contrast to those
of Europe, were to be strong, proud and no longer a vulnerable anomaly in the
world of nation states. The approximately 250,000 survivors of the Holocaust
who settled in Israel were a dissonant presence within this context. Their
tattoos and psychological scars were reminders of a traumatic past that
most Israelis raised in the pre-state *yishuv* preferred to suppress beneath a

future-oriented drive to develop the new state in accordance with the prevalent social democratic hopes and values of the era.[124] The only segment of
Jewish society that found meaning in the Holocaust in the immediate postwar
period were the ultra-Orthodox, for whom the event was a confirmation of the
heretical nature of the Zionist project. Putting forward more vociferously their
already established critique of Zionism as an illegitimate attempt to meddle
in the divinely determined timing of the messianic end of days, the Satmar and
other ultra-Orthodox groups argued that the Nazi extermination had been
God's punishment of the Jews for this sinful impudence.[125]

From the early 1960s, however, the Holocaust emerged as a focus of public
attention and increasingly as a touchstone of historical meaning. The initial cata-
lyst for this change was the trial, in Jerusalem in 1961, of one of the leading Nazi
overseers of the extermination, Adolf Eichmann. David Ben-Gurion staged this
trial at least as much for international as for domestic audiences, seeking to connect the Holocaust to the continued threat he perceived was posed to Jews by
the Arab states that surrounded the young nation. In the years leading up to the
1967 Six-Day War, the Egyptian president Gamal Abdel Nasser was repeatedly
compared with Hitler.[126] The Israeli Holocaust institution Yad Vashem, which
opened as a museum in the same year as the Eichmann trial, grew steadily in
size and prominence, and is today the most visited museum in Israel. Also from
the 1960s, the Holocaust was increasingly interpreted by historians in Israel and
elsewhere as the culmination of a relentless and in essence unchanging history
of European antisemitism. Whereas most earlier interpreters of modern political antisemitism had regarded it as a distinctive phenomenon emerging in the
late nineteenth century, by the end of the twentieth century this approach
had been strongly challenged by a conception of antisemitism as 'the longest
hatred', placing the Holocaust at the heart of a history of Jewish embattlement
and persecution extending from antiquity to the present.[127]

No longer associated with shame or repressed pain, the Holocaust has become the linchpin of Israeli self-presentation in global politics. The memory
of the genocide, brought to the attention of almost all visiting dignitaries at Yad
Vashem, underwrites expectations of empathy with Israel's sense of continued
existential vulnerability. Jewish suffering has thus been restored to the centre
of a renewed account of Jewish world-historical purpose. The realization and
achievements of the state of Israel, on this account, stand as the most compelling example of the resilience and tenacity of the Jews in the face of their suffering. The survival and protection of the Jewish state has thus become almost
inextricably bound up with opposition to antisemitism. These twin causes have

together been imbued, in the light of the Holocaust, with a unique aura of moral indispensability and purpose.

Israel's dramatic military victory in 1967 led to an international surge of Jewish identification with Israel, closely followed by and entwined with a dramatic growth of interest in the Holocaust. In America in particular, the social integration that Jews had so eagerly sought in the 1950s was by the late 1960s leading to alarm that declining religious observance and very high rates of intermarriage posed a new threat to Jewish cultural survival. The fraying, also from the late 1960s, of the cross-ethnic solidarity between Blacks and Jews in the early civil rights era in America occurred in parallel with the wider international challenge to traditional Euro-American historical and political perspectives, through the rise of decolonization movements, second-wave feminism and other outsider voices. In the 1970s and 1980s, as the patrician consensus politics of the postwar years across much of the West increasingly gave way to a more cacophonous and disputatious environment of 'competitive victimhood', Jews, like others, sought to focus and amplify their collective voice. Identification with both Israel and the Holocaust enabled them to do so in a way that was both readily accessible and morally authoritative. These newly foregrounded badges of Jewish identity did not require religious observance or even affiliation, and thus in a sense drew back into the Jewish fold many of those who had seemed to have left it through secularization or intermarriage. The enormity of the Holocaust, and its occurrence at the heart of European civilization, placed the Jewish historical experience as central in almost any comparative discussion of the horrors of the past. Over these decades the Jewish genocide widely assumed unique moral status and pedagogical purpose, as the prime benchmark of human atrocity.[128]

Before the 1967 war, there was little appetite, outside the Jewish ultra-Orthodox world, for finding meaning in the Holocaust. In his *The Face of God after Auschwitz* (1965), however, Ignaz Maybaum (1897–1976), a refugee from Nazi Germany and in the postwar decades a prominent Reform rabbi in London, argued that the genocide had in some way been part of the divine plan. Basing his interpretation on the references to the 'suffering servant' in the book of Isaiah, Maybaum connected the Holocaust to the two great calamities of ancient Jewish history: the destruction of the First and Second Temples. Both these events, he argued, had led to progress in human history crucially facilitated by the Jews, who through these episodes of destruction had been jolted into the next phase of their historical mission. Like Nebuchadnezzar, the Babylonian destroyer of the First Temple, Hitler had, despite his monstrousness, been an agent of the divine will. The sacrificial deaths of six million Jews, May-baum wrote, had, 'in awful efficiency', purged the Jewish people of its outdated medievalism, leaving the surviving community almost entirely 'in the Western camp', and aligned with its values of freedom and progress. These Jews—the surviving 'Remnant preserved by God'—must, he argued, sustain their pro-phetic mission to serve humanity, by interpreting Auschwitz as 'an awful portent in the exodus from our past into the future': from the barbarism and idolatry that Nazism had epitomized, to the future advance of Western civiliza-tion, cherished and defended by the Jewish people.[129] Maybaum was strongly influenced by Rosenzweig, who as we have noted also emphasized the 'suffering servant' idea in his wider conception of the messianic significance of the Jews. *The Face of God after Auschwitz* bears witness to the almost subterranean con-tinuation of the tradition of theological thinking on suffering and Jewish pur-pose represented by Rosenzweig. It has today, however, been almost entirely forgotten. Maybaum's sacrificial conception of Jewish purpose was so pro-foundly at odds with the postwar mood that it could barely be accommodated within Jewish intellectual memory.

In the 1970s, a significantly different Jewish theology of the Holocaust rose to prominence, in which the meaning of the genocide was linked above all to the imperative of Jewish survival. This was formulated most influentially in the '614th commandment' of another Reform rabbi and refugee from Nazism, the Canadian philosopher Emil Fackenheim (1916–2003). The Holocaust, accord-ing to Fackenheim, was a unique event of such epoch-making significance that it demanded the addition of one further imperative to the 613 *mitzvot* of Jewish law: a commandment to sustain Jewish collective life so as not to grant Hitler a posthumous victory. He first put forward this argument in 1967, and devel-oped it most fully in his book *To Mend the World* (1982).[130] The Zionist project and the security of Israel were for Fackenheim unambiguously covered by this supplementary commandment: Israeli sovereignty marked the 'Jewish emer-gence from powerlessness', and was 'a moral achievement of world-historical import'.[131] The existential vulnerability of Israel, which in the wars of 1967 and 1973 stirred the emotions of most Jews across the diaspora and also of many Christians, provided Fackenheim's argument with its political focus and sense of urgency. His rhetoric of Jewish purpose, however, was set within a universalist framework. Emphasizing the kabbalistic notion of *tikkun olam*, he presented the repair of Jewish trust in their Gentile neighbours as a deeply significant heal-ing of the post-Holocaust world. This mending, while taking on a special shape and importance in the aftermath of the Holocaust, was part of the Jews' continued messianic mission. Concluding his book with a classic formulation of Jewish purpose, Fackenheim declared that despite their fatigue and suffering the Jews cannot leave their 'singled-out post', because 'the world . . . cannot do without Jews—the accidental remnant that, heir to the holy ones, is itself bidden to be holy'.[132]

The 1970s was also the key decade for the emergence of Christian interpretations of the meaning of the Holocaust. The Catholic theologian Rosemary Radford Ruether, in her *Faith and Fratricide* (1974)—building on earlier work, particularly, since the 1930s, of the Anglican James Parkes—influentially argued that Christian supersessionist theology was no longer tenable. The 'message of Auschwitz addressed to the Church', Ruether argued, was that its monopolistic claim to divine truth required profound rethinking, because it had stoked the antisemitism that had led to the Nazi genocide.[133] This process of theological reassessment has in most Christian denominations been protracted and difficult. It has stimulated, however, a widespread move away from supersessionism and toward a view of Christianity and Judaism as closely associated rather than as rival faiths. Endeavours to develop positive relations between Christians and Jews have since the 1970s been built upon a strong belief in the importance of learning the lessons of the Holocaust, and of putting them into practice. Organizations such as, in Britain, the Council of Christians and Jews have particularly emphasized a keen vigilance toward the 'light sleeper' of antisemitism and the vulnerability of Israel to its manifestations.[134]

In 1978, US president Jimmy Carter initiated the governmental process that culminated with the opening, in 1993 in Washington, DC, of the United States Holocaust Memorial Museum. This federally supported institution placed the Holocaust in the front tier of American official memory, and quickly established itself as one of the most visited sites in the nation's capital. By the late 1990s, there were more than one hundred museums and other institutions in North America dedicated to public Holocaust education.[135] This boom in Holocaust consciousness, particularly in America but also in Europe and elsewhere, coincided with the period between the end of the Cold War and the attacks of 11 September 2001, during which the absence of ideological rivalry briefly gave rise to an optimistic belief that a peaceful and consensual 'end of history' might be within reach. This cultural mood was particularly receptive to the millenarian overtones of the idea of redemptive suffering as Jewish purpose. The public and pedagogical emphasis was on the drawing of moral lessons for the future from the Jewish suffering of the past, fusing together Christian, Jewish and liberal approaches to the genocide. The millenarian resonance of this vista to a healed future was heightened by the heady symbolism of the collapse of the Iron Curtain (which also made the Nazi death camps and the historic heartlands of European Jewry newly accessible to international visitors as sites of memory and mourning), and by the approaching turn of the millennium. The forward-looking meaning and purpose of Holocaust memory was officially encoded in the foundational 'Stockholm Declaration' (2000) of the intergovernmental International Holocaust Remembrance Alliance (IHRA), which affirmed its member states' 'commitment to plant the seeds of a better future amid the soil of a bitter past'.[136]

In our new millennium this approach to the moral and pedagogical significance of the Holocaust has diffused across all regions of the world. Some scholars have argued that the Holocaust now provides a cosmopolitan touchstone or 'moral forum' for global memory and ethical reflection.[137] It is certainly the case that this event can serve in many contexts not simply as a privileged measure of horror but as an analogical or conceptual gateway for the discussion of other instances of mass violence in history. It is equally clear, though, that the memory of the Holocaust, far from being a politically neutral presence in today's world, is a central element in the rhetorical and psychic battle between Israelis and Palestinians. In this struggle for political support and public sympathy, the Holocaust has often been pitted against the Palestinian *Nakba* (refugee crisis) of 1948, the traces and commemoration of which have been strongly repressed in Israel.[138]

The special signification of the Holocaust in today's global culture, however, is rooted in structures of thought that far pre-date the genocide itself. The exceptional resonance of the event is for this reason largely unaltered by comparative or contextual arguments that seek to understand it in non-exceptionalist terms, within the wider history of hatred and mass killing in modern history. This sense of special significance is based above all on the deeply rooted notion of the meaningfulness of Jewish suffering. This idea, from its biblical roots and Augustinian interpretation to its various iterations in nineteenth- and early twentieth-century literature and thought, has been a fundamental component of the wider conceptualization of Jewish purpose. Jews have persistently been seen as marked apart by their suffering, which has in many different contexts been understood as intimately associated with their special role in ushering the world from division and strife to a future state of harmony and cosmopolitan wisdom. In the late 1940s and 1950s, it briefly seemed that the enormity of the Nazi genocide had overwhelmed the extreme resilience of this idea. Since the 1960s, however, the meaningfulness of Jewish suffering, despite seldom being directly identified in these terms, has, with the rise of Holocaust consciousness, returned to prominence. Over recent decades, the Nazi genocide of the Jews has increasingly moved to the centre of Western and global attempts to establish a shared structure of morally purposive learning from history.

Jews, the Left and the Politics of Hope

For many of the Jews drawn to the political Left in the late nineteenth and early twentieth centuries, socialism held out the promise not only of social justice and decent living standards, but also of cultural normalization. Socialist Zionists, as we have noted, hoped that Jewish settlement in Palestine would lead to the establishment of a normal Jewish proletariat there, enabling a class struggle within Jewish society along the same lines as in other societies. Their leading rivals on the Jewish Left, the non-Zionist Bundists, demanded cultural autonomy for the Jews as a 'transnational nation', envisioning their nationhood as similarly as possible to the other cultural groups of eastern Europe. The universalist scope of socialism was widely perceived in both camps as an excitingly expansive contrast to the confines of traditional Judaism. The New York Yiddish socialist journalist and writer Abraham Cahan vividly captured this attitude in his proud reflection, in 1895, on the increasing displacement of the insular 'little Jewish soul' of the Old World by the strengthening commitment of the Jewish masses to the advancement of happiness for all humanity.[139]

Numerous Jewish thinkers in this period nonetheless ascribed to the Jews a special role in the realization of universal social justice. Hermann Cohen, for example, as we have also noted, regarded socialism as the political expression of the ethical core of Judaism, while Moses Hess, Bernard Lazare and many other socialist Zionists believed that a Jewish state would diffuse justice and fraternalism across the world. Beyond the communal spheres Jewish politics and theology, secular Jews have been strikingly prominent in the intellectual and organizational leadership of the Left in much of Europe and beyond. Several explanations have been offered for this. The vulnerability of the Jews to antisemitism may have inspired a particularly intense sense of solidarity with other downtrodden groups; the ethical message of the biblical prophets may have continued, even unconsciously, to inspire these secular Jewish radicals; the welfare institutions of the traditional Jewish community may have offered some sort of practical socialist model.[140] According to Isaac Deutscher (1907–67), these radical leaders stood in a long tradition of 'non-Jewish Jews', stretching back to Spinoza, Heine and Marx. In their rebellion against Judaism, Deutscher argued, these individuals followed a characteristic Jewish pattern. Straddling the borderlines of religious and national cultures, they were able to transcend the usual confines of thought, and to embrace a more expansive vision of 'the ultimate solidarity of man'. They also attained an intensity of political optimism to which, Deutscher commented barely a decade after the Holocaust, it was 'not easy to ascend in our times'.[141]

Deutscher's own life fits the model he described, and can be taken almost as an 'ideal type' of the twentieth-century radical Jew. Born into a Hasidic family in western Galicia, in his teenage years Deutscher left this world, acquiring a secular university education in Kraków and in the 1930s becoming a leading opponent of Stalinism within the Polish Communist Party. In 1939, he left Poland for London, where he worked as a historian and political writer, and by the 1960s a leading New Left critic of the Vietnam War. He is best known for his three-volume biography of Leon Trotsky, in which he cast his subject, in quasi-biblical terms, as a heroic and sacrificial prophetic leader.[142] Trotsky and Rosa Luxemburg, Deutscher argued, were in spirit and temperament the closest disciples of Marx. This affinity lay in their common background as non-Jewish Jews, which was expressed through the rhetorical intensity and unwavering universalism and internationalism of their engagement with the class struggles of the world.[143] The non-Jewish Jew, for Deutscher, was profoundly shaped by the particularity of his or her Jewish background, but precisely because of this was profoundly committed to the transformation of all humanity, firmly rejecting any special interest in the fate of the Jews. Deutscher thus recast the idea of Jewish purpose in the political language of secular radicalism. The (non-Jewish) Jew, once again, pointed the way to a utopian and universalist future, heralded and embodied by the inversion of Jewish particularism.

Already in the final quarter of the nineteenth century, in centres of immigrant radicalism such as London, New York and Chicago, Jews were not only numerically very significant on the Left, but also widely perceived by others as particularly fervent and idealistic in their politics. Jewish radicalism in London was energized by Aaron Lieberman, who in 1875 had fled there from Vilna to escape the Russian police, and who believed that socialism represented the true mystical core of Judaism. The Yiddish polemics and poetry of Morris Winchevsky, who arrived from Lithuania in 1879, further stirred the political imagination and activism of London's Jewish East End.[144] The German, Catholic-born radical Rudolf Rocker (1873–1958), arriving in London in 1895, was struck by the intensity of the Jewish political meetings he encountered in Whitechapel, where both men and women listened 'with rapt attention', and constituted in his

opinion 'an intellectual elite'. Rocker went on to devote himself until the outbreak of the First World War to the political organization of the London
Yiddish-speaking community.[145] Even though this linguistic barrier led to the
early Jewish Left in Britain and America operating largely through its own
separate structures, there was a widespread sense both on the wider Left and
beyond that the world of Yiddish radicalism possessed a particular intensity and
vigour.

In Germanic Europe, where linguistic differences were not significant, Jews
had featured prominently across the Left since the early nineteenth century. It
was here, in the first half of the twentieth century, that a cross-fertilization between Jewish messianism and revolutionary radicalism most vividly
emerged.[146] This reached its moment of greatest conspicuousness in the short-
lived Bavarian Free State, which was declared in Munich in November 1918
amid the collapse of the German Imperial regime and the Bavarian monarchy
at the end of the First World War, and was crushed by predominantly Prussian
right-wing *Freikorps* troops in May 1919. Political leadership in revolutionary
Munich was dominated by radical Jewish writers and intellectuals: the theatre
critic Kurt Eisner, head of the state until his assassination in February 1919;
the dramatist Ernst Toller, who in April 1919 briefly also took the helm; and
the anarchist theorist Gustav Landauer (1870–1919), who in that late phase
took the role of 'Commissioner of Enlightenment and Public Instruction'.[147]

These were heady months of idealism and experimentation, but also of extreme division, uncertainty and material hardship. The overthrow of the Left
was greeted with relief by most in Munich, many of whom subsequently avenged
their suffering and humiliation over the preceding months and years by focusing blame on the Reds and the Jews. Among those who embraced this simplistic
clarity was the young Adolf Hitler, who had held a minor leadership position
in the army of the revolutionary regime during its final month, and whose antisemitism seems to have become entrenched in his worldview immediately
following its fall, when he swiftly changed sides and eagerly denounced his former comrades.[148] The nodal historical significance of these Bavarian upheavals
has cast an evasive awkwardness over their memory. There was indubitably a
connection between the widespread labelling of the radicalism of this period
as 'Jewish' and the genocide of Jews little more than two decades later. This has
led later historians to avert their gaze from this traumatic entwinement, or to
focus on critiquing exaggerated perceptions of the Jewishness of the Left. In 1919,
though, this perception was far from entirely mythical. Jewish radicalism came
into tight focus in that year both as a nucleus of progressive political hope and

as a target of hatred among reactionary opponents of those universalistic ideals.

The central ideal of Gustav Landauer's utopian anarchism was 'community' (*Gemeinschaft*), conceived in Ferdinand Tönnies's influential sense as an organic social bond undermined by the divisive forces of commerce and capitalism. Landauer repeatedly invoked medieval Christian ideals of community in support of his romantic socialist vision, revering in particular the fourteenth-century German mystic Meister Eckhart. His early writings barely touch on Jews or Judaism, but his utopian, quasi-messianic fervour nonetheless focuses on the core transition of the idea of Jewish purpose: the eclipse of all human separation through a spiritually transformative embrace of the universal connectivity of true community. Spinoza, he noted, was the modern philosopher who had most profoundly grasped the living unity of humanity, God and nature. Landauer did not claim that this insight was rooted in Spinoza's Jewishness, suggesting instead that he had adopted it from the medieval Christian mystics. However, his emphasis on Spinoza links Landauer's argument to the long tradition of interpreting the seventeenth-century philosopher as a secular messiah, whose personal status as a post-Jewish Jew mirrored his intellectual achievement in overcoming the particularisms and oppositions of the past, and signalling the pathway to the unity of the future.[149]

While always seeking to ground his political ideas in the popular history of Germany, Landauer was never in flight from his Jewish origins. It was not until the final decade of his life, though, that he wrote explicitly about Jewish themes. He was inspired to do so by his close friend Martin Buber, whose romantic account of the eighteenth-century originator of Hasidism, *The Legend of the Baal Shem* (1908), offered Landauer a Jewish spiritual and communal idiom that was broadly similar to the resources he found in medieval Christian mysticism.[150] The essence of Judaism, Landauer argued, was a communal struggle for purification, distinctive from the spiritual life of other peoples because it was unmediated and truly collective—'led by no representative, no pioneer, no saviour, no saint, and no priest'—and, because of the Jews' dispersal, directed only inward, and never in rivalry or aggression against others.[151]

To be a nation, Landauer declared, meant to have a purpose. 'What is a nation', he rhetorically asked, 'other than a union of those who, united though their connected spirit, feel in themselves a special task for humanity?'[152] While all nations required a sense of their distinctive role, the special mission of the Jews was both enabled and signified by their stateless diasporic existence. Whereas other nations placed boundaries around themselves, and defined their neighbours across those borders as their enemies, Jews lived among their non-Jewish neighbours, whom they knew only as friends. The Jewish mission was thus to diffuse this amicable peace and unity among all nations. This was a task of the highest importance, constituting no less than 'the revolution and regeneration of humanity'.[153] Landauer was not implacably hostile to Zionism: he contributed to *Der Jude*, the monthly Zionist journal founded by Buber in 1916, and believed that his friend's brand of cultural Zionism could valuably foster the spiritual and creative particularity of the Jewish people. He emphasized, however, that Jewish aspirations both within Zionism and outside it must be selfless and universalist: 'to allow Jews to give themselves to humanity'.[154] These values were equally central to Landauer's broader ideals of political ethics and purpose. His notion of Jewish mission was imbued with a particular intensity, but in practical terms was indistinguishable from his wider utopian commitment, with comrades of all religions and ethnicities, to the immediate building of a world of peace and freedom for everyone.

An improbably important crucible of modern Jewish messianic utopianism was the Heidelberg home of Max Weber, who, on Sunday afternoons in the years before and during the First World War, hosted a discussion group involving his sociologist colleagues Simmel, Sombart and Tönnies as well as others. Two of the most prominent Jewish intellectuals of the twentieth century, Georg Lukács (1885–1971) and Ernst Bloch (1885–1977), were regular participants in this 'Heidelberg Circle', where they first met in 1910. Whereas the four leading sociologists in the group, each with his own distinctive nuance, associated Judaism with rationalism, the young Lukács and Bloch reacted against this. Establishing in Heidelberg a close intellectual friendship, they stimulated each other's growing interest in mystical and messianic thought, particularly though by no means only in relation to Judaism.[155]

Both men shared Landauer's enthusiasm for Buber's writings on Hasidism, and also for medieval Christian mystics such as Meister Eckhart and Joachim of Fiore.[156] They were also united in their opposition to militarism and imperialism, which in 1914 alienated them from the patriotic support of the Heidelberg sociologists for the German war effort. Lukács soon returned to his native Budapest, where, like Landauer in Munich, he assumed a role overseeing education in the even more short-lived and predominantly Jewish-led Hungarian Soviet Republic of 1919. Lukács's major later work on social and literary theory retained a messianic streak, but this was constrained by his formal allegiance to Marxist orthodoxy and was at most only implicitly connected to his early interest in Jewish themes.[157] For Bloch, however, this fascination remained central to his later political development. Christian, Jewish and also non-European traditions of mysticism were the principal resource for his riposte to the caution and conventionality of the Heidelberg Circle sociologists. This challenge was signalled in the nod to Weber's *Protestant Ethic and the Spirit of Capitalism* in the title of his Bloch's first book: *The Spirit of Utopia* (1918).

In this often impenetrably oblique but stirringly passionate text, Bloch evoked a messianic sense of emancipatory transformation as the spiritual essence of radical politics. An intense mood of revolutionary romanticism and apocalyptic expectancy pervades the book, in which Marxism and cultural analysis are intertwined with references to the Bible, medieval mystics and an eclectic range of other sources. In its first edition, *The Spirit of Utopia* contained numerous reference to the Kabbalah and Hasidism. It also explicitly ascribed to the Jews, alongside the revolutionary Russians and (he believed) incipiently revolutionary Germans, a special role in ushering in the messianic utopianism of the future. These references are considerably attenuated in the book's more widely diffused second edition of 1923.[158] These changes were undoubtedly motivated by the raw memory of recent events in Munich and Budapest, in the bloody aftermath of which many revolutionary Jews, including Landauer, were killed. The Jewishness of radical politics was now a delicate subject, and Bloch unsurprisingly chose to reduce its prominence in his writing. He did not, though, remove it entirely. Sprinkled references to Jewish mysticism remain in the later edition, including climactic allusions to the esoteric knowledge of the messianic future contained within the Zohar and other kabbalistic sources.[159]

In his next book, *Thomas Münzer as Theologian of Revolution* (1921), Bloch focused on an abiding hero of the German Left: the radical leader of the Peasants' War of 1525. While emphasizing the visionary importance of this German popular icon, Bloch connected Münzer to a wider subterranean history of revolutionary millenarianism, including medievals such as Joachim of Fiore as well as Isaac Luria's circle of sixteenth-century kabbalists. Münzer's importance for Bloch lay above all in the immediacy of his revolutionary action and utopian expectancy. This anticipated moment of revolutionary fulfilment was imminent, Bloch believed in 1921, in both Russia and Germany. Casting this at the climax of his book in Jewish terms, he wrote that 'Princess Shabbat' was about to appear, bringing with her 'the spirit of an ineradicable utopia'.[160] Bloch, like Landauer and Lukács, aspired above all to animate revolutionary hopefulness and commitment in as wide a readership as possible. He had no interest in addressing Jews in particular, and after 1919 had powerful strategic reasons to thrust German Christian inspirational figures to the fore in his writing. The strand of

Jewish messianism in Bloch's thought was nonetheless irrepressible, and played a crucial role in imbuing his work with its transformative urgency.

Bloch's *magnum opus*, his three-volume *The Principle of Hope*, was drafted in American exile from the Nazis, but revised and published in the 1950s in East Germany, where, from 1949 until leaving for the West in 1961, Bloch held an academic post in Leipzig. This sprawling work is in places at least as bafflingly enigmatic as *The Spirit of Utopia*. It is, though, by far the most ambitious discussion of hope in the Marxist tradition. Bloch's insistence on the ubiquity of hope as an inextinguishable presence in human consciousness stands in contrast to the scientific solemnity of much Marxist writing, particularly in the embattled Cold War atmosphere of the 1950s. His exploration of human hopes and dreams of a better world extends far beyond history. Just in that domain, though, his connective range is vast, linking together the biblical sources of optimistic and utopian thinking, in both the Old and the New Testaments, with the reprise of these ideals in medieval mystics, early modern theorists such as Thomas More and pioneers of socialism such as Robert Owen and the Saint-Simonians.[161]

Leipzig in the 1950s was a very inhospitable environment for the discussion of Jewish utopianism. Bloch did not, though, shy away from including Zionism in his history of the utopian imagination. Moses Hess's *Rome and Jerusalem*, he wrote, was 'the most moving Zionist dream-book', inspired by moral and prophetic ideals—although this had lamentably been transformed into a bourgeois vision by Herzl, sponsored by British imperialism since 1917, and most recently turned into a state ideology based on the invasion of Arab territory.[162] The early nationalist utopianism of the Jews was similar, Bloch argued, to the expressions of hope of other peoples, such as Czechs, Poles or indeed Germans. Straining against this normalization, however, he also noted a 'unique feature' of Jewish utopianism: 'the obligation posited along with it . . . to act in accordance with the intention of the prophets'. This higher calling, he suggested, implied a transcendence of nationalist particularism, which he evoked in personal and loftily universalistic Marxist terms: 'To line up with the movement towards the light, in every country to which we belong: this seems the genuine homeland of the Jews . . . ubi Lenin, ibi Jerusalem.'[163]

The most influential twentieth-century thinker of Jewish radical messianism, Walter Benjamin (1892–1940), was importantly influenced by his close friendship, from 1919 onwards, with Ernst Bloch.[164] Stimulated by Bloch's radical critique of Weber, Benjamin in his fragment 'Capitalism as Religion' (1921) suggested that capitalism was not, as Weber would have it, a coldly rational ideology, but was itself a uniquely merciless religion, demanding cultic worship from its anxious followers every day of the week: 'Christianity in the time of the Reformation did not encourage the emergence of capitalism, but rather changed itself into capitalism.'[165] Unlike Bloch, however, Benjamin did not embrace a redemptive current within the radical Christianity of Thomas Münzer or others. He placed his hopes instead in a more politically unruly and philosophically mysterious form of messianism. In another early fragment, Benjamin praised Bloch for his vehement repudiation of theocracy, against which the demand for an alternative 'order of the profane', grounded on 'the idea of happiness', was paradoxically also a striving for a messianic consummation of the end of history. The method of this striving, he declared, 'must be called nihilism'.[166] In contrast to Bloch's syncretic utopianism, the sources of Benjamin's messianism were not only non-Christian, but specifically Jewish.

Benjamin's juxtaposition of Jewish messianism to Christianity-as-capitalism was a reaction not only to the general analytical coldness of Weberian 'value free' sociology, but also to the association by Sombart, following Marx, of Judaism with capitalism. Benjamin had been raised in a highly assimilated bourgeois environment in Berlin, and Judaism was of little significance for him until his early adulthood. In 1912, however, when debates over Sombart's work and the relationship between German and Jewish culture were at their height, he encountered a Zionist youth leader who made a strong impression on him. He soon rejected Zionism, but a fascination with the cultural and spiritual significance of Jewish esotericism became at this point an enduringly central strand of his thought. Through his intense friendship from 1915 onwards with Gershom Scholem, he became aware of the disruptive antinomianism of Sabbatianism, Frankism and other episodes in the history of Jewish messianism.[167] This theological and political disruptiveness was extremely compelling for him, and became an important stimulus to his rethinking of the nature of time itself.

Benjamin's writings on time and history are almost inexhaustibly suggestive and complex. A key element within them, though, is the idea that history should not be understood as linear and even. Rejecting this conventional model, he returned repeatedly to the irruptive energy, at any moment, of messianic revolutionary transformation. He did not in any sense regard this as a proprietorially Jewish idea: in his 'Critique of Violence' (1921), for example, he linked it to the class struggle, in the power of a general strike calling not for specific demands but for undefined and absolute change.[168] Benjamin's highly idiosyncratic Marxist notion of the hopefulness and revolutionary motion of history was nonetheless most fundamentally underpinned by his valorization of the transformative force and unpredictability of Jewish messianism.

Benjamin's messianic conception of time is most vividly conveyed in his 'Theses on the Philosophy of History' (1940). He here introduces his famous 'angel of history': facing the past with wings spread open, the angel is propelled backwards into the future by a 'storm blowing from Paradise', and is only able to stare at the wreckage and debris of history that increasingly comes into view.[169] Benjamin then contrasts the conventional understanding of time—'homogeneous, empty time', advancing sequentially and processionally—with the messianic fullness of 'now time' (*Jetztzeit*).[170] He introduces this section with an epigraph—'Origin is the goal!'—from Karl Kraus, one of Benjamin's heroes, whom in a reverential essay he had compared to an angel. Kraus, the anti-journalist of journalism, was for Benjamin the truest messenger (or, otherwise put, angel) of the era. He saw Kraus as Kraus saw himself: as a clarion voice of piercing candour and non-conformism, relentlessly exposing the hypocrisy and corruption of others while retaining the clear vision of an outsider perspective.[171] This outsider position matched Benjamin's own sense of self, and also his implicit understanding of the purpose of Jews and Judaism, both personally and metaphysically. True Jewish messengers, whether as intellectuals or angels, stand for him outside the mainstream of history but not aloof from it. They observe the accumulating detritus of human life with acuity and engaged concern, and without false or naïve expectations of the future.

This past-facing perspective is nonetheless one of hope. It is only in the final lines of the essay, in introducing this hopeful vista, that Benjamin explicitly connected his angel to Judaism:

> We know that the Jews were prohibited from investigating the future. The Torah and the prayers instruct them in remembrance, however. This stripped the future of its magic, to which all those succumb who turn to the soothsayers for enlightenment. This does not imply, however, that for the Jews the future turned into homogeneous, empty time. For every second of time was the strait gate through which the Messiah might enter.[172]

The hopefulness of the angel of history is linked precisely to its fixed orientation toward the past. The messianic arrival cannot be predicted, planned or anticipated—but it is a possibility in every moment, regardless of how desolate the accumulating rubble of history might appear. Benjamin contrasts this Jewish messianic hope with the 'magic' of the 'soothsayers' who attempt to predict the future. He is clearly disdainful of these predictive superstitions, which provide, he implies, the dominant source of hope for those worldviews—such as Marxism, Christianity and classical sociology, to name those with which he was primarily in dialogue—that did not observe the Jewish injunction on futurological speculation. Jewish hope, Benjamin suggests, offers an escape from the delusions and disappointments to which these speculations readily lead. It also offers a more resilient defence against despair, because hope for the future is eternal, and is impervious to the legacies of the past.

On 26 September 1940, in the Spanish border town of Portbou, Benjamin lost hope for himself, though seemingly not for the world. Fleeing Nazi Europe with the intention of sailing from Lisbon to the United States, his journey was intercepted by border officials just after walking across the Pyrenees. Expecting to be sent back into the hands of the Gestapo, it appears that Benjamin, after struggling to ensure the survival of a cherished and now lost work-in-progress manuscript that he had been carrying in his briefcase, took his own life. His 'Theses on the Philosophy of History' has been preserved thanks to the copy he had recently given to Hannah Arendt (1906–75), while they both were arranging travel visas in Marseille.[173] Arendt soon afterwards successfully escaped by the same route, reaching New York in 1941. From her new home in America, Arendt—a German Jewish refugee from a cultural background very similar to that of Benjamin and Scholem—emerged as the most distinctive articulator in the postwar decades of the position of the Jewish outsider intellectual.

In her essay 'The Jew as Pariah: A Hidden Tradition' (1944), Arendt put forward her own more firmly historical and political conception of the Jewish outsider perspective. Since the era of their supposed emancipation, she argued, Jews have faced the choice of living either as 'parvenus', seeking to rise in the dominant Christian society, imitatively adopting its styles and values and transferring allegiance to the political agenda of its leaders, or as 'pariahs', refusing this bargain and accepting the consequences. Arendt borrowed the term 'conscious pariah' from Bernard Lazare, who had denounced emancipation as a false promise. The gaining of political rights, in his view, had simply made western Jews more sensitive to the disdain of their non-Jewish peers, in contrast to unemancipated eastern Jews, who thanks to their more assured sense of their Jewishness were largely indifferent to these prejudices. Only the fulfilment of Zionism, Lazare had argued, could bring the Jews true freedom and self-respect.[174] Arendt's primary interest, though, was not in this remedy, but in the value of pariah consciousness itself, and in Lazare's political critique of the relationship between pariahs and parvenus. She praised Lazare's condemnation of Jewish parvenus for allying with the non-Jewish rich in the oppression of the

Jewish (and non-Jewish) poor, and of most Jewish pariahs for deferring to these parvenus, and lowering themselves to the position of the *schnorrer* who accepts their charity. The Jewish 'conscious pariah' rejects this subservience. Arendt saw Lazare as an exemplar of this type of universalist Jew, who proudly embraces outsider status in solidarity with the struggle of all oppressed people for dignity and justice.[175]

The failure of emancipation, for Arendt, was that it had offered rights to Jews only in abstract and individualist terms, failing to recognize the distinctiveness or even the meaningfulness of Jews as a collectivity. This pushed Jews into a different sort of pariah existence, characterized by a profound isolation both from each other (because the severance of bonds between Jews was part of the exchange for emancipation) and from others (because Jews were nowhere really accepted as part of the wider national community). The parable-like stories of Franz Kafka (1883–1924) were for Arendt the most brilliant depictions of this lonely pariah existence. Kafka had also been much admired by Walter Benjamin, and Arendt linked the two men together, along with Karl Kraus, as supremely sharp critics of the ills of their era, and of the inauthenticity and political irresponsibility of the Jewish parvenu bourgeoisie in particular.[176]

A sense of peoplehood in some form, Arendt believed, was indispensable for human flourishing: 'only within the framework of a people can a man live as a man among men'.[177] Kafka's tales captured the cold emptiness of modern existence, in which bureaucratic abstraction had crushed this sense of affective communality. Human bonds, according to Arendt, could not be subordinated to universalist abstractions. In a 1959 speech, delivered in Hamburg in acceptance of the prestigious Lessing Prize, awarded by that city in commemoration of the Enlightenment dramatist and philosopher, she applied this argument to the subject of friendship. The expansive solidarity of fraternity, she declared, emerges among pariah groups. In a sense more noble, though, was the necessarily selective and partisan gesture of friendship, across barriers of disagreement and cultural difference. Lessing's notion of friendship, she asserted, was of this nature, characterized by a 'forever vigilant partiality' rather than confused with the universalizing uniformity of fraternity.[178]

Lessing's iconic intimacy with Moses Mendelssohn, and his idealized dramatic representation of his Jewish friend as Nathan the Wise, was, however, as we have noted, almost the epitome of universalization. Lessing saw Mendelssohn, and depicted Nathan, as an expression of Lessing's own highest universal values, and in neither context showed any interest in traces of Jewish individuation or difference. At an award ceremony symbolic of the preservation of friendship between Germans and Jews, which had so recently been almost extinguished, it is hard not to suspect that Arendt deliberately declared what she wished had been Lessing's style of friendship in place of what it in fact had been, at least with respect to Mendelssohn. Friendship with Jews, just like political inclusion of them, needed in her view to be based not on their assimilation into normative or universalist abstractions, but on a recognition of their Jewish difference and particularity.

Exiled in Paris from 1933 to 1940, Arendt worked with a range of Zionist organizations to facilitate the migration of young Jews to Palestine. This was her practical response to a situation of crisis. Her Zionism, however, was always shaped by her ethical and political commitment to justice. She aligned herself with Lazare's solidaristic and progressive vision of Zionism, and with the advocacy by Judah Magnes and others for a binational polity in Palestine in which equal rights for Jews and Arabs were assured. In an outspoken article in 1944, she powerfully critiqued the tendency of the Zionist leadership to distrust the emancipatory power of the wider Jewish people, and to perpetuate old 'parvenu' habits in currying favour with the leading imperial powers. Only a political solution based on federations, she argued, 'would give the Jewish people, together with other small peoples, a reasonably fair chance of survival'. The alternative imperial model, to which the Zionist movement had since 1942 effectively been committed, threatened, she predicted, a renewal of nationalist hatred and violence.[179]

The violence and ensuing Palestinian refugee crisis of 1948 for Arendt constituted a tragic Jewish moral failure. Lamenting the death of Magnes in 1952, she described him as 'the conscience of the Jewish people', and wrote that 'much of that conscience has died with him—at least for our time'. His values reflected the essence of what Arendt regarded as the long-standing ethically lofty 'Jewish national character'. In the final years of Magnes's life, though, that character had profoundly and wrenchingly changed: 'A people that for two thousand years had made justice the cornerstone of its spiritual and communal existence has become emphatically hostile to all arguments of such a nature, as though these were necessarily the arguments of failure. We all know that this change has come about since Auschwitz, but that is little consolation.'[180]

Arendt's later work mostly approached universal political themes approached through Christian and ancient Greek rather than Jewish intellectual traditions. She eschewed all conventional categorizing labels, and was not straightforwardly aligned with the Left.[181] Her position as a Jewish refugee philosopher was nonetheless crucial to her thought. Politics, she argued in her major work *The*

Human Condition (1958), must be rooted in human action—the '*vita activa*'—and must respond most fundamentally to the 'plurality' of human existence: the fact that no two individuals are ever the same.[182] Her own political activity in Paris in the 1930s, and her critique of the lack of political responsibility of the parvenu and of the non-conscious pariah, both instantiate in a Jewish context her emphasis on engaged action. Her prioritization of plurality, meanwhile, clearly builds upon her earlier critique of the failure of the Enlightenment and the project of Jewish emancipation to recognize Jewish distinctiveness.

The source of political hope that Arendt put forward was less obviously but more profoundly connected to the submerged Jewish current in her thinking. She introduced in *The Human Condition* her key concept of 'natality': the new beginning offered by birth. She describes this as 'the miracle that saves the world', in bringing to human existence its two 'essential characteristics' of faith and hope.[183] This idea of the renewal of birth also represented, in the politically numb mood of the 1950s, her hopeful vision of renewal after the Holocaust. Her reference to natality as a miracle almost injects a hint of messianism into Arendt's generally firmly secular philosophy. She does not hold out hope for any messianic transformation of the world—but her political interpretation of the repeating miracle of birth is nonetheless reminiscent of Benjamin's notion of the irruption into the world, at any time, of new and unpredictable forces of change. Arendt makes almost no reference to Judaism in *The Human Condition*, and associates natality specifically with Christianity: the most succinct and glorious expression of faith and hope, she writes, was in the gospels' announcement that 'a child has been born unto us'.[184] From Arendt's non-Christian perspective, though, this messianism of the past is significant simply as a powerful example, emerging from Judaism, of a spirit of hope that continues in the present and looks to the future. In her pluralistic framework of natality, this power is diffused throughout humanity, and is present in every new life. In this highly distinctive way Arendt reconfigured, in secular and universal terms, the idea of Jewish purpose as a horizon of future hope.

In 1961, Arendt witnessed the trial of Adolf Eichmann. In her analysis, published as *Eichmann in Jerusalem: A Report on the Banality of Evil* (1963), she sought to understand Eichmann as a human being, rather than simply to condemn him as a monster. She also critiqued David Ben-Gurion's politicization of the trial, and the Israeli decision to try Eichmann for 'crimes against the Jewish people', instead of delivering him to an international court to be charged with crimes against humanity. Arendt's approach provoked an outcry within the Jewish world, bringing her close to pariah status for many. Gershom

Scholem accused her in a famous letter of a lack of 'love for the Jewish people'. Arendt responded sharply, rejecting the idea of such love of a collective as dangerous and suspect. She extended her suspicion, though more guardedly, to the idea of patriotism. She accepted, however, a form of critical patriotism, which she described in personal terms: 'wrong done by my own people naturally grieves me more than wrong done by other peoples'.[185]

The rift between Arendt and the Jewish mainstream was a harbinger of much future bitterness between Zionist and universalist Jews, and much angst within individuals drawn to both perspectives and organizations in which these orientations have tussled and collided. The 1967 war rallied unprecedented Jewish support for Israel. However, the construction of Jewish settlements on the occupied Palestinian territories, and repeated Israeli military incursions since the outbreak of the First Intifada in 1987, have led many Jews to share Arendt's sentiment of acute grieving. The polarization of Jewish politics over the past five decades has to a considerable extent stemmed from the fundamental disagreement between Scholem and Arendt in 1963. A loyalist conception of 'love of the Jewish people' has rallied many Jews in support of Israel and in opposition to its perceived enemies and detractors. A significant minority, though, has followed Arendt in rejecting this prioritization of Jewish collective solidarity, and in responding to the conflict between Israel and the Palestinians not from a position of partisanship, but of what might be understood as 'critical patriotism', generating a sense of particular responsibility to speak out against unwarrantedly violent Israeli actions.

For most of the twentieth century, Jews on the Left battled for universal causes, regarding their Jewishness as irrelevant in political terms, even if their milieux of political activity were culturally extremely Jewish, or if Jewish perspectives had played an important role in inspiring their political activity. In some contexts, such as the struggle against apartheid in South Africa, this 'non-Jewish Jewish' political activity was particularly notable.[186] Since the 1960s, though, and even more so as optimism over the Oslo peace process has dwindled since the late 1990s, many Jews on the Left have adopted Arendt's understanding of the relationship of political sentiments and actions to collective identity. This has led them to taking a stand, as Jews, against Palestinian suffering for which they believe Jews bear responsibility. Jewish Voice for Peace, founded in California in 1996, has grown into a substantial Jewish organization campaigning for a just peace for all in the Middle East, alongside many other initiatives through which progressive Jews have spoken out as Jews against particular Israeli actions and policies.[187]

These shifts of outlook among Jews are also related to social transformations and political events beyond the Middle East. American Jewry in the 1960s was divided by the great domestic political battles of the decade: the Black struggle for civil rights and the movement against the Vietnam War. Many Reform and secular Jews committed much energy to both causes. Conservative and Orthodox Jews were generally more cautious on civil rights, and often supportive of the war, although Abraham Joshua Heschel (1907–72), a rabbi and professor at the Jewish Theological Seminary, was a nationally prominent progressive voice on both issues.[188] In the aftermath of these struggles, however, the wider political engagement of the institutionally organized Jewish community weakened. By the mid-1970s, with the waning of the political alliance between Blacks and Jews and the rise of Israel-oriented and other secular community activities, there had been a clearly perceptible inward turn in the concerns of American Jewry.

The Reform 'San Francisco Platform' of 1976—updating the pre-Holocaust Columbus Platform of 1937—reflected this shift, carefully balancing a reaffirmation of universal Jewish purpose with an emphasis on intra-Jewish concerns. Brief references to messianic hope for the redemption of all humanity were retained, but this was presented as a legacy from the early Reform movement, which now needed to be tempered in the light of recent history. 'The Holocaust shattered our easy optimism about humanity and its inevitable progress', while the achievements of the state of Israel 'raised our sense of the Jews as a people'. Whereas early Reform Jews 'regularly spoke of Jewish purpose in terms of Jewry's service to humanity', in recent years 'we have become freshly conscious of the virtues of pluralism and the values of particularism'. In its final clause, entitled 'Hope: Our Jewish Obligation', the platform affirmed an understanding of Jewish purpose as a source of hope for all. It grounded this, however, not in the values of social justice and peace that had been so prominent in the original Pittsburgh Platform of 1885, but in the indomitability of Jewish survival, which not only withstood the catastrophe of the Holocaust but almost immediately afterwards enabled the startling achievements of Israel: 'The existence of the Jew is an argument against despair; Jewish survival is warrant for human hope.'[189]

The radical theologian Marc H. Ellis, in his *Toward a Jewish Theology of Liberation* (1987), put forward a powerful call for a Jewish return to universalist and emancipatory causes. Drawing inspiration from Black and Latin American Christian liberation theologies, and highlighting their use of the biblical Exodus narrative of deliverance from slavery to freedom, Ellis argued that Jews needed to stand in solidarity with oppressed groups across the world, and oppose American and Israeli complicity in their oppression. In the new millennium, as Israeli politics has moved rightward and prospects of peace in the Middle East have receded, Ellis has increasingly focused on the ethical challenge of that conflict, insisting that the Jewish prophetic tradition demands an urgent and active response to Israeli oppression of Palestinians.[190] Other public intellectuals—such as Jacqueline Rose and Brian Klug in Britain—have also drawn on Jewish resources in order to critique recent Israeli policies and actions. For Rose, the only escape from continued violence and a possible future calamity may be through a return to the arguments of the various early dissident voices within Zionism: Ahad Ha'am, Hannah Arendt, Martin Buber and others, who emphasized Jewish culture and ethics rather than Jewish power, and peaceful and respectful coexistence with Palestinians rather than victory over them.[191] Self-criticism, Brian Klug has argued, is the heart of any meaningful understanding of Jewishness. It is only through the ethical striving of self-criticism that Jews can aspire to fulfil their side of the covenantal bargain, as an exemplary 'chosen people'; this necessitates, in his view, a vocal critique of injustices perpetrated by Israel.[192] These arguments are today rejected, often vociferously, by most communally affiliated Jews. They nonetheless stand in continuity with a long tradition of Jewish universalist politics that has looked toward a utopian vision of a just and harmonious world for everyone.

The American philosopher Judith Butler has noted that the memory of the Holocaust provides many progressive Jews with the ethical undergirding of their criticism of Israel, impelling them to reject silent complicity in illegitimate violence or with the dispossession of refugees.[193] The invocation of 'Jewish values' as a basis for the critique of Zionism is nonetheless in her view problematic. While the resources of the Jewish tradition might play some partial role, to ground ethical arguments on them would, she argues, perpetuate a Jewish 'exclusionary framework' in the intellectual realm. The communitarian focus of Judaism has, according to Butler, 'fostered a concern only with the vulnerability and fate of the Jewish people'; a true break with this requires not only that all suffering be equally lamented and all deaths considered equally grievable, but also the translation of ethical principles beyond boundaries of cultural particularity.[194]

Is the idea of a special Jewish ethical or political purpose inherently exclusionary? This question has vexed Jews, and especially progressive Jews, from the late nineteenth century up to the present. Avowedly secular and universal ideals of social justice have displaced religion or ethnicity as the primary framework of meaning and political commitment for many Jews across this period. However, a submerged Jewishness has remained an important aspect of much

Jewish involvement on the Left. This derives above all from the messianic kernel of the idea of Jewish purpose: a sense of expectancy and hope for a universalist and utopian future, envisaged as in some sense springing from the overcoming of Jewish particularity. The political and ethical ideas contained within
the Jewish tradition were widely felt not to require 'translation' into other terms,
because they were in themselves universal, either directly, or incipiently through
their negation. This has enabled many Jews, particularly but not only in America and in the first half of the twentieth century, to combine commitment to a
political vision of equality and universalism with an enduring belief in some
form of Jewish exemplarity—even if considerably attenuated, hazily conceived
or mutedly expressed—in the present.

Over recent decades, though, against the backdrop of a widespread Jewish
reassertion of particularity, progressive Jewish universalism has become a less
readily comprehensible and more embattled outlook. The association of Jews
with the Left is most likely today to be discussed as a dangerous stereotype or
a distorting myth—and it is certainly the case that the fantasy notion of 'Judaeo-
Bolshevism' has played a significant role in the fear- and hate-filled rhetoric of
twentieth-century antisemitism.[195] Jewish individuals, organizations and ideas
have nonetheless indeed figured prominently in the history of the modern Left.
Complex and sometimes passionate entanglements with Jewishness, and in particular with aspects of the Jewish purpose question, are an important intellectual lineage of the Left, and cannot be neatly expunged or extricated from
its patterns of thought and hope. For most of the twentieth century, the nation
state was the primary context for grappling with the challenge of combining
universal commitments with particular identities, with widespread hopes vested
in Jewish nationalism as a potential exemplary model for this. Increasingly,
though, and very conspicuously in many parts of the world in the second decade of our new millennium, these universalist aspirations have lost favour
among nationalists, and have become more closely associated with their internationalist political adversaries. These progressive movements, in keeping
with this alignment, have shifted their hopes of exemplarity and inspiration away
from Zionism, and more onto what remains of the non-Zionist diasporic and
universalist Jewish Left, and its very rich intellectual heritage.

———

According to the Egyptologist Jan Assmann, the fundamental innovation at the
core of Judaism was the 'Mosaic distinction': the opposition between truth and

falsehood in religion. Building upon Freud's arguments in *Moses and Monotheism*, Assmann contrasts the equivalence between gods that was recognized by the 'pagan' religions of the ancient world to the insistence of monotheistic religions on the sole validity of their own one God. The pharaoh Akhenaten was the first to deny the existence of a plurality of gods, but Moses, on Assmann's interpretation of the biblical narrative, took this a step further, in constructing a political theology for the Jews based on forbidding the recognition as God of any god other than their own. Whereas Akhenaten had created a new cosmology based on belief in the exclusive divine power of the sun, in monotheistic religions, from Moses onward, the true God, and the legal, ethical and political principles derived from that divine authority, was opposed to the falseness of other gods, and frequently also to the principles derived from their false claims to divine authority. The Mosaic distinction, according to Assmann, turned religion into a terrain of antagonism and often violent conflict. This insistence on a sharp distinction between truth and falsehood, and the accompanying interdiction on 'idolatrous' graven images, was not, however, an unambiguously negative development. It also spurred the 'advance in intellectuality' (*Fortschritt in der Geistigkeit*) that Freud had identified, which Assmann expansively interprets as the 'Jewish origin of the West'.[196]

Assmann's argument has provoked widespread discomfort. The suggestion that the fundamental distinctiveness of Judaism resides in its rejection of other religions, and that this is responsible for introducing religious antagonism into the world, has seemed to some implicitly antisemitic; the crediting of the intellectual cutting edge of Western modernity to the Mosaic legacy has been critiqued as simply the philosemitic other side of the same problematic coin of Jewish exceptionalization.[197] This debate highlights our current profound unease and uncertainty over the idea of Jewish distinctiveness. The exceptional significance of Jews as originators of the Western lineage of monotheism was scarcely questioned from within that lineage until the eighteenth century. Since then, though, and with greater intensity since the late nineteenth century, this status has coexisted with a countervailing desire, among both Jews and non-Jews, for Jewish normalization. Assmann's approach, following the bold cues offered by Freud, resists this desire. He instead probes the double-edged complexity of Jewish distinctiveness, and its association with both particularism and universalist visions of progress, which has marked the entire history of the Jewish purpose question.

Assmann's recounting of the 'Moses the Egyptian' story, from John Spencer and John Toland in the early Enlightenment era through to Freud, is in part a tale of attempts to resolve this tension, and the Mosaic distinction itself, by merging the Jewish tradition with Egyptian and implicitly also other civilizational histories of the world.[198] The tenacious power of the idea of Jewish distinctiveness, however, has in part depended on the enduring strength of a sense among Jews of, in essence, the 'rightness' of being Jewish. Freud's 1939 characterization of Jews as uniquely confident, optimistic and believing in their superiority to others clashes with our contemporary recoil from ethnic chauvinism. Nonetheless, a sense of the distinctive meaning and value of Jewishness has, as we have seen, over the past century been woven through a wide array of ostensibly normalizing or integrationist reflections on the place of Jews in the world.

In his most recent work, Assmann has drawn an important distinction between two different forms of biblical monotheism. The 'monotheism of truth', he points out, is in fact post-Mosaic in origin, and is enunciated most powerfully in Isaiah and other prophetic books of the Bible. The Exodus narrative, however, asserts a 'monotheism of loyalty'. Under the leadership of Moses, the Israelites are sharply marked apart as a people, in contrast to the other nations and to Egypt in particular. Their covenant at Sinai affirms the vital necessity of sustaining their separateness, and the golden calf episode vividly illustrates the disastrous consequences if they fail to sustain their exclusive loyalty to their own singular God. This 'monotheism of loyalty', Assmann argues, has fundamentally shaped the development of modern religion, and particularly its most mobile, purposively energetic and tightly communal forms, from the early modern Protestants of the Dutch Republic, England and New England to the twentieth-century civil rights and liberation theology movements.[199] His distinction between these two concepts of monotheism brings into relief the biblical roots of the perennial tension in Western thought between the religious and cultural emphasis on Jewish separateness and collective loyalty, and the countervailing fascination, in the name of the universalist monotheism of truth, with the overcoming of Jewish separatism as a crucial step in the overcoming of all separatisms. In the twenty-first century, this tension has once again moved to the fore in multiple political and cultural debates, resonating far beyond the Jewish case alone.

The association of Jews and Judaism with the fundamental defining characteristics of Western civilization and religion raises profound difficulties in the context of global history. This extends beyond the issue highlighted by Assmann of the relationship between strict monotheism and the emergence of conflict between religions. The self-righteousness of the 'Mosaic distinction' forbade the cross-cultural 'translation' between gods and their associated ethical systems: according to a rigorous 'monotheism of truth', thoroughly true ethics could only be derived from the revelation of the one true God. This precludes, or at least limits, the recognition of ethical communality across different religions and cultural outlooks, which is precisely the process that Judith Butler has identified as necessary for freeing ourselves from exclusionary frameworks of thought. In Western thought, not only for Assmann but within a long tradition of philosemitic admiration for the supposed intellectuality and philosophical acumen of Jews, the oppositional sharpness of the 'Mosaic distinction' has been widely associated with the advance of human analytical and scientific inquiry.[200] Viewed from outside these Western traditions, however, this special status accorded to Jewish modes of thinking sits less comfortably. The apparent arrogance—the *chutzpah*—of ascribing a special role to the development of Jewish intellectuality within Western culture readily appears from this vantage point to nest within the colonialist reproduction of this arrogance on a global scale, in the form of the Western assertion of intellectual superiority over the rest of the world.

What if, though, these intellectual lineages are approached from a different angle, and regarded as a non-proprietorial cultural resource for everybody? For the Palestinian public intellectual Edward Said (1935–2003), Freud's work on Moses was compelling not as an exploration of Jewish distinctiveness, but as in a sense the opposite. In presenting Moses as an Egyptian, Freud had, for Said, crucially blurred the boundary between European and non-European cultural traditions, underscoring the complexity and fluidity of all cultural identities, and the permeability of divisions between peoples. In an interview in 2000, Said famously described himself as 'the last Jewish intellectual' and as 'a Jewish-Palestinian'; he also emphasized the importance of Palestinian reflection on the Jewish experience and memory of the Holocaust.[201] Seen from this perspective, the heritage of Jewish distinctiveness is to a large extent untethered from Jews themselves, becoming instead a humanistic repository for cosmopolitan identification and empathy.

The actual place of Jews in the world—politically, socio-economically and culturally—is nonetheless of fundamental importance in shaping the possible meanings of Jewish distinctiveness and Jewish purpose. The multicultural vision of social pluralism, while heavily indebted to Horace Kallen's much earlier orchestral metaphor, came to the fore in the United States and elsewhere in 1970s, in the wake of the civil rights struggle and other upheavals of the previous decade. This coincided with the inward turn of mainstream Jewish life. In some respects, this fitted well with multiculturalism, which enabled Jews to pre-sent their own particularism as one identity among many in the mosaic of modern Western society. However, the rhetoric of multiculturalism emphasized the uplift of marginalized and disadvantaged groups, such as Blacks in America. Jewish Americans, by the 1970s mostly comfortably integrated in white suburbia, clearly did not fit within this targeting. The relationship of Jews to multicul-turalism has therefore been varied and at times confused, encompassing a strategic embrace of its ethos, contestation of its criteria of inclusion and exclu-sion, and rejection of it in favour of an alternative celebratory narrative of unas-sisted and successful Jewish integration and normalization.[202]

The place of Jewish perspectives within the field of postcolonial studies, es-tablished in the wake of multiculturalism, has been a tangled and sometimes controversial issue. Various Jewish thinkers have been held up as foreshadow-ing the postcolonial critical encounter of non-Western or diasporic writers with the hegemonic assumptions of European thought: Moses Mendelssohn's re-sponse to the challenges he faced from Friedrich Jacobi and other Christian thinkers; the critique by Abraham Geiger and later rabbis of Protestant theo-logians' historical assumptions; Hannah Arendt's political reflections on per-secution, exile and statelessness.[203] Both in those historical contexts and in the present, though, Jews have in general not embraced the position of critical mar-ginality that characterizes the postcolonial vantage point. The tight entwine-ment of Judaism and Jewishness within Western thought, and also the long Jew-ish quest for a position of normalcy in the world, complicate any attempt to consider Jews as postcolonial voices.

In his *The Dignity of Difference* (2002), Jonathan Sacks, then the Orthodox chief rabbi of Britain and the Commonwealth, set out his own view of the place and significance of Judaism in modern multicultural society. At the heart of the Jewish outlook, he argued, was a belief in pluralism. In contrast to the Western Platonic tradition of universalism, the particularity of the Jewish covenant was God's way of 'teaching humanity to make space for difference', by affirming that different peoples should worship God differently.[204] In historical terms, Juda-ism represents a living alternative to empires and to their drive to impose on the diversity of humanity a single form of truth and power. Under all five of the great universalist cultures of the West—Alexandrian Greece, ancient Rome, medieval Christianity and Islam, and the Enlightenment—Jews, Sacks declared, have suffered. The Jewish covenant, with the pioneering prophetic reflections on ethics and justice that followed in its wake, in his view offers the source for an alternative pluralistic vision of human coexistence. It is also a crucial wellspring of hope for humanity. The covenantal promise that the righteous, of all nations, will be redeemed provides, according to Sacks, an indispensible religious underpinning for human belief in our capacity to dream of and work for a better world.[205]

Sacks offered a powerfully inclusive Jewish voice of hope in the anxious aftermath of the '9/11' terrorist attacks. His book nonetheless sparked controversy. Some ultra-Orthodox rabbis accused him of heretically suggesting that Judaism recognized the validity of other religions; in response to this Sacks issued a revised edition in which he removed direct references to the truth of other faiths.[206] It's hard to distil a clear view of non-Jews and their religions from traditional Jewish sources, because discussion of this is sparse: the concept of the seven ethical 'Noachide laws', established by God for all peoples, did not emerge until after the destruction of the Second Temple in 70 CE, and these precepts were not considered as a rational moral law until Moses Mendelssohn made this argument in the eighteenth century.[207] More fundamentally, though, Sacks's assertion of the Jewish origins of pluralism amounts to a self-undermining particularistic claim. If the Jews alone have brought an appreciation of difference into the world, then this idea is itself not truly universal, but in some sense a proprietorial 'Jewish value'. Beneath a superficial veneer of multicultural modesty, Sacks rearticulates for the twenty-first century the classic pedagogical formula of Jewish purpose. Jews, tenaciously steadfast in their beliefs through their long history of suffering, are once again, on his account, the unique teachers to the world of the most essential ethical values.

Many Jews across the long twentieth century sought to loosen their cultural ownership over the values and characteristics associated with their purpose in the world. The desire for a more comfortable sense of normality in the wider societies amid which they lived was undoubtedly a leading impetus for this. This aspiration was widely compatible, though, with a sustained sense of purpose that was idealistic and universalistic while also understood as in some sense significantly Jewish. This fusion was confidently asserted in the early decades of the century by politically and socially activist progressive Jewish leaders such as Emil Hirsch in Chicago or Lily Montagu in London. Israel Zangwill and Horace Kallen both attempted, each through his own metaphor, to theorize this distinctive Jewish contribution to the American whole. In the much more embattled environment of Germanic Europe, meanwhile, Theodor Lessing, Karl Kraus and Sigmund Freud, again each in his own way, reconceived Jewish purpose as a form of piercing critique that was necessarily first directed inwardly. The notable Jewish involvement in twentieth-century radical politics brought together these strands of activist energy and probing critique. The political thought and activity of several significant Jews of the Left, from Gustav Landauer and Ernst Bloch to Walter Benjamin and Judith Butler, has been significantly inspired by the long-standing messianic and universalistic future-oriented framework of the idea of Jewish purpose.

This horizon of messianic hope has been an important facet of Jewish thought in all eras. Jonathan Sacks also closes his book with an optimistic invocation of 'a covenant of hope', which he sets out, however, in unabashedly proprietorial terms. Hope, he declares, is a Jewish characteristic: 'Jews have never—despite a history of sometimes awesome suffering—given up hope.'[208] He offers only a vague reference to the insistence on justice of the biblical prophets, though, in contrast to the various concretely political interpretations of that prophetic tradition by both Jews and non-Jews from many strands of the twentieth-century Left. In our new millennium, in the wake of 9/11 and of intensified violence in the Middle East, political conflict has returned to the centre of public debate. The memory of the Holocaust, which rose to such prominence in the more optimistic and consensual 1990s, still figures prominently as a focus of Jewish meaning. We have now entered a more combative era, though, in which the material significance of prophetic or messianic hope has become the crux of intense controversy over the contemporary meaning of the idea of Jewish purpose.

CONCLUSION

So What *Are* Jews For?

JEWS AND CONTEMPORARY PURPOSE

> ANGEL (softly): Forsake the Open Road:
> Neither Mix Nor Intermarry: Let Deep Roots Grow:
> If you do not MINGLE you will Cease to Progress:
> Seek Not to Fathom the World and its Delicate Particle Logic:
> You Cannot Understand, You can only Destroy,
> You do not Advance, You only Trample.
>
> Poor blind Children, abandoned on the Earth,
> Groping terrified, misguided, over
> Fields of Slaughter, over bodies of the Slain:
> HOBBLE YOURSELVES!
> There is No Zion Save Where You Are!
> If you Cannot find your Heart's desire . . .
>
> . . .
>
> PRIOR: Maybe I am a prophet. Not just me, all of us who are dying now.
> Maybe we've caught the virus of prophecy. Be still. Toil no more. Maybe the
> world has driven God from Heaven, incurred the angels' wrath.[1]
>
> —TONY KUSHNER (1992)

THE JEWISH PURPOSE question is a cultural palimpsest: a multi-layered idea, the earlier iterations of which are obscured but not erased by its later formulations. Political, philosophical, social, economic and psychological interpretations of Jewish purpose have been constructed upon each other, all ultimately resting on the theological foundations of the idea. This religious underpinning is never entirely buried without trace. The Jewish purpose question is, at its heart, about the mystery of meaning: it asks how, as part of a collective, people can recognize, understand and fulfil their purpose in the world. This question surpasses the reach of all fields of inquiry, and therefore repeatedly leads back to the religious reference points of the human search for meaning. Modern thinkers, whether they have understood themselves as working within these religious traditions (Bayle, Cohen, Rosenzweig), rejecting them (Spinoza, Voltaire, Marx, Nietzsche), or fundamentally revising them (Hegel, Freud, Scholem, Benjamin), have not slipped free from the special fascination of the Jewish purpose question, or from the essentially religious question of meaning that underlies it. All these individuals, as well as many others, have drawn upon and echoed, consciously and at times unconsciously, the arguments and ideas of the various antecedent layers of this tradition of thought, while adding their own contribution to its further development.

At the root of the idea of Jewish purpose is an account of a specific people, divinely chosen to play a special role in bringing the world to a state of universal betterment. In the Jewish Bible, further details are scanty, but an abundance of verses can be cited in support of an enduringly particularistic relationship between the Jewish people and their protector God. Other verses, though, put forward a universalist vision of Jewish purpose. A sense that God's message, via the Jews, is for all the peoples of the world is most strongly conveyed in the prophetic books: not only the famous 'light unto the nations' references in Isaiah, but also, for example, Micah's prophecy that 'the many nations' will embrace the Jewish divine message when 'instruction shall come forth from Zion' (Micah 4:2), or his declaration that the Jews are required 'only to do justice and to love goodness, and to walk modestly with your God' (6:8). The Apostle Paul developed this universalistic strand into an imperative to transmit the Jewish message to all people, through faith in Christ. In the medieval period, Christianity and Judaism took shape as antagonistic but overlapping religions, sharing, among other things, a belief that at the end of historical time the Jews would play a crucial role in the messianic transformation of the world. This messianic idea has been endlessly refashioned and reimagined, within both Judaism and Christianity and also in avowedly secular visions of utopian expectancy and hope. From Judah Halevi to various forms of Zionism, and from Augustine to certain strands in utopian Marxism, Jews have been cast as ultimately leading all humanity into a better world, and in some sense losing their particularity, or at least its negative aspects, through this process of transformation.

Until the eighteenth century, except during waves of heightened messianic expectancy such as the Sabbatianism of the 1660s, this historical denouement was envisaged at some point in the future. The rationalist optimism of the Enlightenment led some, such as Gotthold Ephraim Lessing, to sense that a new era of human insight and progress might be taking shape, heralded by the exceptional Jewish wisdom of his friend Moses Mendelssohn. It was not until the French Revolution, though, that the temporal separation between the worldly present and the messianic future was profoundly disrupted. After July 1789, a transformed future seemed to be emerging within the present. The transformation of Jews was widely seen as emblematic of these epochal changes, and of the quasi-messianic revolutionary hopes of the moment. With respect to Jewish purpose, the revolutionary era was akin to the emergence of Christianity. Messianic anticipation once again gave rise to a new form of universalistic thinking, encompassing expectations of the imminent dissolution of Jewish difference.

Once again, though, this did not happen. The idea of Jewish purpose was instead renewed, becoming primarily understood not as a signpost to a distant future, but as an active force in the social, economic, cultural and intellectual changes of the present. A messianic underlay remained not far beneath the surface of most of these later modern versions of Jewish purpose. In some incarnations, such as the historical dialectic of Hegelianism, the central importance of this future horizon is explicit. The Zionist idea, as Gershom Scholem emphasized, can aptly be seen as a reanimation of messianism. In the most committedly universalistic currents of modern thought, as with Christianity at the time of its emergence, the significance of Jewish purpose is less readily perceived. On the Left, for example, both Jews and non-Jews have often viewed the idea with suspicion if not outright hostility, because they have regarded it as stamped with the particularism that their universalistic politics sought to overcome.[2] A utopian vision of the future has nonetheless been a key source of inspiration and hope on the Left. Jewish thinkers, drawing on the universalist and prophetic traditions of Jewish purpose, have played a prominent role in articulating and renewing those hopes.

It is too soon to determine with confidence the enduring historical significance of events within living memory. If we consider the Jewish purpose question as a type of intellectual seismometer, though, there is reason to believe that the events of the middle third of the twentieth century led to a change in

thinking on collective purpose that is of equivalent significance to the shift pre-
cipitated by French Revolution. The crimes of Nazism—and in particular the
Jewish Holocaust, understood as the distilled essence of those atrocities—
profoundly shook Western belief in the meaning and purposiveness of human
history, and of Jewish history especially. After a quiet spell in the immediate
postwar period, however, Jewish purpose has since the 1960s found a new foot-
ing, based on the two primary secular concerns of the majority of contemporary
Jewry: support for Israel, and remembrance of the Holocaust. The increasing
focus of mainstream Jewish energies on these twin concerns reflects a move,
since the horrors and the geopolitical transformations of the 1940s, toward an
intellectually and politically narrower conception of Jewish purpose in the
world. The philosophical, pedagogical, ethical, economic and theological
themes that have run through the modern history of the Jewish purpose question nonetheless remain discernible in many contemporary arguments that
imbue the memory of the Holocaust and the security of Israel with special
global significance.

A universalistic vision of human betterment, however, is largely absent
from this contemporary formulation of Jewish purpose. Support for Israel,
in particular, has since 1967 become increasingly dominated by adversarial
rather than idealistic political rhetoric. Ethical universalism remains in general an important force in contemporary Western and global politics. In our
new millennium, though, social democracy and other progressive traditions
linked to this universalistic outlook have been locked in intense conflict with
the growing strength of nationalistic, anti-visionary and inward-looking political movements. The currently dominant ethno-nationalist understanding
of Jewish purpose is also largely inward-looking. The Jewish case is here an
example of this wider trend—but one that carries special significance. The
resonance of the idea of Jewish purpose has invested the state of Israel with
a special fascination not only for evangelical and other Christians, but also
for a wide range of nationalist and other anti-universalist thinkers and groups.
The resources of idealism and universalistic hope contained within the intellectual lineage of Jewish purpose are, also due to this deep historical resonance, often similarly compelling for political movements on the Left that
seek to mobilize around internationalist ideals of social justice. Today's vigorous contestation of Jewish purpose, far from being a matter for Jews alone,
occupies a rhetorically and conceptually central position within the most
fundamental political antagonisms of our era.

Jewish Purpose in Theory and Practice

Who is entitled to answer the Jewish purpose question? Up to the 1930s, this question barely registered. Jews were, for example, divided on the scholarly arguments of Weber and Sombart, but there was no serious suggestion that these non-Jewish scholars ought not to lead public discussion of the place of Jews in the economic history of the world. Since the 1960s, however, as postcolonial critiques of Western intellectual hegemony gathered strength, and narratives of suffering, resilience and resistance assumed importance for subjugated groups as an expression of collective identity and political voice, Jews have also increasingly asserted claims of ownership over their history and representation. The memory of the Holocaust became in the late twentieth century, as we have noted, to some extent a terrain of competitive victimhood, with arguments over the uniqueness or the comparability of the Jewish genocide at times becoming mired in ethnic and political tussles.[3] More broadly, the rise of multiculturalism has promoted the public visibility of minority communities, including Jews, through their own voices and in their own preferred terms.

This approach has often been in tension with certain strands of universalist thought and politics. These complexities have been particularly apparent in France, where since the eighteenth century a strong tradition of Enlightenment universalism has figured prominently in the national political culture. For Voltaire, Judaism stood as a repository of entrenched superstition impervious to universal reason; for the abbé Grégoire, the Jews' political emancipation would lead to their assimilation in the post-revolutionary universalist order; just over a century later, Émile Zola's vision of Jews as fully integrated and patriotic French universalists inflected his famous defence of Alfred Dreyfus. These three thinkers, in different but related ways, positioned Jewish otherness as a negative contrast to their universalistic ideals. This distinctively French intellectual legacy has continued to play an important role in our contemporary era.[4]

French intellectual culture in the postwar period, jolted by the Holocaust, embraced Jewishness as a key locus of resistance to the repressive or falsely self-confident aspects of universalism. For Jean-Paul Sartre, the figure of the Jew, in holding firm to a strong sense of self in the face of the fantastical projections of the antisemite, was a model of existentialist authenticity.[5] The work of Emmanuel Levinas focused attention on Jewish texts and ethical traditions, while Jewish difference loosely aligned with Jacques Derrida's deconstructive *différance*. Other Jewish thinkers, such as Albert Memmi and Alain Finkielkraut, both influenced by Sartre, found significant audiences for their explorations of

Jewish identity.[6] The association of Jews with the critical edge of philosophy was most explicit in the work of the leading theorist of postmodernism, Jean-François Lyotard (1924–98). 'The jews', within quotation marks and with a lower case 'j' to indicate a distinction between this conceptual designation and actual living Jews, were for Lyotard the eternally resistive 'other' of Western thought: 'within its accomplishments, projects, and progress, what never ceases to re-open the wound of the unaccomplished'. This frustration of the Western drive for intellectual domination has generated, he argued, repeated attempts to eliminate the unmasterable otherness represented by the 'the jews', of which Auschwitz is the most recent and horrific example.[7] Lyotard thus gave a postmodern twist to the pedagogical tradition of Jewish purpose. In the place of actual Jews as teachers of the truths of ethical monotheism to the world, he cast 'the jews' as the eternal reminders of the impossibility of any such definitive philosophical certainty.

Interest in Judaic themes and the valorization of Jewish exceptionality remained in vogue among Parisian intellectuals up to the end of the Cold War. For some prominent figures, such as Michel Foucault, this outlook underpinned a supportive stance toward Israel, and a vigilant opposition to antisemitism. Since the 1990s, though, the discussion of Jewish matters in French thought has become increasingly contentious.[8] In an early and influential American critique of Lyotard, Daniel and Jonathan Boyarin accused him of condescendingly appropriating Jewishness for his own philosophical ends. Lyotard's allegorization of Jews as 'jews', they argued, amounted to an intellectual erasure of actual Jews that bore some similarity to the various Western attempts, noted by Lyotard, to eliminate 'jews', up to and including the Holocaust.[9] In the new millennium, these and related charges have been levelled more insistently against Lyotard and other French thinkers.

There is now a widespread unease in the Jewish world, within and beyond France, over the allegorization of Jews and Jewishness, and a tendency for such arguments, when made by non-Jews, to be criticized as a form of appropriation. This recent development marks a notable break with the lineage of the Jewish purpose question. Lessing's idealized allegorization of Jewishness as cosmopolitan wisdom, for example, was a touchstone of German Jewish identificatory pride throughout the nineteenth century, and has not entirely lost this status even today.[10] As we have seen, Jewish thinkers since the seventeenth century have to a large degree shared with non-Jews a common exceptionalist idiom of Jewish purpose. Community leaders, from Menasseh ben Israel in his advocacy for Jewish readmission to England in the 1650s to the efforts of Chaim

Weizmann in securing the Balfour Declaration from the British in 1917, have appealed to these exceptionalist associations with Jews in order to advance their aims.[11] In recent years, however, Lyotard has been criticized for perilously or even antisemitically obscuring actual Jewish voices and experience, while the wider field of 'French theory' has been approached with increasing caution and suspicion, if not disdain, by many scholars of Jewish history and culture.[12]

This intellectual shift has intersected with changes in the wider political environment framing public discussion of Jewish matters. Hopes of peace between Palestinians and Israelis, which were sustained during the 1990s by the Oslo process, have been largely eclipsed by a more pessimistic mood since the outbreak of the Second Intifada in 2000. A major spike in casualties among both Palestinians and Israelis in 2002 brought the tensions of the conflict onto the streets of Europe to an unprecedented degree. The political passions stirred by this conflict were heightened by the aftermath of the New York terror attacks of September 2001, and further inflamed by the bitterly contested US-led invasion of Iraq in 2003. These polarizing issues and emotions were particularly intense in France, home to the largest populations in the European Union of both Jews and Muslims. The complex relationship between these two communities, which had already been frayed following the Gulf War of 1991, became more fraught in the new millennium, as identification with the opposing parties in the Middle East conflict intensified on both sides.[13]

The particular roots of the tension between French Jews and Muslims from North Africa lie in the long-standing French policy of differential treatment of them. This was enshrined most significantly in the Crémieux Decree of 1870, which granted French citizenship to the Jews of Algeria, effectively co-opting them into the colonizing culture and dividing them from the predominantly Muslim indigenous population. The division between the two communities was entrenched in the postwar period of decolonization, during which the overwhelming majority of North African Jews migrated to France or Israel, and did not identify with the anti-colonial cause.[14]

The association of Jews with France in opposition to a Muslim 'other' has intensified since September 2001 ('9/11'). Since that date, popular fear and hostility in France, and across much of the rest of the world, has focused on Muslims. Jewish targets have been singled out in numerous terror and hate attacks in France and beyond, and the continued high tension in the Middle East has also contributed to an inchoate but widespread perception of the dangers facing Jews as the front line of a broader Islamic threat to the security and values of France, Europe and the West. Jewish alarm over Muslim antisemitism, influentially sounded by figures such as Finkielkraut, has resonated with this Islamophobic mood, which has found particular expression in France through repeated waves of polemic and regulation over the wearing of headscarves by Muslim women.[15] Over the opening decades of the new millennium, as the rhetorical protection of the core French national value of secularism (*laïcité*) has focused against Islam, the threat to Jews from Muslim hatred and violence has been readily regarded as emblematic of this wider battle.

This alignment featured prominently immediately following the January 2015 shootings at the editorial offices of the satirical magazine *Charlie Hebdo* and at a kosher supermarket in Paris, in which sixteen people, including four at the supermarket, were killed. In the almost unprecedentedly huge public rallies after these events, the ubiquitous phrase 'Je suis Charlie' was echoed in another extremely popular slogan: 'Je suis juif' ('I am a Jew'). The allegorization of the figure of the Jew in this context was almost universally understood as a spontaneous expression of inclusive solidarity. While this undoubtedly was the primary sentiment behind the phrase, 'Je suis juif' nonetheless drew its rhetorical strength from the deeply rooted Western tradition of imbuing Jewish suffering with special significance. The twinning of these two identificatory slogans also reflected a wider linking of the protection of Jews with the defence of the core values of the French state (the *laïcité* and freedom of speech represented by *Charlie Hebdo*), in both cases primarily from the radicalized Islam identified with the attackers.[16] An undeclared, but nonetheless quietly potent, notion of Jewish purpose was thus in evidence in this mass mobilization. The allegorizing structure of this deployment of the idea echoed Lyotard's argument, but inverted its political valence. 'The jew', when placed alongside 'Charlie', was not a figure of resistance to Western thought, but on the contrary a fundamental symbol of the core values of French republicanism, and a sacrificial victim for them.

The security concerns of the Jewish community, which were placed close to the heart of the French national debate following these attacks, have also loomed large in shaping the internal mood of Jewish life in France. The communal focus on safety and survival appears on the surface broadly similar to the inward turn of European Jewry in the immediate postwar years, when collective energies were largely absorbed by the labour of reconstruction after the Holocaust. Unlike that period, however, the idea of Jewish purpose has not in recent decades been buried beneath more straightforward imperatives of Jewish existence and survival. Despite the widespread Jewish unease over theoretical allegorizations of Jews, the 'Charlie' moment has highlighted a realignment, rather than an eclipse, of the place of Jewish purpose in the national collective consciousness. Political and institutional support for the protection of Jews from both physical and rhetorical attacks has significantly rested upon the association of these concerns with the broader philosophical principles and sense of cultural mission of France and the West. This alignment has however been intensely contested. Since the millennium, there has been a resurgence in France of the intellectual tradition of Left universalism, which has placed very different claims on the idea of Jewish purpose. This notion has therefore once again emerged as a terrain of heated political argument. The underlying matter of contention is not the validity of the idea of Jewish purpose itself, or even simply whether this should be defined and expressed only by Jews, but rather which political values and lines of solidarity should frame the idea in contemporary debate.

The pronouncements of the philosopher Alain Badiou on Jews and Judaism have provoked particularly intense controversy. Inspired above all by the Marxist tradition of politically engaged thought, Badiou's 'philosophy of the event' seeks to reanimate universal ideals of truth and love, which he understands as emerging through commitment to the encounters and events of emancipatory political struggle.[17] He has grounded his affirmation of universalism on a reclaiming of Paul, whose message he distils to a committed and inclusive affirmation of optimism and love: 'not the cult of death but the foundation of a universal "yes".[18] Badiou interprets Paul's rejection of the Jewish law as his decisive and life-affirming act of faith—in Badiou's terminology, the 'event'—that makes possible the activation of political agency in the name of all.[19] Paul's vision of the transcendence of difference was not, Badiou argues, an attempt to abolish Jewish particularity; he aimed, rather, to recast its significance, by bringing to the fore the universalistic essence of God's initial covenant with Abraham. Paul put forward this argument, Badiou reminds his readers, as a dissident position within the Jewish fold, from which he did not seek to disaffiliate: 'A Jew among Jews, and proud of it, Paul only wishes to remind us that it is absurd to believe oneself a proprietor of God.'[20] Badiou's reassertion of Pauline universalism has brought back into contemporary political debate the fundamental controversies of the Jewish purpose question from two millennia ago. Paul is once again here positioned as the originary 'radical Jew', drawing from the unique covenantal heritage of the Jewish people the fundamental intellectual and political resources that point the way to redemption and liberation for all.

Badiou, like Lyotard but in a much more incendiary fashion, has also put forward his own meaning of the term 'Jew'. The self-appointed guardians of the word in the mainstream Jewish community, he has argued, seek to permit its association only with the particularist triplet 'SIT' (Shoah/Israel/Torah)—but they have no legitimate monopoly over its use and definition.[21] Declaring that '"Jews" is ... a glorious name of our philosophical, scientific, artistic and our revolutionary history', he has alleged that the oppression of Palestinians by Israel amounts to an 'inversion of meaning' of this name, and that therefore Israel could in a sense be considered as the country in the world in which there are the fewest Jews.[22] While explicitly asserting his entitlement, as a non-Jew, to define the word 'Jew' and even to claim that identity for himself—'le juif, c'est moi'[23]—Badiou has repeatedly collaborated with dissident Jews on this topic, publishing their work alongside or even subsumed within his own, or engaging enthusiastically in support of their voices.[24] In his uninhibitedly polemical provocations, Badiou has clearly set out and pugnaciously defended some of the core arguments of the Western intellectual tradition of Jewish purpose. This idea, he insists, is the property of everyone, and an indispensible source of political direction and hope for everyone. Jews, however, occupy a privileged position in this conception of human purpose. This is due to their status not only as the point of origin of this idea, but also as the continued bearers, at least by default, of the 'glorious name', and of its accompanying sense of political expectancy and hope, which Badiou, like so many earlier thinkers, associates with the quasi-messianic promise of universalism's future triumph.

Badiou's arguments have been widely and often vociferously criticized as implicitly or even explicitly antisemitic. He has been accused in particular of 'Jew splitting': fêting 'good Jews' who share his views in order more thoroughly to discredit the 'bad Jews' who reject his demand that they should abandon their own understanding of their Jewish identity.[25] Utopian and universalist currents within Jewish life and thought have themselves, however, repeatedly split from the Jewish mainstream. This applies, for example, to Spinoza and the Sabbatian movement in the seventeenth century, to Felix Adler's Ethical Culture movement in the late nineteenth century and to the many 'non-Jewish Jews' of the modern political Left. In the biting satire of Karl Kraus, dissident critique of the mainstream, and especially of the Jewish mainstream, was elevated to the art and essence of Jewish purpose. Condemnations of Badiou's 'Jew splitting' offer no account of these forms of Jewish dissidence. They also repeat his rhetorical act in reverse, in condemning his Jewish allies as inauthentic and in effect 'bad' Jews. Badiou's polemical contestation of the word 'Jew' is a notably outspoken but far from isolated intervention in a much wider debate: the intense argument currently raging—among both Jews and non-Jews, and in France and beyond—between particularist and universalist visions of Jewish purpose.

This conceptual dispute has been profoundly shaped by the material reality of the conflict between Israel and the Palestinians. The high levels of Palestinian casualties during the Israeli ground invasions of the Gaza Strip in 2009 and 2014, and the severe deterioration of living conditions there, have kept this conflict to the fore as a focus of internationalist solidarity, particularly but by no means only within Arab and Muslim communities in Europe. For many supporters of Israel, meanwhile, Hamas and other organizations in Gaza are regarded as particularly dangerous elements of the wider international threat posed by Islamist terrorism. From both these perspectives, the Israeli–Palestinian conflict is freighted with special symbolic and geopolitical meaning. The linking of Zionism with Western imperialism, which figured prominently in nineteenth-century Zionist advocacy by Herzl and others, is now most powerfully asserted by Israel's critics. For Houria Bouteldja, for example—the leading spokesperson of the Indigènes de la République, a new anti-racist and anti-colonial movement in France—opposition to Zionism is central to any such politics. Zionism has also, she argues, imprisoned Jews, in perpetuating and extending the time-honoured French policy of dividing them from Arabs, with whom they historically and culturally have much in common and still could choose to stand in solidarity.[26] Current defenders of Israel usually argue that matters relating to Jews and Jewishness in the West should be considered entirely separately from the conflict in the Middle East. The shadow of this conflict is however, inescapable. The situation in Israel and Palestine plays a key role not only in the continued evolution of the meanings of Jewishness for both Jews and Muslims or Arabs, but also in the wider contestation of the idea of Jewish purpose across the West and beyond.

Zionism, Antisemitism and the Contemporary Politics of Jewish Purpose

In September 2018, the Israeli newspaper *Haaretz* published an opinion poll that aimed to probe 'Israel's muddled Jewish soul'. In response to the question 'Do you believe the Jewish people is a chosen people?', 56% of the canvassed Israeli Jews answered 'yes', while 32% declared 'no'. These answers correlated very strongly with the political and religious outlooks of the respondents. 79% of those who identified with the Right answered 'yes' to this question, but only

13% of those who aligned with the Left.[27] These statistics for Israel reflect apparent trends across the Jewish world. The chosen people idea remains today a core belief for religious Jews, who tend to position themselves on the Right, but it has been overwhelmingly rejected by secular Jews, who are much more likely to consider themselves on the Left. With regard to Jewish purpose, however, this political polarization is more complicated. The idea of Jewish purpose is grounded on the biblical account of the election of Israel, so it would seem natural for it to hold its appeal most strongly among more right-wing and religious Jews. In these circles, though, the notion of Jewish world-historical purpose has been increasingly handled with wariness, and has to a large extent been displaced by an inward-looking focus on collective security and self-reliance. On the predominantly secular Jewish Left, meanwhile, rejection of the idea of chosenness has brought with it an associated rejection, or at least a deep suspicion, of any claim that Jews have a special role to play in the construction of the future. Nonetheless, the universalistic ideals that have figured so prominently in the history of the Jewish purpose question retain a particular animating presence on the Left. The division between these two camps, then, is not so much over the validity of that question, but over contrasting particularistic and universalistic visions of the idea of collective purpose itself.

The election of Israel, as we noted at the start of this book, inescapably begs the question of why God singled out the Jews, or indeed any one people, for special divine intimacy. For the Orthodox theologian Michael Wyschogrod (1928–2015), the mystery of election begins with God 'falling in love' with Abraham. God, for Wyschogrod, is not a distantly impartial judge, but a father-like figure who recognizes and responds to the uniqueness of his children, and 'loves some more than others'.[28] This view has been critiqued by the Conservative rabbi and theologian David Novak, for whom, as Mordecai Kaplan argued in the 1930s, the idea that God loves the Jews more than others can readily appear dangerously similar to the hate-filled chauvinism of the Nazis.[29] Central to Novak's theory of the election of Israel is the mysterious purpose of the Jews in the final redemption of humanity. Renewing for the modern era traditional Jewish teachings on this subject, he emphasizes that this redemption will centrally involve the Jews, in a way that it is impossible for us to foresee, but will be for everybody, ending all estrangement between the world and God: 'God's redemption of Israel will be central to this cosmic redemption.' Jewish chosenness for Novak therefore carries no connotations of superiority or privilege, but simply charges them with an enigmatic but critical role in the ultimate emergence of the redeemed future.[30]

In his most recent book, Novak closely links Jewish election and purpose with Zionism. A sense of purpose, he argues, is a 'basic human need', which brings us into community, and underlies the existence of the Jewish people. God's choosing of one particular people—the Jews—provides divine affirmation of the indispensability of purposive community. The precise purpose of God's choice is known only to God, and is in essence messianic: the Jews have been chosen because of 'what they will be in the future', and their task is to live up to this responsibility, before God, themselves and the world.[31] God also, Novak argues, chose the land of Israel as the homeland of the Jews. The divine commandment to acquire and settle the land of Israel is in his opinion binding on all Jews. In obeying this commandment, Jews contribute to furthering Zionism, which is a central component in the 'great purpose' of Jewish existence.[32] While not explicitly abandoning the universalist horizon of the messianic future, Novak places this in the realm of divine unknowability, leaving Jews to focus in the present on their collective Zionist endeavour. In his argument, as in the thinking of many messianic religious Zionists in contemporary Israel, there is little trace of the idealistic 'light unto the nations' rhetoric that was prominent in so many early articulations of Zionism. Despite his disavowal of the implicit chauvinism he detected in Wyschogrod's theological interpretation of the election of Israel, Novak's own position suggests a similarly self-interested and particularistic perspective with respect to contemporary politics.

On the progressive wing of the Jewish world, meanwhile, particularly in America, universalistic conceptions of Jewish purpose have retained their vitality. The rise since the 1970s of the non-denominational Jewish Renewal movement, inspired by egalitarian values and neo-Hasidic spiritual practices, has been linked with the emergence in America of a new form of 'post-Judaism'. Reflecting and embracing the highly mixed and increasingly 'post-ethnic' nature of contemporary American society, this new model of Jewish identity emphasizes its openness and blurred boundaries, rather than traditional notions of ethnic difference. The Jewish Renewal and neo-Hasidic movements also embrace a 'post-parochial' involvement, from a Jewish perspective, in the betterment of the world as a whole.[33] For the scholar-rabbi Arthur Green, a leading voice in these movements, the election of the Jews should be understood not as an act of preferential selection by God, but as a particular Jewish response to the universality of divine revelation, and a particular form of collective acceptance, through the covenant, of its responsibilities.[34]

Green emphasizes the non-chauvinistic nature of his conception of Jewish chosenness, stressing that other religious traditions, each with its own response to the same universality of revelation, also have much to contribute to the world. The Jewish covenant, however, in designating the Jews as a 'kingdom of priests', charges them with a special mission to all, as 'teachers of humanity'.[35] Green's understanding of the purpose of the Jews as ethical witnesses and pedagogues to others bears a strong underlying similarity to the arguments of the leading Reform rabbis of nineteenth-century Germany and America, such as Abraham Geiger and Emil Hirsch. Green's wider intellectual framework is, of course, somewhat different: Geiger and Hirsch did not feel the need to temper their invocation of the 'mission of Israel' with a humble genuflection to cultural relativism. Just as Hirsch had responded to the radical universalist challenge of Felix Adler's Ethical Culture movement, though, Green similarly argues that the universalistic purpose of the Jews justifies their continued existence as a people, and notes that despite the recent trauma of the Holocaust, the understandable inwardly-focused Jewish concern with collective survival should not be allowed to overwhelm their wider message and purpose. He also engages critically with the opposite wing of Jewish opinion: those who, in the name of Zionism, have a 'blatantly higher regard for Jewish life and Jewish rights than for those of others'. This view, he argues, deeply offends the most sacred 'Jewish values' of diaspora liberals, particularly in America.[36]

The rise of Jewish Renewal has played a significant role in the broader rise of the phrase *tikkun olam*—'repair of the world'—as an expression of Jewish commitment to social and ecological activism. Widely adopted as a rallying slogan in American Jewish youth education movements in the 1970s, the use of the term has boomed since the 1980s. *Tikkun* magazine, founded in 1986, has become the leading forum of the American Jewish Left, and has played an important role in the diffusion of the term into the idiom of American progressive politics more broadly.[37] The meaning of *tikkun olam* today is in some respects very different from its original significance within the sixteenth-century kabbalistic theology of Isaac Luria. For Luria's disciples, and for the devotees of Sabbatai Zevi a century later, this aspiration formed part of an eschatological and millenarian worldview: they anticipated a mystical and utopian transformation of the world within the context of the final denouement of human history. In contemporary parlance, *tikkun* usually refers to practical ameliorative measures in response to the environmental and social justice concerns of the moment.[38] Despite these more modest horizons, and the discontinuity of the concept's recent history, *tikkun olam* today is nonetheless an inheritor of some of the long-standing hallmarks of the Jewish purpose question. Invoked by the leading Liberal rabbi Leo Baeck in the interwar period as a fresh way of conveying the idealism of progressive 'mission of Israel' theology, in postwar North America *tikkun olam* was used, most notably by Emil Fackenheim, to describe the repair of Jewish trust and sense of purpose in the fractured post-Holocaust world.[39]

Most mentions of *tikkun olam* today do not consciously embrace a sense of messianic expectancy, or a belief in a special Jewish role in the building of a better future. Both these ideas, however, are quietly implicit in the term. If there were no Jewish particularity associated with *tikkun olam*, and no relationship between its contemporary and its sixteenth-century meaning, then there would be no clear reason to use the Hebrew phrase rather than a vernacular alternative. The Jewish Left, long uneasy about its relationship to the idea of Jewish purpose, has to some extent found through the language of *tikkun olam* a more comfortable mode of connection with this historical lineage. Blurring the distinctions between religion and secularism and between particularism and universalism, the messianic overtones of this phrase remain fundamental to its inspirational and political power.

Tikkun olam has also been embraced by some twentieth-century Orthodox Jews. Abraham Kook, as we have noted, was strongly influenced by Lurianic Kabbalah, arguing in the interwar period that that ingathering of Jews in Palestine would herald universal redemption and repair of the world. Today, however, arguments over the concept are at the fore of the intellectual battle between competing conceptions of Jewish purpose in the world. In his *To Heal the World? How the Jewish Left Corrupts Judaism and Endangers Israel* (2018), Jonathan Neumann has argued that *tikkun olam*, as it is understood today, has no authentic roots in the Jewish tradition, and has been promoted, through highly selective and wilful interpretations of biblical and other religious texts, to advance a leftist political agenda that is not only alien to Judaism but injurious to it. For many on the Jewish Left, according to Neumann, the sole purpose of the Jewish people is to preach liberal politics to others. This has led them to a hypocritical rejection of their own particularity, while celebrating diversity in others; a special hostility to Israel; and abandonment of the true duty and purpose of Jews, which is to support or live in Israel, and to prioritize the security and welfare of Jews in the diaspora. According to one Anglo-Jewish admirer of Neumann's book, American Jewry's 'secular religion' of *tikkun olam* is 'a fraud', salvation from which can only come from the rejection of universalism and the strengthening of inwardly-focused Orthodoxy.[40] These writers' polemical assaults on *tikkun olam* are driven by a sense that the commitment of many Jews to liberal universalism, and their association of these values with their

Jewishness, poses a serious challenge to the emphasis of the opposing wing of the Jewish political spectrum on the primacy of intra-communal solidarity and Zionism.

In both the United States and Britain, intra-Jewish quarrels over Zionism and Israel have grown particularly acrimonious since the Israeli military assault on Gaza in January 2009, which met with widespread international criticism. Howard Jacobson's comic novel *The Finkler Question*, winner of the prestigious Man Booker Prize in 2010, depicts a contemporary Britain beset with various forms of antisemitism, but lampoons with particular relish the leftist anti-Zionism of a Jewish group, 'ASHamed Jews', which is clearly based on an actual organization founded in London in 2007.[41] Also in 2010, the prominent lawyer Anthony Julius devoted over a quarter of his history of English antisemitism since the medieval period to contemporary anti-Zionism, dedicating more pages to his critique of Jewish anti-Zionism than to either the Muslim or the Christian variants of the phenomenon.[42] Since the election of Jeremy Corbyn as its leader in 2015, the British Labour Party has been riven by internal allegations over antisemitism, with rival Jewish groups within the party taking contrasting positions on the issue. In April 2018, Corbyn's attendance at a Passover seder (festival meal) organized by a radical diasporist Jewish group in his constituency triggered an outcry from the mainstream Anglo-Jewish leadership, which was extensively and sympathetically reported by much of the British press.[43] Controversies over Zionism and antisemitism have also recently been extremely heated in the United States, particularly over the terms in which it is acceptable or appropriate to refer to the influence of pro-Israel lobbying groups in American politics.[44]

Recent public debates on antisemitism have largely focused on its relationship to criticism of Israel. The 'Working Definition of Antisemitism' issued by the International Holocaust Remembrance Alliance (IHRA) in 2016, and since endorsed by many organizations around the world, includes eleven 'contemporary examples of antisemitism', six of which concern attitudes toward Israel. Controversy over this definition, for example within the British Labour Party, has focused on whether freedom of speech might be infringed by the requirement, in these examples, that a broadly 'normal' tone and frame of reference be maintained in any criticism of Israel.[45] The application of 'double standards', by requiring of Israel 'behaviour not expected or demanded of any other democratic state', is one instance of potential antisemitism listed in the Working Definition. It has been widely argued on this basis that the avoidance of investments in companies that profit from the Israeli occupation of

Palestinian territories—'Boycott, Divestment and Sanctions'—should be considered as antisemitic.[46] In May 2019, the German Bundestag endorsed this view. This issue is currently having an extremely polarizing impact in several countries, as campaigns for targeted boycotts and ethical investment screening policies in support of Palestinian rights have grown in strength, while their most committed adversaries have sought through various channels to delegitimize those strategies, including suggesting that it is antisemitic to question their equation with antisemitism.[47]

This close and highly charged scrutiny of statements relating to Israel seems strangely at odds with the Working Definition's demand for normality in this domain. The issue of antisemitism, however, is in fact almost always treated in in exceptional terms. Strongly linked in public debate with the remembrance of the Holocaust, the struggle against antisemitism is today widely understood as an extension of the unique pedagogical lessons of the Nazi genocide. Often described, in the light of that history, as 'the canary in the coal mine'—an early warning of wider and deeper perils—the persistence of antisemitism in contemporary Europe stirs exceptionally intense fear and alarm. Opposition to antisemitism is therefore often given particular prominence, even if its impact on the lives of Jews might not be as severe as that of other, less prioritized, prejudices on other minority groups. In Britain, for example, there has in recent years been considerable public attention paid to antisemitism, particularly on the Left and on university campuses. There has been much less media emphasis on Islamophobia, despite abundant evidence that it is widespread across the political spectrum, but particularly on the Right, and little interest in documented experiences of alienation and discrimination among Muslim students.[48]

The special interest of the educated British public in Jews and in antisemitism is satirized in Jacobson's *Finkler Question*, and underscored by its prize-winning success. In a passage in the novel described by one critic as 'oddly heartfelt', its eponymous Jewish protagonist, disillusioned with 'ASHamed Jews', fantasizes sleeping with and then sadistically killing one of its leading female members, whose hostile characterization is clearly based on a living individual well known in London literary and academic circles.[49] Rather than finding this graphic personal attack repellent, or perhaps despite finding it so, the British literary establishment fêted the novel, reflecting an enduring highbrow cultural fascination with matters Jewish. The content and reception of Jacobson's novel sit rather oddly alongside the core demand of critics of Left anti-Zionism: that Jews and Israel be regarded no differently than other ethnic groups and countries, and that stereotypes and exaggerations be carefully avoided. *Finkler* is replete with stereotypes of Jewish intellectuality, sexuality and self-absorption, and of non-Jewish envious admiration of these traits. Its success suggests that these ideas retain considerable allure, and that the Anglophone literary public, at least, views with widespread interest and some uninhibited relish the internecine battle between Jews over the nature of Jewish purpose in the world.

This strikingly intense and at times even voyeuristic phenomenon echoes the keen interest of earlier generations of non-Jewish intellectuals in the disputes within the Jewish world over Enlightenment and reform in the late eighteenth and early nineteenth centuries, and with Spinoza's earlier rupture with his fellow Jews. In our own time, once again, arguments among Jews exert particular fascination, because they provide a unique distillation of the wider question of human collective purpose as a concern for everybody. Contemporary controversies over Zionism and antisemitism, in pitting two opposing visions of Jewish purpose against each other, stage in vivid and historically resonant microcosm a broader battle of ideas: the tussle between all inward-looking and outward-looking, or particularist and universalist, rival conceptions of the role of any religious, national or other affinity group in the making of our shared future.

The former chief rabbi Jonathan Sacks, asked on BBC television in September 2018 whether accusations of antisemitism in the Labour Party might be aiming to 'close down criticism of Zionism', emphatically responded that this notion was 'absolute nonsense'. 'Nobody is more open to criticism and self-criticism than Jews,' he continued. 'It's something we've been practising for four thousand years: the most self-critical people in history.'[50] Sacks here invoked an association of Jews with unvarnished truth-telling that stretches back to the biblical prophets, and which, as we've seen, was put forward in 1930 by Theodor Lessing as the essence of the Jewish mission to the world: the Jews, for Lessing, were the first to learn, and then to teach to others, how to thrive in the face of suffering by embracing a critical self-awareness. Sacks's critical arguments, however, are much more often directed outwardly rather than reflexively, emphasizing in particular the threat posed to Jews by antisemitism.[51] The tradition of internal critique and ethical stringency within Zionism, associated with Ahad Ha'am, Judah Magnes, Hannah Arendt and many others, is less prominent today. These ideals continue to circulate widely, however, as a descriptive assertion: for example, in the claim that the Israel Defence Forces are 'the most moral army in the world'.[52] The resonance of this superlative, like Sacks's structurally similar statement about Jewish self-criticism, reflects the continued trace of the outward-oriented ideals of Jewish purpose within the rhetoric and collective self-understanding of inward-oriented mainstream Jewry. Even while generally rejecting exceptionalist views of Jews as implicitly antisemitic, and presenting Israel as a 'normal' state in which Jews have attained self-determination like any other people, many Zionists today continue to associate Jews with lofty intellectual and ethical ideals. The universalistic implications of these ideals, however, is often lost amid their transposition from their traditional status as exacting aspirations to their use as self-congratulatory descriptors of current Jewish or Israeli reality.

Since the collapse of the Oslo peace process, and even more so since the events in Gaza in 2009 and 2014, the division between outward- and inward-oriented visions of Jewish purpose has widened and hardened. We are now witnessing something akin to an intellectual Jewish civil war between these outlooks: a war that involves plenty of non-Jewish belligerents as well as onlookers. The universalistic, outward-oriented idea of Jewish purpose is today rallied above all in solidarity with Palestinians and in opposition to Israeli actions and policies. This mobilization also holds together complex conceptual tensions, bringing together Jews, Christians and those who identify as neither, and encompassing a wide range of motivations for placing special emphasis on the possibility of the politics of Jewish collective identification and action being something other than what it predominantly is today. This impulse is not necessarily anti-Zionist: for some, the ethically lofty tradition within Zionism is a primary inspiration for their critique of the current state of the movement.[53]

More diffusely perceived lineages of the Jewish purpose question lead others to criticize contemporary Zionism. The 'singling out' of Israel, as we have just noted in relation to investment policies, is sometimes held to be inherently problematic or even antisemitic. Stretching back to the biblical covenant and its theological legacy, however, the idea of 'singling out' has been intimately associated with the Jewish people, who have therefore, as this book has demonstrated in detail, been the continual primary focus of modern Western reflection on singularity and peoplehood. This multifaceted intellectual tradition is today a pervasive and indelible presence within global political and cultural thought, even when, both on the Left and on the Right, there is only a very dim awareness of its influence and complexity.

The mainstream rhetoric of Zionism today, which functions as the primary binding agent both of Israeli society and of much of the Jewish diaspora, has largely dropped its early vision of itself as a fundamental positive force for the world as a whole. The 'light unto the nations' argument, prominent in the speeches and writings of David Ben-Gurion up to the 1960s, has given way to an emphasis on the entitlement of Jews to collective security and an environment free of antisemitism, and to define for themselves the essential terms of both those two things. This Jewish shift toward particularistic self-assertion has taken place alongside the rise in recent years of a broadly similar political outlook within strengthening nationalist movements across much of the world. Israel has therefore become the focus of increasing interest and admiration from nationalist parties and governments in Europe, North America and beyond. Under Benjamin Netanyahu, Israel has reciprocated, conducting a foreign policy reminiscent of Jabotinsky's admiring respect in the 1930s for other right-wing nationalist movements even when they clearly encompassed a strain of antisemitism.[54] The continuing conflict between Israel and the Palestinians is therefore of key significance, not only in relation to the geopolitical rivalries between various powers and the antagonism between the West and Islam, but also as a symbolic and rhetorical focus of the most fundamental line of division between Left and Right across much of the world. In the precarious and polarized global conjuncture at the beginning of the third decade of the new millennium, the Jewish purpose question, despite seldom being articulated in explicit terms, has most certainly not lost its resonance and importance.

———

'There are no angels in America', declares Louis, an earnestly self-absorbed gay Jewish New Yorker, in *Millenium Approaches*, the first part of Tony Kushner's two-part *Angels in America* (1991–92).[55] He is soon proved wrong. At the end of the play an angel crashes through the bedroom ceiling of Louis's ex-boyfriend, Prior—who is of venerable Anglo-Norman ancestry, and has AIDS—and announces cryptically: 'Greetings, Prophet; / The Great Work begins: / The Messenger has arrived.'[56] In the second part of the drama, *Perestroika*, the angel appears to Prior again, delivering, among other things, the enigmatic pronouncement that is the first epigraph at the start of this concluding chapter. At first terrified and bewildered by the angel, Prior is also transformed by her. Maybe he is indeed a prophet, he muses in our second epigraph: and not only him, but all those dying in the New York AIDS crisis in 1986, who might, he wonders, be infected with the 'virus of prophecy'.

But Prior does not die. He is saved, possibly by the angel, or perhaps by the angel-like ministry of his African American ex-drag queen ex-lover, and of

Louis's new lover's Mormon mother. *Angels in America* ends with an affirmation of the forward motion of history, and of human tenacity, resilience and hope. It is now February 1990; the Berlin Wall has fallen, and the play's central characters are gathered beneath the vast angel of the Bethesda Fountain in Central Park. Prior, who has been living with AIDS for five years, in the drama's final line assumes his own prophetic voice: 'Bye now. / You are fabulous creatures, each and every one. / And I bless you: *More Life.* / The Great Work Begins.'[57]

Kushner's angel, like the angelic pair in Wim Wenders's kindred cinematic meditation on Berlin, *Wings of Desire* (1987), evokes Walter Benjamin's 'angel of history'.[58] As in Benjamin's famous essay, *Angels in America* presents a historical horizon that is both messianic and material: open to the transformative interruption at any moment of the angelic divine, while registering the impact of this irruption as a concrete and worldly healing of broken human lives. The pseudo-biblical language of Kushner's angel seems archaically distant, but she is also an active force in the world, bestowing, among other things, overwhelmingly intense orgasms. Echoing Benjamin's thesis that the angel of history can only gaze upon the past because Jews are 'prohibited from investigating the future', the angel in *Angels in America* tells Prior, in our first epigraph, to reject speculative utopian dreaming: 'There is no Zion Save Where You Are!'

After this encounter, Prior seizes the 'now time' (*Jetztzeit*) of Benjamin's political messianism. His hunger for life galvanized, he and his human saviours make their own future, most significantly by stealing a supply of AZT from the ruthless and closeted lawyer Roy Cohn, who does die of AIDS, both in historical reality and in the play: Louis and the ghost of Ethel Rosenberg, in whose prosecution and execution for passing nuclear secrets to the Soviet Union Cohn had played a significant role in the early 1950s, say *Kaddish* (the Jewish mourners' prayer) for him.[59] The Jewish inspiration of *Angels* is unambiguous, and is clearly anchored to its cultural source: at Cohn's deathbed, for example, two Jews say *Kaddish* for a third. The political vision of the drama, however, is universal. Prior, to whom the angel appears, is not Jewish, and neither are the angel's human surrogates; the hopeful conclusion of *Perestroika* looks forward to a better future for all. Kushner's masterpiece remains the most politically powerful reworking in the past thirty years of the outward-oriented conception of Jewish purpose.[60]

The most sustained and elaborate contemporary secular rearticulation of the traditional nineteenth- and twentieth-century themes of Jewish purpose, meanwhile, runs through the work of the writer and literary scholar George Steiner.

The Jews' enforced but nonetheless cherished rootlessness makes them, for Steiner, exemplary cosmopolitans. They have also persistently—above all through the three transformative systems of thought of Moses, Jesus and Marx—posed to the rest of humanity the profound challenge of ethical ideal-ism. This challenge, which Steiner describes as 'the blackmail of the ideal', is put forward 'with that Jewish intensity . . . which non-Jews often find it so hard to live with', and is at times almost unbearable for them to bear. The consequent non-Jewish recoil from the rigorous ethical idealism posed by Jews underlies the persistence of antisemitism, including, he suggests in his novella *The Portage to San Cristobal of A. H.* (1979), the Holocaust.[61] The association of Jews with the dissemination of lofty and demanding ideals of intellectual abstrac-tion and ethical universalism pervaded, as we have seen, nineteenth-century articulations of Jewish mission and purpose. The inevitability and nobility of Jewish suffering was also a widespread nineteenth-century idea, and in the early twentieth-century writings of Hermann Cohen and Franz Rosenzweig was closely linked to the Jews' ethical distinction and diasporic purpose. Steiner transposes these arguments into the idiom of secular humanism, placing par-ticular emphasis on the idea of an exceptional Jewish textual and literary sen-sibility, which he sees as fundamental to the Jewish role in the world and at odds with the normalizing project of Zionism: the true Jewish homeland, in his view, is 'the text'.[62]

Steiner's idealization of Jewish textual cosmopolitanism has been trenchantly criticized, on grounds of elitism, historical selectivity and intellectual reckless-ness. His rarefied conception of Jewish identity, the Israeli scholar Moshe Idel has argued, was embraced by only a small minority of Jews, mostly bourgeois modern Europeans wholly or partially alienated from Judaism. Idel also puts forward a practical critique: if Steiner is right that the idealistic intensity of the Jews is a perennial cause of antisemitic hatred toward them, would it not be prudent, rather than persisting in their vulnerably dispersed labour of cultural edification, for them to consolidate their presence in their own physical home-land?[63] Steiner's commitment to the continuation of the intellectually lofty Jewish diasporic presence does indeed seem to lack a vista of hope. The mes-sianic idea, which has been a fundamental element throughout the history of the Jewish purpose question, leaves no trace in his secular humanist outlook. His notion of Jewish purpose is therefore elusive—aligning neither with the outward- nor the inward-oriented versions of the idea—and thin. Whereas Rosenzweig and Cohen both looked forward to a messianic future in which the suffering of Jews and the divisions between peoples would no longer pertain, and Kushner in *Angels in America* also focuses our gaze in this redemptive direction, Steiner holds out no such hope. It is unclear whether, according to his account, any ultimate purpose is served, either for Jews themselves or for the world as a whole, by the Jewish 'blackmail of the ideal', beyond the perpetuation of the elite traditions of intellectual rigour and cultural efflorescence that he regards as both distinctively Jewish and of inherent value in themselves.

Messianism has, in contrast, been extremely prominent in recent decades within the most dynamic resurgent force of postwar Judaism: the Brooklyn-based Hasidic movement Habad-Lubavitch. The teachings of the seventh and final Lubavitcher rebbe, Menachem Mendel Schneerson (1902–94), were rich in allusions to imminent messianic transformations. A significant proportion of his followers, to the alarm of some Jewish religious authorities, have continued since Schneerson's death to identify him as the messiah.[64] Habad, under Schneerson's leadership and since, has energetically promoted the recognition among non-Jews of the seven universal 'Noachide laws', motivated by a belief that the Gentile observance of these precepts, as well as the Jewish observance of the Torah, is a necessary preparation for the messianic age. This outward-oriented interest in the ethical behaviour of non-Jews should not, though, be misunderstood as implying an ecumenically egalitarian worldview. In keeping with his characteristic theological strategy of inverting or transposing binary oppositions, Schneerson asserted that while it is the responsibility of Jews to disseminate the Noachide laws among non-Jews, it is reciprocally incumbent on non-Jews to provide material support to Jews. Non-Jews, according to Elliot Wolfson—the leading scholarly interpreter of Schneerson—are thus 'treated as a means to benefit the Jews'.[65] The purpose of the Jews, in the Habad tradition, is to play a unique role, as God's chosen people, in the redemption of the world. Through their religious observance they hasten the messianic advent of a new era, in which all oppositions and boundaries will be overcome, including in some sense, and with particular symbolic significance, the distinction between Jew and non-Jew. Meanwhile, however, this distinction pertains, not only in terms of divine priority, but also ontologically: like Judah Halevi in the twelfth century, Schneerson regarded Jews as different in kind from non-Jews. On this basis, the rebbe adopted consistently hawkish positions on Israel, refusing for example to accept the return of any captured territory to the Palestinians.[66]

There is, then, no absolute separation between the outward- and inward-oriented currents of contemporary thinking on the Jewish purpose question, and no invariable derivation of specific political positions from these outlooks. A closer examination of Schneerson's thought blurs still further the distinction between these perspectives. The 'open secret' of his 'postmessianic messianism', as Wolfson puts it, is that, at the most profound level, redemption is timeless, and the messiah is already here: it remains only for us to open our eyes and recognize this divine presence.[67] This theology resembles Walter Benjamin's insistence on the possible arrival of the messiah at any moment, and Prior's discovery, following the angelic appearance to him in *Angels in America*, of his ability to create his own destiny. The appeal of Hasidism, as relayed by Martin Buber to early twentieth-century Jewish left-wing radicals such as Gustav Landauer, Georg Lukács and Ernst Bloch, lay above all in the messianic sense these thinkers found within it of the proximity and possibility of utopia. Habad-Lubavitch have sustained in their messianic theology this tradition of universalistic utopianism, which we have also noted in early modern Sabbatianism and Frankism, nineteenth-century 'mission of Israel' rhetoric and the Zionism of Abraham Kook. While in this respect standing against the recent mainstream Jewish turn away from outward-oriented messianism and universalism, in political terms Habad has fully supported, and unabashedly underpinned with theological reasoning, an uncompromisingly inward-oriented emphasis on Jewish collective interests.

In the endemic 'post-ness' of our contemporary world—in the wake not only of modernism, but also postmodernism, the Holocaust and 9/11, and now grappling with 'post-truth'—messianic hope seems at a historically low ebb, both in political and in religious terms, other than within communities such as Habad and similarly fervent movements in other religions. The desire to draw a dramatically different and better future into the present, and the will to believe that this is possible, nonetheless remain potently seductive and perhaps politically and emotionally crucial human impulses. This insistently hopeful demand for 'the future in the present' has been a recurrent hallmark of the Jewish purpose question. It has been perceived in the ethical rationalism of Spinoza and the messianic antinomianism of Sabbatai Zevi; the embodiment of Enlightenment cosmopolitanism in Moses Mendelssohn and his fictional *alter ego* Nathan the Wise; the regeneration of western European Jewry that was anticipated in the wake of political emancipation; the various modern theories of Jewish economic, intellectual or psychological precocity; multiple Zionist and Leftist visions of a better world; and the many activist iterations of the idea of a Jewish mission to humanity. It is sustained both in the restructuring of the world evoked at the end of *Angels in America*—an ideal of *perestroika* far more resonant than

Mikhail Gorbachev's sense of the word—and also by the messianic Habad slogan 'Moshiach Now!'

Exceptionalist images of Jews today raise widespread unease. This applies particularly to repetitions or resemblances of stereotypes used by the Nazis: associating Jews with exceptional power, wealth, influence or focus on their collective self-interest is often regarded as implicitly antisemitic, and this view is reflected in the IHRA 'Working Definition'. Jews themselves, however, as we have seen, have in many different contexts regarded themselves in highly exceptional terms. The final Lubavitcher rebbe's theology of the relationship between Jews and non-Jews is a particularly pronounced expression of this. Exceptionalist understandings of the place of Jews in the world have been a central feature of the palimpsest of layered and interpenetrating ideas that constitute the shared Jewish and non-Jewish history of the Jewish purpose question. The claim that Jews possess exceptional attributes is closely intertwined with this history, and assertions that today are readily deemed unacceptable were viewed very differently in the relatively recent past: the early twentieth-century celebration by German Zionists of Werner Sombart's sociological exposition of the prodigious economic impact and acumen of Jews is a notable example.

The idea of Jewish purpose is itself underpinned by a notion of Jewish exceptionalism. This is the case not only when, as in the 'mission of Israel' idea, this exceptionalism is expressly stated, but also in outward-oriented and secular responses to the Jewish purpose question that formally disavow Jewish exceptionality. From Spinoza to *Angels in America*, Jewish perspectives and resources have offered a privileged point of access, precisely through the inversion of their generally perceived particularity, to the universalist ideals that have animated modern progressive politics. A thorough disavowal of all forms of exceptionalist thinking with regard to Jews—which the logic of much contemporary 'anti-antisemitism' appears to demand—therefore seems both impossible and undesirable. This thinking is diffused, in many different forms, throughout the history of Jewish purpose question, which is in turn intricately threaded through Western thought on peoplehood, purpose and politics. Jewish exceptionalism is also profoundly embedded in the many strands of Jewish self-understanding, both religious and secular, that have developed from the starting-point of the biblical covenant and its designation of Jews as a chosen people. It is hard to imagine, to say the least, how this idea could be disentangled and removed either from Jewish or from broader Western thought. Even if it could, though, this would entail the excision from our intellectual heritage of a lineage that has played a profound, multifaceted and often inspiring role in the world up to the present.

The Jews provide the most culturally and historically resonant example in Western thought of what the American political scientist Rogers Smith has described as 'political peoplehood'. Narratives of meaning and belonging, Smith argues, underpin all collective political identities. These stories of peoplehood ubiquitously include claims of special significance in the world, based on a particular sense of ethical worth, and often of providential chosenness.[68] Europeans and Americans, in forming their own collective narratives of identity and purpose, have, as we have seen, repeatedly drawn on the Jewish case as an infusive source or an exemplary model of ethically lofty peoplehood. The Exodus narrative of the passage of the Jews from slavery in Egypt to freedom in their Promised Land is the most immediately accessible example of this, inspiring a rich tradition of Christian 'deliverance politics', extending from the political radicals of the English Revolution of the 1640s through to the stirring civil rights rhetoric of Martin Luther King.[69]

At a deeper level, however, the Jewish purpose question focuses attention on a horizon beyond our contemporary reality of competing nations and interest groups. The idea of exemplary peoplehood, in general but particularly with respect to the association of this idea with Jews, implies, as we have also discussed, an aspiration to transcend the divisions that are constitutive of peoplehood itself. This cosmopolitan ideal has in the twenty-first century retained its paradoxical association with Jewish particularity.[70] The idea that Jews—or a select radical vanguard or intellectual elite among them—have already transcended particularism is, however, misplaced. This is not simply because this congratulatory stance might suggest a problematically exceptionalist view of Jews, a negation of the legitimacy of Jewish particularity or an obliviousness to the inward-looking conception of Jewish purpose that currently predominates in the Jewish world. All these objections are cogent, but proclaiming that Jews have already fulfilled their exemplary potential, as cosmopolitans or otherwise, most fundamentally misses the central challenge of the Jewish purpose question. This idea directs us beyond the present, and toward the possibility of a future in which we, as part of whatever collectivity we might feel we belong to, might be something more than we are in the present, and part of bringing about a different and better world.

If Jewish purpose can be distilled to one word, then the choice is clear. Jews are for hope. Hope for what, though? This question takes us back to our point of departure: God's twice-forged covenant with Abraham and Moses. God chose the Jews, but seemed to leave to them, and equally to everyone else, the task of figuring out why. The history of the Jewish purpose question sets out, in rich complexity, the various interconnected human attempts to answer that question. It cannot, though, provide any definitive answer. The provisional answers we have encountered in this historical exploration were all, inevitably, shaped by the contexts in which they were forged, and by the outlooks and priorities of the people who formulated and in some cases devoted their lives to them. The Jewish purpose question continues today, and will remain in the future, a potent source of inspiration, but also a charged terrain of contestation.

The formulation of our shared hopes stands at the heart of our collective social and political life. Amid the combative post-ideological populism of our contemporary moment, this collective aspiration is itself perhaps now unprecedentedly questioned and vulnerable. In this context, seen from the vantage point of the beginning of the third decade of the new millennium, the intellectual resources offered by the long history of cogitation on the Jewish purpose question, by Jews and non-Jews both together and separately, seem particularly worthy of careful and respectful attention. These reflections and debates testify to the historical and philosophical depth, inspirational power and cross-cultural complexity of Western thought on the nature of peoplehood and collective purpose, in the past, present and future. Despite the profound uncertainties facing us and our planet, the Jewish purpose question still spurs us to think beyond our differences, and always to carry on hoping.

NOTES

Introduction. What Are the Jews For?
History and the Purpose Question

1. Gershom Scholem, 'Judaism', in Arthur A. Cohen and Paul Mendes-Flohr, eds, *Contemporary Jewish Religious Thought* (New York: Free Press, 1987) 505–8, at 508 [based on transcribed conversations in 1973 at the Center for the Study of Democratic Institutions, Santa Barbara, CA].

2. Amélie Kuhrt, *The Ancient Near East, c. 3000–300 BC* (London: Routledge, 1995) 469–72; Daniel C. Snell, *Religions of the Ancient Near East* (Cambridge: Cambridge University Press, 2011) 95–114.

3. Mark R. Cohen, *Under Crescent and Cross: The Jews in the Middle Ages* (Princeton, NJ: Princeton University Press, 1994) 145–54.

4. Immanuel Kant, *The Conflict of the Faculties*, trans. Mary J. Gregor (Lincoln, NE: University of Nebraska Press, 1992 [1798]) 95.

5. Arnold M. Eisen, *The Chosen People in America* (Bloomington, IN: Indiana University Press, 1983) 127–82.

6. Louis Jacobs, *A Jewish Theology* (London: Darton, Longman & Todd, 1973) 269–75.

7. David Novak, *The Election of Israel* (Cambridge: Cambridge University Press, 1995) esp. 241–55.

8. Adam Sutcliffe and Jonathan Karp, 'Introduction: A Brief History of Philosemitism', in Jonathan Karp and Adam Sutcliffe, eds, *Philosemitism in History* (Cambridge: Cambridge University Press, 2011) 1–26.

9. Daniel Boyarin, *Border Lines: The Partition of Judaeo-Christianity* (Philadelphia: University of Pennsylvania Press, 2004); Israel Yuval, *Two Nations in Your Womb: Perceptions of Jews and Christians in Late Antiquity and the Middle Ages* (Berkeley and Los Angeles: University of California Press, 2003).

10. Boyarin, *Border Lines*, esp. 1–33, 202–26.

11. Susannah Heschel, 'Jewish Studies as Counterhistory', in David Biale, Michael Galchinsky and Susannah Heschel, eds, *Insider/Outsider: American Jews and Multiculturalism* (Berkeley and Los Angeles: University of California Press, 1998) 101–15; Willi Goetschel and Ato Quayson, 'Introduction: Jewish Studies and Postcolonialism', *The Cambridge Journal of Postcolonial Literary Inquiry* 3 (2016) 1–9.

12. David Nirenberg, *Anti-Judaism: The History of a Way of Thinking* (New York: W. W. Norton, 2013); Albert S. Lindemann and Richard S. Levy, eds, *Antisemitism: A History* (Oxford: Oxford University Press, 2010).

13. Zygmunt Bauman, *Modernity and Ambivalence* (Cambridge: Polity, 1991); Siân Jones, Tony Kushner and Sarah Pearce, eds, *Cultures of Ambivalence and Contempt: Studies in Jewish–non-Jewish Relations* (London: Vallentine Mitchell, 1997).

14. Jehuda Reinharz and Walter Schatzberg, eds, *The Jewish Response to German Culture: From the Enlightenment to the Second World War* (Hanover, NH: University Press of New England, 1985); Michael Mack, *German Idealism and the Jew: The Inner Anti-Semitism of Philosophy and German Jewish Responses* (Chicago: University of Chicago Press, 2003).

15. Bernard-Henri Lévy, *The Genius of Judaism* (New York: Random House, 2017) 115–56, 226.

16. Ibid., 3–94, 157–204.

17. Henri Atlan, 'Chosen People', in Cohen and Mendes-Flohr, eds, *Contemporary Jewish Religious Thought*, 55–9; Novak, *Election of Israel*, 10–14. All Jewish Bible quotations are from the Jewish Publication Society translation, and all New Testament quotations from the King James version, in both cases occasionally very slightly modified.

18. Michael Walzer, *In God's Shadow: Politics in the Hebrew Bible* (New Haven, CT: Yale University Press, 2012) 1–15; Michael Walzer, Menachem Lorberbaum and Noam J. Zohar, eds, *The Jewish Political Tradition, vol. 1: Authority* (New Haven, CT: Yale University Press, 2000) 6–27.

19. The others are Isaiah 49:6 and 60:3.

20. John Sawyer, *The Fifth Gospel: Isaiah in the History of Christianity* (Cambridge: Cambridge University Press, 1996) esp. 100–125; Adolf Neubauer and Samuel R. Driver, eds, *The Fifty-Third Chapter of Isaiah according to the Jewish Interpreters*, 2 vols (Oxford and London, 1876–77).

21. Daniel Boyarin, *A Radical Jew: Paul and the Politics of Identity* (Berkeley and Los Angeles: University of California Press, 1994) 85.

22. Ibid., 39–56; Martin Hengel, *The 'Hellenization' of Judaea in the First Century after Christ* (London: SCM Press, 2012). For key Christian correctives to this traditional view of Paul, see James Parkes, *The Conflict of the Church and the Synagogue: A Study in the Origins of Anti-Semitism* (London: SCM Press, 1934); E. P. Sanders, *Paul and Palestinian Judaism* (London: SCM Press, 1977).

23. Boyarin, *Radical Jew*, 136–57; Robert Chazan, *From Anti-Judaism to Anti-Semitism: Ancient and Medieval Constructions of Jewish History* (Cambridge: Cambridge University Press, 2016) 23–46.

24. Martin Goodman, *The Roman World, 44 BC to 180 AD* (London: Routledge, 1997), 302–14; Tessa Rajak, 'Judaism and Hellenism Revisited', in *The Jewish Dialogue with Greece and Rome: Studies in Cultural and Social Interaction* (Leiden: Brill, 2000) 3–10.

25. See Giorgio Agamben, *The Time That Remains: A Commentary on the Letter to the Romans* (Stanford, CA: Stanford University Press, 2005) 44–58.

26. Boyarin, *Radical Jew*, 29–32.

27. *Sifre Deuteronomy* 343, in *Sifre: A Tannaitic Commentary on the Book of Deuteronomy*, trans. Reuven Hammer (New Haven, CT: Yale University Press, 1986) 352–3; Walzer, Lorberbaum and Zohar, eds, *Jewish Political Tradition* 1, 33–4.

28. Babylonian Talmud, *Avodah Zarah* 2a–3b, trans. in Michael Walzer, Menachem Lorberbaum and Noam J. Zohar, eds, *The Jewish Political Tradition, vol. 2: Membership* (New Haven, CT: Yale University Press, 2003) 20–3.

29. Moshe Halbertal, 'The Last Judgment—a Talmudic Account', in Walzer, Lorberbaum and Zohar, eds, *Jewish Political Tradition* 2, 23–9.

30. Boyarin, *Border Lines*, esp. 89–147.

31. Jacob Neusner, *Judaism and its Social Metaphors: Israel in the History of Jewish Thought* (Cambridge: Cambridge University Press, 1989) 142, 145–204.

32. Ibid,, 105.

33. Augustine, *City of God*, ed. and trans. R. W. Dyson (Cambridge: Cambridge University Press, 1998 [426]) 891 [bk 18, ch. 46].

34. Jeremy Cohen, *Living Letters of the Law: Ideas of the Jew in Medieval Christianity* (Berkeley and Los Angeles: University of California Press, 1999) 23–65; Chazan, *Anti-Judaism to Anti-Semitism*, 76–106.

35. Robert Wilken, *John Chrysostom and the Jews: Rhetoric and Reality in the Late 4th Century* (Berkeley, CA: University of California Press, 1983); Wendy Mayer, 'Preaching Hatred? John Chrysostom, Neuroscience, and the Jews', in Chris de Wet and Wendy Mayer, eds, *Revisioning John Chrysostom: New Approaches, New Perspectives* (Leiden: Brill, 2019) 58–136.

36. Alain Badiou, *Saint Paul: The Foundation of Universalism* (Stanford, CA: Stanford University Press, 2003 [1997]).

37. Éric Marty, *Radical French Thought and the Return of the "Jewish Question"* (Bloomington, IN: Indiana University Press, 2015 [2007–13]) 53–95; Maurice Samuels, *The Right to Difference: French Universalism and the Jews* (Chicago: University of Chicago Press, 2016) 172–85; Vivian Liska, *German-Jewish Thought and Its Afterlife: A Tenuous Legacy* (Bloomington, IN: Indiana University Press, 2017) 153.

38. Dow Marmur, *Beyond Survival: Reflections on the Future of Judaism* (London: Darton, Longman & Todd, 1982) esp. 187–207; Bernard Wasserstein, *Vanishing Diaspora: The Jews in Europe since 1945* (London: Hamish Hamilton, 1996).

39. Alasdair MacIntyre, *Whose Justice? Which Rationality?* (Notre Dame, IN: University of Notre Dame Press, 1988) esp. 389–403; Mark Salber Phillips and Gordon Schochet, eds, *Questions of Tradition* (Toronto: University of Toronto Press, 2004).

40. Nathan Rotenstreich, 'Universalism and Particularism in History', *Review of Metaphysics* 37 (1983) 21–36; Ernesto Laclau, 'Universalism, Particularism, and the Question of Identity', *October* 61 (1992) 83–90.

Chapter One. Religion, Sovereignty, Messianism: Jews and Political Purpose

1. Baruch Spinoza, *Theological-Political Treatise* (1670), trans. Samuel Shirley in *Spinoza: Complete Works* (Indianapolis: Hackett, 2002) 504 [ch. 12].

2. Carl Schmitt, *Political Theology: Four Chapters on the Concept of Sovereignty*, trans. George Schwab (Chicago: University of Chicago Press, 2005 [1922]) 8–9.

3. Schmitt, *Political Theology*, 36–48; Schmitt, *The Leviathan in the State Theory of Thomas Hobbes*, trans. George Schwab (Chicago: University of Chicago Press, 2008 [1938]).

4. Isaiah Gafni, 'Babylonian Rabbinic Culture', in David Biale, ed., *Cultures of the Jews: A New History* (New York: Schocken, 2002) 223–65.

5. Mark R. Cohen, *Under Crescent and Cross: The Jews in the Middle Ages* (Princeton, NJ: Princeton University Press, 1994) 52–4.

6. Ross Brann, 'The Arabized Jews', in Maria Rosa Menocal, Raymond P. Scheindlin and Michael Sells, eds, *The Cambridge History of Arabic Literature: The Literature of al-Andalus* (Cambridge: Cambridge University Press, 2000) 435–54.

7. Adam Shear, *The Kuzari and the Shaping of Jewish Identity, 1167–1900* (Cambridge: Cambridge University Press, 2008) viii–xii.

8. Judah Halevi, *The Kuzari*, trans. Hartwig Hirschfeld (New York: Schocken Books, 1964 [c. 1140]) 73–4, 79 [part 1, §§ 103, 115].

9. Ibid., 47–9 [1:31–47].

10. Ibid., 109–11 [2:36–44].

11. Ibid., 226–8 [4:23].

12. Menachem Kellner, *Maimonides on Judaism and the Jewish People* (Albany, NY: State University of New York Press, 1991) 81–95.

13. Moses Maimonides, *The Book of Knowledge* [*Mishneh Torah*, vol. 1] (c. 1170), trans. Bernard Septimus in Michael Walzer, Menachem Lorberbaum and Noam J. Zohar, eds, *The Jewish Political Tradition, vol. 2: Membership* (New Haven, CT: Yale University Press, 2003) 32–4, at 32.

14. Ibid., 33.

15. Moses Maimonides, *The Guide of the Perplexed*, trans. Shlomo Pines (Chicago: University of Chicago Press, 1965 [c. 1190]) 364 [part 2, § 33]; Menachem Kellner, 'Chosenness, not Chauvinism: Maimonides on the Chosen People', in Daniel H. Frank, ed., *A People Apart: Chosenness and Ritual in Jewish Philosophical Thought* (Albany, NY: State University of New York Press, 1993) 51–75, esp. 66.

16. Shear, *Kuzari*, esp. 311–13.

17. Kellner, 'Chosenness', 56.

18. Robert Chazan, 'Philosemitic Tendencies in Medieval Western Christendom', in Jonathan Karp and Adam Sutcliffe, eds, *Philosemitism in History* (Cambridge: Cambridge University Press, 2011) 29–48, at 31–3; Jeremy Cohen, *Living Letters of the Law: Ideas of the Jew in Medieval Christianity* (Berkeley and Los Angeles: University of California Press, 1999) 74–9, 150–1.

19. Michael A. Signer, 'God's Love for Israel: Apologetic and Hermeneutical Strategies in Twelfth-Century Biblical Exegesis', in Michael A. Signer and John Van Engen, eds, *Jews and Christians in Twelfth-Century Europe* (Notre Dame, IN: University of Notre Dame Press, 2001) 123–49, at 133–4; Elazar Touitou, 'Rashi's Commentary on Genesis 1–6 in the Context of Judeo-Christian Controversy', *Hebrew Union College Annual* 61 (1990) 159–83.

20. Israel Yuval, *Two Nations in Your Womb: Perceptions of Jews and Christians in Late Antiquity and the Middle Ages* (Berkeley and Los Angeles: University of California Press, 2006) 92–130.

21. Cohen, *Living Letters*, 159–61.

22. Ibid., 221–45; Robert Chazan, *Church, State, and Jew in the Middle Ages* (West Orange, NJ: Behrman House, 1980) 100–106; Chazan, 'Philosemitic Tendencies', 33–7.

23. Cohen, *Living Letters*, 317–89.

24. Hyam Maccoby, *Judaism on Trial: Jewish-Christian Disputations in the Middle Ages* (London: Littman, 1993).

25. Miri Rubin, *Gentile Tales: The Narrative Assault on Late Medieval Jews* (New Haven, CT: Yale University Press, 1999) esp. 5; Anthony Bale, *Feeling Persecuted: Christians, Jews and Images of Violence in the Middle Ages* (London: Reaktion, 2010) esp. 27–9, 160–5.

26. Rubin, *Gentile Tales*, 93–103; Bale, *Feeling Persecuted*, 168–89; Yuval, *Two Nations*, 130–4.

27. Abraham Melamed, 'The Revival of Christian Hebraism in Early Modern Europe', in Karp and Sutcliffe, *Philosemitism*, 49–66, at 53–4; Elisheva Carlebach, *Divided Souls: Converts from Judaism in Germany, 1500–1750* (New Haven, CT: Yale University Press, 2001) 47–56.

28. Lyndal Roper, *Martin Luther: Renegade and Prophet* (London: Bodley Head, 2016) 93–4.

29. Ibid., 389–96; David Nirenberg, *Anti-Judaism: The History of a Way of Thinking* (New York: W. W. Norton, 2013) 246–68; Thomas Kaufmann, *Luther's Jews: A Journey into Anti-Semitism* (Oxford: Oxford University Press, 2017) 54–75, 94–124.

30. Roper, *Martin Luther*, 79–90; Jerome Friedman, *The Most Ancient Testimony: Sixteenth-Century Christian-Hebraica in the Age of Renaissance Nostalgia* (Athens, OH: Ohio University Press, 1983) 168–9.

31. Stephen G. Burnett, 'Reassessing the "Basel–Wittenberg Conflict": Dimensions of the Reformation-Era Discussion of Hebrew Scholarship', in Alison P. Coudert and Jeffrey S. Shoulson, eds, *Hebraica Veritas? Christian Hebraists and the Study of Judaism in Early Modern Europe* (Philadelphia: University of Pennsylvania Press, 2004) 181–201.

32. Friedman, *Ancient Testimony*, 190–251; Stephen G. Burnett, *From Christian Hebraism to Jewish Studies: Johannes Buxtorf (1564–1629) and Hebrew Learning in the Seventeenth Century* (Leiden: Brill, 1996).

33. Anthony Grafton and Joanna Weinberg, *"I Have Always Loved the Holy Tongue": Isaac Casaubon, the Jews, and a Forgotten Chapter in Renaissance Scholarship* (Cambridge, MA: Harvard University Press, 2011) 164–230.

34. Ibid., 67.

35. Theodor Dunkelgrün, 'The Christian Study of Judaism in Early Modern Europe', in Jonathan Karp and Adam Sutcliffe, eds, *The Cambridge History of Judaism, vol. 7: The Early Modern World, 1500–1815* (Cambridge: Cambridge University Press, 2018) 316–48, esp. 322–5; Adam Sutcliffe, *Judaism and Enlightenment* (Cambridge: Cambridge University Press, 2003) 148–55.

36. Dunkelgrün, 'Christian Study', 333–40; Adam Sutcliffe and Jonathan Karp, 'Introduction: A Brief History of Philosemitism', in Karp and Sutcliffe, *Philosemitism*, 1–26, at 7–8; Aaron L. Katchen, *Christian Hebraists and Dutch Rabbis: Seventeenth Century Apologetics and the Study of Maimonides' Mishneh Torah* (Cambridge, MA: Harvard University Press, 1984).

37. Simon Schama, *The Embarrassment of Riches: An Interpretation of Dutch Culture in the Golden Age* (New York: Knopf, 1987) 93–125; Lea Campos Boralevi, 'Classical Foundational Myths of European Republicanism: The Jewish Commonwealth', in Martin van Gelderen and Quentin Skinner, eds, *Republicanism: A Shared European Heritage, vol. 1: Republicanism and Constitutionalism in Early Modern Europe* (Cambridge: Cambridge University Press, 2002) 247–61, at 248–51.

38. Miriam Bodian, 'The Biblical "Jewish Republic" and the Dutch "New Israel" in Seventeenth-Century Dutch Thought', *Hebraic Political Studies* 1 (2006) 186–201, esp. 190–6; Christopher Hill, *The English Bible and the Seventeenth-Century Revolution* (London: Allen Lane, 1993); Alexandra Walsham, *Providence in Early Modern England* (Oxford: Oxford University Press, 1999) 281–325; Achsah Guibbory, *Christian Identity, Jews, and Israel in Seventeenth-Century England* (Oxford: Oxford University Press, 2010) 21–120; Kevin Killeen, *The Political Bible in Early Modern England* (Cambridge: Cambridge University Press, 2017) esp. 105–34.

39. Niccolò Machiavelli, *The Prince* (1532), in David Wootton, ed. and trans., *Machiavelli: Selected Political Writings* (Indianapolis: Hackett, 1994) 18–21 [ch. 6]; Abraham Melamed, *The*

Philosopher-King in Medieval and Renaissance Jewish Political Thought (Albany, NY: State University of New York Press, 2003) 149–66; John H. Geerken, 'Machiavelli's Moses and Renaissance Politics', *Journal of the History of Ideas* 60 (1999) 579–95.

40. Petrus Cunaeus, *The Hebrew Republic*, trans. Peter Wyetzner (Jerusalem: Shalem Press, 2006 [1617]) 6; Adam Sutcliffe, 'The Philosemitic Moment? Judaism and Republicanism in Seventeenth-Century European Thought', in Karp and Sutcliffe, *Philosemitism*, 67–89, at 71–3.

41. J.G.A. Pocock, *The Machiavellian Moment: Florentine Political Thought and the Atlantic Republican Tradition* (Princeton, NJ: Princeton University Press, 1975) esp. 169–72, 183–211.

42. Cunaeus, *Hebrew Republic*, 48.

43. Ibid., 128; Sutcliffe, 'Philosemitic Moment', 75.

44. Phyllis S. Lachs, 'Hugo Grotius' Use of Jewish Sources in *On the Law of War and Peace*', *Renaissance Quarterly* 30 (1977) 181–200; Richard Tuck, *The Rights of War and Peace: Political Thought and the International Order from Grotius to Kant* (Oxford: Oxford University Press, 1999) 78–108.

45. Eric Nelson, *The Hebrew Republic: Jewish Sources and the Transformation of European Political Thought* (Cambridge, MA: Harvard University Press, 2010) 97–107.

46. Richard Tuck, 'Grotius and Selden', in J. H. Burns, ed., *The Cambridge History of Political Thought 1450–1700* (Cambridge: Cambridge University Press, 1991) 95–131; Paul Christianson, *Discourse on History, Law and Governance in the Public Career of John Selden, 1610–35* (Toronto: University of Toronto Press, 1996).

47. John Selden, *De jure naturali et gentium juxta disciplinarum Ebraeorum* (London, 1640) 109; Richard Tuck, *Philosophy and Government 1572–1651* (Cambridge: Cambridge University Press, 1993) 215–16.

48. John Selden, *History of Tithes* (1618), in his *Opera Omnia*, 3 vols (London, 1726) III: 1075–88.

49. John Selden, *Uxor Ebraica*, ed. and trans. Jonathan Ziskind (Leiden: Brill, 1991 [1646]).

50. Jason P. Rosenblatt, *Renaissance England's Chief Rabbi: John Selden* (Oxford: Oxford University Press, 2006) esp. 3–5, 161, 181.

51. John Selden, *On the Jews Sometimes Living in England*, n.d., in *Opera Omnia*, III: 1461.

52. Anthony Grafton, '"Pandects of the Jews": A French, Swiss and Italian Prelude to John Selden', in Scott Mandelbrote and Joanna Weinberg, eds, *Jewish Books and their Readers: Aspects of the Intellectual Life of Christians and Jews in Early Modern Europe* (Leiden: Brill, 2016) 169–88, at 171–2.

53. Arthur Eyffinger, '"How Wondrously Moses Goes Along with the House of Orange!" Hugo Grotius' *De Republica Emendata* in the Context of the Dutch Revolt', *Hebraic Political Studies* 1 (2005) 71–109.

54. John Selden, *Table-Talk*, 3rd edn (London, 1716) 47; Reid Barbour, *John Selden: Measures of the Holy Commonwealth in Seventeenth-Century England* (Toronto: University of Toronto Press, 2003) 270–82; Sutcliffe, 'Philosemitic Moment', 71–81.

55. Thomas Hobbes, *Leviathan* (London: Penguin, 1968 [1651]) 442–51 [ch. 35].

56. Nelson, *Hebrew Republic* (2010) 122–30; Graham Hammill, *The Mosaic Constitution: Political Theology and Imagination from Machiavelli to Milton* (Chicago: University of Chicago Press, 2012) 212–19; Alison McQueen, 'Mosaic Leviathan: Religion and Rhetoric in Hobbes's Political Thought', in Robin Douglas and Laurens van Apeldoorn, eds, *Hobbes on Politics and Religion* (Oxford: Oxford University Press, 2018) 116–34.

57. Hobbes, *Leviathan*, 511–12 [ch. 40].

58. Ibid., 230 [ch. 18]; A. P. Martinich, *Two Gods of Leviathan: Thomas Hobbes on Religion and Politics* (Cambridge: Cambridge University Press, 1992) 143–6.

59. Guibbory, *Christian Identity*, 186–219; Christopher Hill, *The World Turned Upside Down: Radical Ideas During the English Revolution* (London: Penguin, 1975).

60. James Harrington, *The Prerogative of Popular Government* (1658), in J.G.A. Pocock, ed., *The Political Works of James Harrington* (Cambridge: Cambridge University Press, 1977) 516–38. See also Harrington, *The Commonwealth of Oceana* (1656) and *The Art of Lawgiving* (1659), both in Pocock, *Works of Harrington*; Sutcliffe, *Judaism and Enlightenment*, 51–5; Hammill, *Mosaic Constitution*, 219–42.

61. Nelson, *Hebrew Republic*; Fania Oz-Salzberger, 'The Jewish Roots of Western Freedom', *Azure* 13 (2002) 88–132.

62. Christopher Hill, *The English Bible and the Seventeenth-Century Revolution* (1993) 196–250.

63. Ariel Hessayon, *'God Tried in the Fire': The Prophet TheaurauJohn Tany and the English Revolution* (Abingdon: Ashgate: 2007).

64. John Rogers, *Ohel, or Beth-Shemesh: A Tabernacle for the Sun* (London, 1653) 521; Guibbory, *Christian Identity*, 191–5.

65. Thomas Collier, *A Brief Answer to Some of the Objections and Demurs against the Coming-in and Inhabiting of the Jews in this Common-wealth* (London, 1656) 8–9.

66. William Prynne, *Short Demurrer to the Jews* (London, 1655).

67. Collier, *Brief Answer*, 13.

68. Harrington, *Oceana*, 159.

69. David S. Katz, *Philo-Semitism and the Readmission of the Jews to England* (Oxford: Oxford University Press, 1982); Eliane Glaser, *Judaism without Jews: Philosemitism and Christian Polemic in Early Modern England* (Basingstoke: Palgrave, 2007) 113–29.

70. Sutcliffe and Karp, 'Brief History of Philosemitism', 2–6.

71. Menasseh ben Israel, *Mikveh Israel: esto es, Esperança de Israel* (Amsterdam, 1650); Thomas Thorowgood, *Jewes in America* (London, 1650).

72. Ernestine G. A. van der Wall, 'The Amsterdam Millenarian Petrus Serrarius (1600–1699) and the Anglo-Dutch Circle of Philo-Judaists', in J. van den Berg and Ernestine G. A. van der Wall, *Jewish–Christian Relations in the Seventeenth Century: Studies and Documents* (Dordrecht: Kluwer, 1988) 73–94; Yosef Kaplan, Henri Méchoulan and Richard H. Popkin, eds, *Menasseh ben Israel and his World* (Leiden: Brill, 1989).

73. Harold Fisch, 'The Messianic Politics of Menasseh ben Israel', in Kaplan, Méchoulan and Popkin, *Menasseh*, 228–43; Glaser, *Judaism without Jews*, 9–13.

74. Gershom Scholem, *Sabbatai Sevi, the Mystical Messiah* (Princeton, NJ: Princeton University Press, 1973); Matt Goldish, *The Sabbatean Prophets* (Cambridge, MA: Harvard University Press, 2004); Goldish, 'Sabbatai Zevi and the Sabbatean Movement', in Karp and Sutcliffe, *Cambridge History* 7, 491–521.

75. Goldish, 'Sabbatai Zevi', 499; Richard H. Popkin, 'Christian Interest and Concerns about Sabbatai Zevi', in Matt Goldish and Richard H. Popkin, *Millenarianism and Messianism in Early Modern European Culture, vol. 1: Jewish Messianism in the Early Modern World* (Dordrecht: Kluwer, 2001) 91–106; Michael Heyd, 'The "Jewish Quaker": Christian Perceptions of Sabbatai Zevi as an Enthusiast', in Coudert and Shoulson, *Hebraica Veritas?*, 234–65.

76. Gershom Scholem, *Major Trends in Jewish Mysticism* (New York: Schocken, 1961 [1941]) esp. 244–324; Scholem, *The Messianic Idea in Judaism* (New York: Schocken, 1971) esp. 15–17.

77. See Richard H. Popkin and Gordon M Weiner, eds, *Jewish Christians and Christian Jews: From the Renaissance to the Enlightenment* (Dordrecht: Kluwer, 1994).

78. Paweł Maciejko, *Sabbatian Heresy: Writings on Mysticism, Messianism, and the Origins of Jewish Modernity* (Lebanon, NH: University of New England Press, 2017) 67–86.

79. Ibid., xxv.

80. Ibid., xiv–xv, 47–66; Marc David Baer, *The Dönme: Jewish Converts, Muslim Revolutionaries, and Secular Turks* (Stanford, CA: Stanford University Press, 2010).

81. Maciejko, *Sabbatian Heresy*, xxii.

82. Baer, *The Dönme*, 1–82.

83. See Ada Rapoport-Albert, *Women and the Messianic Heresy of Sabbatai Zevi, 1666–1816* (Oxford: Littman, 2011).

84. Scholem, *Sabbatai Sevi*, 519–30.

85. Steven Nadler, *Spinoza: A Life* (Cambridge: Cambridge University Press, 1999) 155–63, 251–4; Richard H. Popkin, 'Spinoza's Relations with the Quakers in Amsterdam', *Quaker History* 37 (1984) 14–28.

86. Lodowijk Meyer, *La philosophie interprète de l'écriture sainte*, ed. and trans. Jacquéline Langrée and Pierre-François Moreau (Paris: Intertextes, 1988 [1666]) 249; Adriaan Koerbagh, *Een Ligt schijnende in duystere plaatsen*, ed. H. Vandenbossche (Brussels: VVW, 1974 [1668]) esp. 1–2, 319–20; Adam Sutcliffe, 'Judaism in Spinoza and his Circle', *Studia Rosenthaliana* 34 (2000) 7–22.

87. Nadler, *Spinoza*, 167–73, 294–9; Jonathan I. Israel, *Radical Enlightenment: Philosophy and the Making of Modernity 1650–1750* (Oxford: Oxford University Press, 2001) 175–205.

88. Spinoza, *Theological-Political Treatise*, 414 [ch. 2].

89. Ibid., 415–16 [ch. 3].

90. Amos Funkenstein, *Theology and the Scientific Imagination: From the Middle Ages to the Seventeenth Century* (Princeton, NJ: Princeton University Press, 1986) 213–71; Stephen D. Benin, *The Footprints of God: Divine Accommodation in Jewish and Christian Thought* (Albany, NY: State University of New York Press, 1993).

91. Spinoza, *Theological-Political Treatise*, 417–20 [ch. 3].

92. Spinoza, *Ethics* (1677), trans. Samuel Shirley in *Spinoza: Complete Works*, 321 [part 4, preface].

93. Spinoza, *Theological-Political Treatise*, 422–3 [ch. 3].

94. Ibid., 425 [ch. 3].

95. Adam Sutcliffe, 'The Spirit of Spinoza and the Enlightenment Image of the Pure Philosopher', in Geoffrey Cubitt and Allen Warren, eds, *Heroic Reputations and Exemplary Lives* (Manchester: Manchester University Press, 2000) 40–56.

96. Leszek Kołakowski, *Chrétiens sans église: la conscience religieuse et le lien confessionel au XVII siècle* (Paris: Gallimard, 1969 [1965]).

97. Spinoza to Albert Burgh, December 1675, in A Wolf, ed., *The Correspondence of Spinoza* (London: Allen & Unwin, 1928) 353–4.

98. Adam Sutcliffe, 'Judaism in the Anti-Religious Thought of the Clandestine French Early Enlightenment', *Journal of the History of Ideas* 64 (2003) 97–117.

99. Wiep van Bunge and Wim Klever, eds, *Disguised and Overt Spinozism around 1700* (Leiden: Brill, 1996); Israel, *Radical Enlightenment*, 285–327.

100. J. M. Lucas, 'The Life of the Late Mr. de Spinosa', in A. Wolf, *The Oldest Biography of Spinoza* (London: Allen & Unwin, 1927 [1719]) 69.

101. Ibid., 69.

102. Sutcliffe, 'Spirit of Spinoza'; Sutcliffe, *Judaism and Enlightenment*, 133–47.

103. Steven B. Smith, *Spinoza, Liberalism and the Question of Jewish Identity* (New Haven, CT: Yale University Press, 1997) 166–96; Israel, *Radical Enlightenment*, 157–328; Israel, *Enlightenment Contested: Philosophy, Modernity, and the Emancipation of Man 1670–1752* (Oxford: Oxford University Press, 2006) 43–51, 224–39; Israel, *Democratic Enlightenment: Philosophy, Revolution, and Human Rights 1750–1790* (Oxford: Oxford University Press, 2011) 8–12.

104. Yirmiyahu Yovel, *Spinoza and Other Heretics: The Marrano of Reason* (Princeton, NJ: Princeton University Press, 1989); Yovel, *The Other Within—The Marranos: Split Identity and Emerging Modernity* (Princeton, NJ: Princeton University Press, 2009).

105. David Nirenberg, '"Judaism" as Political Concept: Toward a Critique of Political Theology', *Representations* 128 (2014) 1–29.

106. Killeen, *Political Bible*, 10–11, 241–2; Sutcliffe, *Judaism and Enlightenment*, 181–4; Israel, *Radical Enlightenment*, 591–8.

107. Charles Taylor, *A Secular Age* (Cambridge, MA: Harvard University Press, 2007) 221–98; Mark Lilla, *The Stillborn God: Religion, Politics, and the Modern West* (New York: Random House, 2007) 55–103.

108. Carl Schmitt, *The Leviathan in the State Theory of Thomas Hobbes: Meaning and Failure of a Political Symbol*, trans. George Schwab (Chicago: University of Chicago Press, 2008 [1938]) 53.

109. Schmitt, *Leviathan*, 53–7; Hobbes, *Leviathan*, 476–8 [ch. 37].

110. Schmitt, *Leviathan*, 57.

111. Raphael Gross, *Carl Schmitt and the Jews: The "Jewish Question," the Holocaust, and German Legal Theory* (Madison, WI: University of Wisconsin Press, 2008 [2000]).

112. Peter C. Caldwell, 'Controversies over Carl Schmitt', *Journal of Modern History* 77 (2005) 357–87.

113. Victoria Kahn, *The Future of Illusion: Political Theology and Early Modern Texts* (Chicago: University of Chicago Press, 2014) esp. 115–46.

Chapter Two. Religion, Toleration, Messianism: Jews and Philosophical Purpose

1. Henri Grégoire, *Essai sur la régénération physique, morale et politique des juifs* (Metz, 1789) 193–4.

2. Jonathan Israel, *The Dutch Republic* (Oxford: Oxford University Press, 1995) 660–9; Tad M. Schmaltz, *Early Modern Cartesianisms: Dutch and French Constructions* (New York: Oxford University Press, 2016) 35–50.

3. Steven Shapin, *The Scientific Revolution* (Chicago: University of Chicago Press, 1996); Anne Goldgar, *Impolite Learning: Culture and Community in the Republic of Letters 1680–1750* (New Haven, CT: Yale University Press, 1995).

4. Theodor Adorno and Max Horkheimer, *Dialectic of Enlightenment*, trans. John Cumming (New York: Continuum, 1989 [1947]) 186.

5. William J. Bulman, 'Introduction: Enlightenment for the Culture Wars', in William J. Bulman and Robert G. Ingram, eds, *God in the Enlightenment* (Oxford: Oxford University Press, 2016) 1–41.

6. Jonathan Israel, *Democratic Enlightenment: Philosophy, Revolution, and Human Rights 1750–1790* (Oxford: Oxford University Press, 2011) 8–17; for the contrary view, Dmitri Levitin, *Ancient Wisdom in the Age of the New Science* (Cambridge: Cambridge University Press, 2015) 5–9, 542–3.

7. Jürgen Habermas, *The Structural Transformation of the Public Sphere*, trans. Thomas Burger (Cambridge, MA: MIT Press, 1989 [1962]) 14–26; James van Horn Melton, *The Rise of the Public in Enlightenment Europe* (Cambridge: Cambridge University Press, 2001) esp. 1–16; Clifford Siskin and William Warner, eds, *This Is Enlightenment* (Chicago: University of Chicago Press, 2010).

8. Daniel Brewer, *Enlightenment Past: Deconstructing Eighteenth-Century French Thought* (Cambridge: Cambridge University Press, 2008) 24–40.

9. Dan Edelstein, *The Enlightenment: A Genealogy* (Chicago: University of Chicago Press, 2010) 24–74.

10. Jonathan Sheehan, *The Enlightenment Bible: Translation, Scholarship, Culture* (Princeton, NJ: Princeton University Press, 2005) 27–30.

11. Richard Simon, *Histoire critique du Vieux Testament* (Paris, 1678) ii–viii.

12. Peter van Rooden, *Theology, Biblical Scholarship and Rabbinical Studies in the Seventeenth Century* (Leiden: Brill, 1989) 222–7.

13. Jean Le Clerc, *Sentiments de quelques théologiens d'Hollande sur l'Histoire critique du Vieux Testament* (Amsterdam, 1685).

14. J. van den Berg, 'Proto-Protestants? The Image of the Karaites as a Mirror of the Catholic–Protestant Controversy in the Seventeenth Century', in J. van den Berg and Ernestine G. E. van der Wall, eds, *Jewish–Christian Relations in the Seventeenth Century: Studies and Documents* (Dordrecht: Kluwer, 1988) 33–49.

15. Jacques-Bénigne Bossuet, *Discourse on Universal History*, trans. Elborg Foster (Chicago: University of Chicago Press, 1976 [1681]) 206.

16. Ibid., 292.

17. Pierre-Daniel Huet, *Demonstratio Evangelica* (Paris, 1679) esp. 73–88, 95–9.

18. Adam Sutcliffe, *Judaism and Enlightenment* (Cambridge: Cambridge University Press, 2003) 60–73; Livitin, *Ancient Wisdom*, 154–80.

19. John Spencer, *De legibus Hebraeorum ritualibus et earum rationibus*, 2 vols (Cambridge, 1685) esp. I: 21ff., 519–635.

20. Guy Stroumsa, 'John Spencer and the Roots of Idolatry', *History of Religions* 41 (2001) 1–23, at 23.

21. Dmitri Levitin, 'John Spencer's *De legibus Hebraeorum* (1683–85) and "Enlightened" Sacred History: A New Interpretation', *Journal of the Warburg and Courtauld Institutes* 76 (2013) 49–92, at 60–73.

22. Spencer, *De legibus*, I: 156–7.

23. Jan Assmann, *Moses the Egyptian: The Memory of Egypt in Western Monotheism* (Cambridge, MA: Harvard University Press, 1997) 55–90.

24. John Toland, *Origines Judaicae* (The Hague, 1709) esp. 104–9.

25. Ibid., 157–8; Toland, *Christianity not Mysterious* (London, 1696).

26. Toland, *Origines*, 117; Justin Champion, 'Toleration and Citizenship in Enlightenment England: John Toland and the Naturalization of the Jews, 1714–53', in Ole Peter Grell and Roy Porter, eds, *Toleration in Enlightenment Europe* (Cambridge: Cambridge University Press, 2000) 133–56, at 149–51.

27. John Toland, *Nazarenus, or Jewish, Gentile, and Mahometan Christianity*, ed. Justin Champion (Oxford: Voltaire Foundation, 1999 [1718]).

28. John Toland, 'Two Problems Concerning the Jewish Nation and Religion' (1709), in ibid., 235–40, at 240.

29. Justin Champion, 'Introduction' to Toland, *Nazarenus*, 1–106; Sutcliffe, *Judaism and Enlightenment*, 197–205.

30. William J. Bulman, *Anglican Enlightenment: Orientalism, Religion and Politics in England and its Empire, 1648–1715* (Cambridge: Cambridge University Press, 2015) 1–13, 97–103.

31. Alan Charles Kors, *Naturalism and Unbelief in France, 1650–1729* (Cambridge: Cambridge University Press, 2016).

32. Pierre Bayle, *Dictionnaire historique et critique*, 1st edn (Rotterdam, 1697), article 'Pyrrhon', remark C [partial trans. in Richard Popkin, ed. and. trans., *Historical and Critical Dictionary: Selections* (Indianapolis: Hackett, 1991) 205–6].

33. Elizabeth Labrousse, *Bayle* (Oxford: Oxford University Press, 1993), 42.

34. Bayle, *Dictionnaire*, article 'David', remark H. [The lettering of remarks for this article follows the 1697 first edition: the lettering was altered in the expurgated version published in subsequent editions.]

35. Ibid., remark D.

36. Ibid., remark I.

37. Pierre Bayle, *Commentaire philosophique* (Amsterdam, 1686); John Christian Laursen, 'Baylean Liberalism: Tolerance Requires Nontolerance', in John Christian Laursen and Cary J. Nederman, eds, *Beyond the Persecuting Society: Religious Toleration Before the Enlightenment* (Philadelphia: University of Pennsylvania Press, 1998) 197–215.

38. Adam Sutcliffe, 'Spinoza, Bayle, and the Enlightenment Politics of Philosophical Certainty', *History of European Ideas* 34 (2008) 66–76; Anton M. Matytsin, *The Specter of Skepticism in the Age of Enlightenment* (Baltimore: Johns Hopkins University Press, 2016) 52–65.

39. Bayle, *Dictionnaire*, article 'Abimelech', remark C.

40. For an extension of this argument, see Sutcliffe, *Judaism and Enlightenment*, 89–99; Sutcliffe, 'Bayle and Judaism', in Wiep van Bunge and Hans Bots, eds, *Pierre Bayle (1647–1706), 'Le Philosophe de Rotterdam': Philosophy, Religion and Reception* (Leiden: Brill, 2008) 121–34.

41. Labrousse, *Bayle*; Jonathan Israel, *Enlightenment Contested* (Oxford: Oxford University Press, 2006) 264–78; Michael Heyd, 'A Disguised Atheist or a Sincere Christian? The Enigma of Pierre Bayle', *Bibliothèque d'humanisme et renaissance: travaux et documents* 39 (1977) 157–65; Thomas M. Lennon, *Reading Bayle* (Toronto: University of Toronto Press, 1999) esp. 28–31.

42. Miriam Yardeni, 'La vision des juifs et du judaïsme dans l'oeuvre de Pierre Bayle', in Yardeni, ed., *Les juifs dans l'histoire de France* (Leiden: Brill, 1980) 86–95; R. H. Popkin, 'Introduction' to Bayle, *Historical and Critical Dictionary*, xxvi.

43. Bayle, *Dictionnaire*, article 'Abimelech', remark C.

44. Stephen Bird, *Reinventing Voltaire: The Politics of Commemoration in Nineteenth-Century France* (Oxford: Voltaire Foundation, 2000).

45. Voltaire, *Remarques sur les Pensées de Pascal* (1728), in Louis Moland, ed., *Oeuvres complètes de Voltaire*, 52 vols (Paris, 1877–85) XXII: 45; Harvey Mitchell, *Voltaire's Jews and Modern Jewish Identity: Rethinking the Enlightenment* (London: Routledge, 2008) 10–113.

46. Roland Barthes, *Critical Essays*, trans. R. Howard (Evanston, IL: Northwestern University Press, 1972 [1964]) 83–4.

47. Voltaire, *Sermon du rabbin Akib* (1761), in *Oeuvres complètes*, XXIV: 282.

48. David Levy, *Voltaire et son exégèse du Pentateuque* (Oxford: Voltaire Foundation, 1975) 223.

49. Karen O'Brien, *Narratives of Enlightenment: Cosmopolitan History from Voltaire to Gibbon* (Cambridge: Cambridge University Press, 1997) 21–55.

50. Voltaire, *Essai sur les moeurs* (1765), in *Oeuvres complètes*, XI: 73, 145.

51. Voltaire, *Dictionnaire philosophique* (1764), in *Oeuvres complètes*, XIX: 179.

52. For an extension of this argument, see Adam Sutcliffe, 'Myth, Origins, Identity: Voltaire, the Jews and the Enlightenment Notion of Toleration', *The Eighteenth Century: Theory and Interpretation* 39 (1998) 107–26.

53. Voltaire to Isaac de Pinto, 21 July 1762, in Theodore Besterman, ed., *Voltaire's Correspondence*, 107 vols (Geneva: Institut Voltaire, 1953–65) XLIX: 131–2.

54. Adam Sutcliffe, 'Can a Jew be a Philosophe? Isaac de Pinto, Voltaire, and Jewish Participation in the European Enlightenment', *Jewish Social Studies* 6 (2000) 31–51.

55. Arthur Hertzberg, *The French Enlightenment and the Jews: The Origins of Modern Anti-Semitism* (New York: Columbia University Press, 1968) 280–313.

56. John Robertson, *The Case for the Enlightenment: Scotland and Naples 1680–1760* (Cambridge: Cambridge University Press, 2005) esp. 28–44.

57. Voltaire, *Letters Concerning the English Nation*, ed. Nicholas Cronk (Oxford: Oxford University Press, 1994 [1733]) 30 [letter 6].

58. Ibid.

59. Ibid.

60. John Locke, *A Letter Concerning Toleration*, ed. John Horton and Susan Mendus (London: Routledge, 1991 [1689]) 51; Bayle, *Commentaire philosophique*, 377 [part 2, ch. 7].

61. John Locke ['Philanthropus'], *Second Letter on Toleration* (London, 1690) 2; John Marshall, *John Locke, Toleration and Early Enlightenment Culture* (Cambridge: Cambridge University Press, 2006) 593–617.

62. John Toland, *Reasons for Naturalizing the Jews in Great Britain and Ireland* (London, 1714); Champion, 'Toleration and Citizenship'; Jonathan Karp, *The Politics of Jewish Commerce: Economic Thought and Emancipation in Europe, 1638–1848* (Cambridge: Cambridge University Press, 2008) 43–66; Diego Lucci, 'Deism, Freethinking and Toleration in Enlightenment England', *History of European Ideas* 43 (2017) 345–58, esp. 347–51.

63. Toland, *Reasons for Naturalizing*, 50–1.

64. Ibid., esp. 11–16; Simone Luzzatto, *Discorso circa il stato de gl'Hebrei* (1638), esp. 8–32, 46–51.

65. Karp, *Politics of Jewish Commerce*, 65.

66. Todd M. Endelman, *The Jews of Britain 1656–2000* (Berkeley and Los Angeles: University of California Press, 2002) 73–6; Dana Rabin, 'The Jew Bill of 1753: Masculinity, Virility and the Nation', *Eighteenth-Century Studies* 39 (2006) 157–71.

67. Shmuel Feiner, *The Jewish Enlightenment*, trans. Chaya Naor (Philadelphia: University of Pennsylvania Press, 2004) 36–67; David Sorkin, 'The Early Haskalah', in Shmuel Feiner and David Sorkin, eds, *New Perspectives on the Haskalah* (London: Littman, 2001) 9–26.

68. King Frederick II of Prussia, *Rividiertes Generalprivilegium und Reglement* (1750), in Ismar Freund, *Die Emanzipation der Juden in Preußen*, 2 vols (Berlin: M. Poppelauer, 1912) II: 22–55; Tobias Schenk, 'Die Preussische Weg der Judenemanzipation', *Zeitschrift für Historische Forschung* 35 (2008) 449–82, esp. 460–3; Schenk, *Wegbereiter der Emanzipation? Studien zur Judenpolitik des 'Aufgeklärten Absolutismus' in Preußen, 1763–1812* (Berlin: Duncker & Humblot, 2010) 82–95.

69. Gad Freudenthal, 'Aaron Solomon Gumpertz, Gotthold Ephraim Lessing, and the First Call for an Improvement of the Civil Rights of Jews in Germany (1753)' *AJS Review* 29 (2005) 299–353, at 325.

70. Sorkin, 'Early Haskalah', 17–25.

71. Gotthold Ephraim Lessing, *Die Juden* (1749), in Wilfried Barner, ed., *Werke und Briefe*, 12 vols (Frankfurt: Deutscher Klassiker Verlag, 1985–2003) I: 485; Ritchie Robertson, *The 'Jewish Question' in German Literature 1749–1939* (Oxford: Oxford University Press, 1999) 34–6; Wilfried Barner, 'Lessings *Die Juden* in Zusammenhang seines Frühwerks', in E. Bahr, E. P. Harris and L. G. Lyon, eds, *Humanität und Dialog: Lessing und Mendelssohn in neuer Sicht* (Detroit: Wayne State University Press, 1979) 189–209.

72. Lessing to Michaelis, 16 October 1754, in *Werke und Briefe*, XI/1: 58.

73. Gotthold Ephraim Lessing, *Nathan der Weise* (1779), in *Werke und Briefe*, IX: 614–15.

74. Ibid., 625.

75. Robertson, *'Jewish Question'*, 42–5.

76. Ritchie Robertson, '"Dies hohe Lied der Duldung"? The Ambiguities of Toleration in Lessing's *Die Juden* and *Nathan der Weise*', *Modern Language Review* 93 (1998) 105–20; Adam Sutcliffe, 'Lessing and Toleration', in Ritchie Robertson, ed., *Lessing and the German Enlightenment* (Oxford: Voltaire Foundation, 2013) 205–25.

77. Jonathan M. Hess, 'Lessing and German-Jewish Culture: A Reappraisal', in Robertson, *Lessing and the German Enlightenment*, 179–204.

78. Gotthold Ephraim Lessing, *Die Erziehung des Menschengeschlechts* (1780), in *Werke und Briefe*, X: 78, trans. H. B. Nisbet in *Philosophical and Theological Writings* (Cambridge: Cambridge University Press, 2005) 217–40, at 221 [§§ 16, 18].

79. Ibid., 88, trans. Nisbet, 230 [§ 51].

80. David Hill, 'Enlightenment as a Historical Process: *Ernst und Falk* and *Die Erziehung des Menschengeschlechts*', in Robertson, *Lessing and the German Enlightenment*, 227–44, esp. 240–1.

81. Lessing, *Erziehung*, 92–3, 97, trans. Nisbet, 234, 238 [§§ 70–1, 86].

82. Robert Lerner, *The Feast of Saint Abraham: Medieval Millenarianism and the Jews* (Philadelphia: University of Pennsylvania Press, 2001) 23–37; Brett Whalen, 'Joachim of Fiore, Apocalyptic Conversion, and the "Persecuting Society"', *History Compass* 8 (2010) 682–91.

83. Adam Sutcliffe, 'Spinoza and Friends: Religion, Philosophy and Friendship in the Berlin Enlightenment', in Laura Gowing, Michael Hunter and Miri Rubin, eds, *Love, Friendship and Faith in Europe, 1300–1800* (Basingstoke: Palgrave, 2005) 197–220, at 202.

84. Ursula Goldenbaum, 'Mendelssohns schwierige Beziehung zu Spinoza', in Eva Schürmann, Norbert Waszek and Frank Weinreich, eds, *Spinoza im Deutschland des achtzehnten Jahrhunderts* (Stuttgart: Fromann-Holzboog, 2002) 265–317; John H. Zammito, '"The Most Hidden

Conditions of Men of the First Rank": The Pantheist Current in Eighteenth-Century Germany "Uncovered" by the Spinoza Controversy', *Eighteenth-Century Thought* 1 (2003) 335–68, esp. 351–4.

85. Moses Mendelssohn, *Philosophische Gespräche* (1755), in *Gesammelte Schriften—Jubiläumsausgabe*, 38 vols (Stuttgart: Frommann-Holzboog, 1971–2020) I: 13–19. See also Mendelssohn, *Morgenstunden* (1785), in *Jubiläumsausgabe*, III/2: 104–13; Jeffrey Librett, *The Rhetoric of Cultural Dialogue: Jews and Germans from Moses Mendelssohn to Richard Wagner and Beyond* (Stanford, CA: Stanford University Press, 2000) 89–96.

86. Mendelssohn, *Philosophische Gespräche*, 14.

87. Alexander Altmann, *Moses Mendelssohn: A Biographical Study* (Tuscaloosa, AL: University of Alabama Press, 1973), 36–7.

88. Georg Wachter, *Spinozismus in Judenthumb* (1699), ed. Winfried Schröder (Stuttgart: Frommann-Holzboog, 1994); Wachter, *Elucidarius cabalisticus* (1706), ed. Schröder (Stuttgart: Frommann-Holzboog, 1995); Sutcliffe, *Judaism and Enlightenment*, 155–62.

89. Moses Mendelssohn, *Phädon, oder über die Unsterblichkeit der Seele* (1767), in *Jubiläumsausgabe*, III/1: 5–128, trans. Patricia Noble (New York: Peter Lang, 2007).

90. Altmann, *Mendelssohn*, 194–263.

91. [August Cranz], 'Das Forschen nach Licht und Recht in einem Schreiben an Herrn Moses Mendelssohn' (1782), in *Jubiläumsausgabe*, VIII: 75–87, trans. Curtis Bowman in Michah Gottlieb, ed., *Moses Mendelssohn: Writings on Judaism, Christianity, and the Bible* (Waltham, MA: Brandeis University Press, 2011) 55–67.

92. Moses Mendelssohn, *Jerusalem, oder über religiöse Macht und Judenthum* (1783), in *Jubiläumsausgabe*, VIII: 99–204, trans. Allan Arkush (Hanover, NH: University Press of New England, 1983) 87.

93. Ibid., 138.

94. Ibid., 89–102, esp. 90.

95. Michah Gottlieb, 'Introduction' to Gottlieb, ed., *Mendelssohn: Writings*, xviii–xxi; Gottlieb, *Faith and Freedom: Moses Mendelssohn's Theological-Political Thought* (Oxford: Oxford University Press, 2011); Gideon Freudenthal, *No Religion without Idolatry: Mendelssohn's Jewish Enlightenment* (Notre Dame, IN: University of Notre Dame Press, 2012).

96. Mendelssohn, *Jerusalem*, 118.

97. Ibid., 117–20; Freudenthal, *No Religion*, 135–59.

98. Mendelssohn, *Jerusalem*, 138–9; Freudenthal, *No Religion*, 235–45.

99. Friedrich Heinrich Jacobi, *Concerning the Doctrine of Spinoza* (1785), trans. George di Giovanni in *The Main Philosophical Writings and the Novel 'Allwill'*, (Montreal: McGill-Queen's University Press, 1994) 187.

100. Jeffrey S. Librett, 'Humanist Antiformalism as a Theopolitics of Race: F. H. Jacobi on Friend and Enemy', *Eighteenth-Century Studies* 32 (1999) 233–45; Gérard Vallée, *The Spinoza Conversations Between Lessing and Jacobi: Texts with Excerpts from the Ensuing Controversy* (Lanham, MD: University Press of America, 1988); Adam Sutcliffe, 'Quarreling over Spinoza: Moses Mendelssohn and the Fashioning of Jewish Philosophical Heroism', in Ross Brann and Adam Sutcliffe, eds, *Renewing the Past, Reconfiguring Jewish Culture: from al-Andalus to the Haskalah* (Philadelphia: University of Pennsylvania Press, 2004) 167–88.

101. Jacobi, *Doctrine of Spinoza*, 187–8.

102. Frederick C. Beiser, *The Fate of Reason: German Philosophy from Kant to Fichte* (Cambridge, MA: Harvard University Press, 1987) 44–5.

103. Carsten Schapkow, *Die Freiheit zu philosophieren: Jüdische Identität in der Moderne im Spiegel der Rezeption Baruch de Spinozas in der deutschsprachigen Literatur* (Bielefeld: Aisthesis, 2001) 65–84; Martin Bollacher, *Der junge Goethe und Spinoza* (Tübingen: Niemeyer, 1969).

104. Emperor Joseph II, *Toleranzedikt*, 2 January 1982, in Alfred Pribram, ed., *Urkunden und Akten zur Geschichte der Juden in Wien*, 2 vols (Vienna and Leipzig: W. Braumüller, 1918) II: 494–500, trans. in Paul Mendes-Flohr and Jehuda Reinharz, eds, *The Jew in the Modern World: A Documentary History*, 2nd edn (New York: Oxford University Press, 1995) 36–40.

105. Christian Wilhelm von Dohm, *Über die bürgerliche Verbesserung der Juden* (Hildesheim: Georg Olms, 1973 [1781–83]); Altmann, *Mendelssohn*, 450–4; Shmuel Feiner, *Moses Mendelssohn: Sage of Modernity* (New Haven, CT: Yale University Press, 2010) 135–7.

106. Feiner, *Jewish Enlightenment*, 135–62; Altmann, *Mendelssohn*, 455–7; Dohm, *Verbesserung*, part 1: 124.

107. Mendelssohn, *Jerusalem*, 74–5; Freudenthal, *No Religion*, 219–23.

108. Dohm, *Verbesserung*, part 1: 18–24, 105–9, 143; see also Jonathan Karp, *Politics of Jewish Commerce*, 94–134; Robert Liberles, 'Dohm's Treatise on the Jews: A Defence of the Enlightenment', *Leo Baeck Institute Year Book* 33 (1988) 29–42; Jonathan M. Hess, *Germans, Jews and the Claims of Modernity* (New Haven, CT: Yale University Press, 2002) 25–49.

109. Dohm, *Verbesserung*, part 1: 144.

110. Emmanuel Eze, *Race and the Enlightenment* (Oxford: Blackwell, 1997) 79–90; Daniel Pick, *Faces of Degeneration: A European Disorder, c. 1848–c. 1918* (Cambridge: Cambridge University Press, 1989) esp. 11–33.

111. Alyssa Sepinwall, *The Abbé Grégoire and the French Revolution: The Making of Modern Universalism* (Berkeley and Los Angeles: University of California Press, 2005) 57–8; Mona Ozouf, 'Regeneration', in François Furet and Mona Ozouf, eds, *A Critical Dictionary of the French Revolution* (Cambridge, MA: Harvard University Press, 1989) 771–90.

112. Hess, *Claims of Modernity*, 69–79.

113. Johann David Michaelis, *Herr Ritter Michaelis Beurtheilung* (1782), in Dohm, *Verbesserung*, part 2: 31–71, at 41–51.

114. Reinhart Koselleck, *Futures Past: On the Semantics of Historical Time* (New York: Columbia University Press, 2004 [1979]) 222–54.

115. Avi Lifschitz, *Language and Enlightenment: The Berlin Debates of the Eighteenth Century* (Oxford: Oxford University Press, 2012) 114–17.

116. Johann Gottfried Herder, *On the Spirit of Hebrew Poetry*, 2 vols (Burlington, VT, 1833 [1782]) I: 21, 46.

117. Lifschitz, *Language and Enlightenment*, 181–7.

118. David Feuerwerker, *L'Émancipation des Juifs en France* (Paris: Albin Michel, 1976) 49–142; all three winning entries are reprinted in *La Révolution française et l'émancipation des Juifs*, 8 vols (Paris: EDHIS, 1968) II–IV.

119. Grégoire, *Essai*, 95–9; Ronald Schechter, *Obstinate Hebrews: Representations of the Jews in France, 1715–1815* (Berkeley and Los Angeles: University of California Press, 2003) 87–95; Sepinwall, *Abbé Grégoire*, 56–80.

120. Alyssa Goldstein Sepinwall, 'A Friend of the Jews? The Abbé Grégoire and Philosemitism in Revolutionary France', in Jonathan Karp and Adam Sutcliffe, eds, *Philosemitism in History* (Cambridge: Cambridge University Press, 2011) 111–27; Paulo L. Bernardini and Diego Lucci, *The Jews, Instructions for Use: Four Eighteenth-Century Projects for the Emancipation of European Jews* (Boston: Academic Studies Press, 2012) 165–96.

121. Schechter, *Obstinate Hebrews*, 154.

122. Achille-Edmond Halphen, ed, *Receuil des lois: décrets, ordonnances, avis du conseil d'état, arrêtés et règlements concernant les Israélites depuis la revolution de 1789* (Paris, 1851) 9–10.

123. Schechter, *Obstinate Hebrews*, 150–93; Gary Kates, 'Jews into Frenchmen: Nationality and Representation in Revolutionary France', in Ferenc Fehér, ed., *The French Revolution and the Birth of Modernity* (Berkeley and Los Angeles: University of California Press, 1990) 103–16.

124. Jay R. Berkovitz, 'The French Revolution and the Jews: Assessing the Cultural Impact', *AJS Review* 20 (1995) 25–86, at 50–3.

125. Diogène Tama, *Collection des Actes de l'Assemblée des Israélites de France et du royaume d'Italie* (Paris, 1807); *Transactions of the Parisian Sanhedrin . . . Translated from the original published by M. D. Tama, with a preface and notes by F. D. Kirwan* (London, 1807); Simon Schwarzfuchs, *Napoleon, the Jews and the Sanhedrin* (London: Littman, 1979).

126. Pierre Birnbaum, *L'Aigle et la Synagogue: Napoléon, les Juifs et l'État* (Paris: Fayard, 2007); Schechter, *Obstinate Hebrews*, 226–35.

127. Jay R. Berkovitz, *Rites and Passages: The Beginnings of Modern Jewish Culture in France* (Philadelphia: University of Pennsylvania Press, 2004) 136–43; Phyllis Cohen Albert, *The Modernization of French Jewry: Consistory and Community in the Nineteenth Century* (Hanover, NH: Brandeis University Press, 1977) 50–61.

128. Marcin Wodzinski, 'Good Maskilim and Bad Assimilationists, or Toward a New Historiography of the Haskalah in Poland', *Jewish Social Studies* 10 (2004) 87–122.

129. David Friedländer, 'Sendschreiben an . . . Probst Teller' (1799), in Richard Crouter and Julie Klassen, ed. and trans., *A Debate on Jewish Emancipation and Christian Theology in Old Berlin* (Indianapolis: Hackett, 2004) 41–78.

130. Friedrich Schleiermacher, 'Briefe bei Gelegenheit . . . des Sendscheibens Jüdische Hausväter' (1799), in Crouter and Klassen, *Debate on Jewish Emancipation*, 80–122; Avi Lifschitz, 'From the Civic Improvement of the Jews to the Separation of State and Church: Languages of Reform in Brandenburg-Prussia, 1781–1799', in M. Albertone, T. Maissen and S. Richter, eds, *Languages of Reform in Eighteenth-Century Europe* (London: Routledge, 2019) 296–320.

131. Deborah Hertz, *Jewish High Society in Old Regime Berlin* (New Haven, CT: Yale University Press, 1988); Hertz, *How Jews Became Germans: The History of Conversion and Assimilation in Berlin* (New Haven, CT: Yale University Press, 2007) 51–123; Steven M. Lowenstein, *The Berlin Jewish Community: Enlightenment, Family and Crisis* (Oxford: Oxford University Press, 1994) 104–33.

132. Brian E. Vick, *The Congress of Vienna: Power and Politics after Napoleon* (Cambridge, MA: Harvard University Press, 2014) 166–92; Reinhard Rürup, 'The Tortuous and Thorny Path to Legal Equality: "Jew Laws" and Emancipatory Legislation in Germany from the Late Eighteenth Century', *Leo Baeck Institute Year Book* 31 (1986) 3–33.

133. Jacob Katz, 'The Term "Jewish Emancipation": Its Origin and Historical Impact', in Alexander Altmann, ed., *Studies in Nineteenth-Century Jewish Intellectual History* (Cambridge, MA: Harvard University Press, 1964) 1–25.

134. Linda Colley, *Britons: Forging the Nation 1707–1837* (New Haven, CT: Yale University Press, 1992) 350–60; Seymour Drescher, *Abolition: A History of Slavery and Antislavery* (Cambridge: Cambridge University Press, 2009) 245–66; Abigail Green, 'The British Empire and the Jews: An Imperialism of Human Rights?', *Past & Present* 199 (2008) 175–205; David Sorkin, *Jewish Emancipation: A History Across Five Centuries* (Princeton, NJ: Princeton University Press, 2019) 210–12

135. Jonathan Frankel, *The Damascus Affair: "Ritual Murder", Politics, and the Jews in 1840* (Cambridge: Cambridge University Press, 1997); Andrea Schatz, *L'Affaire de Damas (1840): Perspectives franco-allemandes* (Paris: L'Éclat, 2017) 32–4; Lisa Moses Leff, *Sacred Bonds of Solidarity: The Rise of Jewish Internationalism in Nineteenth-Century France* (Stanford, CA: Stanford University Press, 2006) 120–6.

136. Schleiermacher, 'Briefe bei Gelegenheit', in Crouter and Klassen, *Debate on Jewish Emancipation*, 97.

137. Paul W. Franks, 'Jewish Philosophy after Kant: The Legacy of Salomon Maimon', in Michael L. Morgan and Peter Eli Gordon, eds, *The Cambridge Companion to Modern Jewish Philosophy* (Cambridge: Cambridge University Press, 2007) 53–79; Abraham P. Socher, *The Radical Enlightenment of Solomon Maimon* (Stanford, CA: Stanford University Press, 2006) 85–108; Christoph Schulte, *Die jüdische Aufklärung* (Munich: Beck, 2002) 157–71.

138. Lazarus Bendavid, *Etwas zur Charackteristick der Juden* (Leipzig, 1793); Adam Sutcliffe, 'The Philosophy of Sociability in the Life and Work of Lazarus Bendavid', in Avi Lifschitz and Conrad Wiedemann, eds, *Jüdische und christliche Intellectuelle in Berlin c. 1800*, forthcoming.

139. Immanuel Kant, *The Conflict of the Faculties*, trans. Mary J. Gregor (Lincoln, NE: University of Nebraska Press, 1992 [1798]) 95; Klaus Berghahn, *Grenzen der Toleranz: Juden und Christen im Zeitalter der Aufklärung* (Köln: Böhlau, 2001), 216–22.

140. Kant, *Conflict of the Faculties*, 95.

141. Immanuel Kant, *Religion within the Boundaries of Mere Reason*, ed. and trans. Allen Wood and George di Giovanni (Cambridge: Cambridge University Press 1998 [1793]) 139.

142. Michael Mack, *German Idealism and the Jew* (Chicago: University of Chicago Press, 2003) 23–41; Paul Lawrence Rose, *German Question/Jewish Question: Revolutionary Antisemitism in Germany from Kant to Wagner* (Princeton, NJ: Princeton University Press, 1990) 91–116.

143. Johann Gottlieb Fichte, *Beitrag zur Berichtung der Urteile des Publicums ueber die Franzoesische Revolution* (1793), trans. in Mendes-Flohr and Reinharz, *Jew in the Modern World*, 309; Anthony J. La Vopa, *Fichte: The Self and the Calling of Philosophy, 1762–1799* (Cambridge: Cambridge University Press, 2001) 131–49.

144. Saul Ascher, *Eisenmenger der Zweite* (1794), in *Saul Ascher: Vier Flugschriften* (Berlin: Aufbau, 1991) 37, 57–9; Ascher, *Leviathan, oder Über Religion in Rücksicht des Judenthums* (1792), in Renate Best, ed., *Saul Ascher: Ausgewählte Werken* (Köln: Böhlau, 2010) esp. 178–81.

145. Paweł Maciejko, *The Mixed Multitude: Jacob Frank and the Frankist Movement, 1755–1816* (Philadelphia: University of Pennsylvania Press, 2011); Ada Rapoport-Albert, *Women and the Messianic Heresy of Sabbatai Zevi, 1666–1816* (London: Littman, 2011) 157–235.

146. Paweł Maciejko, 'Sabbatian Charlatans: The First Jewish Cosmopolitans', *European Review of History* 17 (2010) 361–79; Marsha Keith Schuchard, 'Dr Samuel Jacob Falk: A Sabbatian

Adventurer in the Masonic Underground', in Matt D. Goldish and Richard H. Popkin, eds, *Jewish Messianism in the Early Modern World* (Dordrecht: Kluwer, 2001) 203–26.

147. For such an attempt, see Shmuel Feiner, *The Origins of Jewish Secularization in Eighteenth-Century Europe* (Philadelphia: University of Pennsylvania Press, 2010); for a broad corrective, see Charles Taylor, *A Secular Age* (Cambridge, MA: Harvard University Press, 2007) 221–97.

Chapter Three. Teachers and Traders: Jews and Social Purpose

1. Rabbi David Einhorn, 'Was bedeutet der Berg Sinai den Reformbestrebungen der Gegenwart?', inaugural sermon at Temple Har Sinai, Baltimore, September 29, 1855, in Kaufman Kohler, ed., *David Einhorn Memorial Volume* (New York: Bloch, 1911) 31–44, trans. in W. Gunther Plaut, *The Rise of Reform Judaism* (Philadelphia: Jewish Publication Society, 2015 [1963]) 244.

2. Reinhart Koselleck, *Futures Past: On the Semantics of Historical Time* (New York: Columbia University Press, 2004 [1979]) 222–54; Peter Fritzsche, *Stranded in the Present: Modern Time and the Melancholy of History* (Cambridge, MA: Harvard University Press, 2004) 11–54.

3. David Sorkin, 'The Genesis of the Ideology of Emancipation', *Leo Baeck Institute Year Book* 32 (1987) 11–40, esp. 21–4.

4. Stefi Jersch-Wenzel, 'Population Shifts and Occupational Structure, 1780–1847', in Michael A. Meyer, ed., *German-Jewish History in Modern Times, vol. 2: Emancipation and Acculturation, 1780–1871* (New York: Columbia University Press, 1997) 50–89; David Sorkin, *The Transformation of German Jewry 1780–1840* (Detroit: Wayne State University Press, 1999 [1987]) 107–55; Paula E. Hyman, *The Jews of Modern France* (Berkeley and Los Angeles: University of California Press, 1998) 53–76.

5. Ian McCalman, 'New Jerusalems: Prophecy, Dissent and Radical Culture in England, 1786–1830', in Knud Haakonssen, ed., *Enlightenment and Religion: Rational Dissent in Eighteenth-Century Britain* (Cambridge: Cambridge University Press, 1996) 312–35; Eitan Bar-Yosef, *The Holy Land in English Culture 1799–1917* (Oxford: Oxford University Press, 2005) 48–57.

6. Miriam Leonard, *Socrates and the Jews: Hellenism and Hebraism from Moses Mendelssohn to Sigmund Freud* (Chicago: University of Chicago Press, 2012) 17–64.

7. David Nirenberg, *Anti-Judaism: The History of a Way of Thinking* (New York: W. W. Norton, 2013) 430–45.

8. Friedrich Lenger, *Werner Sombart, 1863–1941: Eine Biographie* (Munich: Beck, 1994) 384.

9. Reiner Grundmann and Nico Stehr, 'Why is Werner Sombart not Part of the Core of Classical Sociology?', *Journal of Classical Sociology* 1 (2001) 257–87; Rebecca Kobrin and Adam Teller, eds, *Purchasing Power: The Economics of Modern Jewish History* (Philadelphia: University of Pennsylvania Press, 2015) esp. 1–24; Gideon Reuveni and Sarah Wobick-Segev, eds, *The Economy in Jewish History* (New York: Berghahn, 2011) esp. 1–22.

10. Zygmunt Bauman, 'Allosemitism: Premodern, Modern, Postmodern', in Bryan Cheyette and Laura Marcus, eds, *Modernity, Culture and 'the Jew'* (Cambridge: Polity, 1998) 143–56; Bauman, *Modernity and the Holocaust* (Cambridge: Polity, 1989) 31–82.

11. Georg Wilhelm Friedrich Hegel, *The Spirit of Christianity and Its Fate* (1799), in T. M. Knox, ed. and trans., *Hegel: Early Theological Writings* (Chicago: University of Chicago Press, 1948) 182–205; Frederick C. Beiser, 'Hegel's Historicism', in Beiser, ed., *The Cambridge Companion to Hegel* (Cambridge: Cambridge University Press, 1993) 270–300, esp. 273–4.

12. Hegel, *Spirit of Christianity*, 195–6.

13. Yirmiyahu Yovel, *Dark Riddle: Hegel, Nietzsche, and the Jews* (Cambridge: Polity, 1998) 32–47; John Edward Toews, *Hegelianism: The Path toward Dialectical Humanism, 1805–1841* (Cambridge: Cambridge University Press, 1980) 30–48.

14. G.W.F. Hegel, *Lectures on the History of Philosophy*, 3 vols (1840–44), trans. E. S. Haldane and F. H. Simson (Lincoln, NE: University of Nebraska Press, 1995 [1892–96]) esp. I: 146; III: 26–36, 252.

15. G.W.F. Hegel, *Lectures on the Philosophy of History* (1837), trans. J. Sibree (Kitchener, ON: Batoche Books, 2001 [1857]) 213–17, esp. 214; Yovel, *Dark Riddle*, 60–101; Steven B. Smith, 'Hegel and the Jewish Question: In Between Tradition and Modernity', *History of Political Thought* 12 (1991) 87–106; Francesco Tomasoni, *Modernity and the Final Aim of History: The Debate over Judaism from Kant to the Young Hegelians* (Dordrecht: Kluwer, 2003) 107–58.

16. Hegel, *Philosophy of History*, 339–40.

17. Ibid., 341–2.

18. Ibid., 342–53, 358ff.; Hegel, *Elements of the Philosophy of Right*, ed. Allen W. Wood, trans. H. B. Nisbet (Cambridge: Cambridge University Press, 1991 [1821]) 379 [§ 358].

19. Saul Ascher, *Die Germanomanie* (1815), in *Saul Ascher: Vier Flugschriften* (Berlin: Aufbau, 1991); Jonathan M. Hess, *Germans, Jews and the Claims of Modernity* (New Haven, CT: Yale University Press, 2002) 137–68.

20. Immanuel Wolf, 'The Concept of a Science of Judaism' (1822), trans. Lionel Kochan, *Leo Baeck Institute Year Book* 2 (1957) 194–204, at 201.

21. Sven-Erik Rose, *Jewish Philosophical Politics in Germany, 1789–1848* (Waltham, MA: Brandeis University Press, 2104) 44–89.

22. Wolf, 'Science of Judaism', 199–200, 203–4.

23. Ibid., 195.

24. Ibid., 198–9.

25. Ibid., 199–200; Rose, *Jewish Philosophical Politics*, 94–9; Ismar Schorsch, *From Text to Context: The Turn to History in Modern Judaism* (Hanover, NH: University Press of New England, 1994) 223.

26. Norbert Waszek, *Eduard Gans (1797–1839): Hegelianer—Jude—Europäer* (Frankfurt: Peter Lang, 1991); Norbert Waszek, 'Eduard Gans on Poverty and on the Constitutional Debate', in Douglas Moggach, ed., *The New Hegelians: Politics and Philosophy in the Hegelian School* (Cambridge: Cambridge University Press, 2006) 24–49; Toews, *Hegelianism*, 126–34; Schorsch, *Text to Context*, 207–10, 215–18.

27. Eduard Gans, *Zweite Rede vor dem 'Kulturverein'* (1822), in Waszek, *Eduard Gans*, 62–75, esp. 65, trans. J. Henning (extracts) in Paul Mendes-Flohr and Jehuda Reinharz, eds, *The Jew in the Modern World: A Documentary History*, 2nd edn (New York: Oxford University Press, 1995) 215–18; Jonathan Karp, *The Politics of Jewish Commerce: Economic Thought and Emancipation in Europe, 1638–1848* (Cambridge: Cambridge University Press, 2008) 224–31.

28. Gans, *Zweite Rede*, 67, trans. Henning, 217.

29. Rose, *Jewish Philosophical Politics*, 119–21, 310.

30. Shmuel Feiner, *Haskalah and History* (Oxford: Littman, 2002) 115–25.

31. Nachman Krochmal, *Moreh Nebukhe ha-Zeman* [*Guide for the Perplexed of Our Time*] (1851), trans. Michael A. Meyer (extracts) in Meyer, ed., *Ideas of Jewish History* (Detroit: Wayne State

University Press, 1987) 189–216, esp. 201, 208; Gershon Greenberg, *Modern Jewish Thinkers: From Mendelssohn to Rosenzweig* (Brighton, MA: Academic Studies Press, 2011) 81–120; Jacob Taubes, 'Nachman Krochmal and Modern Historicism', *Modern Judaism* 12 (1963) 150–64; Jay M. Harris, *Nachman Krochmal: Guiding the Perplexed of the Modern Age* (New York: New York University Press, 1991) esp. 103–55.

32. Ismar Schorsch, 'The Production of a Classic: Zunz as Krochmal's Editor', *Leo Baeck Institute Year Book* 31 (1986) 281–315.

33. Michael A. Meyer, *Response to Modernity: A History of the Reform Movement in Judaism* (New York: Oxford University Press, 1988) 43–61, 99–142.

34. Salomon Formstecher, *Religion des Geistes* (Frankfurt, 1841) 365–412, esp. 411; George Y. Kohler, ed., *Der jüdische Messianismus im Zeitalter der Emanzipation* (Berlin: de Gruyter, 2014) 31–7, 99–119; Greenberg, *Modern Jewish Thinkers*, 139–70; Meyer, *Response to Modernity*, 70–2.

35. Samuel Hirsch, *Die Religionsphilosophie der Juden* (Leipzig, 1842) 105–528, esp. 502–13; Emil L. Fackenheim, 'Samuel Hirsch and Hegel', in Alexander Altmann, ed., *Studies in Nineteenth-Century Jewish Intellectual History* (Cambridge, MA: Harvard University Press, 1964) 171–201.

36. Hirsch, *Religionsphilosophie*, 840–84, esp. 861–8.

37. Samuel Hirsch, *Die Messiaslehre der Juden* (Leipzig, 1843), extracts in Kohler, *Jüdische Messianismus*, 121–45; Christian Wiese, 'Von Dessau nach Philadelphia: Samuel Hirsch als Philosoph, Apologet und radikaler Reformer', in Giuseppe Veltri and Christian Wiese, eds, *Jüdische Bildung und Kultur in Sachsen-Anhalt von der Aufklärung bis zum Nationalsozialismus* (Berlin: Metropol, 2009) 363–410, esp. 364–6.

38. Hirsch, *Religionsphilosophie*, 868–79; Hirsch, *Messiaslehre*, in Kohler, *Jüdische Messianismus*, 121–9.

39. Hirsch, *Religionsphilosophie*, 882; Formstecher, *Religion*, 449–52.

40. Robin E. Judd, 'Samuel Holdheim and the German Circumcision Debates, 1843–1876', in Christian Wiese, ed., *Redefining Judaism in an Age of Emancipation: Comparative Perspectives on Samuel Holdheim (1806–60)* (Leiden: Brill, 2007) 127–42; Judd, *Contested Rituals: Circumcision, Kosher Butchering, and Jewish Political Life in Germany, 1843–1933* (Ithaca, NY: Cornell University Press, 2007) 21–57.

41. Samuel Holdheim, *Predigten über die jüdische Religion* (Berlin, 1853), trans. in W. Gunther Plaut, ed., *The Rise of Reform Judaism: A Sourcebook of its European Origins* (Philadelphia: Jewish Publication Society, 2015 [1963]) 138–40; Michael A. Meyer, '"Most of My Brethren Find Me Unacceptable": The Controversial Career of Samuel Holdheim', *Jewish Social Studies* 9 (2003) 1–19, esp. 10.

42. Meyer, *Response to Modernity*, 89–99.

43. David Friedrich Strauss, *Das Leben Jesu, kritisch bearbeitet* (Tübingen, 1835–36).

44. David Friedrich Strauss, *Das Leben Jesu für das deutsche Volk bearbeitet* (Leipzig, 1864); Ernest Renan, *Vie de Jésus* (Paris, 1863).

45. Abraham Geiger, *Das Judenthum und seine Geschichte*, 3 vols (Breslau, 1865) I: 163–87; Susannah Heschel, *Abraham Geiger and the Jewish Jesus* (Chicago: University of Chicago Press, 1998) 1–22, 108–11, 146–61.

46. Geiger, *Judenthum*, I: 12–26.

47. Ibid., 27–36, esp. 36.

48. Ibid., 41.

49. Ibid., passim; Geiger, *Judaism and Islam* (Madras, 1898 [1833]).

50. Geiger, *Judenthum*, I: 159–60.

51. Ibid., 161.

52. Samson Raphael Hirsch, *Nineteen Letters on Judaism*, trans. Bernard Drachman (New York: Philipp Feldheim, 1960 [1836]) esp. 55, 64–5.

53. Samson Raphael Hirsch, 'Religion Allied to Progress' (1854), trans. I. Grunfeld in *Judaism Eternal: Selected Essays from the Writings of Rabbi Samson Raphael Hirsch*, 2 vols (London: Soncino Press, 1956) II: 224–44, esp. 237–8; Meyer, *Response to Modernity*, 77–9.

54. Elijah Benamozegh, *Jewish and Christian Ethics* (San Francisco, 1873 [1867]) 101–3; Benamozegh, *Israel and Humanity*, ed. and trans. Maxwell Luria (New York: Paulist Press, 1995 [1885]) esp. 330–1.

55. Alessandro Guetta, *Philosophy and Kabbalah: Elijah Benamozegh and the Reconciliation of Western Thought and Jewish Esotericism* (Albany, NY: SUNY Press, 2009).

56. Nicholas Guyatt, *Providence and the Invention of the United States, 1607–1876* (Cambridge: Cambridge University Press, 2007); Todd Gitlin and Liel Liebovitz, *The Chosen Peoples: America, Israel, and the Ordeals of Divine Election* (New York: Simon and Schuster, 2010) 65–120; Meyer, *Response to Modernity*, 227.

57. Christian Wiese, 'Samuel Holdheim's "Most Powerful Comrade in Conviction": David Einhorn and the Debate Concerning Jewish Universalism in the Radical Reform Movement', in Wiese, *Redefining Judaism*, 306–73, esp. 344–51; Meyer, *Response to Modernity*, 244–50.

58. Naomi W. Cohen, *What the Rabbis Said: The Public Discourse of Nineteenth-Century American Rabbis* (New York: New York University Press, 2008) 62–9.

59. Wiese, 'Holdheim's "Comrade"', 364–6.

60. Cohen, *What the Rabbis Said*, 115; Meyer, *Response to Modernity*, 255–8; Wiese, 'Von Dessau nach Philadelphia', 401–2.

61. Gershon Greenberg, '*Religionswissenschaft* and Early Reform Jewish Thought: Samuel Hirsch and David Einhorn', in Andreas Gotzmann and Christian Wiese, eds, *Modern Judaism and Historical Consciousness: Identities, Encounters, Perspectives* (Leiden: Brill, 2007) 110–44.

62. Cohen, *What the Rabbis Said*, 177–97.

63. Ludwig Feuerbach, *The Essence of Christianity*, trans. Marian Evans [George Eliot] (London, 1854 [1841]) 87; Warren Breckman, *Marx, The Young Hegelians, and the Origins of Radical Social Theory* (Cambridge: Cambridge University Press, 1999) 71–80, 90–130; Toews, *Hegelianism*, 141–99, 327–55.

64. Massimiliano Tomba, 'Exclusiveness and Political Universalism in Bruno Bauer', in Douglas Moggach, ed., *The New Hegelians: Politics and Philosophy in the Hegelian School* (Cambridge: Cambridge University Press, 2006) 91–113; Douglas Moggach, *The Philosophy and Politics of Bruno Bauer* (Cambridge: Cambridge University Press, 2003) 59–79, 139–44.

65. Bruno Bauer, *Die Judenfrage* (Braunschweig, 1843) esp. 12–14, 48.

66. Ibid., 19.

67. Ibid., 16, 21, 48.

68. Ibid., 44, 115; Douglas Moggach, 'Republican Rigorism and Emancipation in Bruno Bauer', in Moggach, ed., *New Hegelians*, 114–35.

69. Bauer, *Judenfrage*, e.g., 5.

70. Samuel Hirsch, *Das Judenthum, der christliche Staat und die modern Kritik: Briefe zur Beleuchtung der Judenfrage von Bruno Bauer* (Leizpig, 1843); Nathan Rotenstreich, 'For and Against Emancipation: The Bruno Bauer Controversy', *Leo Baeck Institute Year Book* 4 (1959) 3–36, esp. 11–12.

71. David Nirenberg, *Anti-Judaism*, 433–4; David Leopold, 'The Hegelian Antisemitism of Bruno Bauer', *History of European Ideas* 4 (1999) 179–206, esp. 202–3.

72. Albert S. Lindemann, 'The Jewish Question', in Albert S. Lindemann and Richard S. Levy, eds, *Antisemitism: A History* (Oxford: Oxford University Press, 2010) 17–33, at 17; Jonathan Judaken, 'Antisemitism and the Jewish Question', in Mitchell B. Hart and Tony Michels, eds, *The Cambridge History of Judaism, vol. 8: The Modern World, 1815—2000* (Cambridge: Cambridge University Press, 2017) 559–88, at 560–1; Holly Case, *The Age of Questions* (Princeton, NJ: Princeton University Press, 2018) 115–19.

73. Bauer, *Judenfrage*, 24, 61–2.

74. Ibid., 10–12.

75. Michael Ragussis, *Figures of Conversion: "The Jewish Question" and English National Identity* (Durham, NC: Duke University Press, 1995) 57–88; Nadia Valman, *The Jewess in Nineteenth-Century British Literary Culture* (Cambridge: Cambridge University Press, 2007) 21–2; Julie Kalman, *Rethinking Antisemitism in Nineteenth-Century France* (Cambridge: Cambridge University Press, 2010) 1–4.

76. Heinrich Heine, *Zur Geschichte der Religion und Philosophie in Deutschland* (1835), in Manfred Windfuhr, ed., *Historisch-kritische Gesamtausgabe*, 16 vols (Hamburg: Hoffmann & Campe, 1973–97) VIII/1: 54.

77. Walter Scott, *Ivanhoe: A Romance* (Boston, MA: D. C. Heath, 1905 [1819]) 236 [ch. 24], 388 [ch. 36].

78. Ibid., 496–500 [ch. 44]; Valman, *The Jewess*, 20–34.

79. Georg Lukács, *The Historical Novel*, trans. Hannah and Stanley Mitchell (Lincoln, NE: University of Nebraska Press, 1983 [1937]) 30–63; Fritzsche, *Stranded in the Present*, 51–2, 174–7.

80. Valman, *The Jewess*, 34–43; Jonathan M. Hess, *Deborah and her Sisters* (Philadelphia: University of Pennsylvania Press, 2018).

81. Richard I. Cohen, *Jewish Icons: Art and Society in Modern Europe* (Berkeley and Los Angeles: University of California Press, 1998) 154–85.

82. Jonathan Skolnik, *Jewish Pasts, German Fictions: History, Memory, and Minority Culture in Germany, 1824–1955* (Stanford, CA: Stanford University Press, 2014) 23–44; Maurice Samuels, *Inventing the Israelite: Jewish Fiction in Nineteenth-Century France* (Stanford, CA: Stanford University Press, 2010) 154–92.

83. Samuels, *Inventing the Israelite*, 37–73; Lisa Moses Leff, *Sacred Bonds of Solidarity: The Rise of Jewish Internationalism in Nineteenth-Century France* (Stanford, CA: Stanford University Press, 2006) 102–15.

84. Valman, *The Jewess*, 51–84, 92–115; Ragussis, *Figures of Conversion*, 127–52.

85. Grace Aguilar, *Vale of Cedars, or, The Martyr* (London, 1850) 286; Valman, *The Jewess*, 103–9.

86. Jefferson S. Chase, 'The Homeless Nation: The Exclusion of Jews in and from Early Nineteenth-Century German Historical Fiction', in Bryan Cheyette and Nadia Valman, eds, *The*

Image of the Jew in European Liberal Culture 1789–1914 (London: Valentine Mitchell, 2004) 61–74.

87. Nadia Valman, 'Manly Jews: Disraeli, Jewishness and Gender', in Todd M. Endelman and Tony Kushner, eds, *Disraeli's Jewishness* (London: Valentine Mitchell, 2002) 62–101; Daniel R. Schwarz, 'Disraeli's Romanticism: Self-Fashioning in the Novels', in Charles Richmond and Paul Smith, eds, *The Self-Fashioning of Disraeli 1818–1851* (Cambridge: Cambridge University Press, 1998) 42–65.

88. Benjamin Disraeli, *Coningsby, or The New Generation* (London, 1844) 114, 117–41, 215.

89. Benjamin Disraeli, *Tancred, or The New Crusade*, 3 vols (London, 1847) II: 3.

90. Disraeli, *Coningsby*, 133–5; Valman, 'Manly Jews', 87–9.

91. Jonathan Skolnik, 'Heine and Haggadah: History, Narration and Tradition in the Age of *Wissenschaft des Judentums*', in Ross Brann and Adam Sutcliffe, eds, *Renewing the Past, Reconfiguring Jewish Culture: from al-Andalus to the Haskalah* (Philadelphia: University of Pennsylvania Press, 2004) 213–25, esp. 217–22; Skolnik, *Jewish Pasts*, 45–66.

92. Heinrich Heine, *Ludwig Börne: A Memorial*, ed. and trans. Jeffrey L. Sammons (Rochester, NY: Camden House, 2006 [1840]) 10; Willi Goetschel, *The Discipline of Philosophy and the Invention of Modern Jewish Thought* (New York: Fordham University Press, 2013) 21–38.

93. Ludwig Börne, *Briefe aus Paris* 74 (7 February 1832), in *Sämtliche Schriften*, ed. Inge and Peter Rippmann, 5 vols (Dreieich: Melzer, 1977) III: 511–12; Adam Sutcliffe, 'Ludwig Börne, Jewish Messianism, and the Politics of Money', *Leo Baeck Institute Year Book* 57 (2012) 213–37, esp. 220–2.

94. Heine, *Börne*, 10.

95. Jean-Pierre Lefebvre, 'Heine, Hegel et Spinoza', *Cahiers Spinoza* 4 (1983) 211–29; George S. Williamson, *The Longing for Myth in Germany: Religion and Aesthetic Culture from Romanticism to Nietzsche* (Chicago: University of Chicago Press, 2004) 112–18.

96. Felicité de Lamennais, *Worte des Glaubens*, trans. Ludwig Börne (1834), in *Sämtliche Schriften*, II: 1159–1240; Sutcliffe, 'Börne', 231–2.

97. Heine, *Börne*, 95.

98. Matthew Arnold, *Culture and Anarchy*, ed. Stefan Collini (Cambridge: Cambridge University Press, 1993 [1869]) 126–37, esp. 127–8.

99. Ibid., 136; Leonard, *Socrates and the Jews*, 105–38; Tessa Rajak, *The Jewish Dialogue with Greece and Rome* (Leiden: Brill, 2001) 548–54.

100. Maurice Olender, *The Languages of Paradise: Aryans and Semites—A Marriage Made in Heaven* (Cambridge, MA: Harvard University Press, 1992) esp. 6–20.

101. Ibid., 52–7.

102. Ernest Renan, *The Life of Jesus* (London, 1864 [1863]) 309; Olender, *Languages of Paradise*, 68–79; Alan Pitt, 'The Cultural Impact of Science in France: Ernest Renan and the *Vie de Jésus*', *Historical Journal* 43 (2000) 79–101.

103. Edward W. Said, *Orientalism: Western Conceptions of the Orient* (London: Penguin, 1991 [1978]) 130–50.

104. Shlomo Sand, 'Introduction' to Ernest Renan and Shlomo Sand, *On the Nation and the 'Jewish People'* (London: Verso, 2010) 25.

105. Ernest Renan, 'What is a Nation?' (1882), in Renan and Sand, *On the Nation*, 39–69.

106. Ernest Renan, 'Judaism as Race and Religion' (1883), in Renan and Sand, *On the Nation*, 71–100, esp. 77–80, 93–5.

107. Ibid., 100.

108. Steven E. Aschheim, 'Thinking the Nietzsche Legacy Today', in Aschheim, *In Times of Crisis: Essays on European Culture, Germans, and Jews* (Madison, WI: University of Wisconsin Press, 2001) 13–23; Michael F. Duffy and Willard Mittelman, 'Nietzsche's Attitudes toward the Jews', *Journal of the History of Ideas* 49 (1988) 301–17; Weaver Santaniello, *Nietzsche, God, and the Jews* (Albany, NY: State University of New York Press, 1994); Christian J. Emden, *Friedrich Nietzsche and the Politics of History* (Cambridge: Cambridge University Press, 2008) 308–16.

109. Friedrich Nietzsche, *The Anti-Christ*, trans. R. J. Hollingdale (London: Penguin, 1990 [1888]) 162–3 [§ 40]; Nietzsche, *On the Genealogy of Morals*, trans. Walter Kaufmann (New York: Random House, 2000 [1887]) 509–12, 557–61 [§§ II:11, III:14].

110. Friedrich Nietzsche, *Beyond Good and Evil*, trans. Walter Kaufmann (New York: Random House, 2000 [1886]) 298 [§ 195]; Nietzsche, *Genealogy of Morals*, 469–70 [§ I:7].

111. Nietzsche, *The Anti-Christ*, 144–5 [§ 24].

112. Nietzsche, *Beyond Good and Evil*, 376–9 [§ 251]; Nietzsche, *Human, All Too Human*, trans. R. J. Hollingdale (Cambridge: Cambridge University Press, 1986 [1878]) 174–5 [§ I:475].

113. Friedrich Nietzsche, *Daybreak*, trans. R. J. Hollingdale (Cambridge: Cambridge University Press, 1997 [1881]) 124 [§ 205].

114. Karl Marx, *On the Jewish Question* [*Zur Judenfrage*] (1844), in Joseph O'Malley, ed. and trans., *Marx: Early Political Writings* (Cambridge: Cambridge University Press, 1994) 28–56, at 29.

115. Ibid., 34, 37–8.

116. Ibid., 52, 56 (emphasis in original).

117. Ibid., 56.

118. Ibid., 52–6; Karp, *Politics of Jewish Commerce*, 239–54; Breckman, *Marx*, 292–7.

119. Julius Carlebach, *Karl Marx and the Radical Critique of Judaism* (London: Routledge, 1978) 261–358; Robert S. Wistrich, *Socialism and the Jews* (London: Littman, 1982) 25–35; David Leopold, *The Young Karl Marx* (Cambridge: Cambridge University Press, 2017) 163–80.

120. Gareth Stedman Jones, *Karl Marx: Greatness and Illusion* (London: Penguin, 2016) 8–18, 165–7; Sander L. Gilman, *Jewish Self-Hatred: Anti-Semitism and the Hidden Language of the Jews* (Baltimore: Johns Hopkins University Press, 1986) 188–208; Enzo Traverso, *The Marxists and the Jewish Question: The History of a Debate, 1843–1943* (Atlantic Highlands, NJ: Humanities Press, 1994) 13–17.

121. Karl Löwith, *Meaning in History* (Chicago: University of Chicago Press, 1949) 33–51, esp. 44.

122. Marx, *Jewish Question*, 55–6.

123. Feuerbach, *Essence of Christianity*, 111–18.

124. Max Stirner, *The Ego and Its Own*, ed. David Leopold (Cambridge: Cambridge University Press, 1995 [1845]) esp. 23–5; Lawrence Stepelevich, 'Max Stirner and the Jewish Question', *Modern Judaism* 34 (2014) 42–59.

125. Stedman Jones, *Karl Marx*, 188–90.

126. Kalman, *Rethinking Antisemitism*, 23–45.

127. Joseph Salvador, *Histoire des institutions de Moïse et du peuple hébreu*, 2 vols (Paris, 1862 [1828]) I: 288–303; Leff, *Sacred Bonds of Solidarity*, 84–102; John Tresch, *The Romantic Machine: Utopian Science and Technology after Napoleon* (Chicago: University of Chicago Press, 2012) 191–222.

128. Alphonse Toussenel, *Les Juifs, rois de l'époque* (Paris, 1847); Kalman, *Rethinking Antisemitism*, 128–54.

129. Niall Ferguson, *The House of Rothschild: Money's Prophets, 1798–1848* (London: Penguin, 1998) 379–439.

130. Albert S. Lindemann, *Esau's Tears: Modern Anti-Semitism and the Rise of the Jews* (Cambridge: Cambridge University Press, 1997) 104–16; Werner E. Mosse, *The Jews in the German Economy: The German-Jewish Economic Elite, 1820–1935* (Oxford: Oxford University Press, 1987) esp. 383–4.

131. Wilhelm Marr, *Der Sieg des Judenthums über das Germanenthum* (Bern, 1879) esp. 32, 39–44; Richard S. Levy, 'Political Antisemitism in Germany and Austria, 1848–1914', in Lindemann and Levy, *Antisemitism*, 121–35; Lindemann, *Esau's Tears*, 127–31; Moshe Zimmermann, *Wilhelm Marr: The Patriarch of Antisemitism* (Oxford: Oxford University Press, 1986) 70–95.

132. Lindemannn, *Esau's Tears*, 221–7, 337–47; Richard S. Levy, *Antisemitism in the Modern World: An Anthology of Texts* (Lexington, MA: Heath, 1991) 49–144.

133. Heine, *Börne*, 20.

134. Anthony Trollope, *The Way We Live Now* (Oxford: Oxford University Press, 1982 [1875]) 30–1; Valman, *The Jewess*, 136–44; Bryan Cheyette, *Constructions of 'the Jew' in English Literature and Society: Racial Representations, 1875–1945* (Cambridge: Cambridge University Press, 1993) 38–42; Jonathan Freedman, *The Temple of Culture: Assimilation and Anti-Semitism in Literary Anglo-America* (Oxford: Oxford University Press, 2000) 79–88.

135. Eliyahu Stern, 'Marx and the Kabbalah: Aaron Shemuel Lieberman's Materialist Interpretation of Jewish History', *Journal of the History of Ideas* 79 (2018) 285–307; *Jewish Materialism: The Intellectual Revolution of the 1870s* (New Haven, CT: Yale University Press, 2018) 114–46.

136. Stern, *Jewish Materialism*, 71; Nicolas Berg, *Luftmenschen: Zur Geschichte einer Metapher* (Göttingen: Vandenhoeck & Ruprecht, 2008) esp. 81–145.

137. Jonathan Bushnell Bakker, 'Deborin's Materialist Interpretation of Spinoza', *Studies in Soviet Thought* 24 (1982) 175–83.

138. Lars Fischer, *The Socialist Response to Antisemitism in Imperial Germany* (Cambridge: Cambridge University Press, 2007) esp. 21–36; Michele Battini, *Socialism of Fools: Capitalism and Modern Anti-Semitism* (New York: Columbia University Press, 2016) 6–11; Robert S. Wistrich, *Socialism and the Jews* (London: Associated University Presses, 1982) 116–26.

139. Arthur Mitzman, *Sociology and Estrangement: Three Sociologists of Imperial Germany* (New Brunswick, NJ: Transaction Press, 1973) esp. 3–26, 137–61; Harry Liebersohn, *Fate and Utopia in German Sociology 1870–1923* (Cambridge, MA: MIT Press, 1988) esp. 1–10.

140. Adam Sutcliffe, 'Anxieties of Distinctiveness: Werner Sombart's *The Jews and Modern Capitalism* and the Politics of Jewish Economic History', in Kobrin and Teller, *Purchasing Power*, 238–57; Chad Alan Goldberg, *Modernity and the Jews in Western Social Thought* (Chicago: University of Chicago Press, 2017) 43–75.

141. Werner Sombart, *Der moderne Kapitalismus* (Leipzig: Duncker & Humblot, 1902); Max Weber, *The Protestant Ethic and the Spirit of Capitalism*, trans. Peter Baehr and Gordon C. Wells (London: Penguin, 2002 [1905]); Martin Riesebrodt, 'Dimensions of the *Protestant Ethic*', in William H. Swatos and Lutz Kaelber, eds, *The Protestant Ethic Turns 100* (Boulder, CO: Paradigm Publishers, 2005) 23–51.

142. Werner Sombart, *The Jews and Modern Capitalism*, trans. M. Epstein (New Brunswick, NJ: Transaction Press, 1982 [1911]) 191–2, 249.

143. Max Weber, *Ancient Judaism* (New York: The Free Press, 1952 [1917–19]) 336–55; Weber, *Economy and Society* (Berkeley, CA: University of California Press, 1978 [1925]) 611–23.

144. Reiner Grundmann and Nico Stehr, 'Why is Werner Sombart not Part of the Core of Classical Sociology?' *Journal of Classical Sociology* 1 (2001) 257–87.

145. Rolf Rieß, 'Werner Sombart under National Socialism: A First Approximation', in Jürgen Backhaus, ed., *Werner Sombart (1863–1941): Social Scientist. Vol. 1: His Life and Work* (Marburg: Metropolis, 1996) 193–204.

146. Sombart, *Jews and Modern Capitalism*, 13; Matthew Lange, *Antisemitic Elements in the Critique of Capitalism in German Culture* (Bern: Peter Lang, 2007) 215–27.

147. Francesca Trivellato, *The Promise and Peril of Credit: What a Forgotten Legend about Jews and Finance Tells Us about the Making of European Commercial Society* (Princeton, NJ: Princeton University Press, 2019) 205–15.

148. Sombart, *Jews and Modern Capitalism*, 30.

149. Mitchell Hart, *Social Science and the Politics of Modern Jewish Identity* (Stanford, CA: Stanford University Press, 2000) 28–55; Hart, 'Jews, Race and Capitalism in the German-Jewish Context', *Jewish History* 19 (2005) 49–63; Etan Bloom, 'What "The Father" Had in Mind? Arthur Ruppin (1876–1943), Cultural Identity, Weltanschauung and Action', *History of European Ideas* 33 (2007) 330–49, esp. 338–41.

150. Lenger, *Sombart*, 210–14; Marjorie Lamberti, "From Coexistence to Conflict: Zionism and the Jewish Community in Germany, 1897–1914', *Leo Baeck Institute Yearbook* 271(1982): 53–86, esp. 72.

151. Georg Simmel, *The Philosophy of Money*, trans. Tom Bottomore and David Frisby (London: Routledge, 2004 [1900]) 223–5.

152. Ibid., 435.

153. Pierre Birnbaum, *Geography of Hope: Exile, the Enlightenment, Disassimilation* (Stanford, CA: Stanford University Press, 2008) 127–35.

154. Søren Blak Hjortshøj, 'Georg Brandes' Representations of Jewishness: Between Grand Recreations of the Past and Transformative Visions of the Future', PhD thesis (Roskilde University, 2017) 171–222.

155. Georg Simmel, 'The Stranger' ['Exkurs über den Fremden'] (1908), in Donald N. Levine, ed., *Georg Simmel on Individuality and Social Forms* (Chicago: University of Chicago Press, 1971) 143–9.

156. Hermann Cohen, *Religion of Reason out of the Sources of Judaism*, trans. Simon Kaplan (New York: Frederick Ungar, 1972 [1919]) 127–8 [ch. 8, § 24]; Dana Hollander, 'Some Remarks on Love and Law in Hermann Cohen's Ethics of the Neighbor', *Journal of Textual Reasoning* 4 (2005) (online only).

157. Cohen, *Religion of Reason*, 143 [ch. 8, § 53].

158. Ibid., 253, 266–7 [ch. 13, §§ 38, 65].

159. Ibid., 338–70 [ch. 16]; Andrea Poma, 'Hermann Cohen: Judaism and Critical Idealism', in Michael L. Morgan and Peter Eli Gordon, eds, *The Cambridge Companion to Modern Jewish Philosophy* (Cambridge: Cambridge University Press, 2007) 80–101, esp. 89–91.

160. Cohen, *Religion of Reason*, 283–4 [ch. 14, § 27]; Lawrence Kaplan, 'Suffering and Joy in the Thought of Hermann Cohen', *Modern Judaism* 21 (2001) 15–22.

161. Heinrich Graetz, *History of the Jews*, 6 vols (Philadelphia, 1891–98 [1853–76]) e.g., I: 4–5, II: 141, V: 705–17; Michael Brenner, *Prophets of the Past: Interpreters of Jewish History* (Princeton, NJ: Princeton University Press, 2010) 53–79; Esther Benbassa, *Suffering as Identity: The Jewish Paradigm* (London: Verso, 2010) 85–7.

162. David N. Myers, *Resisting History: Historicism and its Discontents in German-Jewish Thought* (Princeton, NJ: Princeton University Press, 2003) 51–6; Michael A. Meyer, 'Heinrich Graetz and Heinrich von Treitschke: A Comparison of their Historical Images of the Modern Jew', *Modern Judaism* 6 (1986) 1–11.

163. Salo Baron, 'Ghetto and Emancipation: Shall We Revise the Traditional View?', *Menorah Journal* 14 (1928) 515–26; Schorsch, *Text to Context*, 376–88; David Engel, 'Crisis and Lachrymosity: On Salo Baron, Neobaronianism, and the Study of Modern European Jewish History', *Jewish History* 20 (2006) 243–64.

Chapter Four. Light unto the Nations: Jews and National Purpose

1. David Ben-Gurion, 'The Call of Spirit in Israel', *Israeli Government Year Book* (1951), in David Ben-Gurion, *Rebirth and Destiny of Israel* (New York: Philosophical Library, 1954) 399–41, at 437 [biblical citation: Isaiah 49:6].

2. Johann Gottlieb Fichte, *Addresses to the German Nation*, ed. Gregory Moore (Cambridge: Cambridge University Press, 2008 [1808]); Rogers Brubaker, *Citizenship and Nationhood in France and Germany* (Cambridge, MA: Harvard University Press, 1992) 35–72.

3. Patrick Geary, *The Myth of Nations: The Medieval Origins of Europe* (Princeton, NJ: Princeton University Press, 2002) 15–40; Peter Heather, 'Race, Migration and National Origins', in Anna Maerker, Simon Sleight and Adam Sutcliffe, eds, *History, Memory and Public Life: The Past in the Present* (London: Routledge, 2018) 80–100.

4. Anthony D. Smith, *Chosen Peoples* (Oxford: Oxford University Press, 2003) 44–65; Adrian Hastings, *The Construction of Nationhood: Ethnicity, Religion and Nationalism* (Cambridge: Cambridge University Press, 1997) 35–65.

5. Linda Colley, *Britons: Forging the Nation 1707–1837* (New Haven, CT: Yale University Press, 1992) 11–54.

6. Adam Sutcliffe, *Judaism and Enlightenment* (Cambridge: Cambridge University Press, 2003) 248–9; David A. Bell, *The Cult of the Nation in France: Inventing Nationalism, 1680–1800* (Cambridge, MA: Harvard University Press, 2003) 22–49.

7. Philip Lockley, *Visionary Religion and Radicalism in Early Industrial England: From Southcott to Socialism* (Oxford: Oxford University Press, 2013).

8. Donald M. Lewis, *The Origins of Christian Zionism: Lord Shaftesbury and Evangelical Support for a Jewish Homeland* (Cambridge: Cambridge University Press, 2010) 173–89.

9. Moses Mendelssohn, 'Anmerkung zu des Ritters Michaelis Beurtheilung . . .' (1780), in Christian Wilhelm von Dohm, *Über die bürgerliche Verbesserung der Juden* (Hildesheim: Georg Olms, 1973 [1781–83]) part 2: 72–7; Alexander Altmann, *Moses Mendelssohn: A Biographical Study* (Tuscaloosa, AL: University of Alabama Press, 1973) 424–6, 466; Aviezer Ravitzky,

Messianism, Zionism and Jewish Religious Radicalism (Chicago: University of Chicago Press, 1993) 11–13.

10. Ravitzky, *Messianism*, 13–32.

11. Leo Pinsker, *Autoemanzipation! Mahnruf an seine Stammesgenossen von einem russischen Juden* (Berlin: Jüdischer Verlag, 1936 [1882]); David Vital, *The Origins of Zionism* (Oxford: Oxford University Press, 1975) 122–32.

12. Abigail Green, *Moses Montefiore: Jewish Liberator, Imperial Hero* (Cambridge, MA: Harvard University Press, 2010) 258–81; David L. Kertzer, *The Kidnapping of Edgardo Mortara* (New York: Random House, 1997) 162–72.

13. Abigail Green, 'Intervening in the Jewish Question, 1840–1878', in Brendan Simms and D.J.B. Trim, eds, *Humanitarian Intervention: A History* (Cambridge: Cambridge University Press, 2011) 139–58; Adam Mendelsohn, 'Not the Retiring Kind: Jewish Colonials in England in the Mid–Nineteenth Century', in Ethan B. Katz, Lisa Moses Leff and Maud S. Mandel, eds, *Colonialism and the Jews* (Bloomington, IN: Indiana University Press, 2017) 81–100; Lisa Moses Leff, *Sacred Bonds of Solidarity: The Rise of Jewish Internationalism in Nineteenth-Century France* (Stanford, CA: Stanford University Press, 2006) 157–99.

14. Joseph Salvador, *Paris, Rome, Jérusalem; ou, la question religieuse au XIX siècle*, 2 vols (Paris, 1860) II: 481; Paula E. Hyman, 'Joseph Salvador: Proto-Zionist or Apologist for Assimilation?', *Jewish Social Studies* 34 (1972) 1–22; L. Scott Lerner, 'Joseph Salvador's Jerusalem Lost and Jerusalem Regained', in Sheila Jelen, Michael P. Kramer and L. Scott Lerner, eds, *Modern Jewish Literatures: Intersections and Boundaries* (Philadelphia: University of Pennsylvania Press, 2010) 44–65.

15. Salvador, *Paris, Rome, Jérusalem*, II: 190–6, 221–5.

16. Ernest Laharanne, *La nouvelle question d'Orient: Empires d'Égypte et d'Arabie—Reconstitution de la nationalité juive* (Paris, 1860) 34.

17. Ibid,, 40, 42.

18. Ibid., 42.

19. Moses Hess, *The Revival of Israel: Rome and Jerusalem, the Last Nationalist Question*, trans. Meyer Waxman (Lincoln, NE: University of Nebraska Press, 1995 [1862]) 150–9.

20. Isaiah Berlin, 'The Life and Opinions of Moses Hess', in Ezra Mendelsohn, ed., *Essential Papers on Jews and the Left* (New York: New York University Press, 1997 [1979]) 21–57, esp. 22–31.

21. Hess, *Rome and Jerusalem*, 43, 226.

22. Moses Hess, *The Holy History of Mankind*, ed. and trans. Shlomo Avineri (Cambridge: Cambridge University Press, 2004 [1837]) 85–96, esp. 95; Shlomo Avineri, *Moses Hess: Prophet of Communism and Zionism* (New York: New York University Press, 1985) 21–46; Adam Sutcliffe, 'From Moses unto Moses: Thinking with Spinoza from Mendelssohn to Hess', *Leipziger Beiträge zur jüdischen Geschichte und Kultur* 2 (2004) 41–56, esp. 50–4.

23. Sidney Hook, *From Hegel to Marx: Studies in the Intellectual Development of Karl Marx* (New York: Columbia University Press, 1994 [1936]) 186–7.

24. Moses Hess, *Über das Geldwesen* (1844), in Wolfgang Mönke, ed., *Moses Hess: Philosophische und Sozialistische Schriften, 1837–1850* (Berlin [GDR]: Akademie Verlag, 1961) 345–6.

25. Hess, *Rome and Jerusalem*, 186–211.

26. Ibid., 52.

27. Ibid., 165.

28. Ibid., 119, 157–9.

29. Ibid., 114–18.

30. Ibid., 124–5.

31. George Eliot, *Daniel Deronda* (London: Penguin, 1995 [1876]) 530 [ch. 42].

32. Ibid., 525, 527.

33. Ibid., 531–2.

34. Ibid., 538.

35. Ibid., 537.

36. Ibid., 546 [ch. 43].

37. Ibid., 803 [ch. 69]; Amanda Anderson, 'George Eliot and the Jewish Question', *Yale Journal of Criticism* 10 (1997) 39–61, esp. 44–7; Nadia Valman, *The Jewess in Nineteenth-Century British Literary Culture* (Cambridge: Cambridge University Press, 2007) 144–59.

38. George Eliot, *Impressions of Theophrastus Such* (London: William Pickering, 1994 [1879]) 148.

39. Ibid., 160.

40. Ibid. 162–5.

41. David Feldman, *Englishmen and Jews: Social Relations and Political Culture, 1840–1914* (New Haven, CT: Yale University Press, 1994) 94–105; Eitan Bar-Yosef, *The Holy Land in English Culture 1799–1917* (Oxford: Oxford University Press, 2005) 202–25; Bernard Semmel, *George Eliot and the Politics of National Inheritance* (Oxford: Oxford University Press, 1994) 103–32.

42. Vital, *Origins of Zionism*, 13–14, 246–7; David Engel, *Zionism* (Harlow: Pearson, 2009) 48.

43. Theodor Herzl, *The Jewish State*, trans. Sylvie d'Avigdor (New York: Dover, 1988 [1896]) 99.

44. Ibid., 164.

45. Max Nordau, *Degeneration* (Lincoln, NE: University of Nebraska Press, 1993 [1892]) 209–11; Nordau, 'Speech to the First Zionist Congress' (1897), in Arthur Hertzberg, *The Zionist Idea: A Historical Analysis and Reader* (Philadelphia: Jewish Publication Society, 1997) 235–41.

46. George L. Mosse, 'Max Nordau: Liberalism and the New Jew', in Mosse, *Confronting the Nation: Jewish and Western Nationalism* (Hanover, NH: Brandeis University Press, 1993) 161–75; Michael Berkowitz, *Zionist Culture and West European Jewry before the First World War* (Chapel Hill, NC: University of North Carolina Press, 1996) 99–118; Todd Samuel Presner, 'Generation, Degeneration, Regeneration: Health, Disease and the Jewish Body', in Mitchell B. Hart and Tony Michels, eds, *The Cambridge History of Judaism, vol. 8: The Modern World, 1815–2000* (Cambridge: Cambridge University Press, 2017) 589–610.

47. Bernard Lazare, *Antisemitism: Its History and Causes* (Lincoln, NE: University of Nebraska Press, 1995 [1894]) 17–18 [ch. 1].

48. Ibid., 141–63, esp. 157 [ch. 13].

49. Ibid., 180–3 [ch. 15].

50. Bernard Lazare, 'Le nationalisme juif' (Paris, 1898) 16; Nelly Wilson, *Bernard-Lazare: Antisemitism and the Problem of Jewish Identity in Late Nineteenth-Century France* (Cambridge: Cambridge University Press, 1978) 222–52.

51. Steven J. Zipperstein, *Elusive Prophet: Ahad Ha'am and the Origins of Zionism* (Berkeley and Los Angeles: University of California Press, 1993) esp. 1–104; David J. Goldberg, *To the Promised Land: A History of Zionist Thought* (London: Penguin, 1996) 92–112.

52. Ahad Ha'am, 'Slavery in Freedom' (1891), in Louis Simon, ed. and trans., *Selected Essays* (Philadelphia: Jewish Publication Society, 1912) 171–94, at 193–4.

53. Ahad Ha'am, 'The Transvaluation of Values' (1898), trans. Leon Simon in Brian Klug, ed., *Words of Fire: Selected Essays of Ahad Ha'am* (Honiton: Notting Hill Editions, 2015) 100–124, at 112–13.

54. Ibid., 111–12.

55. Ibid., 115–16; Jacob Golomb, *Nietzsche and Zion* (Ithaca, NY: Cornell University Press, 2004) 113–57.

56. Ahad Ha'am, 'Priest and Prophet' (1893), in Klug, *Words of Fire*, 22–35, esp. 34–5; 'When Messiah Comes' (1907), in *Words of Fire*, 149–54.

57. Theodor Herzl, *Old New Land*, trans. Lotta Levensohn (Princeton, NJ: Markus Wiener, 1997 [1902]); Zipperstein, *Elusive Prophet*, 194–9.

58. Zipperstein, *Elusive Prophet*, 319–20.

59. Judah Magnes, 'Like All the Nations?' (1930), in Hertzberg, *Zionist Idea*, 443–9, at 444–5.

60. Ibid., 447–9; George Prochnik, *Stranger in a Strange Land: Searching for Gershom Scholem and Jerusalem* (London: Granta, 2017) 170–1, 264–5.

61. Daniel B. Schwartz, *The First Modern Jew: Spinoza and the History of an Image* (Princeton, NJ: Princeton University Press, 2012) 113–53, esp. 114, 146.

62. Ibid., 136–40.

63. Prochnik, *Stranger in a Strange Land*, 289; Gershom Scholem, 'Toward an Understanding of the Messianic Idea' (1959), in Scholem, *The Messianic Idea in Judaism* (New York: Schocken, 1972) 1–36, esp. 7–8.

64. Gershom Scholem, *Major Trends in Jewish Mysticism* (New York: Schocken, 1961 [1941]) 287–324, esp. 304–6; Scholem, 'Redemption through Sin' (1937), in *The Messianic Idea in Judaism*, 78–141, esp. 126–7.

65. Scholem, 'Toward an Understanding', 35–6.; David N. Myers, *Reinventing the Jewish Past: European Jewish Intellectuals and the Zionist Return to History* (New York: Oxford University Press, 1995) 151–76; Benjamin Lazier, *God Interrupted: Heresy and the European Imagination Between the World Wars* (Princeton, NJ: Princeton University Press, 2008) 139–45; David Biale, *Gershom Scholem: Kabbalah and Counter-History* (Cambridge, MA: Harvard University Press, 1982) esp. 71–88, 105–11; Gabriel Piterberg, *The Returns of Zionism: Myths, Politics and Scholarship in Israel* (London: Verso, 2008), 155–91.

66. Scholem, 'Redemption through Sin', 94–9; Paweł Maciejko, *Sabbatian Heresy: Writings on Mysticism, Messianism, and the Origins of Jewish Modernity* (Lebanon, NH: University of New England Press, 2017) xxi–xxv.

67. Gershom Scholem, 'Reflections on Jewish Theology' (1974), in Scholem, *Jews and Judaism in Crisis* (New York: Schocken, 1976) 261–97, at 294–5.

68. Gershom Scholem, 'Judaism', in Arthur A. Cohen and Paul Mendes-Flohr, eds, *Contemporary Jewish Religious Thought* (New York: Free Press, 1987) 505–8, at 508 [based on transcribed conversations in 1973 at the Center for the Study of Democratic Institutions, Santa Barbara, CA].

69. Gershom Scholem, 'A Lecture about Israel' (1967), in *On the Possibility of Jewish Mysticism in Our Time* (Philadelphia: Jewish Publication Society, 1997) 35–9, at 39.

70. Michael Brenner, *In Search of Israel: The History of an Idea* (Princeton, NJ: Princeton University Press, 2018) 83–4; Ravitzky, *Messianism*, 32–5; Eitan Bar-Yosef, 'Spying Out the Land: The Zionist Expedition to East Africa, 1905', in Eitan Bar-Yosef and Nadia Valman, '*The Jew*' in

Late-Victorian and Edwardian Culture: Between the East End and East Africa (Basingstoke: Palgrave Macmillan, 2009) 183–200; Adam Rovner, *In the Shadow of Zion: Promised Lands before Israel* (New York: New York University Press, 2014) 45–77.

71. Ravitzky, *Messianism*, 40–66.

72. Goldberg, *To the Promised Land*, 6–9; Ravitzky, *Messianism*, 26–32; Hertzberg, *Zionist Idea*, 103–14.

73. Abraham Isaac Kook, *Lights* [*Orot*] (1942, but composed 1910–30), extracts in Hertzberg, *Zionist Idea*, 419–31, at 422.

74. Ibid., 423.

75. Ibid., 427.

76. Ibid.

77. Yehudah Mirsky, *Rav Kook: Mystic in a Time of Revolution* (New Haven, CT: Yale University Press, 2014) 92–120; Shlomo Avineri, *The Making of Modern Zionism* (New York: Basic Books, 1981) 187–97.

78. Ravitzky, *Messianism*, 59–78.

79. Ibid., 122–44; Engel, *Zionism*, 165–70.

80. Ber Borochov, 'Program for Proletarian Zionism' (1906), extracts in Hertzberg, *Zionist Idea*, 360–6.

81. Zeev Sternhell, *The Founding Myths of Israel: Nationalism, Socialism, and the Making of the Jewish State* (Princeton, NJ: Princeton University Press, 1998) esp. 74–133.

82. Avineri, *Making of Modern Zionism*, 139–58; Gideon Shimoni, *The Zionist Ideology* (Hanover, NH: Brandeis University Press, 1995) 166–235.

83. Hillel Halkin, *Jabotinsky: A Life* (New Haven, CT: Yale University Press, 2014) esp. 81–94; Avineri, *Making of Modern Zionism*, 159–86; Shimoni, *Zionist Ideology*, 236–49.

84. Biale, *Scholem: Kabbalah and Counter-History*, 101.

85. Halkin, *Jabotinsky*, 163–8; Shimoni, *Zionist Ideology*, 249–66; Engel, *Zionism*, 157–88.

86. David Ben-Gurion, 'Israel among the Nations', *Israeli Government Year Book* (1952), in Ben-Gurion, *Rebirth*, 442–519, at 509; Brenner, *In Search of Israel*, 154–61; David Ohana, *Modernism and Zionism* (Basingstoke: Palgrave Macmillan, 2012) 89–116.

87. Ben-Gurion, 'Israel among the Nations', 479, 506–7.

88. David Ben-Gurion, 'Messianic Vision' (Address to the Third World Congress for the Study of Judaism, Jerusalem, 1961), in David Ben-Gurion, *Ben-Gurion Looks at the Bible* (London: W. H. Allen, 1972) 110–12.

89. David Ben-Gurion, ed., *The Jews and their Land* (London: Aldus, 1966) 377.

90. Yaakov Ariel, '"It's All in the Bible": Evangelical Christians, Biblical Literalism, and Philosemitism in Our Times', in Jonathan Karp and Adam Sutcliffe, eds, *Philosemitism in History* (Cambridge: Cambridge University Press, 2011) 257–85, esp. 268–79.

91. Gerald R. McDermott, ed., *The New Christian Zionism: Fresh Perspectives on Israel and the Land* (Downers Grove, IL: IVP Academic, 2016).

92. James Renton, *The Zionist Masquerade: The Birth of the Anglo-Zionist Alliance, 1914–1918* (Basingstoke: Palgrave Macmillan, 2007) 11–42; Bar-Yosef, *Holy Land*, 182; Paul C. Merkley, *The Politics of Christian Zionism 1891–1948* (London: Frank Cass, 1998).

93. Colin Kidd, *The Forging of Races: Race and Scripture in the Protestant Atlantic World, 1600–2000* (Cambridge: Cambridge University Press, 2006) 203–70.

94. Tim Grady, *A Deadly Legacy: German Jews and the Great War* (New Haven, CT: Yale University Press, 2017) 25–48; David Rechter, *The Jews of Vienna and the First World War* (London: Littman, 2001) 201–28; Marsha L. Rozenblit and Jonathan Karp, eds, *World War I and the Jews* (New York: Berghahn, 2017).

95. Hermann Cohen, *Deutschtum und Judentum* (1915), in Cohen, *Jüdische Schriften*, 3 vols (Berlin, 1924) II: 237–91, esp. 269–70, 290.

96. Hermann Cohen, 'Antwort auf das offene Schrieben des Herrn Dr. Martin Buber an Hermann Cohen', in *Jüdische Schriften*, II: 328–40, esp. 335 [biblical citation: Micah 5:6].

97. Hermann Cohen, *Religion of Reason out of the Sources of Judaism*, trans. Simon Kaplan (New York: Frederick Ungar, 1972 [1919]) 216–35 [ch. 12]; Leora Batnitzky, *How Judaism Became a Religion* (Princeton, NJ: Princeton University Press, 2011) 57–9; Andrea Poma, 'Suffering and Non-Eschatological Messianism in Hermann Cohen', in Reiner Munk, ed., *Hermann Cohen's Critical Idealism* (Dordrecht: Springer, 2005) 413–28.

98. Martin Buber, 'Zion, the State and Humanity: Remarks on Hermann Cohen's Answer' (1916), in Arthur A. Cohen, ed., *The Jew: Essays from Martin Buber's Journal Der Jude, 1916–1928* (Tuscaloosa, AL: University of Alabama Press, 1980) 87–96, esp. 94.

99. Martin Buber, 'The Renewal of Judaism' (1911), in Asher D. Biemann, ed., *The Martin Buber Reader* (New York: Palgrave Macmillan, 2002) 145–57.

100. Martin Buber, 'Zionism and Nationalism' (1929), in Biemann, *Buber Reader*, 277–80; Shimoni, *Zionist Ideology*, 345–51, 372–8.

101. Franz Rosenzweig, *The Star of Redemption*, trans. Barbara E. Galli (Madison, WI: University of Wisconsin Press, 2005 [1921]) 351.

102. Ibid., 325.

103. Ibid., 426–8; Dana Hollander, *Exemplarity and Chosenness: Rosenzweig and Derrida on the Nation of Philosophy* (Stanford, CA: Stanford University Press, 2008) 27–39; Richard A. Cohen, *Elevations: The Height of the Good in Rosenzweig and Levinas* (Chicago: University of Chicago Press, 1994) 3–39.

104. Rosenzweig, *Star of Redemption*, esp. 348–9, 404.

105. Ibid., 368, 436–7; Peter Eli Gordon, *Rosenzweig and Heidegger: Between Judaism and German Philosophy* (Berkeley and Los Angeles: University of California Press, 2003) 134–5, 206–10, 229–30.

106. David N. Myers, *Resisting History: Historicism and its Discontents in German-Jewish Thought* (Princeton, NJ: Princeton University Press, 2003) 68–105.

107. Rosenzweig, *Star of Redemption*, 317–19; Stéphane Mosès, *System and Revelation: The Philosophy of Franz Rosenzweig* (Detroit: Wayne State University Press, 1982) 176–83; Hollander, *Exemplarity and Chosenness*, 121–3; Gordon, *Rosenzweig and Heidegger*, 210–14.

108. Rosenzweig, *Star of Redemption*, 401–2.

109. Franz Rosenzweig, *Ninety-Two Poems and Hymns of Yehuda Halevi*, trans. Thomas Kovach, Eva Jospe and Gilya Gerda Schmidt (Albany, NY: State University of New York Press, 2000 [1927]) 217; Hollander, *Exemplarity and Chosenness*, 189–90; Cohen, *Elevations*, 23–8.

110. Yael Zerubavel, *Recovered Roots: Collective Memory and the Making of Israeli National Tradition* (Chicago: University of Chicago Press, 1995) 39–76; Idith Zertal, *Israel's Holocaust and the Politics of Nationhood* (Cambridge: Cambridge University Press, 2005) 9–51.

111. Ernst Cassirer, 'Judaism and the Modern Political Myths' (1944), in *Symbol, Myth, and Culture: Essays and Lectures of Ernst Cassirer, 1935–1945* (New Haven, CT: Yale University Press, 1979) 233–41, at 241; Peter E. Gordon, *Continental Divide: Heidegger, Cassirer, Davos* (Cambridge, MA: Harvard University Press, 2010) 317–18.

112. Max Horkheimer and Theodor W. Adorno, *Dialectic of Enlightenment* (New York: Continuum, 1989 [1947]) 186; Stuart Jeffries, *Grand Hotel Abyss: The Lives of the Frankfurt School* (London: Verso, 2016) 223–36.

113. Jean-Paul Sartre, *Anti-Semite and Jew [Réflexions sur la question juive]* (New York: Schocken, 1948 [1946]) esp. 53–4, 149–53; Jonathan Judaken, *Jean-Paul Sartre and the Jewish Question* (Lincoln, NE: Univesity of Nebraska Press, 2007) 122–46.

114. Jean-Paul Sartre and Benny Lévy, *Hope Now: The 1980 Interviews* (Chicago: University of Chicago Press, 1996 [1991]) 99–110, esp. 106; Sarah Hammerschlag, *The Figural Jew: Politics and Identity in Postwar French Thought* (Chicago: University of Chicago Press, 2010) 68–116.

115. Emmanuel Levinas, *Ethics and Infinity* (Pittsburgh: Duquesne University Press, 1985 [1982]) esp. 117; Levinas, *Difficult Freedom: Essays on Judaism* (Baltimore: Johns Hopkins University Press, 1990 [1963]) 225.

116. Vivian Liska, *German-Jewish Thought and Its Afterlife: A Tenuous Legacy* (Bloomington, IN: Indiana University Press, 2017) 148–9.

117. Emmanuel Levinas, *Unforeseen History* (Urbana, IL: University of Illinois Press, 2004 [1994]) 92–8; Hammerschlag, *Figural Jew*, 159–64.

118. Jacques Derrida, 'Violence and Metaphysics: An Essay on the Thought of Emmanuel Levinas', in Derrida, *Writing and Difference* (London: Routledge, 1978 [1964]) 79–153, esp. 79, 152–3; Hollander, *Exemplarity and Chosenness*, 65–72.

119. Jacques Derrida, 'A Testimony Given . . .', in Elisabeth Weber, *Questioning Judaism* (Stanford, CA: Stanford University Press, 2004 [1994]) 39–58, esp. 40–1; Derrida, 'Circumfession', in Geoffrey Bennington and Jacques Derrida, *Jacques Derrida* (Chicago: University of Chicago Press, 1993) esp. 70–8; Hammerschlag, *Figural Jew*, 206–28.

120. Derrida, 'Testimony Given', 41–2.

121. Fichte, *Addresses to the German Nation*, 85–99, esp. 90–1, 95.

122. Jacques Derrida, 'Onto-Theology of National Humanism (Prolegomena to a Hypothesis)', *Oxford Literary Review* 14 (1992) 3–24, at 13; Fichte, *Addresses*, 97.

123. Derrida, 'Onto-Theology', 16–17; Hollander, *Exemplarity and Chosenness*, 101–5.

124. Cohen, *Deutschtum und Judentum*, in *Jüdische Schriften* II: 275, 282–3; Jacques Derrida, 'Interpretations at War: Kant, the Jew, the German', in Derrida, *Acts of Religion* (New York: Routledge, 2010 [1989]) 135–88, esp. 146, 156, 170–6.

125. Derrida, 'Interpretations at War', 182–3; for a critique of Derrida's reading, see Gillian Rose, *Judaism and Modernity: Philosophical Essays* (Oxford: Blackwell, 1993) 65–87.

126. Derrida, 'Interpretations at War', 186–8; Immanuel Kant, 'Perpetual Peace: A Philosophical Sketch' (1795), in H. S. Reiss, ed., *Kant: Political Writings* (Cambridge: Cambridge University Press, 1991) 93–130, esp. 102–5.

127. Hammerschlag, *Figural Jew*, 162–3, 247–52; Howard Caygill, *Levinas and the Political* (London: Routledge, 2002) 182–93; Michael L. Morgan, *Levinas's Ethical Politics* (Bloomington, IN: Indiana University Press, 2016) 266–98.

128. Eliot, *Daniel Deronda*, 535 [ch. 42].

129. Adam Hochschild, *King Leopold's Ghost* (New York: Houghton Mifflin, 1998) 42–6.

130. Herzl, *Jewish State*, 152.

131. Todd Gitlin and Liel Leibovitz, *The Chosen Peoples: America, Israel, and the Ordeals of Divine Election* (New York: Simon & Schuster, 2010) 183–92.

132. Mark Mazower, *Governing the World: The History of an Idea, 1815 to the Present* (New York: Penguin, 2012) 159–62; Carole Fink, *Defending the Rights of Others: The Great Powers, the Jews, and International Minority Protection, 1878–1938* (Cambridge: Cambridge University Press, 2004).

133. Vladimir Davidovich Medem, 'The Worldwide Jewish Nation' (1911), in Simon Rabinovitch, ed., *Jews and Diaspora Nationalism: Writings on Jewish Peoplehood in Europe and the United States* (Waltham, MA: Brandeis University Press, 2012) 105–24.

134. Ethan B. Katz, 'Crémieux's Children: Joseph Reinach, Léon Blum, and René Cassin as Jews of the French Empire', in Katz, Leff and Mandel, *Colonialism and the Jews*, 129–65; Cathy Gelbin and Sander Gilman, *Cosmopolitanisms and the Jews* (Ann Arbor, MI: University of Michigan Press, 2017) 69–137.

135. James Loeffler, *Rooted Cosmopolitans: Jews and Human Rights in the Twentieth Century* (New Haven, CT: Yale University Press, 2018) 171–294; Samuel Moyn, *The Last Utopia: Human Rights in History* (Cambridge, MA: Harvard University Press, 2010) 84–119, 201–11.

136. Anoosh Chakelian, 'Vince Cable: Theresa May's Tory conference speech "could have been taken out of Mein Kampf"', *New Statesman*, 5 July 2017.

Chapter Five. Normalization and Its Discontents: Jews and Cultural Purpose

1. Sigmund Freud, *Civilization and its Discontents* (1930), trans. James Strachey in *Penguin Freud Library*, 15 vols (London: Penguin, 1985) XII: 302–3, 305 [ch. 5].

2. Ezra Mendelsohn, *On Modern Jewish Politics* (New York: Oxford University Press, 1993); Benjamin Nathans, *Beyond the Pale: The Jewish Encounter with Late Imperial Russia* (Berkeley and Los Angeles: University of California Press, 2002) esp. 1–13; David Engel, 'The New Jewish Politics', in Mitchell B. Hart and Tony Michels, eds, *The Cambridge History of Judaism, vol. 8: The Modern World, 1815–2000* (Cambridge: Cambridge University Press, 2017) 363–89.

3. Richard S. Levy, 'Political Antisemitism in Germany and Austria, 1848–1914', in Albert S. Lindemann and Richard S. Levy, eds, *Antisemitism: A History* (Oxford: Oxford University Press, 2010) 121–35; Todd M. Endelman, *The Jews of Britain, 1656–2000* (Berkeley and Los Angeles: University of California Press, 2002) 158–65.

4. Cornelia Wilhelm, 'Unequal Opportunities: The Independent Order B'nai B'rith in Nineteenth-Century Germany and in the United States', in Christian Wiese and Cornelia Wilhelm, eds, *American Jewry: Transcending the American Experience?* (London: Bloomsbury, 2017) 125–35; Rainer Liedtke and David Rechter, eds, *Towards Normality? Acculturation and Modern German Jewry* (Tübingen: Mohr Siebeck, 2003).

5. Andrew Heinze, *Adapting to Abundance: Jewish Immigrants, Mass Consumption, and the Search for American Identity* (New York: Columbia University Press, 1990) esp. 1–18, 219–23.

6. Freud, *Civilization and its Discontents*, 336–7 [ch. 8].

7. Todd M. Endelman, *Radical Assimilation in English Jewish History, 1656–1945* (Bloomington, IN: Indiana University Press, 1990) 73–143; Michael A. Meyer, *Response to Modernity: A History of the Reform Movement in Judaism* (New York: Oxford University Press, 1988) 212–21.

8. Daniel R. Langton, *Claude Montefiore: His Life and Thought* (London: Valentine Mitchell, 2002) 5–6; Edward Kessler, *An English Jew: The Life and Writings of Claude Montefiore* (London: Valentine Mitchell, 1989) 2.

9. Claude Montefiore, 'The Synoptic Gospels and Jewish Consciousness', *Hibbert Journal* 3 (1905) 649–67, esp. 659–61, 665–7; Langton, *Montefiore*, 247–311; Kessler, *English Jew*, 5–10, 51–86.

10. Claude Montefiore, in Oswald John Simon et al, 'Mission of Israel', *Jewish Quarterly Review* 9 (1897) 177–223, at 197–9.

11. Claude Montefiore, *Outlines of Liberal Judaism* (London: Macmillan, 1912) 158.

12. Lily H. Montagu, 'Spiritual Possibilities of Judaism To-Day', *Jewish Quarterly Review* 11 (1899) 216–31, at 230–1.

13. Nadia Valman, 'From Domestic Paragon to Rebellious Daughter: Victorian Jewish Women Novelists', in Nadia Valman, ed., *Jewish Women Writers in Britain* (Detroit: Wayne State University Press, 2014) 10–34.

14. Anne Summers, *Christian and Jewish Women in Britain, 1880–1940* (London: Palgrave Macmillan, 2017) 63–111, 141–53.

15. Langton, *Montefiore*, 110–24; Meyer, *Response to Modernity*, 335–7.

16. Claude Montefiore, 'Liberal Judaism in England: Its Difficulties and Its Duties', *Jewish Quarterly Review* 12 (1900) 618–50, esp. 637, 642; Montefiore, 'Judaism, Unitarianism and Theism', *Papers for the Jewish People* 4 (1908) 5–10.

17. Ahad Ha'am, 'Judaism and the Gospels' (1910), trans. Leon Simon in *Ten Essays on Zionism and Judaism* (London, 1922) 223–53, esp. 253; Steven J. Zipperstein, *Elusive Prophet: Ahad Ha'am and the Origins of Zionism* (Berkeley and Los Angeles: University of California Press, 1993) 235–6.

18. Tobias Brinkmann, *Sundays at Sinai: A Jewish Congregation in Chicago* (Chicago: University of Chicago Press, 2012) 79–99.

19. Ibid., 131–3; Meyer, *Response to Modernity*, 287.

20. Meyer, *Response to Modernity*, 286–9, 309–14.

21. Ibid., 265–70, 387–8.

22. Arthur Kiron, '"Dust and Ashes": The Funeral and Forgetting of Sabato Morais', *American Jewish History* 84 (1996) 155–84, esp. 163–6; Kiron, 'Heralds of Duty: The Sephardic Italian Jewish Theological Seminary of Sabato Morais', *Jewish Quarterly Review* 105 (2015) 206–49, esp. 222–4, 232–3, 238–9.

23. Benny Kraut, *From Reform Judaism to Ethical Culture: The Religious Evolution of Felix Adler* (Cincinnati, OH: Hebrew Union College Press, 1979) esp. 44–75, 108–18; Brinkmann, *Sundays at Sinai*, 100–119, 128.

24. Kraut, *Felix Adler*, 119–20, 207–10.

25. Eli Lederhendler, *Jewish Immigrants and American Capitalism, 1880–1920* (Cambridge: Cambridge University Press, 2009) 85–119.

26. Tony Michels, *A Fire in Their Hearts: Yiddish Socialists in New York* (Cambridge, MA: Harvard University Press, 2005) 1–2, 69–124.

27. Abraham J. Karp, 'Solomon Schechter Comes to America', *American Jewish Historical Quarterly* 53 (1963) 44–62.

28. Mordecai M. Kaplan, 'The Future of Judaism', *Menorah Journal* (1916), reprinted in Simon Rabinovitch, ed., *Jews and Diaspora Nationalism: Writings on Jewish Peoplehood in Europe and the United States* (Waltham, MA: Brandeis University Press, 2012) 169–81, esp. 178–9.

29. Mordecai M. Kaplan, *Judaism as a Civilization: Toward a Reconstruction of American-Jewish Life* (New York: Macmillan, 1934) 3–15.

30. Mel Scult, *The Radical American Judaism of Mordecai M. Kaplan* (Bloomington, IN: Indiana University Press, 2014) 77–83, esp. 79.

31. Kaplan, *Judaism as a Civilization*, 44–5.

32. Ibid., 280–99.

33. Ibid., 120; Kaplan, *The Meaning of God in Modern Religion* (Detroit: Wayne State University Press, 1994 [1937]) 17–18.

34. Kaplan, *Judaism as a Civilization*, 253–63; Scult, *Mordecai Kaplan*, 46–51; Arnold M. Eisen, *The Chosen People in America* (Bloomington, IN: Indiana University Press, 1983) 89–90; Noam Pianko, *Zionism and the Roads not Taken: Rawidowicz, Kaplan, Kohn* (Bloomington, IN: Indiana University Press, 2010) 95–133.

35. Kaplan, *Meaning of God*, 94–103, esp. 96, 102.

36. Ibid., 188–329, esp. 188, 192.

37. Ibid., 303, 363–4.

38. Ibid., 365–8.

39. David Kaufman, *Shul with a Pool: The Synagogue-Center in American Jewish History* (Waltham, MA: Brandeis University Press, 1999) esp. 228–41.

40. Meyer, *Response to Modernity*, 319–20; 388–91.

41. Kaplan, *The Future of the American Jew* (New York: Macmillan, 1948) 226–30; Eisen, *Chosen People in America*, 73–98.

42. Mordecai Kaplan, *The Purpose and Meaning of Jewish Existence: A People in the Image of God* (Philadelphia: Jewish Publication Society, 1964) 294.

43. Ibid., 318.

44. Israel Zangwill, *Dreamers of the Ghetto* (London, 1898) esp. 205, 369.

45. Neil Larry Schumsky, 'Zangwill's *The Melting Pot*: Ethnic Tensions on Stage', *American Quarterly* 27 (1975) 29–41, esp. 29; Meri-Jane Rochelson, *A Jew in the Public Arena: The Career of Israel Zangwill* (Detroit: Wayne State University Press, 2008) 180–9, esp. 181; David Biale, 'The Melting Pot and Beyond: Jews and the Politics of American Identity', in David Biale, Michael Galchinsky and Susannah Heschel, eds, *Insider/Outsider: American Jews and Multiculturalism* (Berkeley and Los Angeles: University of California Press, 1998) 17–33.

46. Israel Zangwill, *The Melting Pot* (New York: American Jewish Book Company, 1921 [1908]) 54 [Act I].

47. Ibid., 259 [Act IV]; Ben Gidley, 'The Ghosts of Kishinev in the East End: Responses to a Pogrom in the Jewish London of 1903', in Eitan Bar-Yosef and Nadia Valman, eds, 'The Jew' in Late-Victorian and Edwardian Culture: Between the East End and East Africa (Basingstoke: Palgrave, 2009) 98–112, esp. 107–10.

48. Zangwill, *Dreamers of the Ghetto*, viii.

49. Zangwill, *Melting Pot*, 142 [Act II].

50. Israel Zangwill, *Children of the Ghetto: A Study of a Peculiar People*, ed. Meri-Jane Rochelson (Detroit: Wayne State University Press, 1998 [1892]) 478, 489, 501–2; Rochelson, *Jew in the Public Arena*, 51–74; Nadia Valman, 'The East End *Bildungsroman* from Israel Zangwill to Monica Ali', *Wasafiri* 24 (2009) 3–8; Valman, 'Walking Victorian Spitalfields with Israel Zangwill', *19: Interdisciplinary Studies in the Long Nineteenth Century* 21 (2015) (online only).

51. Adam Rovner, *In the Shadow of Zion: Promised Lands before Israel* (New York: New York University Press, 2014) 78–115.

52. Israel Zangwill, 'Mr. Zangwill on modern Jewish problems', *Jewish Chronicle*, 18 March 1898, 8–9; Rochelson, *Jew in the Public Arena*, 118–19.

53. Edward Alsworth Ross, *The Old World in the New: The Significance of Past and Present Immigration to the American People* (New York: The Century Co., 1914) esp. 287–90; Horace Kallen, 'Democracy versus the Melting-Pot: A Study of American Nationality', *The Nation*, 25 February 1915, 217–20, reprinted in Rabinovitch, *Jews and Diaspora Nationalism*, 155–68.

54. Kallen, 'Democracy versus the Melting-Pot', 168.

55. Ibid., 159–62.

56. Ibid., 162–3.

57. Ibid., 166.

58. Jonathan Sarna, 'The Cult of Synthesis in American Jewish Culture', *Jewish Social Studies* 5 (1998/99) 52–79, at 56–7.

59. Daniel Greene, *The Jewish Origins of Cultural Pluralism: The Menorah Association and American Diversity* (Bloomington, IN: Indiana University Press, 2011) 64–7; Louis Menand, *The Metaphysical Club: A Story of Ideas in America* (New York: Farrar, Straus and Giroux, 2001) 388–408; Jakob Egholm Feldt, *Transnationalism and the Jews* (London: Rowman and Littlefield, 2016) 31–4.

60. Greene, *Cultural Pluralism*, 14–29.

61. Horace Kallen, 'Hebraism and Current Tendencies in Philosophy' (1909), in *Judaism at Bay: Essays toward the Adjustment of Judaism to Modernity* (New York: Bloch, 1932) 7–15, at 8.

62. Ibid., esp. 10, 13.

63. Horace Kallen, 'On the Import of "Universal Judaism"' (1909), in *Judaism at Bay*, 16–27.

64. Horace Kallen, 'Judaism, Hebraism and Zionism' (1910), in *Judaism at Bay*, 28–41, esp. 30, 37.

65. Ibid., 39.

66. Ibid., 41.

67. Jeffrey Rosen, *Louis D. Brandeis: American Prophet* (New Haven, CT: Yale University Press, 2016) 146–83; Melvin L. Urofsky, *Louis D. Brandeis: A Life* (New York: Pantheon, 2009) 405–13.

68. Noam Pianko, '"The True Liberalism of Zionism": Horace Kallen, Jewish Nationalism, and the Limits of American Pluralism', *American Jewish History* 94 (2008) 299–329; Pianko, *Zionism and the Roads not Taken*, 26.

69. Horace M. Kallen, 'Culture and the Ku Klux Klan', in *Culture and Democracy in the United States* (New York, 1924) 9–43, esp. 11, 43.

70. Horace M. Kallen, *Cultural Pluralism and the American Idea* (Philadelphia: University of Pennsylvania Press, 1956); William Toll, 'Horace M. Kallen: Pluralism and American Jewish Identity', *American Jewish History* 85 (1997) 57–74, esp. 71–2.

71. Greene, *Cultural Pluralism*, 181–3; Nathan Glazer and Daniel Patrick Moynihan, *Beyond the Melting Pot: The Negroes, Puerto Ricans, Jews, Italians, and Irish of New York City* (Cambridge, MA: MIT Press, 1963).

72. Louis Wirth, *The Ghetto* (Chicago: University of Chicago Press, 1928).

73. Mitchell Duneier, *Ghetto: The Invention of a Place, the History of an Idea* (New York: Farrar, Straus and Giroux, 2016) esp. 3–84.

74. Tobias Brinkmann, 'The Dynamics of Modernity: Shifts in Demography and Geography', in Hart and Michels, eds, *Cambridge History of Judaism 8*, 915–41, at 928–33.

75. Marsha L. Rosenblit, *The Jews of Vienna, 1867–1914: Assimilation and Identity* (Albany, NY: State University of New York Press, 1983); Steven Beller, *Vienna and the Jews 1867–1938: A Cultural History* (Cambridge: Cambridge University Press, 1989).

76. Walther Rathenau, 'Hear, O Israel!' (1897), available online at www.ghdi.ghi-dc.org.

77. Walther Rathenau, *Zur Kritik der Zeit* (Berlin: S. Fischer, 1912) 37–40, 219–43; Shulamit Volkov, *Walther Rathenau: Weimar's Fallen Statesman* (New Haven, CT: Yale University Press, 2012) 104–14, 184–5.

78. Paul Reitter, *The Anti-Journalist: Karl Kraus and Jewish Self-Fashioning in Fin-de-Siècle Europe* (Chicago: University of Chicago Press, 2008) 1–67; Edward Timms, *Karl Kraus: Apocalyptic Satirist*, 2 vols (New Haven, CT: Yale University Press, 1986, 2005) I: 63–93; Ritchie Robertson, *The 'Jewish Question' in German Literature, 1749–1939* (Oxford: Oxford University Press, 1999) 309–23.

79. Karl Kraus, *Eine Krone für Zion* (Vienna, 1898) 12, 20, 31.

80. Ibid., 27.

81. Ibid., 28; Reitter, *Anti-Journalist*, 74–82.

82. Kraus, *Krone*, 30.

83. Ibid., 23.

84. Karl Kraus, *Heine and the Consequences* [*Heine und die Folgen*] (1910), trans. Jonathan Franzen in *The Kraus Project* (New York: Farrar, Straus and Giroux, 2013) 3–133, at 19.

85. Ibid., 41, 61.

86. Ibid., 91–105; Reitter, *Anti-Journalist*, 96–106.

87. Carl E. Schorske, *Fin-de-Siècle Vienna: Politics and Culture* (New York: Knopf, 1980); Beller, *Vienna and the Jews*, esp. 238–44.

88. Karl Kraus, 'Er ist doch ä Jud', *Die Fackel* 386 (1913) 1–8; Leo A. Lensing, '1913: Karl Kraus writes "He's a Jew After All"', in Sander L. Gilman and Jack Zipes, eds, *Yale Companion to Jewish Writing and Thought in German Culture, 1096–1996* (New Haven, CT: Yale University Press, 1997) 313–21.

89. Sander L. Gilman, *Jewish Self-Hatred* (Baltimore: Johns Hopkins University Press, 1986) 233–43; John Theobald, *The Paper Ghetto: Karl Kraus and Anti-Semitism* (Frankfurt: Peter Lang, 1996).

90. Reitter, *The Anti-Journalist*, 69–106; Reitter, 'Karl Kraus and the Jewish Self-Hatred Question', *Jewish Social Studies* 10 (2003) 78–116; Timms, *Kraus*, I: 237–49, II: 208–26.

91. Paul Reitter, *On the Origins of Jewish Self-Hatred* (Princeton, NJ: Princeton University Press, 2012) 5–73.

92. Theodor Lessing, *Der jüdische Selbsthaß* (Berlin: Matthes & Seitz, 2004 [1930]) 64.

93. Ibid., 43–5, 64.

94. Theodor Lessing, 'Georg Simmel: Betrachtungen und Excurse', in *Philosophie als Tat* (Göttingen: Otto Hapke, 1914) 303–43.

95. Theodor Lessing, *Geschichte als Sinngebung des Sinnlosen* (Munich: C. H. Beck, 1919); Friedrich von Petersdorf, 'Die perspektivische Konstruktion von Geschichte in Lessings beiden Büchern *Geschichte als Sinngebung des Sinnlosen*', in Elke-Vera Kotowski, ed., '*Sinngebung des Sinnlosen*': *Zum Leben und Werk des Kulturkritikers Theodor Lessing* (Hildesheim: Georg Olms, 2006) 201–14.

96. Lawrence Baron, 'Theodor Lessing: Between Jewish Self-Hatred and Zionism', *Leo Baeck Institute Year Book* 26 (1981) 323–40; Baron, 'Noise and Degeneration: Theodor Lessing's Crusade for Quiet', *Journal for Contemporary History* 17 (1982) 165–78.

97. Lessing, *Der jüdische Selbsthaß*, 80, 235.

98. Reitter, *Origins of Jewish Self-Hatred*, 90–1, 110–19.

99. Lessing, *Der jüdische Selbsthaß*, 40–2, 52, 235.

100. Karl Kraus, 'Man frage nicht . . .' (1933), trans. Franzen in *Kraus Project*, 312–15.

101. Karl Kraus, *Dritte Walpurgisnacht* (Munich: Kösel, 1952) 9; Timms, *Kraus*, II: 492–515.

102. Karl Kraus, *Pro Domo et Mundo* (Munich: Langen, 1912) 63.

103. Timms, *Kraus*, I: 94–114; Franzen, *Kraus Project*, 213–17.

104. Eliza Slavet, *Racial Fever: Freud and the Jewish Question* (New York: Fordham University Press, 2009) 10–14; Jacqueline Rose, *The Last Resistance* (London: Verso, 2007) 17–25.

105. Sigmund Freud, *Moses and Monotheism* (1938), trans. Strachey in *Penguin Freud Library*, XIII: 333–4 [part 1 D].

106. Ibid., 336.

107. Ibid., 335.

108. Ibid., 351–2.

109. Ibid., 352–3.

110. Ibid., 358; Slavet, *Racial Fever*, 177–81; Jan Assmann, 'The Advance in Intellectuality: Freud's Construction of Judaism', in Ruth Ginsberg and Ilana Pardes, eds, *New Perspectives on Freud's Moses and Monotheism* (Tübingen: Max Niemeyer, 2006) 7–18; Joel Whitebook, '*Geistigkeit*: A Problematic Concept', in Gilad Sharvit and Karen S. Feldman, eds, *Freud and Monotheism: Moses and the Violent Origins of Religion* (New York: Fordham University Press, 2018) 46–64.

111. G.W.F. Hegel, *Lectures on the Philosophy of History* (1837), trans. J. Sibree (Kitchener, ON: Batoche Books, 2001 [1857]) 339–40.

112. Jan Assmann, *Moses the Egyptian: The Memory of Egypt in Western Monotheism* (Cambridge, MA: Harvard University Press, 1997) 144–67, esp. 145–7.

113. Yosef Hayim Yerushalmi, *Freud's Moses: Judaism Terminable and Interminable* (New Haven, CT: Yale University Press, 1991) 37–55, esp. 41–5.

114. Yerushalmi, *Freud's Moses*, 81–100, esp. 97–8; for a penetrating critique of Yerushalmi's arguments, see Jacques Derrida, *Archive Fever: A Freudian Impression*, trans. Eric Prenowitz (Chicago: University of Chicago Press, 1996) 49–81.

115. Slavet, *Racial Fever*, 68–79.

116. Freud, *The Future of Illusion* (1927), trans. Strachey in *Penguin Freud Library*, XIII: 183–241, at 238.

117. Yerushalmi, *Freud's Moses*, 95.

118. Freud, *Moses and Monotheism*, 386.

119. Stefan Zweig, *Jeremias: eine dramatische Dichtung in neun Bildern* (Leipzig: Insel, 1918) 493, 507; Robertson, 'Jewish Question', 116–22.

120. Christopher Clark, *Time and Power: Visions of History in German Politics* (Princeton, NJ: Princeton University Press, 2019) 202.

121. Saul Friedländer, *Nazi Germany and the Jews: The Years of Persecution, 1933–39* (London: Weidenfeld & Nicolson, 1997) 73–122; A. Dirk Moses, 'Redemptive Antisemitism and the Imperialist Imaginary', in Christian Wiese and Paul Betts, eds, *Years of Persecution, Years of Extermination: Saul Friedländer and the Future of Holocaust Studies* (London: Continuum, 2010) 233–354; Clark, *Time and Power*, 201–4.

122. Samuel Moyn, *Human Rights and the Uses of History* (London: Verso, 2014) 87–97; Tony Kushner, *The Holocaust and the Liberal Imagination* (Oxford: Blackwell, 1994) 229–47; Peter Novick, *The Holocaust in American Life* (New York: Houghton Mifflin, 1999) 63–123.

123. Eisen, *Chosen People in America*, 61–72, 99–123.

124. Idith Zertal, *Israel's Holocaust and the Politics of Nationhood* (Cambridge: Cambridge University Press, 2005) 52–90; Tom Segev, *The Seventh Million: The Israelis and the Holocaust* (New York: Hill & Wang, 1993) 153–86, 255–310.

125. Aviezer Ravitzky, *Messianism, Zionism and Jewish Religious Radicalism* (Chicago: University of Chicago Press, 1993) 59–78; Yakov M. Rabkin, *A Threat from Within: A Century of Jewish Opposition to Zionism* (Black Point, Nova Scotia: Fernwood, 2006) 168–75.

126. Zertal, *Israel's Holocaust*, 91–127.

127. David Feldman, 'Toward a History of the Term "Anti-Semitism"', *American Historical Review* 123 (2018) 1139–50; Scott Ury, 'Strange Bedfellows? Anti-Semitism, Zionism and the Fate of "the Jews"', *American Historical Review* 123 (2018) 1151–71; Robert Wistrich, *Antisemitism: The Longest Hatred* (London: Pantheon, 1992).

128. Novick, *Holocaust in American Life*, 127–203; Alan Mintz, *Popular Culture and the Shaping of Holocaust Memory in America* (Seattle: University of Washington Press, 2001) 11–16.

129. Ignaz Maybaum, *The Face of God After Auschwitz* (Amsterdam: Polak & Van Gennep, 1965) 196–201, esp. 200; Nicholas de Lange, 'Introduction' to *Ignaz Maybaum: A Reader* (New York: Berghahn, 2001) xvii–xxxi; Daniel R. Langton, 'God, the Past and Auschwitz: Jewish Holocaust Theologians' Engagement with History', *Holocaust Studies* 17 (2011) 29–62, at 38–40; Esther Benbassa, *Suffering as Identity: The Jewish Paradigm* (2010) 101–2.

130. Emil L. Fackenheim, *To Mend the World: Foundations of Future Jewish Thought* (New York: Schocken, 1982) 9–14; Michael L. Morgan, 'Emil Fackenheim, the Holocaust, and Philosophy', in Michael L. Morgan and Peter Eli Gordon, eds, *The Cambridge Companion to Modern Jewish Philosophy* (Cambridge: Cambridge University Press, 2007) 256–76.

131. Fackenheim, *To Mend the World*, 284–5, 304.

132. Ibid., 330.

133. Gregory Baum, 'Introduction' to Rosemary Radford Ruether, *Faith and Fratricide: The Theological Roots of Anti-Semitism* (Eugene, OR: Wipf and Stock, 1995 [1974]) 8; James Parkes, *The Conflict of the Church and the Synagogue: A Study in the Origins of Anti-Semitism* (London: SCM Press, 1934) esp. 371–8.

134. Rosemary Radford Ruether, 'Anti-Semitism and the State of Israel: Some Principles for Christians', *Christianity and Crisis* 33 (1973) 240–4; Richard Harries, *After the Evil: Christianity*

and Judaism in the Shadow of the Holocaust (Oxford: Oxford University Press, 2003) esp. 88–138, 202–32.

135. Jennifer Hansen-Glucklich, *Holocaust Memory Reframed: Museums and the Challenges of Representation* (New Brunswick, NJ: Rutgers University Press, 2014); Alvin H. Rosenfeld, 'The Americanization of the Holocaust', in Rosenfeld, ed., *Thinking About the Holocaust: After Half a Century* (Bloomington, IN: Indiana University Press, 1997) 119–50, at 137–8.

136. Larissa Allwork, *Holocaust Remembrance between the National and the Transnational: The Stockholm International Forum and the First Decade of the International Task Force* (London: Bloomsbury, 2015); see also the IHRA website, www.holocaustremembrance.com.

137. Daniel Levy and Natan Sznaider, *The Holocaust and Memory in a Global Age* (Philadelphia: Temple University Press, 2006) 18; Sharon Macdonald, *Memorylands: Heritage and Identity in Europe Today* (London: Routledge, 2013) 188–215.

138. Michael Rothberg, *Multidirectional Memory: Remembering the Holocaust in the Age of Decolonization* (Stanford, CA: Stanford University Press, 2009); Dirk A. Moses, 'Genocide and the Terror of History', *Parallax* 17 (2011) 90–108; Jacqueline Rose, *The Question of Zion* (Princeton, NJ: Princeton University Press, 2005) 137–45; Nur Masalha, *The Palestine Nakba: Decolonising History, Narrating the Subaltern, Reclaiming Memory* (London: Zed Books, 2012)

139. Michels, *A Fire in Their Hearts*, 1–2.

140. Michael Walzer, 'The Strangeness of Jewish Leftism', in Jack Jacobs, ed., *Jews and Leftist Politics: Judaism, Israel, Antisemitism, and Gender* (Cambridge: Cambridge University Press, 2017) 29–39; Jerry Z. Muller, *Capitalism and the Jews* (Princeton, NJ: Princeton University Press, 2010) 133–88; Robert S. Wistrich, *Socialism and the Jews* (London: Littman, 1982); Jack Jacobs, 'Jews and the Left', in Hart and Michels, eds, *Cambridge History of Judaism 8*, 390–413.

141. Isaac Deutscher, 'The Non-Jewish Jew', in *The Non-Jewish Jew and Other Essays* (London: Merlin, 1981 [1968, but based on a lecture given in 1958]) 25–41, esp. 27, 36.

142. Tamara Deutscher, 'Introduction: The Education of a Jewish Child', in Isaac Deutscher, *The Non-Jewish Jew*, 1–24; Isaac Deutscher, *The Prophet Armed: Trotsky 1879–1921* (Oxford: Oxford University Press, 1954); *The Prophet Unarmed: Trotsky 1921–1929* (Oxford: Oxford University Press 1959); *The Prophet Outcast: Trotsky 1929–1940* (Oxford: Oxford University Press, 1963).

143. Deutscher, 'Non-Jewish Jew', 32–3.

144. Tony Michels, ed., *Jewish Radicals: A Documentary History* (New York: New York University Press, 2012) 25–69; William J. Fishman, *East End Jewish Radicals, 1875–1914* (London: Duckworth, 1975) 97–162; Vivi Lachs, *Whitechapel Noise: Jewish Immigrant Life in Yiddish Song and Verse* (Detroit: Wayne State University Press, 2018) 91–132.

145. Rudolf Rocker, *The London Years* (Nottingham: Five Leaves, 2005 [1956]) 27; Fishman, *East End Jewish Radicals*, 229–309.

146. Michael Löwy, *Redemption and Utopia: Jewish Libertarian Thought in Central Europe—A Study in Elective Affinity* (London: Athlone, 1992).

147. Volker Weidermann, *Dreamers: When the Writers Took Power, Germany, 1918* (London: Pushkin Press, 2018); Eugene Lunn, *Prophet of Community: The Romantic Socialism of Gustav Landauer* (Berkeley and Los Angeles: University of California Press, 1973) 291–342.

148. Weidermann, *Dreamers*, 199–202, 232–3.

149. Gustav Landauer, 'Through Separation to Community' (1901), in *Revolution and Other Writings: A Political Reader*, ed. Gabriel Kuhn (Oakland, CA: PM Press, 2010) 94–108, at 99–100;

Hanna Delf von Wolzogen, 'Gustav Landauer's Reading of Spinoza', in Paul Mendes-Flohr and Anya Mali, eds, *Gustav Landauer: Anarchist and Jew* (Berlin: De Gruyter, 2015) 155–71.

150. Michael Löwy, 'The Romantic Socialism of Gustav Landauer', in Jacobs, *Jews and Leftist Politics*, 252–66, at 259–64; Paul Mendes-Flohr, 'Messianic Radicals: Gustav Landauer and Other German-Jewish Revolutionaries', in Mendes-Flohr and Mali, *Landauer*, 14–44, at 38–40.

151. Gustav Landauer, 'The Beilis Trial' (1913), in *Revolution and Other Writings*, 295–9, at 298.

152. Gustav Landauer, 'Sind das Ketzergedanken?' in *Vom Judentum: Ein Sammelbuch* (Leipzig: K. Wolff, 1913) 250–7, at 253.

153. Ibid., 254, 256–7.

154. Landauer, 'Beilis Trial', 299.

155. Michael Löwy, '1910: Ernst Bloch and Georg Lukács Meet in Heideberg', in Gilman and Zipes, *Yale Companion*, 287–92; Lars Fischer, 'Marxism's Other Jewish Questions', in Jacobs, *Jews and Leftist Politics*, 67–83.

156. Michael Löwy, 'Interview with Ernst Bloch', *New German Critique* 9 (1976) 35–45; Ivan Boldyrev, *Ernst Bloch and His Contemporaries: Locating Utopian Messianism* (London: Bloomsbury, 2014).

157. Löwy, *Redemption and Utopia*, 144–50.

158. Ibid., 138–42.

159. Ernst Bloch, *Spirit of Utopia*, 2nd edn, trans. Anthony A. Nassar (Stanford, CA: Stanford University Press, 2000 [1923]) 259, 271, 278.

160. Ernst Bloch, *Thomas Münzer als Theologe der Revolution* (Frankfurt: Suhrkamp, 1969 [1921]) 228–9.

161. Ernst Bloch, *The Principle of Hope*, 3 vols (Oxford: Basil Blackwell, 1986 [1955–59]) esp. II: 471–624; Terry Eagleton, *Hope without Optimism* (New Haven, CT: Yale University Press, 2017) 90–111; Wayne Hudson, *The Marxist Philosophy of Ernst Bloch* (New York: St Martin's Press, 1982) 14–17, 104–9; Simon Mussell, *Critical Theory and Feeling: The Affective Politics of the Early Frankfurt School* (Manchester: Manchester University Press, 2017) 115–40.

162. Bloch, *Principle of Hope*, II: 600–609.

163. Ibid., 608, 610.

164. Hudson, *Marxist Philosophy of Bloch*, 8–9; Howard Eiland and Michael W. Jennings, *Walter Benjamin: A Critical Life* (Cambridge, MA: Harvard University Press, 2014) 106–7, 156–7.

165. Walter Benjamin, 'Capitalism as Religion' (1921), trans. Chad Kautzer in E. Mendieta, ed., *Religion as Critique: The Frankfurt School's Critique of Religion* (New York: Routledge, 2005) 259–62, at 261; Michael Löwy, 'Capitalism as Religion: Walter Benjamin and Max Weber', *Historical Materialism* 17 (2009) 60–73.

166. Walter Benjamin, 'Theologico-Political Fragment' (1921), trans. Edmund Jephcott in *Reflections* (New York: Schocken, 2007) 312–13.

167. Eiland and Jennings, *Benjamin*, 45–8, 82–6; Gershom Scholem, *Walter Benjamin: The Story of a Friendship* (London: Faber & Faber, 1982 [1975]); George Prochnik, *Stranger in a Strange Land: Searching for Gershom Scholem and Jerusalem* (London: Granta, 2017) 48–56.

168. Walter Benjamin, 'Critique of Violence' (1921), in *Reflections*, 277–300, at 291–2; Stéphane Mosès, *The Angel of History: Rosenzweig, Benjamin, Scholem* (Stanford, CA: Stanford University Press, 2009 [1992]) 65–100; Peter Fenves, *The Messianic Reduction: Walter Benjamin and the Shape of Time* (Stanford, CA: Stanford University Press, 2011) 208–26.

169. Walter Benjamin, 'Theses on the Philosophy of History' (1940), in *Illuminations* (New York: Schocken, 1968) 253–64, at 257–8.

170. Ibid., 261.

171. Walter Benjamin, 'Karl Kraus' (1931), in *Reflections*, 239–73, esp. 273.

172. Benjamin, 'Theses on the Philosophy of History', 264.

173. Stuart Jeffries, *Grand Hotel Abyss: The Lives of the Frankfurt School* (London: Verso, 2016) 211–19; Hannah Arendt, 'Walter Benjamin, 1892–1940', in *Illuminations*, 1–51, at 17–18, and 266.

174. Bernard Lazare, 'Le nationalisme juif' (Paris, 1898) 8.

175. Hannah Arendt, 'The Jew as Pariah: A Hidden Tradition' (1944), in Jerome Kohn and Ron H. Feldman, eds, *The Jewish Writings* (New York: Schocken, 2007) 275–97, at 283–6.

176. Arendt, 'Jew as Pariah', 288–96; Arendt, 'Walter Benjamin, 1892–1940', 32–4; Walter Benjamin, 'Franz Kafka: On the Tenth Anniversary of his Death' (1934), in *Illuminations*, 111–40.

177. Arendt, 'Jew as Pariah', 297.

178. Hannah Arendt, 'On Humanity in Dark Times: Thoughts about Lessing', in *Men in Dark Times* (New York: Harcourt, 1968) 3–31, at 13, 29–30; Peter Fenves, 'Politics of Friendship—Once Again', *Eighteenth-Century Studies* 32 (1999) 133–55, at 144–8.

179. Hannah Arendt, 'Zionism Reconsidered' (1944), in *The Jewish Writings*, 343–74, at 271; Richard J. Bernstein, *Hannah Arendt and the Jewish Question* (Cambridge: Polity, 1996) 101–22; Eric Jacobson, 'The Zionism of Hannah Arendt: 1941–1948', in Randi Rashkover and Martin Kavka, eds, *Jewish Liberalism and Political Theology* (Bloomington, IN: Indiana University Press, 2014) 127–51.

180. Hannah Arendt, 'Magnes, the Conscience of the Jewish People' (1952), in *The Jewish Writings*, 451–2.

181. Bernstein, *Arendt and the Jewish Question*, 3.

182. Hannah Arendt, *The Human Condition* (Chicago: University of Chicago Press, 1958) 7–8.

183. Ibid., 247.

184. Ibid.; Mary G. Dietz, 'Arendt and the Holocaust', in Dana Villa, ed., *The Cambridge Companion to Hannah Arendt* (Cambridge: Cambridge University Press, 2000) 86–109, at 99–102.

185. Hannah Arendt, letter to Gershom Scholem, 24 July 1963, in *Jewish Writings*, 465–71, at 467; Seyla Benhabib, 'Whose Trial? Adolf Eichmann's or Hannah Arendt's? The Eichmann Controversy Revisited', in *Exile, Statelessness, and Migration: Playing Chess with History from Hannah Arendt to Isaiah Berlin* (Princeton, NJ: Princeton University Press, 2018) 61–79.

186. Gideon Shimoni, *Community and Conscience: The Jews in Apartheid South Africa* (Hanover, NH: University Press of New England, 2003) 73–94.

187. Tony Kushner and Alisa Solomon, eds, *Wrestling with Zion: Progressive Jewish-American Responses to the Israeli–Palestinian Conflict* (New York: Grove Press, 2003); Anne Karpf, Brian Klug, Jacqueline Rose and Barbara Rosenbaum, eds, *A Time to Speak Out: Independent Jewish Voices on Israel, Zionism and Jewish Identity* (London: Verso, 2008); www.jewishvoiceforpeace.org.

188. Meyer, *Response to Modernity*, 364–8; Edward K. Kaplan, *Spiritual Radical: Abraham Joshua Heschel in America* (New Haven, CT: Yale University Press, 2007) 178–234, 298–318; Michael E. Staub, *Torn at the Roots: The Crisis of Jewish Liberalism in Postwar America* (New York: Columbia University Press, 2002) 45–152.

189. Meyer, *Response to Modernity*, 369–70, 384–3, 391–4.

190. Marc H. Ellis, *Toward a Jewish Theology of Liberation* (London: SCM Press, 2002 [1987]) esp. 64–87, 115–16; Ellis, *Finding Our Voice: Embodying the Prophetic and Other Misadventures* (Eugene, OR: Cascade Books, 2018) 50–3, 67–122.

191. Jacqueline Rose, *The Question of Zion* (Princeton, NJ: Princeton University Press, 2005); 'An Interview with Jacqueline Rose', in *The Jacqueline Rose Reader* (Durham, NC: Duke University Press, 2011) 341–59, at 355–8.

192. Brian Klug, *Being Jewish and Doing Justice* (London: Vallentine Mitchell, 2011) 23–4.

193. Judith Butler, *Precarious Life: The Power of Mourning and Violence* (London: Verso, 2004) 103–4; Butler, *Parting Ways: Jewishness and the Critique of Zionism* (New York: Columbia University Press, 2014) 24–5.

194. Butler, *Parting Ways*, 1–27, esp. 7–8, 21, 27.

195. Paul Hanebrink, *A Specter Haunting Europe: The Myth of Judeo-Bolshevism* (Cambridge, MA: Harvard University Press, 2018) esp. 11–45.

196. Assmann, *Moses the Egyptian*, 1–8, 208–18; Assmann, *The Price of Monotheism* (Stanford, CA: Stanford University Press, 2010 [2003]) esp. 31–56, 103.

197. Assmann, *Price of Monotheism*, 5–7; Eliza Slavet, 'A Matter of Distinction: On Recent Work by Jan Assmann', *AJS Review* 34 (2010) 385–93.

198. Assmann, *Moses the Egyptian*, 208–18.

199. Jan Assmann, *The Invention of Religion: Faith and Covenant in the Book of Exodus* (Princeton, NJ: Princeton University Press, 2018) esp. 79–90, 327–38.

200. Adam Sutcliffe and Jonathan Karp, 'Introduction: A Brief History of Philosemitism', in Jonathan Karp and Adam Sutcliffe, eds, *Philosemitism in History* (Cambridge: Cambridge University Press, 2011) 1–26, esp. 8, 13–15.

201. Edward Said, *Freud and the Non-European* (London: Verso, 2003) 11–55; Gil Z. Hochberg, 'Edward Said: "The Last Jewish Intellectual"', *Social Text* 87 (2006) 47–65.

202. David Biale, Michael Galchinsky and Susannah Heschel, 'Introduction—The Dialectic of Jewish Enlightenment', in Biale, Galchinsky and Heschel, *Insider/Outsider*, 1–13; Sander L. Gilman, *Multiculturalism and the Jews* (New York: Routledge, 2006).

203. Aamir R. Mufti, *Enlightenment in the Colony: The Jewish Question and the Crisis of Postcolonial Culture* (Princeton, NJ: Princeton University Press, 2007) 37–90; Susannah Heschel, *Abraham Geiger and the Jewish Jesus* (Chicago: University of Chicago Press, 1998) 14–22; Christian Wiese, *Challenging Colonial Discourse: Jewish Studies and Protestant Theology in Wilhelmine Germany* (Leiden: Brill, 2005) 427–44; Bryan Cheyette, *Diasporas of the Mind: Jewish and Postcolonial Writing and the Nightmare of History* (New Haven, CT: Yale University Press, 2013) 6–18.

204. Jonathan Sacks, *The Dignity of Difference: How to Avoid the Clash of Civilizations*, 2nd edn (London: Continuum, 2003 [2002]) 53.

205. Ibid., 60–2, 203–7.

206. Jonathan Petre, 'Chief Rabbi revises book after attack by critics', *Daily Telegraph*, 15 February 2003.

207. David Novak, *The Image of the Non-Jew in Judaism* (Oxford: Littman, 2011) 11–35, 206–12.

208. Sacks, *Dignity of Difference*, 206.

Conclusion: So What *Are* Jews For? Jews and Contemporary Purpose

1. Tony Kushner, *Angels in America, Part Two: Perestroika* (London: Nick Hern, 1994) 29, 31 [Act II, scene 2].

2. Rosa Luxemburg to Mathilda Wurm, 16 February 1916, trans. George Shriver in *The Letters of Rosa Luxemburg* (London: Verso, 2011) 376.

3. Alan Rosenbaum, ed., *Is the Holocaust Unique? Perspectives on Comparative Genocide* (Boulder, CO: Westview Press, 1996).

4. Maurice Samuels, *The Right to Difference: French Universalism and the Jews* (Chicago: University of Chicago Press, 2016) esp. 17–49, 95–116.

5. Jean-Paul Sartre, *Anti-Semite and Jew* (New York: Schocken, 1948 [1946]) 59–141; Samuels, *Right to Difference*, 139–56.

6. Albert Memmi, *Portrait of a Jew*, trans. Elisabeth Abbott (New York: Orion Press, 1962); Alain Finkielkraut, *The Imaginary Jew*, trans. David Suchoff (Lincoln, NE: University of Nebraska Press, 1997 [1980]); Samuels, *Right to Difference*, 159–61.

7. Jean-François Lyotard, *Heidegger and 'the jews'*, trans. Andreas Michel (Minneapolis: University of Minnesota Press, 1990 [1988]) 3, 22; Geoffrey Bennington, 'Lyotard and "the Jews"', in Bryan Cheyette and Laura Marcus, eds, *Modernity, Culture and 'the Jew'* (Stanford, CA: Stanford University Press, 1998) 187–96.

8. Éric Marty, *Radical French Thought and the Return of the 'Jewish Question'* (Bloomington, IN: Indiana University Press, 2015) 112–24; Bruno Chaouat, *Is Theory Good for the Jews? French Thought and the Challenge of the New Antisemitism* (Liverpool: Liverpool University Press, 2016) xi–xxi.

9. Daniel Boyarin and Jonathan Boyarin, 'Diaspora: Generation and the Ground of Jewish Identity', *Critical Inquiry* 19 (1993) 693–725, at 699–701.

10. Jonathan M. Hess, 'Lessing and German-Jewish Culture: A Reappraisal', in Ritchie Robertson, ed., *Lessing and the German Enlightenment* (Oxford: Voltaire Foundation, 2013) 179–204.

11. Adam Sutcliffe and Jonathan Karp, 'Introduction: A Brief History of Philosemitism', in Jonathan Karp and Adam Sutcliffe, *Philosemitism in History* (Cambridge: Cambridge University Press, 2011) 1–26, at 19–21.

12. Chouat, *Is Theory Good for the Jews?*, esp. 49–51; Marty, *Radical French Thought*; Vivian Liska, *German-Jewish Thought and Its Afterlife: A Tenuous Legacy* (Bloomington, IN: Indiana University Press, 2017) 149–50; Shai Ginsburg, Martin Land and Jonathan Boyarin, eds, *Jews and the Ends of Theory* (New York: Fordham University Press, 2019). See also, for a sympathetic reading of Lyotard, Sarah Hammerschlag, 'Troping the Jew: Jean-François Lyotard's *Heidegger and "the jews"'*, *Jewish Studies Quarterly* 12 (2005) 371–89.

13. Maud S. Mandel, *Muslims and Jews in France: History of a Conflict* (Princeton, NJ: Princeton University Press, 2014) 146–56.

14. Ibid., 35–58.

15. Alain Finkielkraut, *Au nom de l'autre: Réflexions sur l'antisémitisme qui vient* (Paris: Gallimard, 2003); Joan Wallach Scott, *The Politics of the Veil* (Princeton, NJ: Princeton University Press, 2007).

16. Samuels, *Right to Difference*, 186–95; Emmanuel Todd, *Who Is Charlie?* (Cambridge: Polity, 2015) 84–9.

17. Alain Badiou, *In Praise of Love*, trans. Peter Bush (London: Serpent's Tail, 2012 [2009]); Alain Badiou, *The Communist Hypothesis*, trans. David Macey and Steve Corcoran (London: Verso, 2010 [2008]); Nick Hewlett, *Badiou, Balibar, Rancière: Re-thinking Emancipation* (London: Continuum, 2007) 24–46.

18. Alain Badiou, *Saint Paul: The Foundations of Universalism* (Stanford, CA: Stanford University Press, 2003 [1997]) 72.

19. Ibid., 75–85.

20. Ibid., 103; see also, for a related argument, Giorgio Agamben, *The Time That Remains: A Commentary on the Letter to the Romans* (Stanford, CA: Stanford University Press, 2005 [2000]) esp. 44–58.

21. Alain Badiou, 'The Word "Jew" and the Sycophant' (2005), trans. Steve Corcoran in *Polemics* (London: Verso, 2006) 230–47.

22. Alain Badiou, 'Israel: The Country in the World where there are the Fewest Jews?' (1982), in *Polemics*, 167–71.

23. Badiou, '"Jew" and the Sycophant', 247.

24. Alain Badiou, Eric Hazan and Ivan Segré, *Reflections on Anti-Semitism*, trans. David Fernbach (London: Verso 2013 [2009/2011]); Badiou, *Polemics*, 217–29; Udi Aloni, with Slavoj Žižek, Alain Badiou and Judith Butler, *What Does A Jew Want? On Binationalism and Other Specters* (New York: Columbia University Press, 2011) 184–203.

25. Samuels, *Right to Difference*, 172–88, esp. 176–7; Marty, *Radical French Thought*, 66–71; Sarah Hammerschlag, 'Bad Jews, Authentic Jews, Figural Jews: Badiou and the Politics of Exemplarity', in Rudi Rashkover and Martin Kavka, eds, *Judaism, Liberalism and Political Theology* (Bloomington, IN: Indiana University Press, 2014) 221–40.

26. Houria Bouteldja, *Whites, Jews, and Us: Towards a Politics of Revolutionary Love* (Pasadena, CA: Semiotexte, 2016) 53–72, esp. 69–70; Gil Anidjar, *Semites: Race, Religion, Literature* (Stanford, CA: Stanford University Press, 2008).

27. Chemi Shalev, 'For Rosh Hashanah, a picture of Israel's muddled Jewish soul', *Haaretz*, 9 September 2018.

28. Michael Wyschogrod, *The Body of Faith: God in the People Israel* (Northvale, NJ: Jason Aronson, 1996 [1983]) 40–81, esp. 64–5.

29. David Novak, *The Election of Israel: The Idea of the Chosen People* (Cambridge: Cambridge University Press, 1995) 241–8.

30. Ibid., 253, 255.

31. David Novak, *Zionism and Judaism: A New Theory* (Cambridge: Cambridge University Press, 2015) 121–36, esp. 129.

32. Ibid., 16, 139–91.

33. Shaul Magid, *American Post-Judaism: Identity and Renewal in a Postethnic Society* (Bloomington, IN: Indiana University Press, 2013) esp. 10, 240–3; David A. Hollinger, *Postethnic America: Beyond Multiculturalism* (New York: Basic Books, 2005 [1995]).

34. Arthur Green, *Radical Judaism: Rethinking God and Tradition* (New Haven, CT: Yale University Press, 2010) 106–14, esp. 108.

35. Ibid., 110–14, 131–3.

36. Ibid., 133–5, 149.

37. Jonathan Krasner, 'The Place of Tikkun Olam in American Jewish Life', *Jewish Political Studies Review* 25 (2013) 59–98, esp. 60–2, 74–8.

38. Lawrence Fine, 'Tikkun: A Lurianic Motif in Contemporary Jewish Thought', in Jacob Neusner, Ernest S. Frerichs and Nahum M. Sarna, eds, *From Ancient Israel to Modern Judaism: Intellect in Quest of Understanding*, 4 vols (Atlanta, GA: Scholars Press, 1989) IV: 35–53.

39. Krasner, 'Tikkun Olam', 67–72.

40. Jonathan Neumann, *To Heal the World: How the Jewish Left Corrupts Judaism and Endangers Israel* (New York: All Points Books, 2018) esp. 195, 210–28; Melanie Phillips, 'Tikkun Olam, the supposedly Jewish social justice, is a fraud', *Jewish Chronicle*, 7 December 2018.

41. Howard Jacobson, *The Finkler Question* (London: Bloomsbury, 2010); 'Prominent Jews call for open debate on Israel', *The Guardian*, 5 February 2007.

42. Anthony Julius, *Trials of the Diaspora: A History of Anti-Semitism in England* (Oxford: Oxford University Press, 2010) 441–588, esp. 544–60.

43. Jessica Elgot, '"I learned a lot": Corbyn defends taking part in radical Jewish event', *The Guardian*, 3 April 2018; Greg Philo, Mike Berry, Justin Schlosberg, Antony Lerman and David Miller, *Bad News for Labour: Antisemitism, the Party and Public Belief* (London: Pluto, 2019).

44. Sheryl Gay Stolberg, 'Ilhan Omar apologizes for statements condemned as anti-semitic', *New York Times*, 11 February 2019.

45. 'Working Definition of Antisemitism' (2006), at www.holocaustremembrance.com /working-definition-antisemitism; Brian Klug, 'The Code of Conduct for Antisemitism: A Tale of Two Texts', July 2018, at www.opendemocracy.net.

46. Kenneth L. Marcus, *The Definition of Anti-Semitism* (Oxford: Oxford University Press, 2015) 202–14.

47. Nathan Thrall, 'How the battle over Israel and anti-semitism is fracturing American politics', *New York Times Magazine*, 31 March 2019; Melissa Eddy, 'Director of Berlin's Jewish Museum quits after spat over B.D.S.', *New York Times*, 14 June 2019.

48. Dave Rich, *The Left's Jewish Problem: Jeremy Corbyn, Israel and Antisemitism*, 2nd edn (London: Biteback, 2018), esp. 257–8; David Hirsh, *Contemporary Left Antisemitism* (London: Routledge, 2018); Ellie Bothwell, 'Muslims feel they're "under suspicion" on UK campuses', *Times Higher Education*, 6 September 2016; S. Sayyid and AbdoolKarim Vakil, eds, *Thinking through Islamophobia: Global Perspectives* (New York: Columbia University Press, 2011); James Renton and Ben Gidley, eds, *Antisemitism and Islamophobia in Europe: A Shared Story?* (London: Palgrave Macmillan, 2017).

49. Jacobson, *Finkler Question*, 230–7, esp. 231; James Wood, 'Member of the tribe: Howard Jacobson's *The Finkler Question*', *The New Yorker*, 8 November 2010.

50. Jonathan Sacks, on *The Andrew Marr Show*, BBC1, 2 September 2018 [transcript at www .bbc.co.uk].

51. George Eaton, 'Corbyn's "Zionist" remarks were "most offensive" since Enoch Powell, says ex-Chief Rabbi', *New Statesman*, 28 August 2018.

52. Josh Jackman, 'The IDF is the most ethical army in the world, say military experts', *Jewish Chronicle*, 16 December 2015; Avi Shlaim, 'The Debate about 1948', in Benny Morris, ed., *Making Israel* (Ann Arbor, MI: University of Michigan Press, 2007) 124–46, at 125.

53. Peter Beinart, *The Crisis of Zionism* (New York: Henry Holt, 2012); 'The Magnes Zionist', at www.jeremiahhaber.com.

54. Anshel Pfeffer, 'Netanyahu and Orban: An illiberal bromance spanning from D.C. to Jerusalem', *Haaretz*, 18 July 2018.

55. Tony Kushner, *Angels in America, Part One: Millennium Approaches* (London: Nick Hern, 1992) 90 [Act III, scene 3].

56. Ibid., 69 [Act III, scene 8].

57. Kushner, *Perestroika*, 99 [Epilogue].

58. James Fisher, *Understanding Tony Kushner* (Columbia, SC: University of South Carolina Press, 2008) 49–51; Roger F. Cook and Gerd Gemünden, *The Cinema of Wim Wenders: Image, Narrative, and the Postmodern Condition* (Detroit: Wayne State University Press, 1997) 183–7.

59. Kushner, *Perestroika*, 81–3 [Act V, scene 3]; Walter Benjamin, 'Theses on the Philosophy of History' (1940), in *Illuminations* (New York: Schocken, 1968) 253–64, at 264.

60. See also Tony Kushner and Alisa Solomon, eds, *Wrestling with Zion: Progressive Jewish-American Responses to the Israeli–Palestinian Conflict* (New York: Grove Press, 2003) esp. 1–9.

61. George Steiner, 'A Kind of Survivor' (1965), in *Language and Silence: Essays on Language, Literature and the Inhuman* (New York: Atheneum, 1982) 140–54, esp. 152–3; Steiner, *Errata: An Examined Life* (London: Weidenfeld and Nicolson, 1997) 61–2; Steiner, *The Portage to San Cristobal of A. H.* (London: Faber and Faber, 1981 [1979]) esp. 120–6.

62. George Steiner, 'Our Homeland, the Text' (1985), in *No Passion Spent: Essays 1978–1996* (London: Faber and Faber, 1996) 304–27.

63. Moshe Idel, *Old Worlds, New Mirrors: On Jewish Mysticism and Twentieth-Century Thought* (Philadelphia: University of Pennsylvania Press, 2010) 52–78; Asaf Sagiv, 'George Steiner's Jewish Problem', *Azure* 15 (2003) 130–54.

64. David Berger, *The Rebbe, the Messiah, and the Scandal of Orthodox Indifference* (London: Littman, 2001).

65. Elliot R. Wolfson, *Open Secret: Postmessianic Messianism and Mystical Revision* (New York: Columbia University Press, 2009) 229–31.

66. Ibid., 133–4, 231–64, esp. 257–8.

67. Ibid., 265–300, esp. 276, 281.

68. Rogers M. Smith, *Stories of Peoplehood: The Politics and Morals of Political Membership* (Cambridge: Cambridge University Press, 2003) esp. 1–10, 93–102; Smith, *Political Peoplehood: The Roles of Values, Interests, and Identities* (Chicago: University of Chicago Press, 2015) esp. 5–6, 189–217.

69. Michael Walzer, *Exodus and Revolution* (New York: Basic Books, 1985); John Coffey, *Exodus and Liberation: Deliverance Politics from John Calvin to Martin Luther King Jr* (Oxford: Oxford University Press, 2014).

70. Cathy S. Gelbin and Sander L. Gilman, *Cosmopolitanisms and the Jews* (Ann Arbor: University of Michigan Press, 2017) 223–54.

A NOTE ON THE TYPE

This book has been composed in Arno, an Old-style serif typeface in the classic Venetian tradition, designed by Robert Slimbach at Adobe.